AN AUTOBIOGRAPHY
VOLUME II

HERBERT SPENCER'S WORKS.

Synthetic Philosophy:
    FIRST PRINCIPLES. 1 vol. 12mo. $2.00.
    THE PRINCIPLES OF BIOLOGY. 2 vols. 12mo. $4.00.
    THE PRINCIPLES OF PSYCHOLOGY. 2 vols. 12mo. $4.00.
    THE PRINCIPLES OF SOCIOLOGY. 3 vols. 12mo. $6.00.
    THE PRINCIPLES OF ETHICS. 2 vols. 12mo. $4.00.

Essays: Scientific, Political, and Speculative. New edition; 3 vols. 12mo. $6.00.

Social Statics, Abridged and Revised; and THE MAN *versus* THE STATE. 1 vol. 12mo. $2.00.

The Study of Sociology. 1 vol. 12mo. $1.50.

Education. 1 vol. 12mo. Cloth, $1.25; paper, 50 cents.

Facts and Comments. 1 vol. 12mo. $1.20 net; postage, 12 cents additional.

Various Fragments. 1 vol. 12mo. Cloth, $1.25.

The Inadequacy of "Natural Selection." 1 vol. 12mo. Paper, 30 cents.

Descriptive Sociology. A Cyclopædia of Social Facts. 8vo. Folio. $35.00

D. APPLETON AND COMPANY, NEW YORK.

Herbert Spencer
when 78

AN
AUTOBIOGRAPHY

BY
HERBERT SPENCER

ILLUSTRATED

IN TWO VOLUMES
VOL. II

NEW YORK
D. APPLETON AND COMPANY
1904

COPYRIGHT, 1904, BY
D. APPLETON AND COMPANY

Published April, 1904

CONTENTS OF VOL. II.

PART VII.

1856–1860.

CHAPTER		PAGE
XXX.	A System of Philosophy Projected	3
XXXI.	Plans for Executing it	32
XXXII.	A Plan Fixed Upon	55

PART VIII.

1860–1867.

XXXIII.	Writing *First Principles*	67
XXXIV.	An Autumn's Relaxations	88
XXXV.	A Volume of the *Biology*	98
XXXVI.	A Digression	123
XXXVII.	Another Volume of the *Biology*	131
XXXVIII.	Impending Cessation	154
XXXIX.	Sad Events	162

CONTENTS

PART IX.
1867–1874.

CHAPTER		PAGE
XL.	RE-CASTING *FIRST PRINCIPLES*	179
XLI.	AN IMPRUDENCE AND ITS CONSEQUENCES	200
XLII.	A TOUR IN ITALY	208
XLIII.	DEVELOPING THE *PSYCHOLOGY*	232
XLIV.	FINISHING THE *PSYCHOLOGY*	260
XLV.	AN EXTRA BOOK	283
XLVI.	SOME MINOR INCIDENTS	300
XLVII.	THE *DESCRIPTIVE SOCIOLOGY*	305

PART X.
1874–1879.

XLVIII.	A RETROSPECTIVE GLANCE	321
XLIX.	VOL. I. OF THE *SOCIOLOGY*	324
L.	A SERIES OF ARTICLES	354
LI.	*THE DATA OF ETHICS*	369
LII.	*CEREMONIAL INSTITUTIONS*	382

PART XI.
1879–1889.

LIII.	UP THE NILE	393
LIV.	ENDING OF THE *DESCRIPTIVE SOCIOLOGY*	410
LV.	*POLITICAL INSTITUTIONS*	416
LVI.	A GRIEVOUS MISTAKE	443

CONTENTS

CHAPTER		PAGE
LVII.	COMING EVENTS	452
LVIII.	A VISIT TO AMERICA	457
LIX.	CONCLUSION	482

PART XII.

LX.	REFLECTIONS WRITTEN FOUR YEARS LATER	489

APPENDICES.

	A NOTE CONCERNING THE LIFE AND LETTERS OF T. H. HUXLEY	553
A.	PROGRAMME OF THE SYNTHETIC PHILOSOPHY	557
B.	LETTER TO MR. G. H. LEWES	565
C.	DOCUMENTS CONCERNING THE CESSATION OF THE ISSUE OF THE PHILOSOPHY	573
D.	A NEW INVALID-BED	576
E.	ENGLISH FEELING ABOUT THE AMERICAN CIVIL WAR	580
F.	A NEW FISHING-ROD JOINT	591
G.	OBITUARY NOTICE OF J. S. MILL	594
H.	LETTER OF PROF. YOUMANS	598
	INDEX	605

PART VII.

XXX. A SYSTEM OF PHILOSOPHY PROJECTED.
XXXI. PLANS FOR EXECUTING IT.
XXXII. A PLAN FIXED UPON.

CHAPTER XXX.

A SYSTEM OF PHILOSOPHY PROJECTED.

1857—8. Æt. 37—38.

My search for a fit place of abode when I returned to town, ended satisfactorily. Malvern House, otherwise 13, Loudoun Road, St. John's Wood, in which I settled myself, is a good house seated in the midst of a garden walled round. The occupier, who carried on a wholesale business in the city, and who, as I afterward learnt, feared to fall into a state of chronic melancholy, as his father had done before him, had hit on a prophylactic—surrounding himself with a lively circle. In addition to the family, consisting of host and hostess, three daughters and a son, ranging from seven up to about twenty, and a governess, there were as boarders an old retired government official (a commissioner of some kind I think he had been) lively notwithstanding his years—eighty and a wit; a "grass-widow," pleasant to look upon but without an idea in her head, whose husband was in India; and her friend, a vain old lady who played the part of duenna.

Beyond the fitness of the circle and the salubrity of the locality, which is on the backbone of St. John's Wood, the place had the advantage that it was within two minutes' walk of No. 1, Waverley Place, then occupied by Huxley. We had a standing engagement for Sunday afternoons: a walk of a few miles into the country along the Finchley Road, or up to Hampstead, being the usual routine. Many pleasant talks and useful discussions there were between us on those occasions during the succeeding year. I remember that once when, as it would seem, society and human life as at present existing had been topics of somewhat pessimistic comment, I said (not however doing justice to my thought)—"Yes, one cannot hope for much more than to make one's mark and die." Whereupon Huxley, with greater self-abnegation, responded—"Never mind about the mark: it is enough if one can give a push."

Reference to these walks and talks reminds me of an incident connected with one of them. Shortly after I had established myself in Loudoun Road, Buckle called. It was on a Sunday afternoon. Our conversation had not gone far when I intimated that the hour had come for the usual excursion; and, on my answering his inquiry who Huxley was (for then he was not widely known), Buckle agreed to go with me to be introduced. He went with us a short distance up the Finchley Road; but, saying that he had an engagement, presently turned back. We looked after him as he walked away; and Huxley, struck by his feeble, undecided gait, remarked—"Ah, I see the kind of man. He is top-heavy." I have never done more than dip into *The History of Civilization in England;* but I suspect that the analogy suggested was not without truth. Buckle had taken in a much larger quantity of matter than he could organize; and he staggered under the mass of it.

November was occupied chiefly in seeing through the press the volume of *Essays: Scientific, Political, and Speculative;* but its last days, joined with the first part of December, found me busy with a review-article. A letter to my father dated 28th November, contains the paragraph—

"I have undertaken to write a short article on this Banking crisis—perhaps under the title of the bunglings of State-banking—in which I propose showing the evils of meddling and the superiorities of an unrestricted system. It is for the next *Westminster*."

This essay, which appeared under the title of " State Tamperings with Money and Banks," displayed once more my antagonism to over-legislation. It is significant, too, as showing in another direction, an abiding faith in the self-regulation of internal social activities.

An essay on such a subject seems a very unlikely place in which to meet with a biological doctrine; and yet one cropped up. Among reasons given for reprobating the policy of guarding imprudent people against the dangers of reckless banking, one was that such a policy interferes with that normal process which brings benefit to the sagacious and disaster to the stupid. " The ultimate result of shielding men from the effects of folly, is to fill the world with fools," was a belief expressed. This was a tacit assertion, recalling like assertions previously made, that the survival of the fittest operates beneficially in society. It appears that in the treatment of every topic, however seemingly remote from philosophy, I found occasion for falling back on some ultimate principle in the natural order.

But now I come to an event of much moment—an event which initiated a long series of changes and determined my subsequent career.

Already I have, when speaking of each essay or book from time to time written, indicated the way in which it stood related to the general doctrine elaborated in after years. Here, to exhibit more clearly the attitude of mind and stage of thought which had been reached, it will be well briefly to recapitulate in immediate succession the implied steps of mental development.

In the narrative of my boyhood I pointed out that I early became possessed by the idea of causation. My father's frequent questions—" Can you tell me the cause of this?" or—" I wonder what is the cause of that," presented to me now one thing and now another, as due to some identifiable agency, usually physical. Though his religious views prevented him from denying the miraculous, yet so frequently did there recur the interpretation of things as natural, and so little reference did he make to the supernatural, that there grew up in me a tacit belief that whatever occurred had its assignable cause of a comprehensible kind. Such notions as uniformity of law and an established order, were of course not then entertained; but the kind of thinking into which I had been led, and which was in part natural to me, prepared the way for acceptance of such notions in due time. How deep-seated had become the implied kind of consciousness, was shown a little later by the incident I narrated as occurring at Hinton when Arnott's *Physics* was being read aloud; and when I called in question the conception of *vis inertiæ* there set forth, which, as I dimly perceived, was irreconcilable with that conception of causation I had come to entertain. The same mental proclivity displayed itself during the later years of my youth in the discussions continually entered upon. Very rarely if ever did I cite an authority for any opinion expressed; but always the course taken was that of seeking to justify an opinion by reference to natural necessities or probabilities. Doubtless my intellectual leaning towards belief in natural causation everywhere operating, and my consequent tendency to disbelieve alleged miracles, had much to do with my gradual relinquishment of the current creed and its associated story of creation—a relinquishment which went on insensibly during early manhood. Doubtless, too, a belief in evolution at large was then latent; since, little as the fact is recognized, anyone who, abandoning the supernaturalism of theology, accepts in full the naturalism of science, tacitly asserts that all things as they now exist have been evolved. The doctrine of the universality of natural causation, has for its inevitable corollary the doctrine that the Universe and all things in it have reached their present forms through successive stages physically necessitated. No such corollary, however, had at that time made itself manifest to me; and I cannot recall any definite belief then entertained about the origin of the Universe or the origin of living things. The first pronounced convictions on these matters were, as I have said, due to the reading of Lyell's *Principles of Geology* when I was twenty: his arguments against Lamarck producing in me a partial acceptance of Lamarck's view.

Two years after, in *The Proper Sphere of Government*, there was shown an unhesitating belief that the phenomena of both individual life and social life, conform to law; and there was insistence on the progressive adaptation of constitution to conditions: implying the influence of the development hypothesis previously accepted. Eight years later increased consistency and definiteness were given to these views in *Social Statics*. Though, as shown in the chapter on "The Divine Idea," positive theism was implied; and though teleological conceptions were involved; yet, practically, the supernaturalism was almost hidden behind the naturalism. Everything was was referred to the unvarying course of causation, no less uniform in the spheres of life and mind than in the sphere of inanimate existence. Continuous adaptation was insisted on as holding of all organisms, and of mental faculties as well as bodily. For this adaptation, the first cause assigned was the increase or decrease of structure consequent on increase or decrease of function; and the second cause assigned was the killing off, or dying out, of individuals least adapted to the requirements of their lives. The ideally moral state was identified with complete adjustment of constitution to conditions; and the fundamental requirement, alike ethical and political, was represented as being the rigorous maintenance of the conditions to harmonious social co-operation; with the certainty that human nature will gradually be moulded to fit them. The dependence of institutions upon individual character was dwelt on; the reciprocal influences of the two emphasized; and the adjustment of moral ideas to the social state illustrated. A physiological view of social actions was taken; on sundry occasions the expression " social organism " was used; the aggregation of citizens forming a nation was compared with the aggregation of cells forming a living body; the progress from a whole made up of like parts which have but little mutual dependence, to a whole made up of unlike parts which are mutually dependent in a high degree, was shown to be a progress common to individual organisms and social organisms. So that the conception of progress subsequently to be presented in a more generalized form, was evidently foreshadowed.

Thus far, acceptance of the developmental idea had been

tacit only; but soon after the publication of *Social Statics* it was avowed: the essay on the "Development Hypothesis," published in March, 1852, being a profession of faith. Immediately after, in "A Theory of Population," &c., came an argument which, dealing with only one aspect of evolution—the decrease of fertility that accompanies increase of development—nevertheless practically assumed the rest. Assigning for this inverse relation necessary physical causes, it also assigned to necessary physical causes, the anticipated increase of mental development and decrease of fertility pointed out as likely to occur in the human race under that growing competition entailed by pressure of population. Treating though it did of a political question, the essay on "Over-legislation," not long afterwards published, betrayed the same general mode of thinking. It assumed that social arrangements and institutions are products of natural causes, and that they have a normal order of growth.

An additional element of thought of great importance now came into play. When looking through the edition of Carpenter's *Principles of Physiology* published in 1851, for the purpose of writing a notice of it in the *Westminster Review*, I became acquainted with von Baer's statement that the development of every organism is a change from homogeneity to heterogeneity. The substance of the thought was not new to me, though its form was. As above shown, in *Social Statics*, citing facts in illustration from Professors Owen and Rymer Jones, I had emphasized the truth that in ascending grades of organization, " we find a gradual diminution in the number of like parts, and a multiplication of unlike ones. In the one extreme there are but few functions, and many similar agents to each function: in the other, there are many functions, and few similar agents to each function." And there is also emphasized the truth that " just this same increasing subdivision of functions takes place in the development of society "—that " the earliest social organizations consist almost wholly of repetitions of one element;" while, with social progress there goes multiplication of " distinct classes " and " special occupations." But in the first place, the conception thus reached had not a sufficiently consolidated form to make it an efficient factor in further thought; and in the second place, involving as it did the idea of function along with the idea of structure, it was limited to organic phenomena. It was otherwise with the more generalized expression of von Baer. Besides being brief it was not necessarily limited to the organic world; though it was by him recognized only as the law of evolution of each individual organism. Added to my stock of general ideas, this idea did not long lie dormant. It was soon extended to certain phenomena of the super-organic class. At the close of the essay on " The Philosophy of Style," published in October, 1852, it made an unobtrusive first appearance as supplying a measure of superiority in style. Change from homogeneity to heterogeneity, began to be recognized as that change in which progress other than organic, consists. But this mode of expressing the idea did not at once replace the one used in *Social Statics*. The doctrine set forth in the essay on " Manners and Fashion," published in April, 1854, that the ceremonial, political, and ecclesiastical controls, are divergent forms of one original control, again exhibits in its original shape the conception that advance from lower to higher is characterized by increasing multiformity.

How dominant the hypothesis of development had now

become with me, is curiously shown in an essay on "The Universal Postulate," published in the *Westminster Review* for October, 1853. Irrelevant though the hypothesis seems to a discussion concerning the test of truth; yet it came out in the expressed belief that fundamental intuitions of which the negations are inconceivable, are products of organized and inherited effects of experiences: evidently the germ of an evolutionary psychology.

Further extensions in the same fields, accompanied by increased definiteness and the sudden appearance of certain other cardinal ideas of like generality, occurred in the two essays published at midsummer, 1854, on "The Genesis of Science" and "The Art of Education." A leading conception set forth in the first of these essays, was that the sciences neither arise in serial order nor can be arranged in serial order, but that their relations are those of divergence and re-divergence: increasing heterogeneity in the body of science being an implication. Moreover it was shown that as the diverging branches of science inosculate more and more, there is an advancing integration keeping pace with the advancing differentiation. And it was also pointed out that along with growing heterogeneity there is growing definiteness. There were kindred ideas in "The Art of Education." It was contended that as the course of mental development is from the simple to the complex, and from the indefinite to the definite, educational methods must be adjusted to this course of development.

A large step was next made. The belief set forth in the early essay on "The Development Hypothesis," implied that not only had bodily organization been naturally evolved, but mental organization too. In the article on

"The Genesis of Science" I had been led to trace the growth of definite reasoning, and the gradual formation of cardinal scientific ideas, as resulting from the accumulating experiences of mankind. Hence arose the thought of writing a *Principles of Psychology*, tracing out the genesis of mind in all its forms, sub-human and human, as produced by the organized and inherited effects of mental actions. In the survey of so relatively wide a field of phenomena, there of course occurred opportunities for further development of the conceptions already entertained; and further development took place. An early-impressed belief in the increase of faculty by exercise in the individual, and the subsequently accepted idea of adaptation as a universal principle of bodily life, now took, when contemplating the phenomena of mind, an appropriately modified form. Progressive adaptation became increasing adjustment of inner subjective relations to outer objective relations—increasing correspondence between the two. Successive chapters treat of the correspondence as "direct and homogeneous," as "direct but heterogeneous," as "increasing in speciality," as "increasing in complexity," and also of "the integration of correspondences."

Quite naturally then, on thus recognizing throughout a further vast field of phenomena the increase of heterogeneity, of speciality, of integration, previously recognized as traits of progress in various minor groups of phenomena, there was suggested the question—Are not these the traits of progress of all kinds? And it needed but to ask the question to find an affirmative answer. Brief inspection made it manifest that the law held in the inorganic world, as in the organic and super-organic. There resulted forthwith the conception of an essay which should set forth the universal presence of these traits—or rather, the first of them; for my mind was at the time so pre-occupied with the thought of increasing heterogeneity as a universal trait, that no space seems to have been left for recognition of the truth that increasing integration and increasing definiteness were also universal traits. There immediately occurred a further significant advance. After recognition of the truth that increasing heterogeneity is universal, there arose the question—Why is it universal? And a transition from the inductive stage to the deductive stage was shown in the answer—the transformation results from the unceasing multiplication of effects. When, shortly after, there came the perception that the condition of homogeneity is an unstable condition, yet another step towards the completely deductive stage was made. And here it may be remarked that with this change from the empirical to the rational, the theorem passed into the region of physical science. It became now a question of causes and effects reduced to their simple forms—a question of molar and molecular forces and energies—a question of the never-ending re-distribution of matter and motion considered under its most general aspects. Thus it is clear that something like a consolidated system of thought was nearly reached.

On glancing over these stages it is, indeed, observable that the advance towards a complete conception of evolution was itself a process of evolution. At first there was simply an unshaped belief in the development of living things; including, in a vague way, social development. The extension of von Baer's formula expressing the development of each organism, first to one and then to another group of phenomena, until all were taken in as parts of a whole, exemplified the process of integration. With advancing integration there went that advancing heterogeneity implied by inclusion of the several classes of inorganic phenomena and the several classes of super-organic phenomena in the same category with organic phenomena. And then the indefinite idea of progress passed into the definite idea of evolution, when there was recognized the essential nature of the change, as a physically-determined transformation conforming to ultimate laws of force. Not until setting down as above the successive stages of thought, was I myself aware how naturally each stage had prepared the way for the next, and how each additional conclusion increased the mental proclivity towards further conclusions lying in the same direction. It now seems that there was an almost inevitable transition to that coherent body of beliefs which soon took place.

What initiated the unification? No positive answer is furnished by my memory; but there is an answer which, on reviewing the circumstances, may be considered as almost certainly the true one.

As above narrated, I had recently been collecting together, revising, and publishing, a number of essays. The transaction had entailed two readings. There was the preparation of them for the press; and there was the correction of the proofs as they passed through the press. Hitherto the various evolutionary ideas which, during the preceding six years had been from time to time expressed in these essays, had been lying apart in my thoughts; but now they were brought together and twice over contemplated in immediate succession. Obviously this process was one fitted to disclose kinships and connexions before unobserved, and fitted, therefore, to produce consolidation.

With this special cause there probably co-operated a more general cause. The time was one at which certain all-embracing scientific truths of a simple order, were being revealed. Years before had been published the work of Sir William Grove on *The Correlation of Physical Forces;* and now the scientific world was becoming everywhere possessed by the general doctrine of the "Conservation of Force," as it was then called. When writing the *Principles of Psychology* three years previously, and proposing (in the division referred to in the preface as then withheld, but which was added in the second edition) to interpret nervous phenomena as resulting from discharges along lines of least resistance, my tendency to seek for ultimate physical principles as keys to complex phenomena, had shown itself. Apt thus to look at things, and prepared therefore to be especially receptive of such truths as that the various kinds of force are but different forms of one force, and that this one force can in no case be either increased or decreased, but only transformed; it is manifest that I was ready to have the several general conceptions above described, still further unified by affiliation on these ultimate physical principles. There naturally arose the perception that the instability of the homogeneous and the multiplication of effects, must be derivative laws; and that the laws from which they are derived must be those ultimate laws of force similarly traceable throughout all orders of existences. There came the thought that the concrete sciences at large should have their various classes of facts presented in subordination to these universal principles, proximate and ultimate. Clearly the astronomic, geologic, biologic, psychologic, and sociologic groups of phenomena, form a connected aggregate of phenomena: the successive parts having arisen one out of another by insensible gradations, and admitting only of conventional separations. Clearly, too, they are unified by exhibiting in common the law of transformation and the causes of transformation. And clearly, therefore, they should be arranged into a coherent body of doctrine, held together by the fundamental kinships.

Though naturally I cannot say that these were the ideas which actually occurred, and that this was their order; yet that some such ideas occurred in some such order, is proved by the fact that I shortly sketched out a scheme of the kind indicated. Evidently I felt at the time that I had made an important step; for this rough draft, then drawn up as follows, is dated.

6 January, 1858.

Vol. I.
Part I. The Unknowable.
    Chap. 1. Truth generally lies in the co-ordination of antagonistic opinions.
    — 2. Failure of Theological Hypotheses.
    — 3. Limitations and Insufficiency of Science.
    — 4. Reconciliation of Theology and Science lies in the recognition of an Omnipresent Activity.

Part II. The Laws of the Unknowable.
    Chap. 1. Though the Omnipresent Activity is unknowable, experience proves its laws to be uniform and ascertainable (illustrated by the law of all Progress).
    — 2. The first law—Instability of the homogeneous.
    — 3. The second law—All force follows the line of least resistance.

Chap. 4. The third law—Every cause produces more than one effect.
— 5. The fourth law—The correlation of forces.
— 6. The fifth law—The conservation of forces (force indestructible).
— 7. The sixth law—The Equilibration of Forces (tendency to ultimate equilibrium).
— 8. These, being the laws of all force whatever, underlie all phenomena whatever.

PART III. ASTRONOMIC EVOLUTION.
Chap. 1. The Nebular Hypothesis.
— 2. Do. Do. as applying to the Universe.
— 3. The Equilibration of Light and Heat as well as Mechanical force.

PART IV. GEOLOGIC EVOLUTION.
Physical Genesis of the Earth.
Chemical Do. Do.

VOL. II. THE PRINCIPLES OF BIOLOGY.

PART I. LIFE IN GENERAL.

PART II. EVOLUTION OF LIFE IN GENERAL (the Development Hypothesis).

PART III. EVOLUTION OF INDIVIDUAL ORGANISMS.

PART IV. MORPHOLOGY (Law of Organic Symmetry).

PART V. LAW OF MULTIPLICATION (Theory of Population).

Vol. III. THE PRINCIPLES OF PSYCHOLOGY
(OBJECTIVE).

Part I. Mental Dynamics ┐ The unwritten part, in which is to be shown how the genesis of Intelligence conforms to the laws of force, and more particularly the law that force follows the line of least resistance.

Part II. General Synthesis
(as written).

Part III. Special Synthesis
(as written).

Vol. IV. THE PRINCIPLES OF PSYCHOLOGY
(SUBJECTIVE).

Part IV. Special Analysis
(as written).

Part V. General Analysis
(as written).

Vol. V. THE PRINCIPLES OF SOCIOLOGY.

(Divided into several parts, showing how the growth, structure, and actions of societies are determined by the laws of force laid down—how the general force is *sensation* or *desire* which is an actual force expending itself in an *equivalent* of muscular contractions or labour—how it follows the line of least resistance—how all phenomena of *production* and *exchange* result from this force following the line of least resistance—how all the differentiations proceed in conformity with this and the other laws of force—how social progress is an approximation to a state of ultimate equilibrium in virtue of the equilibrium of forces —and how finally this state of equilibrium is the perfect or moral state.)

Vol. VI. THE PRINCIPLES OF RECTITUDE
(PERSONAL).
(Developing in detail the ultimate state of adaptation of constitution to conditions—the equilibration of desires and duties, wants and satisfactions, which civilization is producing.)

Vol. VII. THE PRINCIPLES OF RECTITUDE
(SOCIAL).

PART I. SOCIAL STATICS.

PART II. NEGATIVE BENEFICENCE.

PART III. POSITIVE BENEFICENCE.

Developing in detail the moral equilibration of the social state.

Vol. VIII. ESSAYS.
Vol. IX. ESSAYS.
Vol. X. ESSAYS.

This is reproduced verbatim from the original draft, which had been left without any corrections. Evidently there is much crudity in the portions which are detailed; and the other portions, merely indicated, are not thought out. But it is remarkable that the scheme as at first thus suddenly conceived, should have resembled as much as it does the scheme eventually executed. Three days after the date of this sketch I wrote home as follows:—

"13 Loudoun Road
9 Jany '58.

MY DEAR FATHER

I sent the *Westminster* yesterday. When done with circulate it in the usual order.

Within the last ten days my ideas on various matters have suddenly crystallized into a complete whole. Many things which were before lying separate have fallen into their places as harmonious parts of a system that admits of logical development from the simplest general principles. I send you a brief sketch which will give you some idea of it. In process of time I hope gradually to develop the system here sketched out.

I am very well. After having had a rest I am just beginning the article for the *British Quarterly*.

I wish you had some good news to give me about the Bridgegate property. My mother's cold is by this time I hope quite well.

Affectionately
H. S."

A verification of date is yielded by a subsequent letter from my father. Finding me but a poor correspondent and apt to overlook the questions he asked, he had fallen into the habit of writing out these questions as they occurred to him from time to time on separate half-sheets of note-paper: each question having beneath it a space to contain my answer. Two such separate half-sheets, both dated January 31, 1858, contain these questions and answers.

How do you reconcile your omnipresent activity with the future equilibrium you speak of?

An equilibrium like that of the solar system consists with activity.

Shall you be able to prove that perfect homogeneity is unstable?

Absolute homogeneity extending throughout *infinity* would be stable.

Can you tell me whether the future work alluded to in your Social Statics embraces the Principles of Sociology together with the Principles of Rectitude?

No.

I am puzzled to know how your vol. 7 will be able to take

in with Social Statics Negative Beneficence and Positive Beneficence and retain a moderate size. Shall you take part of the matter of Social Statics from it and put to other chapters?

Yes.

Did you wish me to keep these *crystallized ideas* of yours to myself or do you wish me to divulge them?

Keep them to yourself.

Thus then it is clear that the first days of 1858 saw the inception of the undertaking to which the rest of my life was to be devoted.

An engagement had been made in November, 1857, to write an article for the April number of the *British Quarterly* on the moral discipline of children; and the writing of this essay (which forms one of the chapters in the little volume on *Education*) occupied me during the early part of 1858.

Concerned with the process of mental unfolding, the subject was certain to be treated by me from the point of view now reached. Consciously or unconsciously the theory of evolution furnished guidance. One of the initial conceptions is that since inherited constitution must ever be the chief factor in determining character, it is absurd to suppose that any system of moral discipline can produce an ideal character, or anything more than some moderate advance towards it. " The guiding principle of moral education" especially insisted on, is that there shall habitually be experienced the natural reaction consequent on each action. As the ascent through lower forms of life has been effected by the discipline of enjoying the pleasures and suffering the pains which followed this or that kind of conduct; so further ascent above the form of life now reached must be thus effected. One of the corollaries drawn is that as throughout our converse with surrounding Nature, most of our activities are unrestrained, but those which bring penalties continue to bring penalties whenever they are repeated—Nature accepting no excuses; so, with educational discipline, while there should be no needless restraints, the needful restraints should be unvarying and irresistible.

These leading ideas sufficiently indicate the way in which moral education was conceived as simply a final part of the process by which the emotional nature has been evolved—a process which in the future is to follow the same lines as in the past.

Life in those days was passing not unpleasantly. Some incidents of the time I give in extracts from letters. The first is from one to my mother dated February 19.

"I am going on very well—sleeping better for the last ten days, and writing all morning without thinking about my head. Indeed I have rarely any sensation now. The good living and the lively society here evidently suit me well.

I dined lately at Sir John Trelawney's, in company with Mr. Grote the historian of Greece, and Mr. Buckle, the new historian, whom I knew previously. Mr. Grote I wanted to know. He was very civil and hoped we should meet again.

I saw John Mill lately. He was complimentary about the essays; telling me he had read all those he had not before seen and had re-read the others."

Here is part of a letter to my father dated March 1:—

"The enclosed note is from the Editor of the *Quarterly Review*. The article which I am to write is on 'Physical Training,' in which I am proposing to expose the bad results of under-feeding, under-clothing, and over-education. I have not written for the *Quarterly* before, and as their pay is the same as the *Edinburgh* (£16 per sheet) I am glad to make the connexion."

In a letter to him dated March 22nd occurs the passage:—

"I am day by day developing further the scheme of which I gave you a sketch. Another general law of force has occurred to me since I saw you, viz.—*the universality of rhythm;* which is a *necessary* consequence of the antagonism of opposing forces. This holds equally in the undulations of the etherial medium, and the actions and reactions of social life."

A later note runs:—"I dined with Buckle the other day. Among other guests were Mr. Grote, Sir Henry Holland, Monckton Milnes, M.P." [afterwards Lord Houghton].

The essay on physical training above referred to as having been written for the *Quarterly Review* was not accepted by the editor: at that time the Rev. Mr. Elwin. Possibly its conceptions, anti-ascetic as they were, did not harmonize either with his theological system or with the ideas which public school-life had fostered in him. It was not until April, 1859, that this essay, now forming the fourth chapter of the little book on *Education,* was published in the *British Quarterly Review.*

Though it makes no reference to the doctrine of evolution, its ideas are congruous with the doctrine in so far that the method of nature is emphasized as that which should be kept in view when deciding on methods of physical training. There is an implied recognition of the principle conformed to in the rearing of offspring throughout the animal-world at large; namely that in proportion as growth and organization are incomplete, much must be given and little demanded. It is argued that as with inferior creatures, early life is distinguished by the continual receipt of benefits and absence of labours; so with ourselves, early life, instead of being made often as laborious as adult life, should be so carried on as to favour more the development of the body, and to postpone later such development of the mind as requires any great and continuous effort.* In harmony with this view, it is contended that for bodily welfare the sensations are the most trustworthy guides; and that the mischiefs of bad physical management result from disregard of them. Though it is not so alleged in the essay, this guiding principle, too, is a corollary from a general biological truth—the truth that among all lower forms of life, uncontrolled by commands, traditions, or creeds, there has been no other prompter to right physical actions than obedience to the sensations: the continual killing off of those in which the two were not rightly adjusted to the needs, having maintained and improved the adjustment. Whence it follows that, inheriting as we do adjustments established during the progress through lower forms of life, our sensations are on the whole trustworthy guides to bodily welfare.†

* For elucidations see *Principles of Sociology*, § 322.

† The reader will find explanations in the *Principles of Psychology*, § 124, and in the *Data of Ethics*, §§ 33—6. Study of the passages there found will prevent him from identifying sensations and emotions. Careless use of words, and consequent careless thinking, leads nine people out of ten to confuse together all the feelings in such wise that one who says that sensations are trustworthy guides to bodily welfare, is habitually represented as saying that we ought in all cases to follow the promptings of our feelings: the truth being that we have often other ends than bodily welfare to be pursued; and further, that though the

So that though this essay was not conspicuously evolutionary in its doctrines, yet its doctrines were evolutionary in their unavowed origin.

A few years before this time, the great telescope of Lord Rosse had resolved into stars, sundry nebulæ which were previously regarded as irresolvable. There was drawn the inference that all nebulæ, so called, consist of stars; and that their nebulous appearance is solely the result of extreme remoteness. This inference was at that time generally accepted among astronomers.

As the doctrine of evolution in its widest sense sets out with that state of matter and motion implied by the nebular hypothesis, it naturally happened that this tacit denial of the nebular hypothesis did not leave me unmoved. I saw reasons for questioning the legitimacy of the inferences above described, and was prompted to look more nearly into the matter. Finding abundant grounds for dissent, I set them forth in an article for the *Westminster*, entitled "Recent Astronomy and the Nebular Hypothesis."

The first part of the article, having for its purpose to show that the conclusion which had been drawn from the assigned evidence was logically untenable, was not an inappropriate undertaking for an outsider; but the undertaking grew into an exposition and defence of the nebular hypothesis considered in detail. With a daring which I look back upon with surprise, I set forth sundry suggestions, interpretations, and speculations, in aid of it. There was an attempt to show how nebular rotation

sensations are fairly well adjusted to the requirements, the emotions are by no means thus adjusted.

would be set up in masses of diffused nebulous matter. Arguments were drawn from the distribution of comets; from the inclinations of the orbit-planes of the planets; from the inclinations of the planetary axes to their respective orbit-planes; from the velocities of rotation of the planets; and from the distribution of satellites. An endeavour was made to show that for the various specific gravities of the planets the hypothesis yields an explanation; and that the differences in temperature among them, which there is reason to infer, as well as their general differences from the Sun in respect of temperature, are also such as the hypothesis implies: to which last argument there was added an inference respecting the composition of the solar atmosphere.

An astronomer would have been chary about committing himself to so many speculative views. To propound them needed one who had not an established scientific reputation at stake. Naturally there were errors in the article. Two, however, of the conclusions drawn have since been verified. Mr. Proctor has given abundant further proof that the nebulæ are not remote sidereal systems; and within some three years after the publication of the article, the researches of Kirchhoff and Bunsen proved, by the help of the spectroscope, the truth of the speculation I had ventured concerning the photosphere of the sun. The article was published in the *Westminster Review* for July. Some correspondence ensued with Sir John Herschel and Sir G. B. Airy, then Astronomer Royal, who were good enough to favour me with criticisms. On two points I had the satisfaction of finding the disagreement of the first met by the agreement of the last.

I left town towards the end of June, and before going elsewhere spent a few days at home.

The scheme which had in January taken definite shape in my mind, and indeed on paper, had of course during the spring been the subject of thought in respect of the means for carrying it into effect. I finally decided to consult John Mill on the matter, and wrote to him the following letter.

"17, Wilmot Street,
Derby, 29 July, '58.

My dear Sir,—

May I ask your opinion on a point partly of personal interest, partly of more general interest?

In the essays on "Progress: its Law and Cause" and on "Transcendental Physiology," which I believe you have read, are the rudiments of certain general principles, which, at the time they were first enunciated, I had no intention of developing further. But more recently, these general principles, uniting with certain others whose connexion with them I did not before recognize, have evolved into a form far higher than I had ever anticipated; and I now find that the various special ideas which I had designed hereafter to publish on certain divisions of Biology, Psychology and Sociology, have fallen into their places as parts of the general body of doctrine thus originating. Having intended to continue occupying myself, as hitherto, in writing essays and books embodying these various special ideas, I have become still more anxious to devote my energies to the exposition of these larger views which include them, and, as I think, reduce all the higher sciences to a rational form.

But, unhappily, my books have at present no adequate sale. Not only have they entailed upon me the negative loss of years spent without remuneration, but also a heavy positive loss in unrepaid expenses of publication. What little property I had has been thus nearly all dissipated. And now that

I am more anxious than ever to persevere, it seems likely that I shall be unable to do so. My health does not permit me to spend leisure hours in these higher pursuits, after a day spent in remunerative occupation. And thus there appears no alternative but to desist.

Under these circumstances my question is—Do you think that in the reorganized staff of the Indian Administration I might find some post, rather of trust than of much active duty, which would give me an income sufficing for my modest bachelor needs, while it would allow adequate leisure for the prosecution of these aims? I fear that few if any such posts are likely to exist; and that my political views might render some, even of these few, unavailable; but it appears worth while to inquire. I need hardly say that my object is so exclusively that which I have explained, that a post which did not conduce to it would have no temptation for me, however otherwise desirable.

I ask your advice under the belief that you sympathize in the general views I wish to develop, and may therefore feel some interest in the matter.

Believe me,
Very truly yours,
HERBERT SPENCER."

Mill's reply to this letter, though sympathetic, was disappointing. It held out no encouragement; and I dropped all thought of any such help as an office of the kind described might have given.

Though born in Derby, I had up to this time seen but little of Derbyshire. Matlock I had been to; but had reached no point further north. Mainly I fancy from lack of funds, I decided to limit my summer excursion to a ramble in the Derbyshire dales; hoping to find some fishing as a pastime. Going as far as Buxton, and being disappointed in respect of sport, I turned south again, and settled myself at a picturesque little place, the Briars, Matlock Bank, where I spent about a fortnight: returning thence to Derby.

Already, from an illustration given a few pages back, joined with preceding ones, some will have inferred that I had adopted Danton's motto,—*De l'audace! encore de l'audace! toujours de l'audace!;* and while at Matlock Bank I furnished another illustration. I have named the fact that in 1851, I attended a series of Prof. Owen's lectures on Comparative Osteology; and that in the course of them my scepticism respecting his theory of the archetypal skeleton and archetypal vertebra grew gradually stronger, until at the close of the course it ended in complete disbelief. No occasion had thus far arisen for setting forth this disbelief; nor, in the absence of encouragement derived from finding doubt in others, should I have thought myself warranted in expressing it. Distinguished biologists had shown their adherence to Prof. Owen's doctrine. It was set forth and adopted in Carpenter's *Principles of Physiology;* and the *Archetype and Homologies of the Vertebrate Skeleton* was in use as a text book at University College. Though this endorsement did not cause me to believe; yet even my independence would not have prompted public utterance of dissent had nothing happened. But during the spring, Prof. Huxley, in his Croonian Lecture before the Royal Society on "The Vertebrate Structure of the Skull," attacked Prof. Owen's interpretation of it. Hearing this amount of disagreement expressed, I was encouraged to take up the general theory; and in June arranged with the Editor of the *Medico-Chirurgical Review* to write a criticism on the several works in which Prof. Owen has embodied it. Had the question been one of knowledge, I should not have been absurd enough to criticize a naturalist so profoundly acquainted with the facts; but it was a question of reasoning. Setting out with the remark that " judging whether another proves his position is a widely different thing from proving your own;" the first paragraph of my article ended with the further remark that " if the data put before him do not bear out the inference, it is competent for every logical reader to say so." Thus taking Prof. Owen's various statements and explanations as they stood, the purpose was to show that they involved incongruities so numerous as to make his hypothesis untenable. Though the doctrine of evolution made no overt appearance in the earlier part of the article, it came out at the close; for in the last few pages an endeavour was made to show how the genesis of the vertebrate skeleton is interpretable from the evolution point of view.

Six weeks of Derby proved anything but beneficial. The popular notion about native air was then, as on many other occasions, disproved in my own case. At the end of August, being much below par, I joined the Lotts at Llandudno, and there rapidly improved. The salubrity of the place and the many pleasant excursions were as causes of improvement, aided by the enlivening society of old friends—the only society I much care about. And here I am prompted to remark concerning health, that not by people at large only, but by medical men, the effects of mental influences are under-estimated. The exhilaration produced by novelty; the breaking away from the monotonous routine of daily life at home; the absence of worrying anxieties and the presence of positive gratifications, are usually more potent causes of improvement than are differences in physical circumstances. Even where change of scene with its accompanying increase of enjoyments and decrease of annoyances, is excluded, the effects of agreeable emotions are often surprising. I have had many experiences of the fact that dyspepsia, so far from being necessarily exacerbated by dining out, may even be cured, notwithstanding many dietetic imprudences, if the social surroundings are such as to yield great pleasure.

After three weeks at Llandudno, and an interval at Derby, I returned to town in October; and again took up my abode at 13, Loudoun Road.

CHAPTER XXXI.

PLANS FOR EXECUTING IT.

1858—59. ÆT. 38—39.

I HAD left London before the end of June; and it was not until the first of July that the two papers by Mr. Darwin and Mr. Wallace on the operation of Natural Selection in causing divergence of species, were read before the Linnæan Society. I have but a vague impression of the way in which this event became known to me; but my belief is that I remained in ignorance of it until my return to town in October.

A reason confirming me in this belief is furnished by a paragraph contained in a letter to my mother dated 29 November, which runs as follows:—" I have been distributing a few volumes of my Essays. Enclosed are some of the acknowledgments, from Dr. Latham, Dr. Hooker, and Mr. Charles Darwin." As the volume had been published in December, 1857, I was, when I came upon this passage, at a loss to understand why this distribution had not been made until November, 1858. But the probable explanation is that, when I learnt the nature of Mr. Darwin's paper and learnt that Dr. Hooker accepted his interpretation, I sent copies of the volume to them and to a few others, because of the essay on the Development Hypothesis contained in it. The following is Mr. Darwin's acknowledgment:—

No, it is not as follows; for on consideration I decide to omit it. Notwithstanding the compliments it contains, which seemed to negative publication, I was about to quote it, because it dispels, more effectually than anything else can, a current error respecting the relation between Mr. Darwin's views and my own. But the reproduction of it would be out of taste, and I leave the error to be otherwise corrected.

Here I may fitly comment on certain difficulties which I foresee will from time to time present themselves—difficulties in choosing between two alternatives, each of which is objectionable. If, after long periods of non-success, there came to an autobiographer incidents implying success, and the increased appreciation indicated, mention of these cannot be omitted without partially falsifying the narrative. On the other hand, as they reflect some kind of honour on him, the mention of them appears indicative of vanity; though it may result from a desire to give a complete presentation, or from the feeling that against the debit items of the account it is but fair that the credit items should be placed. What, then, is to be done? At first sight it seems possible for one who narrates his own life and draws his own portrait to be quite truthful; but it proves to be impossible.

There are various media which distort the things seen through them, and an autobiography is a medium which produces some irremediable distortions.

Immediately on my return to town I proposed to the editor of the *Medico-Chirurgical Review* to write an essay on "The Laws of Organic Form" for publication in

January, 1859. The title shows that the essay contained a further extension of evolutionary views. The germinal idea had occurred to me in the course of a country ramble with Mr. G. H. Lewes in the autumn of 1851.

The thesis was that organic forms in general, vegetal and animal, are determined by the relations of the parts to incident forces. Radial symmetry, bilateral symmetry, and asymmetry, alike in stationary and moving organisms, were shown, one or other of them, to become established, according as the parts are similarly disposed towards the environment all round an axis, or similarly disposed on two sides of an axis, or not similarly disposed on any side. The explanation given was that here the necessities entailed by position and there the necessities entailed by locomotion, entailed likenesses between parts which were conditioned in like ways. This general interpretation of external forms was congruous with the more special interpretation of internal forms in the case of the vertebrate skeleton—an interpretation appended to the critique on Prof. Owen's theory.

A systematized and elaborated statement of the hypothesis set forth in this essay, was in later years incorporated in Part IV. of the *Principles of Biology*.

What induced me to take up the subject, I cannot remember; but while at Derby in October, I collected some materials for an article on "The Morals of Trade," and, continuing my inquiries in London, began writing it as soon as the article above named was completed.

This was one of the few exceptions to the general rule. Many examples have made it clear that nearly everything I wrote had a bearing, direct or indirect, on the doctrine of evolution. Here, however, there appears no trace of any such bearing; unless, indeed, it be in the tacit recognition of the moral modifiability of human nature and the moral adaptation of men to the passing social state. The article took for its especial topic, not those multitudinous small dishonesties which characterize retail trade, but those larger and less familiar ones which vitiate the transactions of manufacturers, merchants, and wholesale dealers. A further object of the essay was to show that the dishonesty of the classes not engaged in trade is proved by numerous illustrations to be as great in degree though different in kind. And yet another object was to suggest that a remote cause for such dishonesties, alike of traders and others, is the indiscriminate admiration given to whatever implies wealth.

Originally written for the *Quarterly Review* but not accepted by the editor, the article was published in the *Westminster Review* for April, 1859. I may add, as a curious incident, that many years afterwards the Rev. Canon Lyttelton applied to me for permission to republish it in a pamphlet along with a sermon of his own on the same subject—a permission which I cheerfully gave. That an ecclesiastic should take a step which coupled his name with mine, curiously exemplified the spread of liberality in religious opinion.

In a letter to my father dated 16 November, 1858, there occurs the remark:—" The arrangements at Malvern House are not so good as they were. The number is much smaller—Mr. Parry and myself being the only inmates not of the family:" inconvenient changes of hours being also named. And then a letter of 15 December says of my hosts that:—" They are going to make some arrangements which will make it no longer convenient to have me. They express great regret at the necessity of separation. I, too, am sorry; for I doubt whether I shall find a place altogether as suitable."

Had it not been that Mr. Parry—the old gentleman I have referred to as being eighty and a wit—had also to take his departure, I should have concluded that my host had been prompted by the wish to prevent any further influence exercised by me over his son: a youth of some nineteen or twenty. Not, indeed, that I had knowingly exercised such influence; but the son had got hold of my books, and imbibed from them ideas of a kind his father did not approve. Naturally enough, he desired to prevent what he regarded as a perversion; and his desire, though clearly not the sole cause, may have been a part cause for making the domestic change which took place.

My removal was long postponed, however; for my letters continue to be dated from 13, Loudoun Road up to the beginning of February; at which date, having failed to find a desirable habitat, I went down home for a few weeks.

During the latter part of 1858, as during its earlier part, there had been constantly before me the question—How to carry out my undertaking? The general conception had of course been enlarging, and gaining in definiteness while it gained in fulness; and I was growing eager to find some way of setting it forth after the manner sketched out at the beginning of the year. The difficulties in the way were very great. What little property had come to me from my uncle Thomas, had been nearly all frittered away. Partly it had been spent in the publication of books which were not simply unremunerative, but entailed positive losses. And of what had not thus been sunk, most had gone in costs of living and travelling about during the eighteen months in which my nervous breakdown had prevented me altogether from working. As may be inferred, when these drafts upon it had been met not very much remained of the legacy of £500 left to me in 1853. During the period described in the last two chapters, I was able to work at the best only three hours a day, and often not that; and there occasionally came relapses which forced me to leave off for a time entirely. To these facts must be added the further one, that my essays, not usually of a kind to be written off-hand, but involving much thought and inquiry, brought me but small returns. The articles for the *Medico-Chirurgical Review* were paid for at the rate of either six pounds or six guineas per sheet (sixteen pages); and the others at the rate of ten pounds per sheet. Clearly such being my limited capacity for work, and such being the remuneration for what I did, it was not easy for me, though practising every economy, to meet my expenses.

How then was it possible to execute my project—a project sufficiently extensive and onerous even for one in full health and having income enough to maintain him while devoting himself to non-paying work. What to do, was a question frequently occupying my not very hopeful thoughts, and was a question sometimes discussed with friends. One of the schemes I entertained, not in a sanguine way it is true, shows how hardly pressed I was to find some plan. Chapman, when the *Westminster Review* came into his hands, had established what he called an "Independent Section"—an appended portion in which was published, now and again, a paper of which he thought well, though he did not wish to commit the Review to its conclusions. My proposal was that I should write instalments of the System of Philosophy, or at any rate of the first volume, to be published in this independent section—some two or three sheets per quarter: being paid for them at the ordinary rate. Naturally enough Chapman did not think favourably of this proposal, and it dropped through. Wild as it was, however, it was not so wild as one made by my friend Lewes. Knowing that I was not without mechanical ingenuity, and that I had years before profited by an appliance I had registered, he suggested that I should get my income by small inventions, and devote my leisure time to the work! I remember that George Eliot joined me in laughter at this amusing proposal. It was made by one who little knew how precarious are the proceeds of inventions, and how frequently inventors reap losses rather than gains.

Thus the year ended without disclosing any way of doing that which I now felt to be my work in life.

Before leaving town as above indicated, several small matters of interest occurred, as shown in the following extracts from a letter home, written on January 10.

"I have agreed with Chapman to do an article for him on the relative values of different kinds of knowledge. I have not fixed the title yet. But its chief aim is to go in for more *science*.

I am pretty well—as well as Xmas excitements allow. But I should be all the better for less going out.

The matter of Chapman's business has dropped through. It would not have done unless I had devoted all my time to it. So it is to be carried on by Chapman's late assistants—Birt & Fergusson.

I shall probably leave this house in about a week. I am going to take an advertisement to the *Times* to-day.

I will send you the new number of the *Medico-Chi.* containing my article on the "Laws of Organic Form," shortly. At present Lewes has it.

I did not after all go down to Hastings. Sir J. Trelawney and his family returned to town sooner than was expected.

The Potters are in town, and I spent Saturday evening with them. I am to go and see them in the spring."

The third of the foregoing paragraphs recalls a fact which I had completely forgotten. Chapman, a sanguine speculative man, who, during his career as a publisher, lasting some fourteen or fifteen years, had been losing money, was at this date forced to retire: deciding, at the same time, to resume those studies in preparation for the practice of medicine, which had been interrupted when he became a publisher. Among those who had assisted him with loans was Mr. Octavius Smith; and, judging from what occurred, he had, I presume, become the chief creditor. Now-a-days but few publishers are alarmed by so-called heterodox opinions in the books offered to them; but at that time Chapman was the only respectable publisher through whom could be issued books which were tacitly or avowedly rationalistic. Hence, being broad-minded and anxious that the spread of liberal opinion should not be hindered, Mr. Smith wished the business to be carried on. Having, as it seemed, some confidence in my judgment, he suggested that I should undertake to superintend it: perhaps thinking that after giving it due attention, I should have sufficient leisure to carry out the undertaking which he knew I had at heart. But probably I saw that, difficult as it is even for one fully disciplined to make an enterprise of such a kind answer by devoting to it all energies, it would be impossible to make it answer if neither of those conditions was fulfilled.

The article above named as having been agreed upon, which was eventually entitled "What Knowledge is of most worth?" and now forms the first chapter in the little work *Education*, &c., was commenced either just before my departure for Derby or shortly afterwards. I recall the date because of an important incident connected with it. Before the essay was half done, I suffered one of my not infrequent relapses, and had to suspend work. My father was at the time much troubled by the interference of the Local Sanitary Board with property of his in Derby—some thirteen small houses which, instead of being improved by alterations on which the authorities insisted, had been so much damaged that some of his tenants left. Hence he contemplated a memorial to the Town Council, complaining of the treatment he had received. He was, however, peculiar in the respect that while energetic about small things, he was almost paralyzed by things of moment. Anxious that the proposed memorial should be written, knowing that if left to himself my father would not write it, and yet feeling that my own state of brain would not allow me to write it for him, I said that if he would be amanuensis I would try to do the work for him by dictating. He agreed; and the experiment, being tried, proved successful. It did more—it initiated a practice which I thereafter adopted. I made the satisfactory discovery that my head would bear dictating much more easily than it would bear writing; and I at once foresaw that this discovery would considerably affect my future course.

On my return to town in March I settled myself at 24, Oakley Square. A letter dated 23rd April contains the paragraph:—" I have got an amanuensis, and find the dictation answers. I do fully half as much again or more, and with greater ease."

I may here remark that from the beginning I never experienced any difficulty. Friends to whom I afterwards recommended dictation, asserted either that they should not be able, or that they had not been able, to collect their thoughts under such conditions. One of them who, yielding to my repeated exhortations, tried the experiment, told me on inquiry that it had failed. On asking why, he said that his landlady, not having succeeded in finding, as he requested, a youth to play the part of scribe, suggested that perhaps her daughter might serve. He accepted the proposal; but, on making a trial, confessed that he found himself thinking much more about the girl than about his work. This, it seemed to me, was a very inadequate experience on which to found a generalization. Avoiding a distraction of this kind, I was but little impeded. The disturbance to thought produced by the consciousness that another was waiting for me, though I think I felt it a little at first, soon became inappreciable. Did not the change of method affect my style? is a question which will be asked. Not very greatly I think. After this article, of which the first half had been written and the second half dictated, was published, I put to a competent judge of composition the question whether he could decide where the transition was made. He was unable to do this; and remarked only that he thought the latter part of the essay was more declamatory—I think that was the word—than the earlier part. Nevertheless I believe the practice of dictating, thereafter followed, did injure my style. The general experience is that diffuseness results when the pen is held by another. One who, when writing by proxy, makes it a point to keep his amanuensis going, is obviously more likely to use a defective expression than when, holding the pen himself, he has no external incentive to abridge any pause he makes for thinking. Only where, as in my own case, there is acquired the habit of so far ignoring the amanuensis as to take whatever time may be needed for choosing the best form of words, is the effect on the quality of the product likely to be small. Still, an effect is, I think, traceable. It has been remarked to me more than once that *Social Statics* is better written than my later books. Though doubtless a good deal is due to the nature of subject—though *The Study of Sociology*, akin in matter, approaches more nearly in manner to *Social Statics* than any other work of mine; yet there remains a difference. *Social Statics* was, I remember, characterized as epigrammatic; but none of my later books could be rightly thus characterized.

The essay "What Knowledge is of most worth?" reference to which has called forth these parenthetic remarks, was published in the *Westminster Review* for July, 1859. Since then, the claims of science have received increasing recognition; but when this essay was written, its leading thesis, that the teaching of the classics should give place to the teaching of science, was regarded by nine out of ten cultivated people as simply monstrous. Even now, changed though the general feeling is, more space for science is but reluctantly yielded; and in such places as public schools the space is still very small. To one who never received the bias given by the established course of culture, and on whom the authority of traditions and customs weighs but little, the state of opinion about the matter appears astounding. To think that after these thousands of years of civilization, the prevailing belief should still be that while knowledge of his own nature, bodily and mental, and of the world physical and social in which he has to live, is of no moment to a man, it is of great moment that he should master the languages of two extinct peoples and become familiar with their legends, battles, and superstitions, as well as the achievements, mostly sanguinary, of their men, and the crimes of their gods! Two local groups of facts and fictions, filling a relatively minute space in the genesis of a World which is itself but an infinitesimal part of the Universe, so occupy students that they leave the World and the Universe unstudied! Had Greece and Rome never existed, human life, and the right conduct of it, would have been in their essentials exactly what they now are: survival or death, health or disease, prosperity or adversity, happiness or misery, would have been just in the same ways determined by the adjustment or non-adjustment of actions to requirements. And yet knowledge subserving the adjustment which so profoundly concerns men from hour to hour, is contemptuously neglected; while the best preparation for complete living is supposed to be familiarity with the words and thoughts, successes and disasters, follies, vices, and atrocities, of two peoples whose intelligence was certainly not above ours, whose moral standard was unquestionably lower, and whose acquaintance with the nature of things, internal and external, was relatively small. Still more when from the value of knowledge for guidance we pass to the value it has for general illumination, may we continue to marvel at the perversity with which, generation after generation, students spend their years over the errors of ancient speculators who had no adequate data for their reasonings, while all that modern science, having for materials the accumulated and generalized observations of centuries, can tell respecting ourselves and our surroundings, they ignore; or if they glance at it, do so at leisure hours as at something relatively unimportant. In times to come this condition of opinion will be instanced as one of the strange aberrations through which Humanity has passed.

Concerning this article I may add that, while it had no direct bearing on the doctrine of evolution, its insistence on comprehensive scientific culture, was an insistence on the acquisition of that knowledge from which the doctrine of evolution is an eventual outcome.

Sometime during this spring occurred an incident which I may name partly for its intrinsic interest, and partly as a lesson.

Already I have mentioned the fact that, while yet the first of the *Scenes of Clerical Life* was but partly written, I was told by George Eliot, on whom I had frequently urged the writing of fiction, that she had commenced; and, as I think I have said, I was for some time the sole possessor of the secret. Of course curiosity concerning the authorship of these stories accompanied the interest in them; and amusement was afforded me by the speculations I heard ventured—in some cases by her friends. After the publication of *Adam Bede* the curiosity became greater and the speculation more rife; and it was by-and-by guessed that she was the anonymous author. Chapman, knowing that if anyone knew I did, one day suddenly addressed me—" By the way, Mrs. Dunn told me the other night that Miss Evans is the author of

Adam Bede: is it true?" "Mrs. Dunn!" I replied; "who told Mrs. Dunn any such thing?" "Oh, that she didn't say." "I do not see how Mrs. Dunn should know anything about it; she can have no means of learning." Thus I fenced as well as I could, but all to no purpose. Chapman soon returned to the question—"Is it true?" To this question I made no answer; and of course my silence amounted to an admission.

When next I went over to Wandsworth, I told them what had occurred, and was blamed for not giving a denial: the case of Scott being named as justifying such a course. Leaving aside the ethical question, however, a denial from me would have been futile. The truth would have been betrayed by my manner, if not otherwise. I have so little control over my features that a vocal "No" would have been inevitably accompanied by a facial "Yes."

The lesson which the incident teaches is that a secret cannot safely be committed even to one in whom perfect confidence may be reposed. For, as we see, scrupulous faith will not always prevent unintended disclosure. I may add that fortunately no harm was done. The secret was leaking out; and, moreover, the reason for keeping the secret had no longer much weight.

When thinking about ways of prosecuting my scheme, there sometimes arose the question—Is there any post under Government which I might consistently accept, and which would give me the needful leisure? Of course most of the offices which might else have served were unavailable by one holding the views I did, and still do, concerning the limitations of State-functions. An inspectorship of prisons occurred to me as a position which might be filled without any dereliction of principle; since maintenance of order is a State-function which I have ever insisted upon as essential. It was, however, a foolish hope that such an office would, after I had discharged its duties, leave me any time for writing. But my mood was that of the drowning man who catches at a straw.

There is proof that the thought of obtaining some post of this kind had been entertained towards the close of the preceding year. Then, and during subsequent months, I obtained testimonials from sundry leading men. Among them were Mill, Huxley, Tyndall, Grote, Hooker, Fraser, Sir Henry Holland, and Sir G. C. Lewis. Several were strongly expressed; and especially those of Mill, Huxley, and Tyndall.

Of all posts likely to answer my purpose, that of stamp-distributor was the most promising. It is one of which the duties are in large measure mechanical and can be to a considerable extent performed by a subordinate. Either at the close of 1858 or in the spring of 1859, the stamp-distributorship for Derby fell vacant, and I made an effort to obtain it. Lord Derby was then Prime Minister; and Lord Stanley (the present Lord Derby) was Secretary of State for India. He had read some of my books; and, as I knew from the editor of the *Westminster*, had expressed approval of some of my articles. Hence I hoped something from his friendly intervention: the appointment of an impecunious author to such a place being not without precedent. The claims of party proved too strong, however. The place was given to the editor of a provincial Conservative paper who had been useful in his locality.

A letter from Hooker written at the time proves to me

a fact which I had absolutely forgotten—namely, that I had thought of a foreign consulship as a post which might possibly give me adequate leisure. This was a very erroneous supposition, Hooker told me.

What was my daily life during this period? The question is one I cannot answer more definitely than by saying that, after a walk of half-an-hour or so, the morning was devoted to work—or as much of the morning as the state of my head would allow; and that during the rest of the day I had to kill time as best I might. I suppose I walked a good deal in the afternoon; and did much of my thinking while walking—a habit which was, and has since been, physically injurious, however much otherwise beneficial. A story I have told of myself as a boy, shows how apt I was to become mentally absorbed at an early age; and in later life, states of absorption, different as were the subjects of thought, were scarcely less marked. I once discovered to my dismay that I sometimes passed those living in the same house with me, and, though I looked them in the face, remained unconscious that I had seen them.

It is clear, however, from letters, that my social circle was extending. Beyond mention of engagements to friends already named there are occasionally such passages as:—

"I dined yesterday in company with Mr. Roebuck, his wife and daughter, and some other notabilities." [One of the said notabilities was, I remember, the late Mr. Charles Austen]. "Sir J. Trelawney has invited me to go yachting with him for a few days." "I dined in company with Tyndall on Wednesday. He gave us an account of his night on the top of M. Blanc." . . . "Dr. Arnott called on me yesterday and stayed an hour." [Dr. Arnott, at that time well known by his *Elements of Physics,* liked the article "What Knowledge is of most worth," and had obtained my address from the editor of the *Westminster.*] . . . "I am going to Dr. Carpenter's to-night, to meet Mr. Morell."

Dr. Morell, known at that time by his book on *The Recent Philosophy of Europe,* has long resided in Capri, and has dropped out of public thought. During dinner a story was told about some eccentric member of the Carpenter family, who had adopted a boy with a view to carrying out his own ideas of a good education. He shortly found that the undertaking was more onerous than he expected, and thereupon cast about for a wife: giving one whom he found to understand that the rearing of the boy was to be considered the primary purpose of the marriage. Dr. Morell's comment was—"Ah, I see: Rule of Three inverse."

Of amusements in those days there is but little to say. Now that operas were no longer free to me, I never went —the cost was too great; and I but rarely saw a play. Occasionally some music was heard during the seasons when there were going on the promenade concerts, which were at that time conducted by their promoter, Jullien. Especially on what were announced as classical nights did I go. Even then there was often a good deal which I rather tolerated than enjoyed—much that seemed to me manufacture rather than inspiration. A friend of mine, Pigott, said of orchestral music, that when from any one instrument there came something worth listening to, all the other instruments forthwith entered into a conspiracy to put it down; and though his remark ignored too much the larger effects of orchestral combinations, it pointed to the fact that most orchestral combinations are

not sufficiently coherent. Ballads had ceased to give me the pleasure which they did in the early days; but above all I was, and am still, intolerant of such solos as were performed by Sivori and other celebrities of the kind—mere displays of executive skill. When I go to a concert, I do not go to hear gymnastics on the violin.

I may remark in passing that the applause given to such performances well illustrates the vitiation of opinion. Usually after a display of wonderful mechanical dexterity by an instrumentalist, the members of the orchestra applaud. Observing this, many of the audience, thinking these cultivated musicians must be the best judges, applaud loudly; and the rest of the audience join in the applause, lest they should be thought persons of no taste: the truth being that the brother instrumentalists applaud, not the music produced, but the triumph over difficulties. And thus the mass of hearers, following authority as they suppose, are led to accept as music what is in fact the murder of music. In this case, as in multitudinous other cases, every one says and does what every one else says and does—lacking courage to do otherwise; and so helps to generate or to maintain a sham opinion. Considering that the ordinary citizen has no excess of individuality to boast of, it seems strange that he should be so anxious to hide what little he has.

Early in May, 1859, I left town for Gloucestershire to spend ten days at Standish. It must, I think, have been on this occasion that I initiated my little friends there—a troop of children, all girls, whom I had severally seen grow up from infancy—in Natural History, by establishing an aquarium and giving them lessons in the use of the microscope. Hitherto our afternoon walks had been walks simply; but now they became expeditions in search of interesting objects. My visits being the occasions for rambles further afield and less restrained than those taken in charge of a governess, were, I believe, looked forward to as bringing extended liberties and more varied amusements. The pleasurable associations thus established in early days affected our relations throughout our after lives.

Returning to town for a few days only, I left for Derby some time before the end of the month, and there recommenced work. The lives and deaths of periodicals would form a good topic for an essayist. Annually a considerable number are born, and annually a considerable number die,—now scarcely surviving infancy, now killed by starvation in middle life, and now coming to an end in old age in consequence of that increasing rigidity which will not allow of adaptation to new conditions. Out of the periodicals to which I have contributed, I can count up ten newspapers, magazines and quarterlies, which have thus disappeared. One of them was the *Universal Review*, a then recently established organ of opinion for which I had been asked to write an article. It was one of those which die early; but it survived long enough to publish the essay on "Illogical Geology" which I had undertaken for it. This was written, or rather dictated, during a six weeks' sojourn at Derby.

The topic was one which gave occasion for expressing evolutionary ideas in a new direction; and I presume that the consciousness of this was dominant with me when I undertook the subject. There were the changes of the Earth's crust itself to be considered from a developmental point of view, as well as the changes of the past life on its surface. As originally proposed, the article was to have been a review of the works of Hugh Miller; but these eventually became simply the text for a discussion of what seemed to me the errors of orthodox geology, as exemplified in them as well as in the works of Murchison and Lyell. The title " Illogical Geology " sufficiently shows that the article called in question the legitimacy of current conclusions, considered as following from the evidence assigned. No more in this case than in the case of Prof. Owen's theory, should I have ventured to express dissent concerning matters of fact; but, accepting the facts as stated, an outsider was not unwarranted in considering whether the inferences were legitimately drawn from them.

The assumption made by some that strata in different parts of the Earth, called by the same name, were contemporaneous, and the more defensible assumption made by others, that if not single strata yet systems of strata were everywhere contemporaneous, were shown to be inconsistent with various of the admissions and assertions elsewhere made. The dogma then accepted by geologists, that certain great breaks in the succession of organic remains imply almost complete destructions of living things and creations of new floras and faunas, was contested; and it was argued that the acknowledged course of geological changes would, along with small breaks, necessitate these great breaks. Naturally a chief aim was that of showing that the arguments against the hypothesis of evolution which Hugh Miller and others drew from palæontology, were fallacious. But I was candid enough to admit that while geological evidence did not disprove the development hypothesis, neither did it prove it: contending that the most we can expect is to find congruity between the hypothesis and the evidence yielded by comparatively recent fossil forms. This congruity has since been shown to exist.

In those years and after, a craving for the mountains recurred annually; and when, along with satisfaction of it I could satisfy a craving for the sea, I rejoiced in doing so. Leaving home early in July, I took the coast of Cumberland on my way north; settling myself for a week or so at Drigg, close to the since-established watering-place known as Sea-scales. My artist-friend Deacon joined me there with his two boys. A walk over to Wast-water was one of our excursions; and there was a subsequent migration to St. Bees.

A change of ministry had occurred in June; and Sir G. C. Lewis had become Home Secretary. He was editor of the *Edinburgh Review* at the time I wrote for it the article on " Railway Morals and Railway Policy:" an interview and some correspondence having been thereby occasioned. Moreover he had written me some friendly criticisms on the doctrine set forth in the essay on " Progress: its Law and Cause." So that I was not without hope that, having stamp-distributorships in his gift, I might through him obtain one, and thereby be enabled to live while carrying out my scheme. Before leaving Derby I had forwarded to him the testimonials above named, and while at Drigg received his reply. I cannot now find it; but I remember distinctly enough that it was not encouraging—so little encouraging in fact that I thereafter gave up all hope.

The 19th of July found me at Achranich, the highland paradise of my kind friends with whom I had before spent a delightful two months, and with whom I was now to spend another like interval. As said in a letter home on the 21st—" Fishing, riding, driving, walking, talking and laughing, are capital stimuli, and have given me two good nights:" a sentence I quote partly to indicate the enjoyable life, and partly to show that the question of more or less sleep still remained dominant. I must add that the expression "good nights" is relative only in meaning; for my best night would, by any one in health, be called a bad one.

"The day was one I shall never forget," is the closing sentence of a letter written during the last week of my stay. It describes "the most charming excursion I ever had." This was an excursion by boat " down the Sound of Mull, up Loch Sunart and Loch Teachus; and home by land," which I name not so much for its own sake, though " the scenery was splendid and the colouring marvellous;" as because in our party of twelve there were several of known names. One was Professor Sellar, whose works on Roman literature are of high repute; another was Miss Cross, who some years later published a volume of graceful poems, but, marrying and dying soon afterwards, did not fulfil the promise then made; and a third was Mr. John Cross, who, long afterwards, married George Eliot and wrote her life. Young and vivacious as were nearly all members of the party, and elated as all were by sailing over a sunny sea amid islands and mountains made gorgeous by the autumn colouring of trees, bracken and decaying lichens, the occasion united a variety of pleasures which but rarely come together; so that I remember saying after our return that the day must be marked not by one white stone but by many.

Reaching home about the 20th September, I occupied

myself in fulfilling an engagement made before I left town in the spring. A letter to my father dated 29th April contains the paragraph:—" Dr. Sieveking has asked me to review Bain's new book ' The Emotions and the Will' for the *Medico-Chirurgical;* and I have consented."

This review I undertook mainly because of the connexion which the subject had with the general question of evolution. Its aim was to show that the phenomena presented by the emotions can be truly understood only from the evolution point of view. Bain and I were on terms, if not exactly of friendship, yet of friendly acquaintanceship; but I said in the article all that I thought: giving credit at the same time that I expressed dissent. Some of my criticisms touched fundamentally his method and his general conceptions; but he, in a way unusual with authors, accepted them in good part. Indeed I cannot remember anyone, known to me either directly or indirectly, who has maintained an attitude so purely philosophical; and in whom the interests of truth have so greatly predominated over all personal interests. In after years we became more intimate and eventually established cordial relations.

Towards the end of October I returned to town and again took up my abode in Oakley Square. Though my letters at the time do not betray discouragement, yet I can scarcely have failed to feel it; for now, after the lapse of nearly two years, I seemed no nearer to the execution of my project than on the day when it first took possession of me.

CHAPTER XXXII.

A PLAN FIXED UPON.

1859—60. ÆT. 39—40.

THE closing months of 1859 were occupied in fulfilling several literary engagements. Masson, my acquaintance with whom, made nearly ten years before, had ripened into a friendship which has since continued and increased in warmth, was at that time Editor of *Macmillan's Magazine*, then recently established. He asked me to write an article for him, and I agreed to do so. I had also arranged to write one for the *Westminster* on "The Social Organism," and one for the *British Quarterly* on "Prison Ethics."

Most readers are, I suspect, weary of the analyses, made for the purpose of showing the bearings of successive essays on the general doctrine which occupied my mind; but near as I am now to the end of the series, I may be excused for continuing them. That the conception of the Social Organism is an evolutionary one, is implied by the words; for they exclude the notion of manufacture or artificial arrangement, while they imply natural development. Briefly expressed in *Social Statics*, and having grown in the interval, the conception was now to be set forth in an elaborated form. The leading facts insisted on were, that a social organism is like an individual organism in these essential traits:—that it grows; that while growing it becomes more complex; that while becoming complex its parts acquire increasing mutual dependence; and that its life is immense in length compared with the lives of its component units. It was pointed out that in both cases there is increasing integration accompanied by increasing heterogeneity; to which I might have added increasing definiteness, had my ideas at that time been fully matured. The article appeared in January, 1860; and some attention was drawn by a promulgation of ideas which to the average mind seemed simply whimsical.

The essay on "Prison Ethics," written at this time but not published in the *British Quarterly* until the subsequent July, though not evolutionary in aspect was evolutionary in spirit. Its conclusions were based on the laws of life, considered first in themselves and then as conformed to under social conditions. The right of society to coerce the criminal up to certain limits but not beyond those limits, was a deduction. But the essentially evolutionary characteristic was the doctrine that not only the ethically justifiable treatment but the treatment alone successful in reforming criminals, is that of insisting on self-maintenance while they are under restraint—keeping them subject to those requirements of social life which they have not conformed to. The thesis defended was that with criminals, as with all living beings, there will go on adaptation to circumstances if they are forced to live under those circumstances: a corollary from the doctrine of organic evolution.

The brief paper on the "Physiology of Laughter" which I wrote for *Macmillan's Magazine*, also participated, though not conspicuously, in the family traits. It was evolutionary as being an explanation of laughter in terms of those nervo-muscular actions which are displayed everywhere throughout the animal kingdom from moment to moment; and especially as using for a key the law that motion follows the line of least resistance—a law previously recognized as one needful to be taken account of in the interpretation of evolutionary processes.

While these articles were in hand, the *Origin of Species* was published. That reading it gave me great satisfaction may be safely inferred. Whether there was any set-off to this great satisfaction, I cannot now say; for I have quite forgotten the ideas and feelings I had. Up to that time, or rather up to the time at which the papers by Mr. Darwin and Mr. Wallace, read before the Linnæan Society, had become known to me, I held that the sole cause of organic evolution is the inheritance of functionally-produced modifications. The *Origin of Species* made it clear to me that I was wrong; and that the larger part of the facts cannot be due to any such cause. Whether proof that what I had supposed to be the sole cause, could be at best but a part cause, gave me any annoyance, I cannot remember; nor can I remember whether I was vexed by the thought that in 1852 I had failed to carry further the idea then expressed, that among human beings the survival of those who are the select of their generation is a cause of development. But I doubt not that any such feelings, if they arose, were overwhelmed in the gratification I felt at seeing the theory of organic evolution justified. To have the theory of organic evolution justified, was of course to get further support for that theory of evolution at large with which, as we have seen, all my conceptions were bound up. Believing as I did, too, that right guidance, individual and social, depends on acceptance of evolutionary views of mind and of society, I was hopeful that its effects would presently be seen on educational methods, political opinions, and men's ideas about human life.

Obviously these hopes that beneficial results would presently be wrought, were too sanguine. My confidence in the rationality of mankind was much greater then than it is now.

In a letter to my father dated January 20, occurs the sentence—" I shall send you something that will surprise you in a few days." This sentence referred to the programme of the *System of Philosophy*, then in type.

During the autumn of 1859 I abandoned all thought of obtaining any official position which would give me sufficient means while affording me a share of leisure. What then was I to do?—How was I to execute my project? Among plans despairingly thought over there occurred to me that of issuing by subscription. Favourable opinions were expressed by friends with whom I discussed it—among others by the Leweses. George Eliot's diary shows that I dined with them at Wandsworth on November 19th; and I have a tolerably distinct remembrance that we then talked the matter over. The earliest impression I have of the programme (which is marked " revise ") is dated simply January , 1860: a blank for the day of the month being left until I had obtained the criticisms of various friends—Huxley, Tyndall and others. Along with an outline of the proposed series of works, severally divided into their component parts, and each part briefly described, the programme stated the method of issue as follows:—

"It is proposed to publish in parts of from five to six sheets octavo (eighty to ninety-six pages). These parts to be issued quarterly; or as nearly so as is found possible. The price per part to be half-a-crown; that is to say, the four parts yearly issued to be severally delivered, post free, to all annual subscribers of ten shillings."

A long delay occurred before general distribution of the programme. An authoritative endorsement was needful; and much time was occupied in obtaining weighty names of first subscribers, to be printed on the back. The cheerful aid of friends was afforded me— Huxley being especially helpful; and in the course of some six weeks, an imposing list was got together—the chief men of science, a considerable number of leading men of letters, and a few statesmen. In Appendix A will be found a reprint of this programme; and with it these names of sponsors. The date is March 27, 1860.

Comparison of it with the rough draft drawn up in January, 1858, shows that while the outline of the scheme, in so far as the component works are concerned, is substantially the same; and that while, between the delineated contents of each volume in the one case and in the other, there is in some cases a correspondence of a general kind and in other cases an approach to a specific correspondence; there is an amount of difference showing that during the intervening two years the conception had undergone a marked development. Growth of the series from seven volumes to ten, had resulted from expansion of the *Principles of Biology* from one volume to two, and expansion of the *Principles of Sociology* from one volume to three; while within each volume the divisions had multiplied, and there had been arrived at a mode of dealing with each subject in a systematic manner common to them all.

I may remark here that though during these two years there had thus been an extensive further evolution of the original conception, the evolution which subsequently took place, was but small. On comparing the volumes as summarized in the printed programme, with the volumes as since published, it will be seen that the last correspond with the first, save by containing some relatively small additions. In the *Principles of Psychology* there has been introduced (but not until the edition of 1880) a part entitled " Congruities "; while in the *Principles of Sociology*, beyond a change in the order of two of the divisions, there has been introduced a division dealing with Domestic Institutions; and there will, if I live to complete the second volume, be introduced a division dealing with Professional Institutions.

The plan succeeded fairly well. Thanks, no doubt, to the influential names attached to the circular, the issue of it was followed by numerous responses. In the course of the spring there came in between three and four hundred names of subscribers: the number finally reached being over 440. Assuming my ability to write four numbers per annum, and supposing that all the subscribers paid their subscriptions (which a considerable proportion in such cases never do) the gross proceeds would have been some £200 a year. From this, however, had to be deducted the costs of printing, binding, and issuing; which would have reduced the proceeds to perhaps £120 or £130 a year. I dare say I should have been sanguine enough to proceed on the strength of this calculation, even had no addition to these proceeds been in prospect. But there was an addition in prospect.

Some years previously I had made the acquaintance of an American whose sympathies were enlisted on my behalf by perusal of some of my books or essays—Mr. E. A. Silsbee of Salem, Mass. While yet the circular was in its unfinished state, I sent to him a copy, accompanied by the inquiry whether he thought that subscribers might be obtained in America. His reply, dated February 14, held out much encouragement; and a letter of March 6, written after the circular had been sent to New York, contained a sentence the significance of which was shown by subsequent events. The sentence runs—" Mr. Youmans, a very popular and intelligent lecturer on scientific subjects, well known by his works on Chemistry, Physiology, &c., entered with great enthusiasm into the project." Devoting himself with characteristic vigour to the furtherance of my scheme, this previously-unknown friend succeeded in obtaining more than two hundred subscribers.

The relation thus initiated was extremely fortunate; for Prof. Edward L. Youmans was of all Americans I have known or heard of, the one most able and most willing to help me. Alike intellectually and morally, he had in the highest degrees the traits conducive to success in diffusing the doctrines he espoused; and from that time to this he has devoted his life mainly in spreading throughout the United States the doctrine of evolution. His love of wide generalizations had been shown years before in lectures on such topics as the correlation of the physical forces; and from those who heard him I have gathered that, aided by his unusual powers of exposition, the enthusiasm which contemplation of the larger truths of science produced in him, was in a remarkable degree communicated to his hearers. Such larger truths I have on many occasions observed are those which he quickly seizes—ever passing at once through details to lay hold of essentials; and having laid hold of them, he clearly sets them forth afresh in his own way with added illustrations. But it is morally even more than intellectually that he has proved himself a true missionary of advanced ideas. Extremely energetic—so energetic that no one has been able to check his over-activity—he has expended all his powers in advancing what he holds to be the truth; and not only his powers but his means. It has proved impossible to prevent him from injuring himself in health by his exertions; and it has proved impossible to make him pay due regard to his personal interests. So that towards the close of life he finds himself wrecked in body and impoverished in estate by thirty years of devotion to high ends. Among professed worshippers of humanity, who teach that human welfare should be the dominant aim, I have not yet heard of one whose sacrifices on behalf of humanity will bear comparison with those of my friend.

Returning from this tribute of admiration, it remains only to say that, the number of the American subscribers added to that of the English ones, having produced a total of about six hundred, my hopes appeared to be justified, and I resolved to proceed.

I was just free from all ties to periodicals. The last of them had been an engagement to prepare for the *Westminster Review,* an article on " Parliamentary Reform: the Dangers and the Safeguards," which was published in April. Years passed before I interrupted my chief work to do anything more in the way of essay-writing.

I may fitly say a few words about this article; less because of its evolutionary bearings than because of the well-grounded fears expressed in it. Not, indeed, that it had no evolutionary bearings. Its ultimate thesis that "as fast as representation is extended the sphere of government must be contracted," which is a corollary from the thesis upheld some years before, that representative government is the best possible for the administration of justice and the worst possible for everything else, is a practical application of the general doctrine that social progress is accompanied, and should be accompanied, by increasing specialization of functions; and this is an evolutionary doctrine. But that which may be distinguished as the practical part of the article, was an argument showing that unless with the extension of political power there went such direct imposition of public burdens as caused an unceasing consciousness of the way in which public expenditure weighs upon each, there would be an injurious increase of governmental interference and a multiplication of governmental agencies. And it was contended that whereas in the past the superior few had inequitably used their power in such ways as indirectly to benefit themselves at the cost of the inferior many; so the inferior many, becoming predominant, would inequitably use their power in such ways as indirectly to benefit themselves at the cost of the superior few: such superior few being understood to include not the socially superior only but also the superior among those of lower *status*.

Unhappily this prophecy has been fulfilled,—fulfilled,

too, much sooner than I expected. And another extension of the franchise since made, so great as entirely to destroy the balance of powers between classes, and so made as to dissociate the giving of votes from the bearing of burdens, will inevitably be followed by a still more rapid growth of socialistic legislation.

I was now just forty; and I calculated that at the rate of progress specified in the circular, I should get through the undertaking by the time I was sixty. It would have been a sanguine anticipation even for one well in body and brain; and for one in my state it was an absurd anticipation.

Indeed when I look back on all the circumstances,—when I recall the fact that at my best I could work only three hours daily,—when I remember that besides having not unfrequently to cut short my mornings, I from time to time had a serious relapse; I am obliged to admit that to any unconcerned bystander my project must have seemed almost insane. To think that an amount of mental exertion great enough to tax the energies of one in full health and vigour, and at his ease in respect of means, should be undertaken by one who, having only precarious resources, had become so far a nervous invalid that he could not with any certainty count upon his powers from one twenty-four hours to another!

However, as the result has proved, the apparently unreasonable hope was entertained, if not wisely, still fortunately. For though the whole of the project has not been executed, yet the larger part of it has.

PART VIII.

XXXIII. WRITING *FIRST PRINCIPLES*.
XXXIV. AN AUTUMN'S RELAXATIONS.
XXXV. A VOLUME OF THE *BIOLOGY*.
XXXVI. A DIGRESSION.
XXXVII. ANOTHER VOLUME OF THE *BIOLOGY*.
XXXVIII. IMPENDING CESSATION.
XXXIX. SAD EVENTS.

CHAPTER XXXIII.

WRITING *FIRST PRINCIPLES*.

1860—62. Æt. 40—42.

Up to this date my life might fitly have been characterized as miscellaneous. Here it may not be amiss to pause a moment and ask whether there was any relation between this trait of it and the course subsequently pursued.

From the education ordinarily passed through, mine differed by its comparative variety; and while lacking most of the usual linguistic elements, it included a good deal of physical, chemical, and biological knowledge not commonly gained.

Throughout the years passed in civil engineering many phases of the profession occupied me. Beyond plan-drawing and making designs of various kinds, there came surveying and levelling, secretarial business, drafting of contracts, and over-seeing execution of them, testing of locomotives, preparations of plans and sections for Parliament, joined with superintendence of the required staff and followed by attendance on Parliamentary Committees. And along with these sundry forms of engineering activity, there went the occasional invention of appliances and devising of methods.

During a long unengaged interval, inventing and experimenting in many directions filled a large space.

Some time was given to drawing and modelling. Geology and Botany had shares of attention. Several speculative scientific papers were published. The province of Government was thought about and written about. And a period of active political life was passed through.

After entrance upon a literary career there came, if not variety of occupations, yet variety of subjects treated. With journalism was joined the writing on Political Ethics; and political ethics presently led the way to Psychology. Essays at that time and afterwards written, ranged so widely that they look extremely incongruous when bracketed; as instance—" Over Legislation " and " Gracefulness "; " Population " and " Style "; " Manners " and " Development of Species "; " Geology " and " Laughter "; " Banking " and " Personal Beauty "; " Trade Morals " and " The Nebular Hypothesis "; " The Genesis of Science " and " Railway Policy "; " The Shapes of Organisms " and " Parliamentary Reform "; " The Law of Progress " and " Types of Architecture "; " The Test of Truth " and " The Origin of Music "; " Prison Discipline " and " The Use of Anthropomorphism," &c., &c.

But now this miscellaneousness came to a close, and there commenced something like unity of occupation. I say something like; for though the topics to be successively dealt with in developing the Synthetic Philosophy were many in kind—showing perhaps in this way the influence of the preceding life—yet they derived coherence from the unity of conception and method pursued throughout; and to this extent the life became constant instead of changeable.

In one respect, indeed, the unsettledness continued; for, as before, so for some years after, my abode was variable. As I usually spent from two to three months of the autumn away from London, regard for economy made me give up whatever place I occupied, and on my return to town there was generally some reason why it seemed well to advertise afresh for accommodation: a course which sometimes, though not always, led to change of residence. After a short absence from town in the spring, one of these changes took me to 18 Torrington Square, Bloomsbury.

Here it was that on the 7th of May 1860, I began my undertaking; and here it was that I quickly furnished justification to any who exclaimed against my folly in attempting so great a task with my deranged health. Already in April the extra work which, during the preceding months, had been entailed by the floating of my project, had brought on a relapse, and I had to leave town; first for a ramble in Surrey, whence, being companionless, I returned in two days, and then for a sojourn in Derby. And now having, as I hoped, got again into working order, and made a satisfactory commencement, I broke down before I had got through the first chapter. A letter home of the 21st of May is dated Brighton, where I had manifestly gone to recruit. " I am very much better," says a note written from London on the 26th, and which continues—" I go to the Potters in about a week, and shall doubtless progress there still further. I do not think, however, that it will be prudent to work hard enough to get out my first part in July." Letters written from Standish show that I spent about ten days there. On the 13th I departed for Llandudno, to join my friends the Lotts; and I continued with them up to the end of June. Meanwhile my father and mother, in company with a Derby friend, had betaken themselves to my father's favourite spot, Tréport; and pressure, to which I eventually yielded, was put upon me to follow.

At Tréport I resumed work to a small extent. One sunny afternoon, on the grassy slope which runs up from the town to the cliffs, might have been seen two figures, one writing and the other reclining or lounging. They were my father and myself; and the explanation was that he had undertaken to play the part of amanuensis. Indoors and outdoors, some little progress was made in this way during the first week in July. But the place did not on this occasion suit me; for the reason, I believe, that whereas before I was high up above the sea, I was now close down upon it. The result was that on the 11th of July I returned to London.

Something like my ordinary state having been at last regained, I wrote, or rather dictated, at my usual rate; that is, for three hours daily. The MS. of No. 1 of my serial was completed, partly in London and partly in Derby, before the middle of September.

A letter of the 19th of September is from Achranich, where I had at that date been for a few days, and where I had now another delightful sojourn of nearly a month.

There were two other guests—Mr. Arthur Hugh Clough, the poet, and his wife, who was a niece of Mr. Octavius Smith. *The Bothie of Tober-na-Vuolich* had been lying about the house at Achranich during my previous visits. I had already seen a little of its author in London, and now I saw a good deal of him. Not, indeed, that our intercourse was to much purpose in the way of establishing an intimacy. He was a very reserved, undemonstrative man, who usually took little share in general conversation. His face had a weary expression which seemed to imply either chronic physical discomfort or chronic mental depression—an apparent depression which suggested the thought that he was oppressed by consciousness of the mystery of things. Of the ideas or sentiments he uttered no trace remains with me. One thing only which he said do I remember; and this was a story concerning an ancestor of his. While rambling in North Derbyshire, his father or grandfather—I forget which,—was struck by the picturesqueness of a gorge down which tumbled a small stream. Turning to a man who was at hand, he inquired its name. " Go it Clough " was the startling reply. The explanation of the apparent insult was that the stream was named " the Goit," and that " clough " is the North Derbyshire word for a ravine.

A two days' excursion of the whole party, family and guests, was the only incident which broke the usual routine of out-door sports and in-door pleasures. Some dozen miles or so of mountain road, traversed by vehicles and horses, brought us to Strontian on Loch Sunart. After a night spent there, a drive along the beautiful shores of the loch, and then over the intervening country till we came in sight of Loch Shiel, was followed by a return to the shore of Loch Sunart at Salen. A boat down the remainder of Loch Sunart and up Loch Teachus, brought us back nearly to the boundary of the estate: a scramble in the dusk over the intervening moor, a moonlight row along Loch Arienas, and a drive from Acharn, taking us home. The excursion was not so delightful as that of the preceding year, but it has left vivid memories.

Reference to this excursion reminds me that on my

return I found waiting for me a packet of proofs; and this recalls a typographical error contained in one of them. Most authors occasionally have droll blunders made by printers, and one such occurred in these early proofs of *First Principles*. Where I had written—" the daily verification of scientific predictions," the compositor had put—" the daily versification of scientific predictions."

After some ten days spent at Derby on my way, I reached London again on the 22nd of October. Number 1 of my serial, greatly delayed by printing and postal delinquencies, was on the eve of issue—nearly three months after the date I had originally hoped.

Little work was done before I again left town. My uncle William, the youngest of the brotherhood, whom I had found unwell on my return from Scotland in October, became seriously ill in November. I was in consequence called down to Derby and remained there till his death, which occurred before the close of the month. We had always been on amicable terms from the early days when, to his prompt action, I owed the appointment with which my engineering life commenced; and though at issue on religious questions, there had been a good deal of sympathy between us in our conversations on general topics. But I was quite unprepared for the distribution he made of his property. Appointing me sole executor, his will, making small bequests to other relatives, left to me the remainder of what he possessed, subject to annuities to my father and to an old servant. I believe there were two motives for this course. An eminently friendly man—so much so that he was habitually appealed to by sundry of his intimates for advice and help in their affairs—he was by implication always solicitous for the welfare of relatives, and ever ready to aid. But in proportion to the warmth of this feeling appeared to be the warmth of his resentment when offended; and his resentment was persistent. Some year or two before his death there had arisen a family difference which had, I believe, much to do with the provisions made in his will. My father, however, was of opinion that another motive was dominant. He told me that his brother was solicitous for the credit of the family, and probably thought that the arrangement he made would be most conducive to it.

But whatever may have caused this distribution of his property, not many months elapsed before I became aware that it would have important effects on my career; for experience soon proved that I had miscalculated my resources. While my scheme was still only in contemplation, I was told by a competent judge that there would be great difficulty in getting in the subscriptions; and I quite counted upon suffering some loss from non-payment. I was not, and never had been, among those who labour under the delusion that intellectual culture produces moral elevation; and did not expect to find that those who took in my serial were more honest than uneducated people. The defaulters were, however, more numerous than I expected. I found that which I was told others had found:—a moiety pay promptly; others after the publishers send them reminders; not a few, being several subscriptions in arrear, require repeated notices from the publishers before they discharge their obligations; and a considerable class, deaf to all representations, never pay at all for the parts sent to them year after year, and have at last to be struck off the list.

Having started with a number of subscribers which I concluded would suffice to pay costs of printing &c. and leave a moderate return (a number which, not counting Americans, eventually rose to 430), I was unprepared for the amount of loss suffered.

The extent of these defalcations was such that in the absence of other resources I should have had to stop before the completion of my first volume.

The end of 1860 and the beginning of 1861, passed without any incident calling for mention beyond an illness of my father. Being a nervous subject, he regarded this with greater alarm than it called for. I took him to Brighton, and stayed with him there a good deal during parts of February and March; and he afterwards passed some time with me in London, where he recovered.

Notwithstanding consequent hindrances to my work, it progressed satisfactorily; and, escaping nervous relapses, I managed to issue Parts II and III at the appointed times—intervals of three months. At the end of March, however, my head gave way again and I had to desist. Early in April ten days were spent at Standish, with pleasure and doubtless with benefit, after which I went home for a time. I was not wholly idle during these visits. I had decided to re-publish, in the form of a volume, the four articles on Education which had originally been contributed to the *Westminster*, the *North British*, and the *British Quarterly* Reviews. The revision of these articles, commenced before leaving town and finished while at Derby, was in considerable measure carried on out of doors. I rambled into the country; looked out every now and then for a sheltered or sunny bank on which to recline while correcting a few pages; eventually reached some village where a country inn furnished me with a meal; and then, after a rest, returned home.

In this way I got through a little easy work which otherwise would have been impracticable; and after I completed it, returned to London.

More than a month was passed there before I was able to resume the writing of *First Principles;* and then the resumption was under difficulties, as is shown by the following paragraph from a letter to my father dated London, 14 June, 1861.

"I am much better this week and am doing some work. I am doing it in a very odd way—uniting dictating and rowing. I take my amanuensis on the Regent's Park water, row vigorously for 5 minutes and dictate for a quarter of an hour; then more rowing and more dictating alternately. It answers capitally."

Soon afterwards I was led into another way of keeping off cerebral congestion. Mr. J. F. McLennan, at that time little known, but afterwards well known as the author of *Primitive Marriage,* &c., was a candidate for (I think) a professorship at Edinburgh, and wrote to me for a testimonial: directing my attention to a certain article of his in the *Encyclopædia Britannica* as affording me a means of estimating his competence. Remembering the disaster which had resulted when I read up with the view of writing a testimonial for Professor Fraser, I declined, after giving my reasons. Mr. McLennan took my refusal in good part; and, having himself suffered somewhat from an overworked brain, recommended to me racquets as an exercise. Accepting the suggestion, and discovering an open racquet-court at The Belvidere, Pentonville, I betook myself thither with my amanuensis every morning, and after a game or two adjourned to an adjacent room where I dictated awhile, and then, before head-symptoms set in, returned to the court for another game or two; and so on all the morning.

Though in this way I got through two or three paragraphs daily without making myself worse, I failed to get better; and it became manifest that I should be unable to issue my next part at the appointed date. It became manifest, too, that working against time would never do: the endeavour to keep to fixed intervals must be abandoned. Accordingly I issued a notice to the subscribers stating that the next number would not appear at the end of the three months; and stating, further, that for the future the successive numbers would be severally issued as soon as completed, without regard to dates.

A few lines to my mother, dated Oban, July 9, show that I was unexpectedly detained there by the delay in the arrival of my friends, who had again kindly invited me to visit them. Still below my ordinary state of health, and yet wishing not to let my time pass wholly without result, I sought out a youth of some eighteen or so, sufficiently educated to serve as amanuensis, and when the time came took him over with me to lodge at Loch Aline, whence he came to me daily. A letter dated 28 July, written to my father, then in France, says:—

"I have been at Ardtornish now rather more than a week. In consequence of the Smiths not having arrived, to my great dismay, I had to spend a fortnight in Oban and the neighbourhood. This did me harm, as solitude always does; and I have in consequence not been well. However I am better now than I have been; and the delightful life here will doubtless soon set me right. I have got a decent amanuensis (this being Sunday he is not available) and have done a little work. . . . The writing and boating answers very well, and is very pleasant.

Our weather here is very agreeable—above the average of Scotch weather; and the scenery is charming. All day long there is some beautiful effect on mountains or sea to look at; and the sun-sets are magnificent.

I have set up three aquaria, which give great interest; and the microscope [one which I had bought just before leaving town] also is a source of amusement. The dredge is now made, but we have not used it. The coast is very rich, and I expect to get many novelties. . . .

I went out fishing the evening I arrived, and caught a salmon the first thing. Since then the river has been too low."

I give these extracts at length because they conveniently serve to introduce some explanations and comments. The first concerns the apparent change of name from Achranich to Ardtornish. At the time when Mr. Smith bought the estate of Achranich, the two estates, Acharn and Ardtornish, lying on either side of it, were owned by Mr. Sellar (father of the present Professor Sellar of Edinburgh, Mr. Alexander Craig Sellar, M.P., and other sons), who was desirous of purchasing Achranich and uniting the three estates. He hesitated too long, hoping to get a reduction of price, and Achranich was unawares bought over his head, to his great disgust. Some years afterwards his death brought the estates of Acharn and Ardtornish into the market; and after considerable delay they were, at the close of 1860, purchased by Mr. Smith: the three united estates being thereafter known as Ardtornish. As the Ardtornish house (part of which, as before described, is visible some distance behind the ruins of the castle) was more convenient than the old house at Achranich; and as the new house was still in course of erection; it was decided to occupy the Ardtornish house till the new house was complete.

It was to the views from the Ardtornish house that the expression "charming scenery," used above, referred. Probably I was thinking of a certain bright morning in August. From the smoothly shorn lawn with its flower beds, I was looking over the carefully trimmed hedge, to the mountains on the other side of the Sound, and marking how the cultivated beauty of the one served as a foil to the wild beauty of the other, when there came to me through the open window the first movement from one of Beethoven's finest sonatas: a favourite movement which has since never failed to recall the scene. But there is a still more vivid recollection dating back to one of the evenings of that year. The western part of the Sound of Mull trends a good deal towards the north; so that during the summer months the Sun sets over the hills at its further end. On the evening in question the gorgeous colours of clouds and sky, splendid enough even by themselves to be long remembered, were reflected from the surface of the Sound, at the same time that both of its sides, along with the mountains of Mull, were lighted up by the setting Sun; and, while I was leaning out of the window gazing at this scene, music from the piano behind me served as a commentary. The exaltation of feeling produced was unparalleled in my experience; and never since has pleasurable emotion risen in me to the same intensity.

Other words in the foregoing extract recall the fact that during my stay, what little writing I did was broken by exercise, now on the land and now on the water: sometimes rambling along the shore of Loch Aline and sitting down occasionally to dictate a few sentences, or along the Ardtornish cliffs, where the waterfalls suggested one of the illustrations used in the chapter I was writing on the "Direction of Motion"; and at other times boating—either paddling about in Ardtornish Bay or rowing from Achranich to the ferry, and dictating while I rowed.

Filled with many pleasures and with little work, the time thus passed till the end of August.

The dates of letters imply that, after spending something like a fortnight at home on my way south, I went to London. A letter written from 18 Torrington Square, on September 21, 1861, says:—

"I reached town safely on Wednesday, and you will be surprised to hear left it again next day. Happening to call on Lewes, I was induced by him to join him in a country ramble. We started forthwith for Reigate, and spent Friday and Saturday in walking through a charming country; both of us returning much the better for the excursion.

I had eighty-eight replies to my advertisement for an amanuensis. You see I have found one; and I shall commence work in earnest tomorrow."

The country ramble in question was from Reigate to Dorking, where we slept; thence next day to Ockley, where we slept; and then back over Leith Hill. Though not the last of the excursions we made together, this was, I think, the last but two.

I had evidently not yet got back to the normal level

of my abnormal state. In a letter of the 26th I read:—
"I am much better, and doing my work (on the water) with comfort": the result being that my next number was issued in November, after having been delayed some four or five months.

Mention of its issue recalls an incident affecting my finances, which should be named. In a preceding chapter I have stated that Chapman, with whom I had published *Social Statics*, had, after sinking a good deal of money, been finally compelled to give up his publishing business. It was eventually taken by a Mr. Manwaring —a young man quite inadequately prepared, as it turned out. *The Principles of Psychology* and a volume of *Essays, &c.*, had been published for me by Messrs. Longman; but my business transactions with the firm had been such as rendered me undesirous of continuing them, and still more undesirous of extending them. Consequently I put the issue of my serial into the hands of Mr. Manwaring. It proved an unfortunate step, for there soon came a crash. A letter to my father written on 22nd January, 1862, says:—

"You will see by the enclosed that I have succeeded (though after some difficulty) in coming to an arrangement with Williams & Norgate. Everyone agrees that they are the best people I could have. I shall be very glad to get out of Manwaring's hands; but I expect to lose by him considerably."

This expectation was fulfilled. By Mr. Manwaring were of course received the amounts paid by subscribers, and of the sum accruing from them which was in his hands at the time of his failure (between forty and fifty pounds) I believe no part ever reached me. As I was already suffering loss from defaulting subscribers, it was hard that I should lose also a portion of the amount derived from those who paid. In the absence of other resources the result might have been serious.

The winter months and those of the early spring brought no events worthy of record. In a letter of 23rd January I speak of myself as "still improving" and "pretty nearly up to my average": the effect being that now, after this relapse so long in being recovered from, my work was progressing with but little hindrance.

Certain additions to my social circle must here be named. For some years Mr. and Mrs. George Busk had been among my acquaintances, and before 1862 I had come to count them among my friends—friends with whom the intimacy grew gradually closer. Retiring in nature, and consequently much less known to the world at large than to the scientific world, Mr. Busk, not long afterwards elected President of the College of Surgeons, was one who devoted his leisure (for he had given up practice) to science and to the business of various scientific societies in which he took an active part. And Mrs. Busk, scientifically cultivated in a degree rare among ladies, united with her culture other mental attractions, which gave a never failing interest to her conversation. In after years many pleasant times, short and long, were spent with them and their four daughters.

On several occasions, at their house and elsewhere, I had met at dinner one whose name has since become familiar to most; and the result was the commencement of an intimacy, as witness the following passage in a letter to my father:—

"As you see by this note, I have made some new friends. The writer, well known in the world of science, is the eldest son of Sir John Lubbock, whose name you know very well as an astronomer. I spent a very pleasant two days with them and met Sir John Lubbock there at dinner. . . Last night I had a note from Mrs. Lubbock asking me to go down to them again on the 13th of April."

At that time Mr. and Mrs. Lubbock lived at Lammas, Chislehurst. Many Saturday afternoons and Sundays were afterwards agreeably spent there; and when, a few years later, High Elms, the family seat, descended along with the title to Mr. Lubbock, visits of this kind were continued. Other guests, coming from the worlds of science, literature, and politics, while they made these occasions interesting, made them also somewhat too exciting: especially as all present were habitually drawn out by Lady Lubbock's vivacity and Sir John's versatility. Two unusually bad nights were commonly entailed on me; and consequently, as time went on, I had more and more to avoid these and other such Sunday visits into the country: a further reason for doing this being that on each occasion the Monday morning's work was in large measure sacrificed.

Here the mention of Sir John Lubbock's versatility, conspicuous enough even to readers of newspapers and still more conspicuous to those who know all his many activities, recalls an incident which illustrates his remarkable facility in carrying on many occupations. The incident occurred some four years or so later, at a time when I had been investigating the circulation in plants, and had made a number of preparations for the microscope. These I took with me one Saturday to High Elms, thinking they would prove of interest. On the Monday morning early, Sir John was out cub-hunting with his brothers (a frequent practice with them); on his return he made a diagram for a lecture he was about to give; then he examined under the microscope the preparations I had brought; and finally he came to breakfast. After breakfast there was the drive to the station; a rapid glance through the *Times* on the way up to town; some pages of a book which he had brought with him; and at length came the business of the day, itself sufficiently varied—banking, probably a board-meeting of some kind, political business, attendance at a scientific society: perhaps after a dinner party. And the remarkable peculiarity was that with all these many and varied occupations he never seemed in a hurry; but, by his habitual calm, gave the impression that he was quite at leisure.

On looking back to my social life at this time, I see that its excitements were becoming occasionally too much for me, as witness some sentences in a letter home dated 15th of April:—

"Dining out three days running is always more than I can stand with impunity; and I am hence somewhat below par this morning, but not so much so as I expected. In consequence of this accumulation of excitements I had to excuse myself from the Coopers' invitation, which was for Friday. As I told Mrs. Cooper, I *dare* not accept. I shall call on them in the course of this week."

Let me add, however, that I have often found dining out in moderation, beneficial rather than injurious—especially in a lively circle, as I think I have before remarked. My experiences to a considerable extent justify the advice which Sir Henry Holland told me he gave to his dyspeptic patients. He recommended them to go out to dinner and eat made dishes.

A few words about the Leweses should be added here.

Charles, his father's eldest son, had recently obtained—a post in the Post Office I was about to say, but the cacophony stopped me; and then I was about to say, an office in the Post Office, which is nearly as bad; let me say—a place in the Post Office. Chiefly, I believe, for his benefit, they removed from Wandsworth into town, and took a house in Blandford Square. From time to time I spent an evening with them there—always pleasantly, of course. Occasionally Lewes and I and another friend of theirs, amused ourselves by singing glees. George Eliot, however, never joined us: why, I do not know, for her voice would greatly have improved the harmony.

A change of residence was made towards the end of February. I removed to 29 Bloomsbury Square. The house was a good one, having large rooms and being in other ways desirable. Here I remained for the rest of the season; and here, before the end of June, I completed *First Principles*.

Am I about to write an imaginary review of the work, as of two preceding works? No: like reasons do not exist. The motive for giving, in the manner adopted, an account of *Social Statics*, was that the connexion between its ideas and the ideas which preceded and succeeded them, might be exhibited; and it seemed the more needful thus to exhibit them because, as I have for many years been deterred by consciousness of its defects from issuing new editions of the work, it is difficult of access. Similarly with *The Principles of Psychology*. Save in a few public libraries, no one can now find a copy of the first edition; and only, therefore, by the help of the outline I have given, can any one judge of its relation to antecedent and subsequent phases of thought, as well as of its divergence from contemporary opinion. But in *First Principles*, which from its date of publication has continued in successive editions to be readily accessible, there is exhibited, not a stage in the development of the doctrine, but the developed doctrine itself. Though an unlooked for evolution of considerable importance subsequently took place, as will hereafter be shown, yet the system had now so far approached its final shape that description of it as one of the stages passed through would be superfluous.

But, though I do not intend either to outline the contents of the book or to pass any criticisms upon it, I find occasion to make some comments: partly concerning the reception it met with and partly concerning my entirely erroneous anticipations.

Unlike a book of travels, or a gossiping biography, or a volume of Court scandal, or a fresh translation of some classical author, or the account of some bloody campaign, or a new speculation concerning the authorship of *Junius*, or a discussion of Queen Mary's amours, it offered no temptation to the writer of reviews in literary journals; and hence, as might have been expected, it was comparatively little noticed. Passed over altogether by some critical organs, it got in some others the briefest recognition; as, for instance, in the *Spectator*, which gave to it one of those paragraphs of a score of lines in small type, in which it dismisses ephemeral books. While I was not much surprised at this, my surprise was considerable on finding that in most cases the important part of the book was ignored, and that such notice as was taken, was taken of the part which I regarded as relatively unimportant.

Years before, when there took possession of me the project of developing into a System of Philosophy the conception briefly and crudely set forth in the essay on "Progress: its Law and Cause," I saw that it would be needful to preface the exposition by some chapters setting forth my beliefs on ultimate questions, metaphysical and theological; since, otherwise, I should be charged with propounding a purely materialistic interpretation of things. Hence resulted the first division—"The Unknowable." My expectation was that having duly recognized this repudiation of materialism, joined with the assertion that any explanation which may be reached of the order of phenomena as manifested to us throughout the Universe, must leave the Ultimate Mystery unsolved, readers, and by implication critics, would go on to consider the explanation proposed. To me it seemed manifest that the essential part of the book—the doctrine of Evolution—may be held without affirming any metaphysical or theological beliefs; and though, to avoid the ascription of certain beliefs of these classes which I do not hold, I thought it prudent to exclude them, I presumed that others, after noting the exclusion of them by the first division of the work, would turn their thoughts chiefly to the second division. Nothing of the kind happened. Such attention as was given was in nearly all cases given to the agnostic view which I set forth as a preliminary. The general theory which the body of the book elaborates was passed over or but vaguely indicated. And during the five and twenty years which have since elapsed, I have nowhere seen a brief exposition of this general theory.

It might have been not unreasonably supposed that an alleged law of transformation, everywhere unceasingly displayed by existences of all orders, would have received the amount of consideration required for deciding on its probable truth or probable falsehood; seeing that if false its falsity ought to be shown, and if true it should enter as an important factor in men's conceptions of the world around them. But it did not seem so to those who undertake to guide public opinion.

CHAPTER XXXIV.

AN AUTUMN'S RELAXATIONS.

1862. ÆT. 42.

"WELL, it is a great satisfaction to think that the doctrine is now safely set forth, whatever happens to me," I remarked to a friend after *First Principles* was published; and I doubt not that this satisfaction, partly personal but largely impersonal, added to the zest with which I entered upon the relaxations of the summer and autumn.

I say advisedly the summer and autumn. The year 1862 was the year of the second International Exhibition; and of course, as soon as I was at leisure, I devoted a good deal of attention to it. My father, and afterwards my mother, came up to town; and days were spent there in showing them the things of chief interest. Then there arrived the Lotts and other country friends, to whom also I occasionally played the part of guide. Naturally the pleasures given were not so keen as those given by the first Exhibition; but still they were great.

On the 10th of July I was at Llandudno with the Lotts. We made a fortnight's stay there, during which we one day picnic'd at the Aber Falls. On the left hand, the falls are flanked by a spur of Carned David (or is it Carned Llewellyn?); and this, in the course of the afternoon, Lott and I climbed. The climb had a sequence, as witness the following passage of a letter of 16th July.

AN AUTUMN'S RELAXATIONS

"We made a mountain ramble two days ago, and I found it did me more good than anything since I have been here. So I propose to have a course of mountain rambles. I am moderately well but not brilliant in condition."

The result was that, on our return to Derby, I shortly started on a pedestrian fishing tour in Scotland.

As far as Oban and the lower part of the Caledonian Canal, I kept to familiar routes; but at Invergarry I left the steam-boat, having decided to explore the west and north of Ross.

The remainder of my first day, during which I stopped here and there to make a few casts for trout in the Garry, brought me to Tomdoun Inn; and on the next day, Sunday, walking up the rest of Glengarry and down Glen Quoich, I reached Loch Hourn-head. Loch Hourn is the grandest of the Scotch lochs; and though the part seen in this descent to it is not the best, it delighted me so much that my pleasure became vocal. Perhaps it would not have done so had I known what awaited me. To the name Loch Hourn-head was joined on my map one of the little circles which usually implies at least a village having an inn, if not a larger place. I found, however, that besides some tumble-down fishermen's cottages the only house was a keeper's lodge. Here I was taken in by favour, and had to put up with meagre fare and rude accommodation: a damp bed being part of it. Fortunately I had provided myself with a pocket-waterproof, and here, as at various places stopped at in my tour, this befriended me: on some occasions keeping off the rain by day, it, on other occasions, served, when used as a sheet, to keep off the damp by night.

In the course of the evening I said that on the morrow I intended to cross over into Glen Shiel. My host expressed his fear that he would be unable to give me a guide, as they were busy with the hay. I slighted the notion that I needed a guide: saying that I was accustomed to Scotch mountains. Next morning proved fine; and the keeper, admitting that I should perhaps be able to find my way, directed me where to ford the stream which drains Glen Quoich. In an hour or so, I reached the top of the mountain-ridge whence I expected to look down on Glen Shiel and the high road running through it. To my astonishment I found below me a bare valley with no trace of road or human habitation. The map, which showed a single range of mountains between Glen Quoich and Glen Shiel, had deceived me: there were two ranges. Had the summits of the hills become clouded I should not have known where I was, on descending. Fortunately the day continued fine. Keeping my bearings pretty accurately, I ascended the second ridge, and then, as I expected, saw Glen Shiel. During my scramble down a steep hill side covered with heather so deep that I could not see my footing, I twice slipped one of my legs into a crevice between rocks and might readily have broken it. Had I done so, I should most likely have died there. When I got safely on to the high road I became conscious of the risk that is run by one who, leaving a place to which he will not return, traverses alone a wild tract of country on the way to a place where no one expects him. In case of accident he is not missed, and no search is made. Another thing struck me. Joining my experiences in Switzerland with the experience I had just had, I was impressed with the heavy responsibility which rests on the makers and publishers of guide-books. I suspect that from time to time lives are lost, and every year many illnesses caused, in consequence of their misdirections.

A night passed at Shiel Inn was followed by a day passed in fishing the river which runs down the Glen. Half a dozen or more sea-trout rewarded my efforts; but the water was far too low for good fishing and the inn was uncomfortable, so that I was not tempted to stay. A delightful sunny walk along the picturesque shore of Loch Duich carried me the following morning as far as Loch Alsh Ferry, and thence to Balmacarra. A fishing ramble filled the next day. On the morrow a pleasant walk over the intervening hills brought me to Loch Carron ferry, and a further walk to Jeantown. The morning after found me on the other side of the ridge dividing Loch Carron from the valley which skirts the Applecross mountains—strange looking, and one of them especially remarkable: a mountain situated in the centre of an amphitheatre of precipices, from which it has evidently been cut out by glacier-action. That evening I reached Shieldag, a dreary little fishing hamlet on the shore of Loch Torridon. The western side of Ross is not much frequented by tourists, and probably I was the first that season who had stopped at the miserable little inn. They gave me a bedroom so damp that the paper hung from the walls in festoons. "A sabbath day's journey" to Kinloch Ewe was instructive, as well as picturesque in scenery. The doctrine of denudation receives in these regions striking confirmations. On all sides the mountains, consisting the greater part of the way up of, I think, dull red sandstone, are capped with quartz rock. Evidently quartz rock once extended over the whole district; and these islands of quartz on the mountain tops, have been left there by the eroding agencies which cut out the wide and deep valleys between. Then, among further objects of geological interest is "the valley of a thousand hills": such being, it is said, the literal meaning of the Gaelic name. It contains a vast moraine. An ancient glacier, bearing on its surface many separate lines of *débris*, must have paused from time to time in the course of its slow retreat, so as to deliver each line of *débris* for a long interval on the same spot: thus forming a heap.

A day at Kinlochewe was passed in trying to take some sea-trout out of Loch Maree; but as I lacked a boat, the attempt failed entirely. Next day left behind it two memories. The road to Gairloch runs along the shore of Loch Maree; and, keeping in view the imposing Ben Sleoch on the right, passes on the left, after two or three miles, the mouth of a valley which runs away inland. Some miles down this valley stands a mountain of sub-conical shape, the sides of which are channeled by water-courses. If, imagining these water-courses, deeply cut into the rock, to have originally run straight down, it be supposed that some power adequately great gave the whole mountain a twist round its vertical axis, so as to change these straight water-courses into spiral ones, an idea will be gained of its structure. A sketch of this mountain still exists among my papers. Some miles further on, where there lies between the road and the side of the loch a low bit of rough land, some adjacent cottagers, while digging out peat, had brought into view a large surface of granite, not simply rounded, but retaining the polish given to it by the glacier that once filled the basin of Loch Maree—a polish which had been preserved by the overlying peat for—how long shall we say? perhaps 50,000 years.

At the end of one of those days, common in mountainous countries, during which one is frequently tempted by a gleam of sunshine to take off one's waterproof, and then, ten minutes after, by a sudden shower compelled to put it on again, I reached the Gairloch Hotel; and thence, the morning after, departed for Poolewe, there to await, in a dreary little inn, the expedition of the next day—the most serious in the course of my tour. Ullapool on Loch Broom was the nearest stopping place on the northern coast of Ross. Between it and Poolewe was a wild country traversed by a bad road, with no place where rest or refreshment could be had. But I had either to go on to Ullapool or to return the way I came, which I was reluctant to do.

Hiring a boat down Loch Ewe as far as the point at which my route diverged from its shore, and bidding good morning to the boatmen, I commenced my solitary walk of, I suppose, over thirty miles: stopping after some hours to take my meagre mid-day meal of boiled herrings and bread which I had brought with me. The monotony of the day was beguiled somewhat by the scenery, or perhaps I should say rather by the striking geological traits it presented: especially those of immense glacier-action. I passed over a ridge of hills, probably some four or five hundred feet high, on the top of which all the rocks were rounded; showing that in ancient times the glaciers which had filled the adjacent valleys had also covered this ridge, to a depth, probably, of some hundreds of feet. Late in the afternoon I reached the shore of Little Loch Broom. Here, to cut off a portion of the road, I paid one of the fishermen to row me across: first, however, having an experience of Celtic indolence. The boat was lying on the beach half full of water. The man took out the plug, and he and his daughter stood idly by, waiting until, by a stream the thickness of one's finger, the water should escape. He seemed quite unconcerned when I, in a fit of exasperation, seized the baler and began to empty the boat myself. Shortly after came what might have ended in disaster. By the people of some dilapidated cottages on the opposite shore, I was directed into a path which went over the high moor to Loch Broom. This path continued fairly visible for a time; but, as I got on to the flat top of the moor or mountain bog (for it was entirely formed of deep peat), I found it traversed in all directions by large fissures which the water had made in draining away—fissures three or four feet wide and as deep or deeper, over which I had continually to leap. It was in short a bog full of crevasses, with bottoms of soft-peat mud, out of which I should not easily have got had I fallen in. As the evening was coming down rapidly and the path was no longer discernible, I became somewhat fearful of the result; but fortunately I got across before it became dark, and descended to Loch Broom and to Ullapool.

Letters show that I had intended to go as far north as Loch Assynt in Sutherlandshire; but my companionless excursion, though enjoyable at the beginning, was getting wearisome, and I doubt whether I should have fulfilled my intention even had nothing occurred to prevent me. But something did occur. A letter which I found waiting for me at Ullapool made me turn my face south, and travel as fast as coach, railway, and steamboat would carry me.

The contents of the letter which so precipitately changed my course, may be inferred from the following few lines written home, dated Glasgow, August 17th:— "Mr. and Mrs. Youmans are come. I am just starting off with them for a few days. You will probably see me early next week."

Professor Youmans, who from the outset became so ardent an adherent of mine, and then, as always, was prepared for any amount of labour on my behalf, had come over to England with his wife (being then recently married), partly as he told me to see the Great Exhibition of 1862, and partly to consult with me concerning the management of my affairs in the United States.

Our conversations were carried on in the course of three days spent in taking these new friends round to the chief places of interest that were easily accessible. Edinburgh, of course, came in for immediate attention: the chief streets, Calton Hill, The Castle, and Holyrood being visited. I was but a poor *cicerone* for them, however, as measured by ordinary standards; for I could tell them nothing about the historical associations. I have a vague recollection of amusing Professor Youmans by my response to some remark or question coming from our guide at Holyrood—"I am happy to say I don't know." Probably the remark or question referred to Queen Mary. On this, as on kindred occasions, I thus implied my satisfaction, partly in having used time and brain-space for knowledge better worth having, and partly in expressing my small respect for gossip about people of no intrinsic worth, whether dead or living.

Of course something of Scottish scenery had to be shown; and as my friends could not spare time for anything more distant, I carried them over the ordinary tourists' round—by Callander to Loch Katrine; thence to Inversnaid; across Loch Lomond to Tarbet; and from that place to Arrochar on Loch Long. The night being passed there, we went by steamboat next morning to Greenock, where we parted; they for London on their way to the continent and I, in the course of the day, for Derby.

After a fortnight at home and a few days spent with the Brays at Coventry, I returned to London—not indeed to my previous abode; for I found there no fit accommodation. A letter dated 15 Sept. shows that I was settled in Gloucester Square, Hyde Park. A few weeks' experience, however, so dissatisfied me with the management of the house that I decided upon migrating. Before I had found another suitable place Mr. Silsbee, an American gentleman named in a preceding chapter, who was about to spend the winter in the south of France, pressed me to go as far as Paris with him. Being under obligation to him, and having work enough to occupy me in revising while away, I consented, and we departed on the 17 Oct.

Of incidents during this visit to Paris I recall but one. This was a discussion with Mr. Silsbee in the Louvre before a landscape by Rubens (I think), rendered partly by time, and partly by the artist, unlike anything ever seen—especially in atmospheric effect; while it was also extremely unpicturesque in composition. To me it seemed a picture to be glanced at and passed by; but from Mr. Silsbee it called forth much admiration. Even more than ourselves the Americans are affected by the appearance of antiquity: so much so, in some cases, that I heard an American lady declare that a country without ruins of old castles and abbeys is not worth living in. And in still greater degrees than ourselves, they are thus led to confound those extrinsic traits of objects which show antiquity with those intrinsic traits which characterize them as works of art.

Little given to mental analysis, most people fail to discriminate among the causes of their pleasures—or rather, never try to distinguish; and hence ascribe to an ancient work of art itself, the reverential sentiments which its age and its traditional repute arouse in them. But judgments swayed by these sentiments are anything but trustworthy. The one case in which something like measure is possible —that of relative strength—shows clearly how untrue are men's estimates of the past compared with the present. And doubtless the bias which has so conspicuously perverted current opinion in a matter concerning which there ought to have been the least liability to mistake, has perverted it in other matters, and among them in matters of art.

One may say with some approach to truth that on art questions men's judgments have been paralyzed by authority and tradition as they have been on religious questions. There is reason for hoping, however, that as the paralysis is diminishing in respect of the last it will presently diminish in respect of the first.

CHAPTER XXXV.

A VOLUME OF THE *BIOLOGY*.

1862—64. ÆT. 42—44.

On my return from Paris, some time in the first week of November, I took up my abode at 6 Hinde Street, Manchester Square,—a house which has since been destroyed in the formation of a new street. Here I remained during the winter and early spring.

Is it really a fact that women have better intuitions into character than men have? That they are quicker to divine other's moods of mind, there is, I think, good reason for believing, as I have pointed out in the *Study of Sociology;* and it seems almost an implication that if they perceive more truly the passing mental states in those they observe, they also perceive more truly their permanent mental states or established natures. Yet when ·we remember how multitudinous are the cases in which women are deceived by smooth manners and pretty speeches, we cannot but hesitate about admitting this implication. May not the truth rather be that men and women differ, not so much in these intuitions as in the readiness with which they accept and act upon them? The lines—" I do not like you Dr. Fell," etc., point to a distinction between the two. Speaking generally, women do not question the worth of the impressions made on them; while men, receiving the like impressions, are apt to doubt—often think the feelings produced in them are merely prejudices, and consequently decide to wait for evidence. Now as impressions of these kinds are usually not meaningless, but vaguely represent organized and inherited experiences (as we see in an infant which cries on seeing an ugly face or hearing a gruff voice), it results that women, forthwith guided by such impressions, may not unfrequently escape injuries which men, waiting for evidence, suffer before they have satisfied themselves that their impressions are right.

I am led to make these remarks by an experience in Hinde Street. The first impressions I received from my hostess were of an unfavourable kind. She gave me the idea of a nature anything but attractive, although she put on a manner of great civility. I ignored this natural verdict of my feelings, but I had afterwards reason to regret that I did not yield to it. Though no positive evil resulted, the relation was an unpleasant one.

Not as being illustrative of anything repugnant in her, I may here name for its drollery an incident that occurred during my few months of stay in the house. Vain as well as vulgar-minded, she professed to have a high admiration of Shakspeare: was partial to reading his plays aloud, and considered that she declaimed the speeches extremely well. On one occasion, after enlarging upon her reverence for him, she ended by saying—" Ah, I often wish that he were alive, and I had him here. How we should enjoy one another's conversation!"

I had commenced *the Principles of Biology* immediately on arriving in town in the autumn; and during my brief stay in Gloucester Square had made moderate progress with it. My visit to Paris, though it did not put a stop to revision, stopped dictation. Of course I resumed this as soon as possible after my return. Another interruption, however, though too brief to be mentioned save for its cause, shortly occurred.

Mr. J. S. Mill had just published his book on *Utilitarianism*. In it, to my surprise, I found myself classed as an Anti-utilitarian. Not liking to let pass a characterization which I regarded as erroneous, I wrote to him explaining my position—showing in what I agreed with the existing school of Utilitarians, and in what I differed from them. The essential part of this letter was published by Professor Bain in one of the closing chapters of his *Mental and Moral Science;* but it is not to be found anywhere in my own works. As it seems unfit that this anomalous distribution should be permanent, I decide to reprint it here; omitting the opening and closing paragraphs:—

'The note in question greatly startled me by implicitly classing me with the Anti-utilitarians. I have never regarded myself as an Anti-utilitarian. My dissent from the doctrine of Utility as commonly understood, concerns not the object to be reached by men, but the method of reaching it. While I admit that happiness is the ultimate end to be contemplated, I do not admit that it should be the proximate end. The Expediency-Philosophy having concluded that happiness is the thing to be achieved, assumes that morality has no other business than empirically to generalize the results of conduct, and to supply for the guidance of conduct nothing more than its empirical generalizations.

' But the view for which I contend is, that Morality properly so-called—the science of right conduct—has for its object to determine *how* and *why* certain modes of conduct are detrimental, and certain other modes beneficial. These good and bad results cannot be accidental, but must be necessary consequences of the constitution of things; and I conceive it to be the business of moral science to deduce, from the laws of life and the conditions of existence, what kinds of action necessarily tend to produce happiness, and what kinds to produce unhappiness. Having done this, its deductions are to be recognized as laws of conduct; and are to be conformed to irrespective of a direct estimation of happiness or misery.

'Perhaps an analogy will most clearly show my meaning. During its early stages, planetary Astronomy consisted of nothing more than accumulated observations respecting the positions and motions of the sun and planets; from which accumulated observations it came by and by to be empirically predicted, with an approach to truth, that certain of the heavenly bodies would have certain positions at certain times. But the modern science of planetary Astronomy consists of deductions from the law of gravitation—deductions showing why the celestial bodies necessarily occupy certain places at certain times. Now, the kind of relation which thus exists between ancient and modern Astronomy is analogous to the kind of relation which, I conceive, exists between the Expediency-Morality and Moral Science properly so-called. And the objection which I have to the current Utilitarianism, is, that it recognizes no more developed form of morality—does not see that it has reached but the initial stage of Moral Science.

'To make my position fully understood, it seems needful to add that, corresponding to the fundamental propositions of a developed Moral Science, there have been, and still are, developing in the race, certain fundamental moral intuitions; and that, though these moral intuitions are the results of accumulated experiences of utility, gradually organized and inherited, they have come to be quite independent of conscious experience. Just in the same way that I believe the intuition of space, possessed by any living individual, to have arisen from organized and consolidated experiences of all antecedent individuals who bequeathed to him their slowly-developed nervous organizations—just as I believe that this intuition, requiring only to be made definite and complete by personal experiences, has practically become a form of thought, apparently quite independent of experience; so do I believe that the experiences of utility, organized and consolidated through all past generations of the human race, have been producing corresponding nervous modifications, which, by continued transmission and accumulation, have become in us certain faculties of moral intuition—certain emotions responding to right and wrong conduct, which have no apparent basis in the individual experiences of utility. I also hold that just as the space-intuition responds to the exact demonstrations of Geometry, and has its rough conclusions interpreted and verified by them; so will moral intuitions respond to the demonstrations of Moral Science, and will have their rough conclusions interpreted and verified by them.'

Before leaving the subject I may remark that this difference of view has, I believe, arisen in part from difference of culture. In Bentham's day the knowledge of physical science was confined to a small number; and, as a result, thoughts about causation were, in nearly all men, vague and undeveloped. Education, if not wholly linguistic, included such other subjects only as gave scarcely any material for generating definite ideas of causal relations. That every expended force must work, somehow and somewhere, an equivalent of change, and conversely, was in idea rendered familiar to scarcely any. The like may, I think, be said of Bentham's followers in general. Though, doubtless, causes have been theoretically recognized by all of them; and though in Mr. Mill's *System of Logic*, the doctrine of causation receives full and critical exposition; yet by him, as by the Utilitarians generally, there has not been that study of physical science at large which conduces to an ever-present and vivid consciousness of cause. In the absence of discipline and physical science the search for causes does not become a mental habit. Hence the contented resting in empirical utilitarianism. It was thought that the results of this kind or that kind of action are to be ascertained by induction; and it was tacitly assumed that nothing more remains to be done. That the connexions between conduct and consequence in every case are causal, and that ethical theory remains but rudimentary until the causal relations are generalized, was a truth not recognized by them.

Christmas of this year, as of the preceding year, was spent by my father with me in London. Though now over seventy he remained in fair vigour; having, indeed, in a considerable degree recovered from the nervous disorder of his middle life. I find by letters that the dread of a cold journey was the chief difficulty to be got over in persuading him to come to town.

Concerning my social life at this time, which this visit of my father fitly introduces, there seems nothing to record save some accessions to my circle of friends. One of these is recalled by the following passage in a letter home, dated 25th February, 1863.

"I dined on Saturday with some new friends named Huth, who were great friends of Mr. Buckle's. They are very nice, intelligent people. Dr. Carpenter was one of the guests; and also Mr. Hare, the author of the scheme of representation that has excited so much attention."

All members of the family were worshippers of Mr. Buckle. Two of the sons were with him in the East when he caught the fever which caused his untimely death. Mr.

Henry Huth, the father, an amiable man whose lack of animal energy led to a retiring manner and preference for a quiet life, was noted for his magnificent collection of rare books. This is now in the possession of his son, Mr. Alfred Huth, who has become known as the biographer of Buckle, and also by his work on the results of marriages between relations.

The other addition to my social circle was a gentleman with a remarkable name—Mr. Osmond De Beauvoir Priaulx; the author of a work entitled *Questiones Mosaicæ*. He was famed for giving sumptuous dinners to somewhat select parties. Buckle had been a frequent guest. On the occasion of my first dinner at his house, there were, among others less known, Mr. Higgins, at that time distinguished as a writer of slashing letters in *The Times* signed "Jacob Omnium;" Mr. G. S. Venables, a Parliamentary barrister, and a writer of leaders in *The Saturday Review* and in *The Times,* who, I have been told, had somewhat disappointed his friends: his University career having raised great expectations. Then there was Erasmus Darwin, a brother of Charles Darwin, too feeble in health to display his powers. Thackeray, too, was one of the party. Neither then nor on other occasions when I met him, did he display his powers in any way. The share he took in conversation was not large; and in what he did say, so far as I can remember, no sign of wit or humour was given. I have heard that he could be a lively companion; but it seems possible that usually when in company he was occupied in observing traits of character and manner. A painter of human nature as variously manifested must ordinarily be more a listener than a talker.

Mr. Priaulx was called by his friends an intellectual

sybarite; and while one of these words was justified by the character of his parties, the other was justified by the quality of his dinners, which differed from other dinners, even of an elaborate kind, in that they had always a good deal of the unexpected: there were unusual dishes. Various choice wines, too, eight or ten in kind, came round in the course of dinner and dessert; of which the Chateau Yquem was always looked forward to by the guests as yielding the culminating pleasure of the feast.

Before the end of March, letters show a change of address: I was in my old quarters in Bloomsbury Square, where I suppose I was tempted back by an offer of the accommodation I needed. Later on in April there is a reference to another of my visits to Standish, where it appears that I enjoyed myself as usual and derived benefit.

This season seems to have had no relapse from my ordinary abnormal state of health. Sleeping, now as ever a chief difficulty, had been improved by a course recommended; as witness the following paragraph.

"I have recently been profiting considerably by the advice of a French physician—a Dr. de Mussy to whom Huxley sent me. He has prescribed frequent warm baths—three or more times in the week, with the view of improving my sleeping. I have decidedly slept the better for them."

Here let me add, for the instruction of the sleepless, that some years later Dr. de Mussy told me he had modified his opinion respecting the efficacy of warm baths as soporifics; for he had met with cases in which, though taken at a temperature below blood heat (as they should always be), they produced wakefulness instead of sleepiness. That under some conditions they do this, I can myself testify; for, many years after, owing I suppose to some change in my constitutional state, this reverse effect was produced upon me, so that I dare not take a warm bath late in the day. Unexpected as this experience was, it was congruous with a statement once made to me by the late Dr. Bence Jones respecting other medicinal agents. Speaking of drugs, he said that there is scarcely one which may not under different conditions produce opposite effects. Certainly we have familiar proof that this is the case with alcohol, tea, coffee, tobacco and opium.

This mention of opium reminds me that I had for some time previously made occasional use of it—commonly under the form of morphia. With me sleep brought sleep and wakefulness was habitually followed by more wakefulness; so that after a series of specially bad nights it had been my practice to break the morbid habit, and re-establish the periodicity of sleep by artificial means. Sometimes it was weeks, sometimes months, before I again had recourse to one or other preparation of opium. That the average result was beneficial is an opinion which I here express, because there is, I think, an undue fear of opium; both in the minds of medical men and in those of men at large. Every medicinal agent is liable to abuse; and when it has been greatly abused there arises a reaction, which goes almost to the extent of forbidding its use. In respect of opium a re-reaction is needed.

Health not much disturbed, and work but little interrupted, enabled me to issue three numbers of my serial during the winter and subsequent season: the last of them, however, number IX, retaining me until after the middle of July. I then left London for my holiday. It was not a complete holiday; for, as usual, I took with me work for revision. In this case it was the revision of the various essays published during 1858, 1859 and 1860, which I had decided to collect in a volume.

My first resting place was Scarborough, to which place I went to spend some time with my mother, who was staying there in the hope of recovering from that debility which had been for years coming on. She exemplified the evils resulting from carelessness of self, accompanying undue care of others. Writers on morals do not recognize the fact that excess of self-sacrifice is not only a cause of suffering to the individual making it, but often becomes a cause of suffering to relatives; and if this fact is unrecognized by those who undertake to set forth the principles of right conduct, still less is it recognized by the world at large—or, if recognized, it is not in such way as overtly to influence conduct. A strong sense of duty, partly natural and partly traceable to religious convictions, had, for years, been leading my mother gradually to undermine her system by taxing it too much; and now there was beginning that constitutional prostration which presently made her a confirmed invalid. Many of my letters contain expostulations, but they were useless. She was one of those who exemplify the truth that women's natures, and by implication their beliefs, become fixed at an earlier period of life than do those of men; and her amiable errors were continued in spite of all reasoning.

After ten days at Scarborough I turned my face northwards, and the first indication of my whereabouts is given in a letter which says:—" We have just arrived safely and well at Oban after a fine day's voyage." At first I was puzzled by the " we "; for I had forgotten a tour in the North West Highlands with Lott and one of his Derby friends, well known to me also. Starting next day by fast steamer (the *Mountaineer* I think it was in those days), and taking our course down the Sound of Mull and up the Sleat Sound, we skirted the north east shore of Skye in the afternoon; and, abandoning our original project of exploring Skye, went on to Gairloch. The following morning we took our course by the side of Loch Maree to Kinlochewe: reversing my walk of the previous year. A dog-cart took us next day as far as Loch Torridon, whence, finding a fit guide, we took our way through the mountains to the shore of Loch Carron —a wild and interesting climb—and put up at Jeantown. Balmacarra was our next stopping place; and the day being Sunday we, conforming to the custom of the house, in common with all other guests, whether in private rooms or not, dined at the *table d'hote*. There were present on this occasion Mr. and Mrs. Cardwell (as they then were) and Mr. Robert Lowe (as he then was) : they and ourselves forming the party. Nothing in the conversation was remarkable enough to be remembered. A steam-boat carried us to Glenelg the next morning. There my friends left me, and, prompted by my recommendation, explored Loch Hourne and Glengarry on the way home; while I remained till the 20th, when I became due at Ardtornish.

Thereupon commenced a month more pleasant to me in recollection than the details of its doings would be to the reader in narration. Two extracts from letters written at the time, may, however, be fitly given. One dated early in September says:—

"Some guests have lately arrived—Mr. Charles Buxton, M.P., his wife and two sons, and Mr. Godfrey Lushington.

Mr. and Mrs. Charles Buxton I knew, but have not seen them of late, and am glad to renew the acquaintance. . . .

I have found some treasures in the shape of plants which illustrate my views of morphology. This is the more fortunate because I had lost the specimens I before possessed."

The Mr. Charles Buxton, M.P., mentioned above, an amiable and intelligent man, was one of the sons of Sir Thomas Fowell Buxton, of anti-slavery fame. He did not survive for many years: not having, I think, the strength needed for bearing the stress of public life joined with that of business and social excitements. His face bore the expression of chronic fatigue. One of the sons, who were at that time boys, now sits in Parliament for Poplar. A letter of the 17th September says:—

"I am proposing to take my leave of the Smiths this day week: they have sundry visitors coming in a few days after and will be quite full. . . .

I am *quite* well—better than I have been for years. My sleeping is getting more normal and I hope I am now beyond the liability to relapses. I have caught four more salmon since I wrote—three in one day."

Before the end of the month I was at home, and remained there through a good part of October: no doubt partially occupied in seeing through the press the Essays to be presently re-published.

I had but just settled myself in Bloomsbury Square, and had scarecly got into full work, when I left town again for a short time. The occasion was a visit to Lord Houghton at Fryston Hall, his country place near Pontefract—a town for which he sat in Parliament while he was known as Richard Monckton Milnes. I found a circle of a dozen agreeable people, belonging to the political and literary worlds, only two of whom I knew personally. The surroundings of Fryston have greatly injured it as a residence; nor is the country around picturesque. But the few days spent there on this occasion, and on subsequent occasions, were made pleasant by the social indoor life.

I had known our host as Mr. Milnes since 1851, and had more recently, in London, attended some of his dinners and literary breakfasts—widely known as gatherings of notabilities of all kinds holding all opinions. While partly his catholicity, it was perhaps partly his constitutional love of excitement which prompted him to extend his hospitality to every one who had made a name, and thus to collect these incongruous assemblies; for he seemed unable to lead a quiet life. Even in his later years, when increasing age might have been expected to have a sedative influence, he was ever moving hither and thither, to be present at gatherings, grave and gay, of various natures. About his views one gained but an undecided impression. Whether it was the effect of mental restlessness or whether it was the effect of readiness to listen to ideas of all kinds, however extreme, there seemed in him an unsettled state of opinion upon most things.

There were exceptions, however, to his restlessness. I heard of one at least. A few years later than the time of which I am speaking the English disciples of M. Comte decided to commence Sunday services appropriate to their creed: Dr. Congreve, who was the leader of the body, being priest. Some curiosity was excited for a time among those who were willing to listen to new opinions. One of such, on being asked what he had seen, replied that there was a regular service, having orderly forms. "In fact," said he, "it was just like a church: there was Lord Houghton fast asleep."

He was extremely pleasant and amusing as a companion. His information about people and things, was copious; and he abounded in anecdotes, which he narrated with an enjoyment that was infectious. Full of kindly feeling, too, he was. From many sides I have heard references to his benevolent help quietly given. He was genuinely desirous of aiding whatever he thought good.

Since the publication of *First Principles*, Professor Youmans had been, as before, active in looking after my affairs in the United States: among other things having, as I heard (not from himself but from Mr. Silsbee), written over a hundred letters to negligent and defaulting subscribers.

He was anxious that my already-published works should be circulated in the United States. The Messrs. Appleton had, I believe, undertaken the risk of reprinting the *Education;* but, I presume, did not think that the reprinting of the two volumes of *Essays* and of *Social Statics* would pay. Under these circumstances he proposed a scheme, the nature of which may be gathered from the response I made to it, dated December 17, 1863, which ran as follows:—

"I must really protest against the amount of sacrifice so generously proposed to be made by my American friends. The obligations under which you have placed me, and to which you have been lately adding so greatly, it has been beyond my power to avoid, had I wished to avoid them; but the obligations foreshadowed in your last letter, are, in part, such as I can, and must, avoid. If my American friends, moved by your active efforts, agree to take upon themselves the risk of re-publishing some of my writings—a risk which I dare not run myself—I cannot help it; and while I feel somewhat uneasy at seeing such responsibilities undertaken, I cannot but feel a considerable pleasure in finding so much interest manifested in the success of my aims. But when it is proposed that my friends should supply Messrs. Appleton with the stereotype plates, and that I should begin to reap the profits of the reprint from the outset, as seems to be implied by your statement of the arrangement, I must decline to agree. It is, I think, a quite sufficient generosity on their part, if they save me from a contingent risk, and give me the contingent profit after their expenses have been paid."

This was, I believe, the course eventually adopted. Funds were raised to pay the cost of reprinting the several volumes named, and after those who furnished them had been recouped, I began to receive a royalty on all copies sold.

The topic of arrangements for the publication of my books in America having been here incidentally raised, I may fitly add what has further to be said about it. During subsequent years the course followed was this. A duplicate set of stereotype plates having been, in each case, cast for me by my printers, was sent to New York. From these Messrs. Appleton printed the American edition, under an agreement to pay me a royalty of 15 per cent. of the retail price on all copies sold from the outset: their only risk being the cost of paper and press-work. Of course a considerable sale had to be achieved before the returns repaid me the outlay for the stereotype plates. But after this there resulted a fair profit. To this arrangement, negotiated for me by my friend Youmans, the Messrs. Appleton have loyally adhered.*

Of occurrences during the winter and subsequent season, the first in strict chronological order should have been named before those of the last section, which, by implication, refer to it; namely, the publication of the second series of *Essays, &c.* This occurred at the end of November. There is little to be said about it; for so far as I remember scarcely any notice was taken of the book, and none of my letters mention reviews of it. Republished essays are generally looked coldly upon by critics, and mine were of a kind to excite, in nine out of ten among them, even less warmth of reception than usual.

The year ended without anything more worthy of remark than that my father came to town to visit me at Christmas, and that some time in January I returned with him to Derby, remaining there till the beginning of February. Incidents of succeeding months may be most conveniently indicated by extracts from letters home. One written on March 26 says:—

Bain has sent me a copy of the second edition of his

* The first book by Mr. Spencer which the Messrs. Appleton published was "Education," in November, 1860. Since then twenty-five separate works have been printed by this house, including the "Autobiography." From the start a royalty payment has been made to Mr. Spencer, although he had no legal protection for his writings in the United States. From the records of the house, it appears that, in the early years, plates were imported from England, but in many cases before and in all cases since the International Copyright Act went into effect, the composition and electrotyping have been done at the expense of the American publishers. It may be added here that from the beginning until December 31st, 1903, the Messrs. Appleton have sold 368,755 volumes of Mr. Spencer's writings, but these figures, of course, take no account of the sale of unauthorized editions during the years previous to the adoption of International Copyright.—Publishers' Note.

"Senses and the Intellect," in which he shows much generosity of feeling.

This passage refers to the great candour and good temper with which he received the criticisms I had passed upon the first edition of his work, and the readiness shown by him to modify the expression of his views. The following paragraphs are from a letter dated April 25:—

"The Potters have taken a house in town for the season, and I have seen something of them. I dine with them again next Saturday.

I seem to have been really benefited by the fit of excitement I had a while ago. [The cause of which will be indicated presently]. I bear my work very conveniently, and can do more reading without feeling it."

About this time Mr. Potter had become Chairman of the Great Western Railway Company; and Parliamentary business made it needful for him to be much in town. The taking of a London house for the season, thus initiated, was continued during many subsequent years, with the effect of adding to my social pleasures, and to those far preferable pleasures yielded by a family circle of intimate friends. The next extract, which is from a letter to my mother dated May 18, refers to some kindred gratifications.

"I have been visiting the Lubbocks a good deal lately. ... I have postponed going to spend a week with them because I am unable at present to spare the time."

On May 27 I wrote to my father respecting anticipated arrangements as follows:—

"I shall in all probability go to Scotland. Mr. Smith asked me to do so some two months ago; and though the invitation will need renewal when the time comes, I do not see any reason to doubt that it will be renewed. As to your own movements at Midsummer, I do not see why you should not do as before. At any rate, you can join me here in town during the latter end of June and the beginning of July, and we can discuss further steps."

I may also fitly quote some paragraphs from a letter dated June 9.

"I got the American papers this morning, and was much amused with some of the statements in the biographical notice. Did you recognize all the statements you are credited with?

Enclosed I send a notice of the "Classification," and some other things that may interest you. You will be struck by the continued and thoughtful kindness of my friends the Lubbocks.

I am quite well and getting on satisfactorily with my next number. Only yesterday I arrived at a point of view from which Darwin's doctrine of "Natural Selection" is seen to be absorbed into the general theory of Evolution as I am interpreting it."

Some explanation is called for by the last paragraph. Organic evolution being a part of Evolution at large, evidently had to be interpreted after the same general manner—had to be explained in physical terms: the changes produced by functional adaptation (which I held to be one of the factors) and the changes produced by "natural selection," had both to be exhibited as resulting from the redistribution of matter and motion everywhere and always going on. Natural selection as ordinarily described, is not comprehended in this universal redistribution. It seems to stand apart as an unrelated process. The search for congruity led first of all to perception of the fact that what Mr. Darwin called "natural selection," might more literally be called survival of the fittest. But what is survival of the fittest, considered as an outcome of physical actions? The answer presently reached was this:—The changes constituting evolution tend ever towards a state of equilibrium. On the way to absolute equilibrium or rest, there is in many cases established for a time, a moving equilibrium—a system of mutually-dependent parts severally performing actions subserving maintenance of the combination. Every living organism exhibits such a moving equilibrium—a balanced set of functions constituting its life; and the overthrow of this balanced set of functions or moving equilibrium is what we call death. Some individuals in a species are so constituted that their moving equilibria are less easily overthrown than those of other individuals; and these are the fittest which survive, or, in Mr. Darwin's language, they are the select which nature preserves. And now mark that in thus recognizing the continuance of life as the continuance of a moving equilibrium, early overthrown in some individuals by incident forces and not overthrown in others until after they have reproduced the species, we see that this survival and multiplication of the select, becomes conceivable in purely physical terms, as an indirect outcome of a complex form of the universal redistribution of matter and motion.

Though I had kept up well during the season there came a relapse at Midsummer, caused partly by extra effort in completing, before leaving town, the number of my serial then issued and partly, as a letter confesses, by too many social excitements. I should have forgotten this relapse had not a letter shown that my father and I went early in July to Margate; and this would not have recalled the fact that I was much out of order had there not resulted the memory of an incident there. Mr. T. S. Baynes, then candidate for the professorship at St. Andrews which he afterwards held, wished for a testimonial from me. I had read nothing of his, and dared not undertake the required amount of reading. The difficulty was solved by my father, who read aloud to me several mornings as we sat in a nook under the cliff. After a week's stay he went to France, and I turned my face northwards.

Why narrate in detail my doings during the autumn? Accounts of this kind are occupying too much space. Condensation must be carried as far as consists with due indication of the ways in which my leisure times were spent.

Derby, of course, was my first stopping place. After fetching my mother home from Matlock (she could not now make long journeys) and after spending a few days with her, I joined the Lotts at Penmaenmaur and remained till the end of July. Among the excursions we made was an ascent of Snowdon. When they returned home I went on to Scotland, stopped two days at Corran Ferry, seated myself for a time at Fort William, and from that place took rambles: one of them being up Glen Nevis as far as the amphitheatre into which it widens, another being by Glen Spean to the Brig of Roy and back. Returning as far as Oban, I found that the looked for missive from Ardtornish had not arrived, and I decided to spend the time in a local tour: my route being across the hills to Port Sonachan on Loch Awe; thence to Inverary; thence through Glen Croe to Arrochar on Loch Long; thence to Tarbet, Inverarnon and Tyndrum; from there to Dalmally; and from Dalmally back to Oban: six days being thus occupied. My vexation was great on finding that the invitation for me had been lying in the Post Office since the day after I left. Had I not been so impatient I might have had Highland enjoyments along with charming friends instead of being a lone wanderer among mountains. However, the prospect of a month's pleasures before me soon banished the thought of some pleasures lost. I remained at Ardtornish until the middle of September and then left for Derby. After some three weeks there I departed for London early in October.

A letter saying that I was about to fix myself at 88 Kensington Gardens Square, gives a hopeful account of this new abode; which, internally not unsatisfactory, was externally much more salubrious than my abodes of several previous years. Here I revised the last proofs of my twelfth number, which was sent to subscribers before the close of the month: the issue to the public of the *Principles of Biology,* Vol. I, taking place shortly after.

What am I to say about this second instalment of " The System of Philosophy," as it was at that time named? It seems absurd to pass over without remark the volume which gives the title to the chapter; even though the title merely serves to indicate my special occupation while there passed those two years of my life which the chapter narrates. On the other hand it appears needless to give any account of the contents of a book which is accessible to any one who wishes to learn them; and it would be out of taste to signalize those ideas in it which seem to me of chief value. General comments, however, may not be inappropriate.

Something by way of apology for venturing to deal

with so vast and so difficult a subject seems called for—a subject too vast for any man fully to acquaint himself with as a whole—so vast that even one of its two great divisions is more than a diligent student can master—so vast that even a subdivision furnishes matter for investigation sufficient to occupy a life. Though in boyhood I had been interested in Natural History at large, and more especially in Entomology; and though at that time and in later years I was a constant reader of medical periodicals and books, from which some knowledge of anatomy and physiology was gathered—though I had for some time studied Biology with a purpose; and though a certain natural aptitude for laying hold of cardinal facts enabled me gradually to acquire from what I read, better general conceptions of biological truths than most might have acquired; yet it is manifest that I was inadequately equipped for the task. But I had undertaken to set forth a general theory of Evolution as exhibited throughout all orders of existences. Whoever carries out such an undertaking must either have a knowledge of all the concrete sciences greater than any man has ever had, or he must deal with some sciences of which his knowledge is but partial, if not very imperfect. Either the thing must not be done at all or it must be thus done.

In my own case the presumption was diminished by the consciousness that friends who sympathized with my aims, and whose competence in their respective departments was beyond question, were prepared to aid me by their criticisms. Professor Huxley kindly agreed to read through my proofs for the purpose of checking statements of zoological facts; while Dr. (now Sir Joseph) Hooker did the like for botanical statements.

On the whole the result seems to have shown that the attempt was not unwarranted.

In one respect, indeed, I had, as an outsider, studying the phenomena of organic life as phenomena of Evolution at large, a certain kind of advantage over specialists, dealing after the ordinary manner with their respective separate subjects—plant-life and animal-life. The man of science who limits himself to a department, is apt to overlook, or else not sufficiently to appreciate, those most general truths which the phenomena he studies display in common with other groups of phenomena. The truths exhibited by plant-life and animal-life in common, which neither the pure botanist nor the pure zoologist is called upon to recognize at all, are really truths of the profoundest meaning; and though in most cases there is, on the part of each, such acquaintance with the sister science as discloses some, at any rate, of these most general truths, yet while the attention of each is almost wholly absorbed by his specialty, these most general truths are relegated to the background of thought instead of occupying its foreground. Still more does inattention to orders of phenomena remote in kind, result in either unconsciousness or inadequate consciousness of the truths common to all these orders of phenomena and the phenomena of life—truths of wider significance than those which the phenomena of life themselves display. Of course the study of biological facts, not from the point of view of Organic Evolution only, but from the point of view of Evolution at large, inorganic, organic, and super-organic, entailed the placing of these widest truths in conspicuous positions: thus conducing to a more philosophical conception of biological facts.

One further remark to be made is that this treatment of the subject led incidentally to a method which proved of much service. While the ultimate purpose was to interpret the general facts of structure and function as results of Evolution, it was manifest that, as a preliminary step, it was needful to specify and illustrate these general facts; and needful also to set forth those physical and chemical properties of organic matter which are implied in the interpretation. That is to say, there had to be exhibited the Data of Biology and the Inductions of Biology. Some one has remarked that in philosophizing much depends upon rightly putting a question to Nature; and in this case the deliberate inquiry what are antecedent truths taken for granted in Biology, and what are the biological truths which, apart from theory, may be regarded as established by observation, proved of great advantage. Subsequently, when dealing with Psychology, with Sociology, and with Ethics, a like course of procedure yielded like advantages.

Concerning the reception of the work there is little to be said: the reason being that little notice was taken of it. In 1864, not one educated person in ten or more knew the meaning of the word Biology; and among those who knew it, whether critics or general readers, few cared to know anything about the subject. Probably in many cases the volume received hardly as much attention as is implied by that reviewing humorously described as cutting the leaves and smelling the paper knife. One notice I may refer to, partly as being typical and partly because of its unconscious drollery. In *The Athenæum* of 5 November, 1864, a paragraph concerning the book commenced thus:—" This is but one of two volumes, and the two but part of a larger work:

we can therefore but announce it." If we imagine the critic, many years after, to have had before him the "System of Philosophy" as finished, he might with much greater cogency have said:—"Here are ten volumes on five different subjects, which it is manifestly impossible for us to review. We can therefore but announce them." The argument is neat and conclusive:—This is but a part and cannot be noticed. This complete work is too big and varied for notice. Consequently it must all pass unnoticed.

CHAPTER XXXVI.

A DIGRESSION.

1864. ÆT. 43.

CHRONOLOGICALLY placed, the incidents to be narrated in this chapter should have been narrated some distance back in the preceding chapter; for instead of belonging to the close of 1864, they belong to its opening. But the narrative would have been confused had I adhered strictly to the order of occurrence. I have thought it better to make of these detached incidents the matter for a detached chapter.

Ten years had elapsed since, in the essay on the "Genesis of Science," I had discussed and rejected the classification of the sciences proposed by M. Comte. In the course of the criticism to which the first part of the essay was devoted, I expressed the opinion that the sciences do not admit of serial arrangement, whether considered logically in their natures or historically in their developments; and I expressed the further opinion that they stand in relations of divergence and re-divergence, which may be symbolized by the branches of a tree. More than once during these ten years, I had made attempts to represent on paper their ramifying relations, but without success: none of the diagrams I made came anywhere near satisfying me. But now, my attention having been again drawn to the subject by seeing these diagrams, my thoughts took, it seems, a new direction, and led me to recognize those fundamental distinctions which divide the great groups of sciences, and determine the classification of them.

There is a family of sciences which severally undertake to give accounts of individualized objects—not objects which, like fragments of stone, are in some or many respects indefinite, but objects which are definable, and are known either as solitary individuals or as individual members of a species. Be it nebula, star, the sun, a planet or a satellite, each of the things Astronomy concerns itself with is an identifiable individual. So is the Earth with which Geology deals; and so are all plants and animals. So in a sense are minds; for though not visible entities, they are coherent and organized groups of functions exhibited by certain entities; and each of them is individualized as belonging to one or other kind of creature, and, in a minor degree, to one or other sample of it. And so it is with societies. Each of them is a more or less distinctly incorporated whole, individualized by its structural traits as well as by its name and locality. Moreover, every science of this class is like the others in the respect that it aims to give an exhaustive account of the object or objects forming its subject-matter. Nor is this all. It aims also to give an account of the ways in which each of them became what it is—to give a history of the transformations through which it has passed. Astronomy, Geology, Biology, Psychology, and Sociology, may in fact all of them be properly called Natural Histories; though in current speech a sub-division of one monopolizes the name.

Devoid of these traits, the sciences forming another

family have in common certain other traits. Mechanics, Physics, and Chemistry, none of them treat of definitely individualized objects. The forces with which Mechanics is concerned are not tangible or visible entities at all; nor, in formulating their laws, is absolute quantity of any moment: relative quantity only enters into the inquiry. Similarly, the phenomena of Heat, Light, and Electricity are generalized without reference to specialized portions or particular amounts: the characters which give individuality are absent. The like holds with Chemistry. In their gaseous forms the matters it deals with can scarcely be said to have tangibility or visibility; in their liquid forms they cannot be said to be individualized; and though, in their solid forms, fragments of them have shapes and sizes by which they can be recognized, these are irrelevant to those truths respecting molecular constitutions, combining proportions, and modes of action, which Chemistry sets forth. Moreover these sciences have the peculiarity that they respectively treat of matters and forces, not as they exist in actual objects and actual motions, but as separated, so far as may be, from one another—from impurities and from perturbing actions. And once more, they have, by consequence, the peculiarity that the truths they express are partially ideal: the atomic weights and combining equivalents of the chemist are not verified absolutely by experiments, for impurities cannot be entirely got rid of; and no law of motion or action formulated by the physicist is ever fulfilled completely, because interferences can never be wholly escaped.

Yet more sharply marked off from both of these groups of sciences than they are from one another, is a third group of sciences. This third group is not concerned at all with the real, but with the purely ideal. Though Logic and Mathematics habitually affirm truths respecting existences, yet they are in no case concerned with the existences themselves, but only with certain of their aspects considered as dissociated from them. Logic has to do with the exclusions, inclusions and over-lappings of classes of existences, considered as distinguishable from one another by marks; and it cares neither what the existences are nor what the marks are. The units with which arithmetic and the calculus at large deal, often stand for real objects, but the reality of the objects is quite irrelevant to the numerical truths reached: in any ordinary calculation when one number is multiplied or divided by another, there is no thought of the things which the numbers represent. So it is with geometrical truths. These are concerned with the phenomena of pure space. Though in the expression of these phenomena visible lines are habitually used, yet that which gives the lines visibility is intentionally ignored.

That the conception originally presented itself to me in this shape, I do not say; but this was the outcome of it. It became manifest that, as above shown, the sciences fall into three groups—Concrete, Abstract-Concrete, and Abstract. And it became further manifest that the sciences within each group are to be arranged in the order of decreasing generality.

This view appeared to me important enough to merit prompt publication; and I decided to suspend my ordinary work that I might write an essay setting it forth.

Whether this resolve was made in December 1863, while my father was with me in town, or whether it was made while I was in Derby in January 1864, I cannot decide. But it was evidently in one or the other; for the first letter in which reference is made to it, implies that my father had already been told about it. It is dated February 19, and runs as follows:—

"I am still busy with the Essay on Classification, which I have fully written out, and have nearly done revising. It works out far more completely than I imagined it would. After sundry consultations I have decided not to publish it in a periodical but to publish it separately as a pamphlet."

This decision was, I fancy, in large measure a forced one. Inquiry made it manifest that an essay so purely philosophical would be unreadable by nearly all who take in periodicals, and that editorial acceptance was scarcely to be expected. There was no alternative but to undertake the cost of printing it as an independent publication.

As it happened, this decision was fortunate; for just as the pamphlet, or rather *brochure*, was on the eve of issue, there occurred an incident which made needful an emphatic repudiation of certain doctrines ascribed to me; and while the issue of the pamphlet afforded a fit opportunity for the repudiation, a postscript to it afforded a fit place.

The incident in question was the appearance of a review of *First Principles*, by M. Auguste Laugel, in the *Revue des Deux Mondes*, for 15 February 1864. Highly satisfactory to me as the review was in many respects, there was one respect in which it was unsatisfactory. M. Laugel tacitly implied that I belonged to a school of thought from the doctrines of which I dissent: having, indeed, to sundry of the leading doctrines, a profound aversion.

That body of scientific truths and methods which M. Comte named " Positive Philosophy," he remarked, was analogous to that which had been in England called " Natural Philosophy "; and, by implication, the men of science who had been natural philosophers were regarded by him as positive philosophers. This naming, or re-naming, led to an unfortunate confusion. The philosophy which M. Comte named " Positive Philosophy," came not unnaturally to be spoken of by his disciples as *his* philosophy; and gradually among them, and afterwards among the undiscriminating public, there grew up the notion that those who held the doctrines called by M. Comte " Positive Philosophy " were adherents of M. Comte. M. Laugel, if he did not fall into this error, at any rate used language which seemed to countenance it. He spoke of me as imbued with certain ideas (naming especially the relativity of knowledge) characterizing the Philosophy called Positive; and though these ideas were manifestly not ideas originated by M. Comte, nor claimed by him, yet by calling them ideas of the Positive Philosophy which I accepted, he produced the impression that I was an adherent of M. Comte.

This impression, utterly untrue as it was, I thought it needful to dissipate; and the greater part of March I occupied in setting forth my antagonism to all those doctrines which are distinctive of the Comtean Philosophy. On the 26 March I wrote to my father as follows:—

" I have just got rid of the last revises of my pamphlet, the corrections and modifications of which have caused me a great deal of bother and delay. I expect it will be out towards the end of next week.

You ask about my health. I am happy to say that I am well, in spite of unfavourable circumstances. The writing the Appendix about Comte brought on a fit of excitement, moral and intellectual, which I could not subdue. I could not stop thinking day or night, and was in a great fright lest I should have a serious relapse. However I escaped it; and now seem to be *all the better.* It seems to me that this fit of excitement has done something towards restoring my cerebral circulation, which, ever since my break-down, has been deficient."

The fit of excitement here referred to was not produced wholly by the writing of this postscript setting forth " Reasons for dissenting from the philosophy of M. Comte." A private controversy which resulted had much to do with it. Wishing to be quite fair to Comte, I thought it desirable that the proof of what I had written should be looked through by one who was in sympathy with him. Lewes, if not a disciple in the full sense of the word, was a partial adherent, and was also his expositor. I asked him to oblige me by his criticisms, which he willingly did. Some of the minor ones I accepted and profited by, but against the major ones I protested; and this led to a correspondence between us over which I excited myself in the way indicated. My letter of chief importance, which might fitly have formed a postscript to the postscript, will be found in Appendix B.

The inquiry which led to the digression described in this chapter had a sequence. More important than the theory of the Classification of the Sciences set forth, and much more important than the definite rejection of the Comtean philosophy, for which the opportunity was afforded, was a certain incidental result.

When arranging the divisions and sub-divisions of the Concrete Sciences, and setting out with recognition of the fact that under their most general aspects they all give accounts of the re-distributions of matter and motion, there arose the need for stating the universal trait of all such re-distributions. This trait is that increasing integration of matter necessitates a concomitant dissipation of motion, and that increasing amount of motion implies a concomitant disintegration of matter. Perception of this truth threw a new light on the phenomena of Evolution at large. Here were seen the processes which constitute respectively Evolution and Dissolution under their primordial aspects. It became obvious that the differentiations, with resulting increase of heterogeneity, which I had supposed to be primary traits of Evolution, were but secondary traits. Clearly the first law must be the law in conformity with which aggregates are formed and destroyed; and not the law in conformity with which their complexities of structure arise.

The necessity for re-arranging *First Principles* became manifest. It had been wrongly organized and must be re-organized. This task I decided to undertake as soon as a new edition seemed likely to be called for.

CHAPTER XXXVII.

ANOTHER VOLUME OF THE *BIOLOGY*.

1864—67. ÆT. 44—47.

LETTERS show that before the number which closed the first volume of the Biology was issued, I had commenced the second volume; for I was eager to get completely worked out on paper, ideas which had been long waiting for expression. A letter to my father of October 14, complaining of delays, continues:—

"Meanwhile I am getting ready my materials, and arranging my ideas for commencing the next No. which I shall do to-morrow or on Monday. The subject of Morphological Development grows upon me so much as I examine into it, that I feel somewhat perplexed how to say all that I have got to say within the available space."

I am reminded by this passage of the way in which with me, and I suppose with many others, plans that have been once formed exercise an almost irresistible coercion. Habitually, before I have yet finished rejoicing over my emancipation from a work which has long played the tyrant over me, I make myself the slave of another. The truth is, I suppose, that in the absence of wife and children to care for, the carrying out of my undertakings is the one thing which makes life worth living—even though, by it, life is continually perturbed. I have often said jestingly, that if I could but get over the bad habit of writing books, I might maintain good health. It seems that I declined to have good health on such terms.

Not, indeed, that at the time of which I now speak I had more than usual reason to complain. After having been a week at my new habitat there went a report home speaking of its favourable effects; and a letter written on the 7th November says—

"I am in very tolerable condition now that the weather has become fine again. I felt this time, as I always do, a marked difference between my state during a low atmospheric pressure and my state during a high atmospheric pressure."

This passage I quote mainly to show my sensitiveness to atmospheric changes, which has been a constant trait with me ever since. During subsequent months further improvement in health seems to have resulted from my migration to the suburbs; as witness the following paragraph from a letter dated 7 April 1865:—

"I am tolerably well; having returned on Monday from the Lubbocks with whom I had been spending five days. Last night our Blastodermic Club entertained Colenso at dinner. To-night I dine with Huxley, and to-morrow with the Huths. On the whole I think I am improving in my power of bearing work and excitements."

Reverting to the account of my work, a paragraph in a letter dated November 23, 1864, indicates a new phase upon which it was now entering:—

"I question whether it will be practicable for me to come down before Christmas. I have to get a number of wood-engravings done for my next number, and this involves continual interviews and arrangements with the engraver; which, together with getting up all the facts &c. occupies me very fully just now, and makes it difficult for me to get away. In fact to do so I must suspend my work."

Since the days when I was in the habit of making portraits of friends, more than twenty years previously, I had never taken up my pencil. But now such small skill as I have in delineating objects, became again serviceable. The greater part of the illustrations I required were of a kind which it was needful to make directly from Nature; and the ability to make them myself, instead of employing an artist, saved me not only money but the trouble which would have been required to explain all that I wanted.

These brief extracts and comments may be taken as sufficiently indicating the course of my life during the winter of 1864 and the London season of 1865.

Of more interest to the reader than these details, is an event referred to in the first of the above-quoted letters, dated November 7, 1864. It concerns the earliest meeting of a body much more important by its quality than by its size.

"In pursuance of a long-suspended intention, a few of the most advanced men of science have united to form a small club to dine together occasionally. It consists of Huxley, Tyndall, Hooker, Lubbock, Frankland, Busk, Hirst, and myself. Two more will possibly be admitted. But the number will be limited to ten. Our first dinner was on last Thursday; and the first Thursday of every month will be the day for subsequent meetings."

The increase of the number to ten never took place. One addition was shortly afterwards made—Mr. W. Spottiswoode; but no decision was come to respecting the tenth. From time to time for some years the question was raised and discussed; but no one was found who fulfilled the two requirements—that he should be of adequate mental calibre and that he should be on terms of intimacy with the existing members. For the Club was intended to be, first of all, an assemblage of friends desirous of meeting one another more frequently than their daily avocations and many engagements allowed them to do in the absence of pre-arrangement. Eventually, the subject of a tenth member was tacitly dropped.

Some time elapsed before we named ourselves. "The Thorough Club" was one title suggested; but the historical associations negatived it. In a letter to my father quoted above, I have used the name "Blastodermic"—a figure of speech alluding to the truth that the blastoderm is that part of an ovum in which the rudiments of future organization first appear. Who proposed this I do not remember, but it was not adopted. So long did our anonymous character continue, that at length it was remarked (I believe by the wife of one of the members, Mrs. Busk) that we might as well name ourselves after the unknown quantity. The suggestion was approved, and we became the X Club. Beyond the advantage that it committed us to nothing, this name had the further advantage that it made possible a brief, and, to a stranger, an enigmatical, notice of our meetings. A few days before the first Thursday in the month, the secretary for the time being sent to each member a post-card on which was written $x=5$; or whatever other day of the month the first Thursday fell upon. Doubtless many speculations and many absurd conclusions were caused in the minds of servants who took in these post-cards.

The Club had no rules, save the interdict upon non-attendance for any other reason than illness or absence from town. Nor had it any avowed purpose beyond the periodic assembling of friends. True, we had originally intended to discuss scientific and philosophical questions; and one of our members continued, for some time, to press us to carry out our intention. But though scientific questions often cropped up, and led to conversations, they were never formally introduced. Time was spent chiefly in lively talk, of which *badinage* formed a considerable element.

There did, however, grow up something like a function. It became the custom to discuss, after dinner, the affairs of the scientific societies: sometimes those of the British Association, but more frequently those of the Royal Society. These consultations had their effects, though in what exact way I do not know. In course of time the existence of the Club became known in the scientific world, and it was, we heard, spoken of with bated breath—was indeed, I believe, supposed to exercise more power than it did.

It is not surprising that its influence was felt. Among its members were three who became Presidents of the Royal Society, and five who became Presidents of the British Association. Of the others one was for a time President of the College of Surgeons; another President of the Chemical Society; and a third of the Mathematical Society. To enumerate all their titles, and honours, and the offices they filled, would occupy too much space. Of the nine, I was the only one who was fellow of no society, and had presided over nothing.

As is implied by an instance referred to above, we

occasionally invited men of mark, home or foreign, as guests. Of the one class I may name, Prof. Clifford, Prof. Masson, and Mr. Robert Lowe (afterwards Lord Sherbrooke); and of the other class M. Auguste Laugel, Prof. Helmholtz, and Professor Asa Gray. In the course of many years there were various others whose names I do not recall.

Our monthly meetings extended from October to June, and towards the close of June we had, for many years, a supplementary meeting which was something more than a dinner. On each of these occasions the married members brought their wives; and thus sometimes raised the number of the party to fifteen. We left town early on the Saturday afternoon for some promising place, and boated or rambled before our dinner; drove on Sunday to a pleasant spot where we picnic'd; dined together again on the Sunday evening; and then some returned to town while others remained over Sunday night. On the first occasion we took up our quarters at Skindle's Hotel, on the banks of the Thames at Taplow, and had our picnic-luncheon on the Sunday under Burnham Beeches; and once, if not twice, afterwards, we went to the same place. Another year saw us at Windsor; on which occasion we picnic'd in a distant part of the forest. And when the Oatlands Park Hotel was utilized, St. George's Hill was the place for our Sunday's luncheon. Though most of us at that time were not young, we were in tolerable vigour; and these meetings, enlivened by the presence of ladies, were very enjoyable. Sometimes at our picnics a volume of poems was produced. Either in Windsor Forest or at St. George's Hill, Huxley, I remember, read aloud to us Tennyson's " Œnone." After some ten years, several motives caused the cessation of these meetings in the country.

The Club has now (September 1887) nearly completed its twenty-third year. Time has of late been diminishing our number. Spottiswoode was the first to leave us —dying prematurely: I think, before he was sixty. Last year we lost Busk, but at a good age,—seventy-six I believe. Of the remaining seven there are but three in good health. But our ranks have never been thinned by desertions or by differences. During these twenty-three years nothing has occurred to disturb the harmony of our meetings.

The following is an extract from a letter to Youmans dated 17 December 1864. The last paragraph is the one of chief interest; but, while I am quoting, I may as well quote some preceding ones, which are not without their significance.

"Again let me express my obligations for your unwearied exertions on behalf, both of my books and my pecuniary interests. . . .

There are two things that strike me respecting the accounts. . . . One is that there seems to have been forgotten my protest against being credited with the proceeds of the sale of the re-printed *Essays,* at this early period of the transaction. Let me remind you that I declined receiving the profits of the reprints, until after those gentlemen who had guaranteed the cost of the stereotype plates had been reimbursed. . . . The amount of 242 dollars 81 cents, credited to me should be credited to them. . . .

"The prospects of *The Reader* about which I told you, are highly encouraging. Huxley, Tyndall, Cairns, Galton and Pollock are the editors. And among other proprietors of weight, in addition to those I before named, are Darwin and

Lubbock and Mill, whose consent to become a proprietor I obtained a few days ago."

The Reader, here referred to, was a weekly paper (of *The Spectator* form) predominantly literary, and in a smaller degree scientific, which had been founded a year or two before by Mr. T. Hughes, Q.C., Mr. Ludlow, and others who, dissatisfied with existing papers of the class, were desirous of having one which should be candid and impartial in its criticisms, and liberal in its views of affairs—not political affairs so much as social affairs. As habitually happens with new journals, it inflicted considerable loss upon its founders; and, weary of what I suppose at length seemed to them no longer a hopeful undertaking, they were anxious to get out of it—if possible by sale. Mr. J. N. Lockyer, who edited the scientific department, giving reports of societies &c., was anxious that the paper should not drop, and was energetic in getting together a new proprietary. Among others he came to me, and, entering into his scheme sympathetically, I canvassed sundry of my friends with success. I took a share myself and induced Tyndall to take one. At my instigation Mr. Octavius Smith took several, I forget how many; Mr. Huth took five; a friend at Hendon, Mr. James Campbell took two; and I succeeded in inducing Mr. Mill also to become a proprietor. The following letter to him contains some details concerning our plan.

"The annexed circular briefly indicates an undertaking into which a number of those who have at heart the advance of liberal opinion are entering with much zeal. It is felt that if this opportunity of establishing on a safe footing an organ of scientific thought and of conscientious literary criticism is lost, it may be long before this very desirable object can be achieved.

The editorial organization is highly satisfactory. Professor Huxley will edit the department of Science aided by Prof. Tyndall. Mr. Francis Galton takes the department of Travels and Ethnology. Professor Cairns that of Political Economy and Political Philosophy. And Mr. Frederick Pollock [now Sir Frederick] that of *Belles Lettres*.

The paper is not yet quite paying its expenses; but it is scarcely to be doubted that with the concentration of faculty now about to be engaged upon it, it will soon do so; and may not improbably become a good investment. The paper has been purchased for £2250, and it has been resolved to issue 40 shares of £100: calling up £80 on each; so as to leave about £1000 working capital. Thirty-four are already taken up.

It is proposed at the beginning of the year to commence a new series of the paper; and it is suggested that at that time, along with the prospectus of the paper as re-organized and re-officered, there should be published the names of the proprietors, as an indication of the course which the paper is likely to take. Your name would add greatly to our *prestige*."

I regretted afterwards that I took so active a part in the business; for it ended in disappointment and loss. Just as the new staff was starting, when there was no longer time for consideration, it was found needful to appoint a general editor. Partly because he was an amateur, and partly because he was not fully in sympathy with us, the general editor did not conduct matters as intended; and our own aims, as well as the expectations of our subscribers, were balked. After a period of decline a professional editor was appointed and things improved somewhat; but it was too late. Eventually we made over the paper to a Mr. Bendyshe, I think, in whose hands it died.

It seems that we were not daunted, however, as witness the following extract from a letter to Youmans written on January 14, 1867:—

"An attempt is being made here to establish a scientific journal, to do what *The Reader* was intended to do. My friend Mr. Campbell came to me the other day, proposing to give £1000 towards the capital, if such a thing were attempted. I mentioned it at the X, and the notion was well received. I propose that we shall take a year or so to organize matters, before making a start; and get our scientific friends throughout the kingdom to canvass their localities, so as to get a constituency to start with."

I had utterly forgotten this scheme, and, by implication, do not remember what resulted. Possibly the movement was that which ended in the establishment of *Nature*.

Concerning *The Reader* I have omitted to say that, though I took no part in the management, I gave a little aid in the way of contributions. While it was in our hands I wrote for it four articles—two political and two scientific.

Save the articles just named, which were of course short, no writings for periodicals had been undertaken by me since 1860. A desire to make as rapid progress as my health would permit with my life-work, led me to negative all solicitations. But now, besides the above-named exceptions, there came a more important exception.

The Fortnightly Review had recently been established. Lewes, who was its first editor, had for some time wished me to write for it. I demurred for the reason just assigned; and probably should have continued to demur, had it not been for a cause described thus in a letter home dated 15 May, 1865:—

"Lewes has induced me to reply to Mill's misrepresentation of me in his book on Hamilton. My reply will appear in the *Fortnightly Review* some two months hence."

Not long afterwards, having occasion to write to Mill on some other matter, I named the fact that I was about to answer him. He made this response:—

"Nothing can be more agreeable to me than to hear that you are going to answer me in the Fortnightly Review. I hope you will not spare me. If you make out so strong a case (and no one is more likely to do so if it can be done) as to make it absolutely necessary for me to defend myself, I shall perhaps do so through the same Review; but not without a positive necessity. I have had enough for the present, of writing against a friend and ally."

The following paragraph from a letter to my father, written on July 10, says, in connexion with the matter:—

"I dined with Mill yesterday, along with Bain and some others, and spent a very pleasant evening. As I remarked to him, it is rather curious that the day on which I first paid a visit to him should be the day on which I had just revised the proof of my article against him."

I may here add that on sundry later occasions during Mr. Mill's residence at Blackheath, and subsequently when he took a flat in Victoria Street, Westminster, I had the pleasure of dining with him. Among those whom I met there at intervals were Mr. and Mrs. Grote, Professor Cliffe Leslie, Lord and Lady Amberley, and, several times, Prof. Bain and his wife. These gatherings had not been long commenced or recommenced. Previously, I had seen Mr. Mill only at the

India House; for after their marriage he and Mrs. Mill led a recluse life. It was, I believe, some years after her death before he began to receive friends. In manner he was quiet and unassuming. His face gave constant evidence of the extent to which in later life, as in his earlier life, his nervous system had been overtaxed; for he had frequent twitchings of some facial muscles. Another trait of expression I can recall: there was a certain habitual setting of the lips, implying, as it seemed to me, a conscious self-restraint. Too stern a discipline in his boyhood, and perhaps too serious a view of things in his later years, put, I think, an undue check on the display of pleasurable feelings. I do not remember his laugh; and my impression is that though he appreciated good things he did not laugh heartily. In fact his mental attitude as expressed in manner and conversation, was much the same as that shown by his address as Lord Rector at St. Andrews, which seemed to imply that life is for learning and working. Though, being a Utilitarian, knowledge and action must have been regarded by him as subordinate to the gaining of happiness, immediate or remote; yet, practically, this ultimate purpose seemed to be ignored. But though in him the means to happiness had come to occupy the foreground of consciousness almost to the extent of thrusting out the end, just as it does in the man of business who thinks only of making money, and almost forgets the uses of the money; yet he differed widely in the respect that this absorption in learning and working was not for self-benefit, but for the benefit of mankind.

Reverting to the matter from which this sketch of Mill has led me to digress, I have to add that the article in question was published on the 15th of July. Thereupon he sent me the copy of a note which he proposed to add to a new edition of his work on Hamilton, then in the press, correcting the mis-statement of my view, on which his argument against me in his *Logic* was based. As this note did not rightly recognize the nature of the mis-statement, I wrote to him pointing out more clearly what this was. There presently came a reply acknowledging the error. I quote a sentence for the purpose of exhibiting his candour.

"It is evident that I have again a misapprehension of your opinion to confess and correct, since you do not acknowledge it as yours in the mode in which it is stated by me."

Though it is three months later in date, I may fitly add here a relevant passage from a letter to my father written on October 3:—

"John Mill has just sent me the sixth edition of his Logic, containing, among other changes, considerable modification in the chapter which he devotes to the question at issue between us. He seeks to meet some of the arguments of my article in the *Fortnightly*. . . . I am quite satisfied with the present aspect of the controversy."

And thus ended a discussion which had been commenced by my essay on "The Universal Postulate," published in *The Westminister Review* in 1853.

Soon after the article was issued, I became aware that there existed good reason for writing it. I am reminded of this discovery by the following extract which I find in a letter home dated 15 May:—

"I gave a dinner to Youmans last Friday, and asked, to meet him, Huxley, Tyndall, Hooker, Bain, Lewes, and Masson. It went off very well."

Why this extract serves as a reminder is not very manifest. But it recalls to me the satisfaction which Prof.

Youmans expressed that I had made this rejoinder to Mill's reply; and his satisfaction was due to the fact that the rejoinder would dissipate a misapprehension current in America. That I had said nothing, was there understood to imply that I had nothing to say. Probably here, too, my silence was construed in this way.

One of the punishments of authorship, or, at any rate, authorship of certain kinds, is the almost inevitable subjection to alternative evils—those inflicted by declining controversy, and those inflicted by engaging in it. That which one constantly sees in oral disputes (that he who has the last word leaves on auditors the impression of having had the best of the argument) holds, too, of disputes carried on in print—holds even where the last word is also the first word; that is, where no notice is taken. The tendency to interpret absence of reply into inability to reply, is very general and almost irresistible. Even I have found myself on more than one occasion supposing that when no answer came no sufficient answer could be given; though I well know that there are commonly other causes. One is pre-occupation. Another is the belief that time spent in controversy is usually wasted. Opponents as candid and conscientious as Mill, in whom the love of truth predominates over the love of victory, are rarely met with. Hence the probabilities always are that in defence of the original misrepresentations (and most controversies arise out of misrepresentations), fresh misrepresentations will be made, and new issues raised, time after time; until the original question is lost sight of and the thing ends in unsettled side-issues.

And yet, strong as are the reasons for avoiding controversy, the reasons for entering into it are sometimes even stronger; for an unanswered objection or unrectified mis-statement is often extremely mischievous. For example, I am well aware that criticisms made upon the theory concerning our space-consciousness set forth in the *Principles of Psychology*, which might be effectually disposed of, have for years had a damaging effect on the estimate of the book.

My summer and autumn movements this year will be sufficiently indicated by the following extracts from letters to my father, of which the first, dated July 4, gives a key to the rest.

"I met Mr. Smith last night at an election meeting of J. S. Mill's supporters. [Mill was just then a candidate for Westminster, which he afterwards represented in Parliament]. He asked me to go to Scotland. They are to leave in about a fortnight, and I am to join them early. I shall therefore probably come down to Derby about the close of next week, and spend a week or so with you before going North."

The next was written on the 10th.

"I had given notice to Mrs. Sharpe to leave at the end of this week. But if you will come up here, I will stay for a few days longer, so that you may have a week in town. The Youmanses will probably leave for Switzerland in a week or ten days. You could, after being a week here, go on to Brighton or elsewhere, if you felt so disposed."

He came, and I, after a time, went to Derby. In a letter to him written thence, giving an account of my mother's health, I find the passage:—

"I voted for Evans and Colville on Saturday. You have probably seen before now that they were returned by small majorities."

This was the only vote for a Member of Parliament I ever gave. Certain property which had come to me from my uncle William, gave me a qualification; and when I shortly afterwards sold this property, I was disqualified. Though since that time I have had a qualification in London, and might have registered, I have never done so. Not that the election of Liberal or Conservative has been a matter of indifference to me; for, speaking generally, my sympathies have been with the Liberal candidate. But in most cases my dissent from the beliefs tacitly held by both political parties on the question of the functions of the State, which I regard as the question of most importance, has been such that I have had little motive to support one candidate rather than another. In fact as, of late years, Liberals have vied with Conservatives in extending legislative regulations in all directions, there has been nothing to choose between them, and therefore, to me, no temptation to vote.

Returning from this parenthetic explanation, I may quote next from a letter dated 6 August.

"I arrived at Ardtornish last night and was cordially received. The Earps and I [Mr. Earp was my friend Lott's senior partner] arrived at Oban on the Wednesday evening as intended, and spent Thursday and Friday very pleasantly, partly in showing them the neighbourhood and partly in sea-fishing. The weather was very fine, while with you we hear it was raining. On Saturday they started with me by the steamer that goes to Staffa, which was to drop me at Ardtornish in going, but in consequence of the tides it went round Mull the other way and I had to go to Staffa with them. As I had never before seen it, I was not sorry—it is worth seeing."

Written on the 31st, saying that I was about to leave Ardtornish next day, a letter also said that I thought of going South by the East coast, which I had never seen.

This intention was fulfilled; as witness the following lines sent from Durham on the 4th September:—

"I stopped on my way at Dunbar, Berwick, Newcastle, Tynemouth. From this picturesque old place I think of going to-morrow to Barnard Castle and thence to Richmond. I shall probably be home on Thursday or Friday."

After spending a little time at Derby, I reached town on the 18th of September, and was settled in Kensington Gardens Square on the 22nd.

The first quotable passage from home correspondence after that date, is one written on October 3, as follows:—
"Inclosed I send you a letter from Ernest Renan, the French Professor who has recently obtained so much celebrity by his *Vie de Jesus*. If you can make it all out, you will see that it is very satisfactory—especially the intimation that *First Principles* is likely to be translated into French."

This was the first intimation of the kind which came to me from abroad; but the French did not after all take the initiative. This was taken by the Russians. In the following March I received from St. Petersburg information that translations were in progress, or had been published, I forget which; and several Russian translations had made their appearance during the five years which elapsed before there appeared the first French translation.

Nothing further worthy of record is mentioned in correspondence until December 18, when, in a letter home, there occurs a passage describing something new in the course of my work:—
"I have been very busy lately with the microscope studying the circulating system in plants, and have arrived at some interesting results. I shall probably devote myself to it a good deal while I am at Derby."

This I did. I obtained from the hothouses and greenhouses at Kew, a large number of cuttings, chiefly of aberrant types of plants, and passed much of my time at home in experimenting upon them. After my return to town the investigations continued. A letter of January 30, 1866, says:—

"I am still busy with my microscope: usually working with it at the same time that I am dictating; but, as a result which you may imagine, dictating slowly, and not very well. As I write this, I have under the microscope a very beautiful preparation, serving very admirably as evidence of my hypothesis."

To Professor Youmans on March 2, I described a further phase of the matter:—

"I should have written to you again before this time, but that I have been of late so very busy with certain investigations in Vegetal Physiology, of which your sister [she had remained in England] has possibly by this time told you something; and during the last month more especially I have been compelled to devote myself wholly to them, in consequence of having committed myself to a paper for the Linnæan Society on the subject. This I read last night. It passed off very satisfactorily. I shall of course send you a copy of the paper when it is printed; but as there will be a plate of illustrations it will probably be a long while before you receive it."

The inquiry which came to issue in this manner, had arisen in the course of my work. When treating of physiological development, something had to be said about circulation in plants. Botanical books gave no accounts from which I could frame an intelligible conception; and I found it needful to look into the facts for myself. There was a manifest inadequacy in the accepted statement that the movement of liquid is through the wood; for there arose the question,—What course does it take in young plants which are still succulent, and in those parts of adult plants which have not yet formed wood? Is circulation in these cases carried on by diffusion from cell to cell, or is it carried on through definite canals? If in young tissues definite canals exist, as they do, it would be strange did the moving liquids neglect these and pass through the general substance, which is comparatively difficult to permeate. But I did not argue thus; though a certain friend of mine, who regards me as prone to *a priori* reasoning, would doubtless suppose that I did. My argument was wholly inductive and unguided by hypothesis; for, until observations and experiments had suggested one, no view at all was entertained by me. The result, however, was to show that the inference which might have been drawn *a priori* was true. In young plants; in the leaves and soft shoots of old ones; throughout all parts of adult plants that remain succulent, like the balsams; and in such aberrant plants as cactuses, which, between their joints, are long before they develop wood; the vessels are the channels which the sap follows. But whatever wood is formed or forming, it becomes the channel followed by the sap: the adjacent vessels, deserted by liquid, become filled with air—not, as was supposed, because they are air-carriers, but simply as dead or disused organs.

This inquiry developed into further ones respecting the mechanics of the circulation and the forces which cause and aid it. Incidentally some traits of structure, too, were observed. Details will be found in the Appendix to *Principles of Biology*, Vol. II.*

* One and twenty years have elapsed since the paper above described was published. To my surprise I have nowhere seen mentioned any attempt to either verify or disprove the conclusions it contains. Some

Conforming to its title, this chapter ought, I suppose, to include an account of all that occurred while the second volume of the *Biology* was being written. But, besides entailing undue length, entire conformity to its title would make it include sundry events momentous enough to occupy places by themselves. I therefore pass over a period intervening between the reading of the paper just described, and the completion of the book: thinking it best to say here what little has to be said about the book as eventually published.

Few parts of my work give me more pleasure in the execution. In the first division, "Morphological Development," certain views which had long been waiting for full expression found a place. There came the opportunity for, and indeed almost the necessity for, a specula-

passing references to the paper have, I believe, been made; but the text books continue to repeat substantially the same story as before. I have lately referred to the most recent authoritative work—the translation of Sachs *On the Physiology of Plants;* and in it I find it still stated that the circulation is through the wood: the statement being stretched so as cover the facts by saying that it is always through lignified tissue, and including under that name vascular bundles as well as wood-cells— a proceeding which seems to me about as reasonable as it would be to group a man's ears with his bones because both have a basis of cartilage. Twice during the interval I have myself verified the leading proposition of the paper in a simple and conclusive way. The way is this:—Choose a young plant some three or four inches high, in a greenhouse where it has been grown in soft, prepared soil. Insert a trowel at such distance from it as not to touch its rootlets, and take it up bodily along with the mass of soil imbedding its roots. Immerse the mass in a vessel of water; so that the loose soil may fall away and leave the roots bare. Fill a wide-mouthed bottle with a strong decoction of logwood; insert in it the roots of the young plant; and there leave it, for, say, twelve hours. Then cut through obliquely the stem or a leaf stalk, and apply to the cut surface a little chloride of tin in solution. Immediately the characteristic purple will be seen in the vascular bundles; and microscopic examination will show that the coloured liquid is confined to the vessels.

tion concerning the modes in which the two higher types of plants, endogens and exogens, have been evolved out of a lower type of plant. That there has been such an evolution is an inevitable implication; and a probable mode in which it has taken place had to be shown. Originally standing quite apart from this, but eventually becoming united to it, was a conclusion towards which I had for some years been gravitating respecting the relations between the foliar and axial parts of plants, and in support of which I had collected many specimens: the conclusion being that the two are not primordially distinct, as was alleged, but that the foliar organ is the primitive unit, and the axial organ the derivative. Then, too, there had to be worked out under the general head of "Morphological Differentiation" that hypothesis respecting the shapes of organisms and their parts, which, first reached in 1851, was sketched out in the "Law of Organic Symmetry" in 1858; and beyond the developing of this in relation to the external shapes of organisms and their parts, there came the extension of it to the shapes of certain internal parts.

Scarcely less interesting to me was the subject of "Physiological Development," forming the next division. The point of view from which the phenomena were contemplated, was, of course, the same as that from which the preceding group of phenomena were contemplated. How are physiological differentiations to be interpreted in terms of the re-distribution of matter and motion—as consequent, that is, upon the relations of parts to incident forces? For clearly, if the survival of the fittest among organisms as wholes, is to be regarded as a process of equilibration between actions in the environment and actions in the organism; so must the local modifications of their parts, external and internal, be regarded as survivals of structures the reactions of which are in equilibrium with the actions they are subject to. This general view had to be carried out in the interpretation of such contrasts as those between outer and inner tissues, and those between parts of outer tissues exposed to one set of forces and parts exposed to another. And then, in animals, it had to be similarly carried out in its application to internal organs: especially those of the alimentary canal and its appendages. Throughout all the interpretations there ran the general thesis that, while the majority of these differentiations are indirectly caused by survival of the fittest, there is part of them, and that, too, the primordial part, due to the direct action of incident forces.

Lastly, under the head of "Laws of Multiplication" came a division in which there had to be set forth in detail the idea originally sketched out some fifteen years before, in the "Theory of Population deduced from the General Law of Animal Fertility." Separated from crudities and superfluities, the idea withstood a wider comparison with the facts; and while apparently applicable to the organic world as a whole, seemed also in harmony with the evidence presented by races of men differently conditioned. Here, on recalling the matter, I am struck by the fact, which I have never before observed, that long before reaching the general conception of Evolution as set forth in terms of the re-distribution of matter and motion, there was a manifest tendency to contemplate organic phenomena from this same physical point of view. For the various conclusions reached were so many corollaries from the doctrine that in proportion as the matter and motion expended in maintaining individual life are great in their amounts, the amounts available for the maintenance of the species are small, and *vice versâ:* the implication being that fertility is inversely proportionate to the size and heterogeneity of the species and the activity and complexity of its life.

Am I going to say something about the reception of the volume? No: for a very sufficient reason—it had no reception. In other words it was not sent round to the press. My decision not to send it was made after receiving definite proof that readers had been deterred from looking at my books by the totally wrong conceptions of them they had gained from reviews. This proof was given by Professor Bain. He told me that during a conversation with John Mill, in which the *Principles of Psychology* was referred to, he, Bain, confessed that he had not read it. Mill expressed great surprise; whereupon Bain explained that the impression gained from notices of it had deterred him. He went on to say that when, subsequently, he read the book, he found to his astonishment that the reviews had not given him the remotest conception of its contents. Receiving as I thus did a verification of a belief towards which I was tending, I directed my publishers not to issue any copies of the second volume of the *Biology* to the critical journals.

CHAPTER XXXVIII.

IMPENDING CESSATION.

1866. ÆT. 46.

OF the various occurrences occupying the *hiatus* indicated towards the close of the last chapter, the first in order of time was a crisis in my career which happened at the beginning of 1866.

During the preceding year, my attention was decisively drawn to the fact that my expenditure, though modest in amount, continually outran my income, and forced me to draw upon capital more frequently or more seriously. A letter recalls the fact that early in 1863, the subscribers to my serial, originally 430 in number, had fallen to 350: the ending of *First Principles* having, I presume, been an occasion for the withdrawals of many, and perusal of the early part of the *Biology*, uninteresting to the majority, having caused further withdrawals. Moreover, among the remaining names not a few had to be crossed out after futile efforts made by the publishers to obtain payments of subscriptions in arrear.

The difficulty was becoming otherwise complicated. My father was now 75; and though he maintained his erect carriage and preserved tolerable health, his energies, bodily and mental, were of course flagging. As a consequence, while his professional engagements fell off, those which remained occasionally proved too much for him: so much so, indeed, that in more than one letter I advised him to retire altogether, rather than make himself ill. My mother, too, had now become a confirmed invalid; and illness is always expensive. Thus their requirements were increasing at the same time that the means of meeting them were decreasing; and in the absence of returns from teaching, my father's other sources of income were obviously insufficient. Of course the result was that I had to aid; and the required aid was certain to become greater year by year.

During his then recent stay in England, I had talked the matter over with my friend Prof. Youmans—probably in the course of the week he spent with me in Kensington Gardens Square. Such, at least, is the implication of the following passage from a letter written to him on October 28, 1865.

"Since you left I have obtained from the share-broker at Derby, through whose hands most of my money transactions have gone, the data I needed; and, joining them with my bank account and other memoranda, I have been able to make a tolerably definite calculation of my losses. I found that my guess was not far from the mark. It turns out that since 1850 I have sunk nearly £1,100 in writing and publishing books; and the amount will considerably exceed £1,100 by the time I have finished the volume now in progress. . . .

Not finding the result any more encouraging than I supposed, I have not, as you may expect, found any reason to modify my intention of issuing, along with No. 15, the notice of cessation at the close of the volume."

This intention was carried out. Before the notice was issued, much anxious thought and no little painful feeling were passed through. It was grievous thus to give up my life-work when already a considerable part of it had been satisfactorily executed. But I had either to go on wasting away what little I possessed and neglecting my responsibilities, or else to abandon the undertaking; and I sorrowfully decided upon the last.

It shortly appeared, however, that the undertaking was not to be abandoned without an effort being made to prevent the abandonment. The first indication of such an effort came to me in the shape of a remarkable proposal from Mr. J. S. Mill. Usually I find it desirable to omit unimportant parts of letters quoted; but here it seems as well to give in full Mr. Mill's letter and my reply to it.

"Blackheath Park,
Feb. 4, 1866.

Dear Sir,
On arriving here last week, I found the December livraison of your Biology, and I need hardly say how much I regretted the announcement in the paper annexed to it. What the case calls for, however, is not only regret, but remedy; and I think it is right that you should be indemnified by the readers and purchasers of the series for the loss you have incurred by it. I should be glad to contribute my part, and should like to know at how much you estimate the loss, and whether you will allow me to speak to friends and obtain subscriptions for the remainder. My own impression is that the sum ought to be raised among the original subscribers.

In the next place, I cannot doubt that the publication in numbers though it may have been the best means which presented itself at the time, has had an unfavourable effect on the sale, and that a complete treatise with your name to it would attract more attention, obtain more buyers, and would be pretty sure to sell an edition in a few years. What I propose is that you should write the next of your treatises, and that I should guarantee the publisher against loss, *i.e.*

should engage, after such length of time as may be agreed on, to make good any deficiency that may occur, not exceeding a given sum, that sum being such as the publisher may think sufficient to secure him. With this guarantee you could have your choice of publishers, and I do not think it likely that there would be any loss, while I am sure that it could in no case be considerable. I beg that you will not consider this proposal in the light of a personal favour, though even if it were I should still hope to be permitted to offer it. But it is nothing of the kind,—it is a simple proposal of co-operation for an important public purpose, for which you give your labour and have given your health.

I am
Dear Sir,
Very truly yours
J. S. MILL."

The answer I wrote to this letter ran as follows:—

"88 Kensington Garden Square,
7 *Feby.* 1866

Dear Sir,

I scarcely know how properly to respond to your very kind letter of the 4th; or what to say in due acknowledgment of its very generous proposals. Though you are so good as to represent them as made on public grounds rather than personal ones, I naturally cannot wholly dissociate the two; and cannot avoid, therefore, feeling how much I am indebted to you for so noble a self-sacrifice as that which you offer to make in furtherance of my scheme. I fear, however, that there are insurmountable reasons and feelings of mine, standing in the way of the arrangement you suggest.

In the first place I should be averse to either asking, or having asked on my behalf, any compensation from the subscribers for the losses my work has entailed on me; even were those losses of the kind you infer them to be, which in great part they are not. It is only the volume now in progress that will cost more for printing, paper, illustrations &c. than will be received from the subscribers. Preceding volumes have done something more than repay their expenses—the last of them, however, but very little. The losses which deter me from proceeding, are those resulting from unremunerated labour, and the continual sinking of what property I possess, to meet my necessary expenses. My whole course since 1850, when I began publishing, has been that of doing work that brought either loss or no adequate return; and I have been enabled to continue this course only by the accident that bequests from relations, which have in the meantime come to me, have sufficed to eke out my resources. Had it not been for a legacy from an uncle in 1853, I should not have been able to write the *Principles of Psychology;* and I should inevitably have been brought to a stand by pecuniary difficulties in the middle of *First Principles,* had it not been that another uncle, who died in 1860, left me the greater part of his small property: which is, however, at present so burdened with annuities that it brings me in very little. The result has been that all along I have been obliged to go on eating up my capital—a process which of course advances with increasing rapidity.

This course I have been persevering in, hoping that eventually the tide would turn, and that I should be no longer obliged to continue sinking what little I possess. But finding, in the course of last year, that the list of subscribers was continuing to diminish, and that the sales of the bound volume of the *Biology* had not reached 100 in the lapse of 12 months, I began to hesitate. On getting together all the data, I found that since 1850 I had lost nearly £1,100. Seeing that I was still going on losing, and that my sinking of capital was becoming more and more serious, I resolved that I would desist. Thus you see that the difficulty is considerably greater than the notice of discontinuance had led you to infer; and I fear that the plan you have so kindly proposed will not meet it. Various letters from subscribers, addressed to Messrs. Williams and Norgate, or to me, have proposed arrangements for avoiding the cessation. To these letters I have furnished Messrs. Williams and Norgate with a general form of reply, stating that—1st. The doubling the subscription, as suggested by some, would probably do as much harm as good. 2nd. The raising a publication-fund, as suggested by others, was a proposition I could not entertain. 3rd. That the proposal that each subscriber should obtain one or more others, was one which, if acted upon generally, might be effectual; but that I declined asking the subscribers to do this; and that any such thing, if done, must be done of their own accord.

A few days ago Messrs. Williams and Norgate hinted that something was likely to be done in pursuance of this last proposal. But having assumed an absolutely passive attitude, I do not know who are moving in the matter, or what is likely to result.

While obliged, as you will thus see, to decline the arrangement which you have generously offered to make, I shall ever have pleasurable remembrance of it as a manifestation of feeling between authors that has rarely been paralleled.

      I am, dear Sir,
       Very sincerely yours,
        HERBERT SPENCER."

I ought to have said, rarely, if ever, paralleled. It may be doubted whether there was ever before made a kindred proposal by one author to another: another, too, with whom he was not in complete agreement.

Had Mr. Mill been in England at the time when the notice was issued, a letter from him would probably have been the first indication received by me of an endeavour to avert the impending cessation. But, as is implied towards the close of my reply, before I received the letter above quoted, certain others of my friends had taken action. A letter to Prof. Youmans, dated 2 March, 1866, says:—

"Mill has since called on Williams and Norgate, and is, I believe, co-operating with those who were previously moving in the matter; but who they are, and what they are doing, I do not know."

And then, in a letter of April 10, I find a passage saying what had been done and what was likely to be done. It runs as follows:—

"As to the progress of matters here, though I have been aware from hints dropped for some time past that something was doing among those interested in preventing the impending stoppage, I did not learn until two days ago, what was the nature of the course taken; and when I did learn it, a misapprehension very nearly led me to put a peremptory stop to it. Indeed I was on my way to the printers with the draft of an adverse circular, when I learnt the true state of the case. It is now probable that, after insisting on certain qualifying conditions, I may agree to the arrangement that has been secretly made; and which I find I can hardly resist without quarrelling with my friends who have made it. It seems that the arrangement has resulted under the pressure of a number of persons interested, chiefly wealthy, who were anxious that something should be done to meet the difficulty; and who, under the guidance of Huxley, Tyndall, Busk, Lubbock and Mill, have arranged to take a large number of copies (250) for distribution; and they say that I cannot prevent them. However, I shall refrain from opposing the arrangement only on condition of a large reduction in the number (down to 150) and the erasure of the names of some of those concerned" [who, I thought, ought not thus to tax themselves].

This arrangement, with the qualifications indicated, was agreed upon; and there was issued a circular in conformity with it, signed by Mill, Huxley, Tyndall, Busk and Lubbock (see Appendix C). Naturally my feeling was one of mingled satisfaction and dissatisfaction—satisfaction, that so much sympathy should be shown me by distinguished friends, whose measures thus promised to prevent the suspension; and dissatisfaction, that such measures should be needful.

But neither in its original form nor in its modified form was this arrangement carried out. Before much had been achieved, there occurred a change in my position which led me to write a letter expressing the wish that the circular should be cancelled. This was done by a second circular (see Appendix C).

What reason I had for taking this seemingly-strange step, which undid all that my friends had taken the trouble to do, will be seen in the next chapter.

CHAPTER XXXIX.

SAD EVENTS.

1866—67. ÆT. 46—47.

EARLY one morning towards the close of April, I received a telegram which led me to take the first train to Derby. The cause will be at once inferred; and the issue of that cause will be seen in the following passage from a letter to Professor Youmans, dated May 7:—

"Before you receive this you will probably have received the Derby paper which I posted to you on Friday, containing a paragraph which you will read with melancholy interest: a brief tribute of respect to my late father. I was called down to him by telegraph this day fortnight, and found him seriously ill, but not, as I supposed, or as any one supposed, in immediate danger. He got gradually worse, however, and died on the Thursday night. As you may imagine the shock has been great and has unnerved me greatly. Indeed I found my system running down so rapidly, and such serious symptoms showing themselves, that I have been obliged to come up to town for a few days change of scene, lest I should fall into some nervous condition out of which it would take me a long time to recover.

Fortunately we are able to keep this sad loss from my mother. She has gradually fallen into that state of mental debility and forgetfulness which renders it easy to evade her inquiries. Not remembering things for more than a few hours, and often for not more than a few minutes, she is habitually under the impression that it is but a few hours since she saw my father. It is a great satisfaction that she is saved from the suffering which knowledge of the truth would give her.

I return to Derby probably at the close of this week."

But for an imprudence, my father might well have lived another ten years. Some workmen were altering the drainage on his property, and he, not duly heeding the bitter East wind, stood by giving directions: being at the time in a depressed state, caused by long-continued anxiety about my mother. A resulting congestion, or inflammation, of the lungs quickly became serious. He did not die of the disease, however, but of the treatment. The physician (now long since deceased) believing that he would die of exhaustion unless he got rest, decided to administer morphia. Probably he did not allow sufficiently for the extreme enfeeblement and for the choked state of the lungs: for the dose he gave was an overdose and proved fatal.

I name this detail as introductory to a detail of more significance. My father died in a morphia-dream, the subject of which was the high-handed action of Governor Eyre in Jamaica. Since the days of the anti-slavery agitation he had ever been deeply interested on behalf of the Negroes; and the Eyre-prosecution, then pending, greatly occupied his mind. His last audible words concerned the controversy which was raging at the time; and implied a dim idea of his state mingled with the ideas of his dream; for they expressed the complaint that when he was so ill, it was cruel to draw him into an argument about the matter.

It was not an unfit ending for a consciousness which all through life had been occupied with the interests of his fellows and those of mankind at large. The ambition which, when I was a boy, he so often set before me—to be " a useful member of society "—was an ambition ever dominant in himself: too dominant, indeed, for he sometimes unduly sacrificed personal welfare to public welfare. Would that the world were peopled with such. What a marvellously different world it would be!

Though at the time of his death he was seventy-six, my father had not made a will. I suppose this mattered little; for the disposition of his property by will would probably have been the same as that which resulted from his intestacy.

Of course the settlement of his affairs kept me a good deal at Derby; and there by and bye came detentions caused by the sale of property. A number of small houses possessed by him I promptly decided not to keep. Even when an agent is employed to collect rents and look after minor repairs, small house-property entails on its owner much trouble and vexation. All through life I had seen the way in which my father was worried by matters of business which his agent had to refer to him; and all through the latter part of his life I had seen the way in which he was further worried by the interferences of the sanitary authorities, who were continually insisting on alterations (some of them made necessary by their own blunders) and occasionally driving away tenants by the insanitary results they produced. Not even had I been likely to live permanently in Derby, would I have continued to own property which, troublesome enough otherwise, had become a source of perpetual exasperations.

But the care of my mother, which now devolved upon me, was the chief cause for my frequent presence in

Derby. Though a good nurse, under the oversight of a sister-in-law, was to be trusted to a considerable extent, yet visits by me at short intervals were obviously necessary. The carrying on of my work had of course to be adjusted as best it might. Compromising the requirements enabled me to diminish the hindrances. During a fortnight in London, where I had my amanuensis, materials, and sources of information, I prepared sufficient manuscript to occupy me something like a week at Derby in revising; and then came another fortnight in London, followed by another week at Derby.

Alternations thus arranged, determined the course of my life during the remainder of 1866 and the first half of 1867.

July of this year brought me a great surprise. My friend Youmans arrived, and was the bearer of startling intelligence and something more. It appeared that when the notice of cessation reached him, he determined that my undertaking should not drop if he could prevent it; and with characteristic energy he began to provide for its continuance. Saying nothing to me about the matter, he had, during the intervening six months, busied himself in raising a fund which he arranged should come to me in the form of a testimonial; or rather, in a form which, as it turned out, left me little choice but to accept. He handed me a letter from Mr. Robert B. Minturn, of the firm of Grinnell, Minturn & Co., who had undertaken to act as a kind of trustee, and who, telling me what the sympathy of the Americans had prompted them to do, hoped that I would not prevent their sympathy from taking effect. Unavoidably this action of my American friends eventually became known; and soon after midsummer statements concerning the results had appeared in American journals and had been copied in some English journals. These statements were incorrect; and Prof. Youmans thought it needful to publish in one of the London papers a letter containing a correct statement. As this letter gives the facts in a more authoritative way than any I can give them myself, it will be best to quote it.

"*Aug.* 11. 1866.

Sir,—The paragraph which you lately published on the authority of the American papers, "that Professor Youmans recently left that country in order to present to Mr. Herbert Spencer 5,000 dollars and a very valuable gold watch, as a testimonial from his American admirers," requires some correction; as it mis-states both the amount contributed and my own purpose in coming to this country. The case is this: —Nearly all Mr. Spencer's writings have been republished in America, where they have been both widely read and very highly appreciated. Many of his friends there, feeling a deep indebtedness to him for works by which they knew he had been the loser to a serious amount, thought that they could not more suitably express their gratitude than by a substantial testimonial. But knowing that Mr. Spencer had decisively declined some overtures on the part of his friends in England, having the kindred purpose of preventing the cessation of his philosophical series, and preferring not to be placed in a like predicament, they invested 7,000 dollars in his name in public securities, which, as they belong to no one else, he is of course at liberty either to appropriate or leave to accumulate for the benefit of his heirs.

E. L. YOUMANS."

Thus I was practically put under coercion; for even could I have decided to baulk my American friends, it would have been absurd to do this by letting their gift and its accumulated interest go eventually to an unknown person.

SAD EVENTS

The presentation watch named in Prof. Youman's letter, was one of those manufactured by the Waltham Watch-Company, at the time when they were making their reputation—watches of a quality which they presently ceased to make; as I learned long afterwards from their agent over here. It has proved a great treasure as a time-keeper, and has excited the envy of friends who have known its performances.*

In July 1866 the British Association was at Nottingham. I had never been to one of their meetings. Now, however, partly because it met so near my home but chiefly because my friend Youmans wished to be present, I spent a good many days there: going to and from Derby every day.

While recalling the incidents of the occasion, there comes back to me one which has but little connexion with the occasion. I have above referred to the fact that the Eyre-prosecution was then pending, and that hot controversies were going on concerning it. These controversies arose at times and places often unfit; as I remember happened during a dinner at the house of Dr. Ransom, who entertained daily while the meeting of the As-

---

* I find in a letter, written in December, 1880, after the watch had been in my possession fourteen years, a paragraph respecting it which may fitly be quoted :—" I have several times intended to tell you how wonderfully well my American watch has been going of late. It has always gone with perfect regularity, either losing a little or gaining a little; but of course it has been difficult to adjust its regulator to such a nicety as that there should be scarcely any loss or gain. This, however, was done last summer. It was set by the chronometer-maker in July, and it is now half a minute too slow; never having varied more than half a minute from the true time since the period when it was set. This is wonderful going. As the Admiral says, one might very well navigate a ship by it." [In 1890 it went with equal nicety: lost 42 seconds in half a year.]

sociation continued. I was taking an active part in the matter; having become a member of the Jamaica Committee, formed for carrying on the prosecution: a committee which, headed by John Mill, was remarkable for containing all the leading evolutionists—Darwin, Huxley, Wallace, and myself, besides others less known. Indeed the evolutionists, considering their small number, contributed a far larger proportion to the committee than any other class. I may add here that notwithstanding a charge made by Lord Chief Justice Cockburn to the Grand Jury, thoroughly justifying the prosecution, and emphatically denying the assumed power of a governor to proclaim martial law as Governor Eyre had done, the Grand Jury ignored the bill; and thus tacitly asserted that a deputy ruler may rightly suspend the established law whenever he considers it needful, and set up military tribunals to hang or shoot or otherwise punish as they may think well. That cultivated Englishmen should not have perceived that the real question at issue was whether free institutions were to be at the mercy of a chief magistrate, seems at first marvellous; but it is marvellous only on the supposition that men's judgments are determined by reason, whereas they are in far larger measure determined by feelings.

Of the proceedings of the Association, some few memories remain. There was the presidential address by Mr. (now Sir William) Grove, on "Continuity;" more instructive to the uninitiated than to the advanced. There was a lecture, too, by Dr. (now Sir Joseph) Hooker, narrating some results of the Antarctic Expedition. And then there was the dinner of the Red Lions: an annual occasion on which the saying *Dulce est* etc. is taken to heart.

After the meeting of the Association was over, Prof. Youmans and I started upon a tour in North Wales which I induced him to take with me: his assent being, I suspect, due more to the wish for a favourable occasion for prolonged talks and consultations, than to a desire to see the scenery; for his sight had been so impaired by the chronic ophthalmia which at one time entailed years of blindness, that he was scarcely able to appreciate landscape beauties.

Not pausing till we reached Beaumaris, we spent one day there, another at Carnarvon, and another if not two at Bedgellert. Thence an enjoyable coach-drive by Port-Aberglaslyn, Harlech, and along the sea-coast, brought us to Aberdovey. Here we took lodgings for a week, and Mrs. Youmans joined us from London. Reading and working mainly occupied my energetic friend. Leaving him indoors, busy with an article for the *New Englander*, demolishing a critic who had attacked me, I made use of the out-door opportunities: one day being spent in a bootless fishing excursion, and another in making an expedition with Mrs. Youmans to Aberystwith. The train which, at the end of the week, took my friends back to London, took me as far as Machynlleth; where I bade them a temporary good-bye and set out on a pedestrian tour. The first day's walk, during the greater part of which I had Cader Idris before me, brought me to Dolgelly. Before the end of the next day I reached Bala. And the day after that saw me at Llangollen; whence I took the railway for Chester.

What was my subsequent course I cannot now remember, and there are no letters to remind me. I have long been under the impression that from 1856 onwards until quite recently, I had invariably made an annual visit to some part of Scotland; but I now incline to think that in 1866 an exception occurred. I believe that I returned to Derby, and thence, after a time, to London: possibly having decided that under the circumstances it was needful that I should confine my movements to places within a day's journey of home.

On going back and noting my various changes of residence, the reader might reasonably infer that I am by nature nomadic. But his generalization would be disproved by the single fact now to be named. On my return to town towards the end of September 1866, I settled myself at 37 Queen's Gardens, Lancaster Gate, and have made that my home up to the present time—a period of over 21 years.

The house is situated in a salubrious locality, and has Kensington Gardens within three or four minutes walk. Experience proved it to be quiet and well managed; and it contained a group of inmates above the average of those one finds living *en pension*. There was a retired government officer belonging to the Stores Department —a Mauritian of French extraction, honourable in feeling, a great snuff-taker, and one who regretted that duelling had ceased. Next to him came an admiral, who every day drank the Queen's health, and displayed piety and militancy in a not unusual combination. Another naval officer there was who uttered Radical sentiments, fostered in him, I fancy, by disappointment in his profession, for which he was evidently incompetent; and there was also a captain in the army, occupied in some philanthropic work in London. Then came a maiden lady, between 70 and 80, who had acquired a certain stock of information, ideas, and feelings, in her teens, and had never since added to or modified them. These were fixtures. After them may be named sundry who were semi-settled—the wife of a judge in the West Indies, staying in England for her health, pretty and inane; an Indian tea planter, quiet and not unintelligent; an Australian with wife and daughter, come back to spend his money. From time to time there were other visitors from the Colonies—from New Zealand, from the Cape, from Canada. Occasionally, too, there were Americans; of whom I remember the episcopal bishop of Illinois with his children. And then to these settled and semi-settled, must be added those who came for short periods—for the London season, or for a few weeks. Humdrum was the circle they formed, as indeed are most social circles. But on the whole I was tolerably contented with my surroundings.

I have said that 37 Queen's Gardens was the address of my new abode; but after a few years this address was slightly changed. Our hostess, Miss Shickle, took the next house No. 38, and by a doorway broken through, united the two houses. Thereafter No. 38 became my address. As the dining-room and general drawing-room were in No. 37, No. 38 was quieter; and I was enabled to seclude myself as much as I wished. In fact I saw no more of my fellow guests than one sees of those who daily come to the *table d'hôte* of a Continental hotel. As the arrangements were such as freed me from all trouble and provided for my needs satisfactorily, I was never seriously tempted to make any change.

At the same time that I settled myself in Queen's Gardens, I took, at No. 2 Leinster Place, about three minutes walk off, a room to serve me as a study, with the option of taking an additional room if need be. Here I collected and arranged all my books, papers, and other things needful for work; and here I spent my mornings. I thus protected myself against all interruptions: the servants at Queen's Gardens being forbidden to give any further reply to visitors than that I was not at home.

A blank which occurs here, alike in my memory and in records, extends to January 14, 1867; at which date I find that I sent to my American friend a letter containing the following passage.
"I think it is since I wrote last, that they have been wanting me to become a candidate for the professorship of Mental Philosophy and Logic at University College—a post for which they would not have Martineau, who had offered himself. I declined, however, without hesitation. Since then, I have had to resist similar overtures made by Masson, who wanted me to stand for the Moral Philosophy chair at Edinburgh, which is likely soon to be vacant. One proposal, however, I have assented to. Mr. Grote wishes to nominate me on the senate of the London University, when there occurs an occasion; and as this will not involve much tax on my time, I have made no objection."

This extract yields me conclusive proof that in respect even of interesting occurrences, my memory has in some cases failed utterly. In the absence of the above passage I should have been not simply unconscious that I had ever been asked to become a candidate for a professorship, but should not have believed it had it been alleged.

I may add that Mr. Grote's proposal came to nothing. Whether the nomination was ever made I do not know, for I never heard anything further about the matter.

The next incident to be set down is one of which I

need no reminder. Had I needed one, however, I should have found it in my next letter, dated February 25. Instead of describing it afresh it will be best to describe it in the words then used to my American friend, as follows:—

"I am not sure whether I mentioned to you when you were here, that I had been devising, and was about to have made, an invalid bed on a new principle. During my father's brief illness, I was struck with the amount of suffering and exhaustion entailed on patients when they are very feeble, by turning them over, raising them up, getting them out of bed and into it again &c. Thinking over the matter after my father's death, it seemed to me that it would be very easy to avoid all these evils, and to make a bed that would put a patient in any conceivable attitude, and turn him over, or put him out of bed, without any effort on his part. As my mother was getting very feeble, and the time seemed soon likely to come when such a bed would be of advantage to her, I decided to carry out my idea. In the course of the autumn I put the working drawings into the hands of a man in Derby; and after a great deal of delay, caused partly by my present frequent absence, in London, and partly by the difficulty of getting things done just as I wanted, I succeeded, about a month ago, in getting it completed and put to use. Since then my mother has been in it, and, to my great satisfaction, likes it extremely. Enclosed I send you a set of photographs, which will give you a general idea of its construction and the various things it will do. Considering it is the first made, it answers very well; and in making a second, it can be in several respects so improved as to answer perfectly: being, at the same time, rendered both lighter and cheaper. As you will see it consists of two frame-works; the upper of which is hinged in such ways as to admit of raising the body to any inclination and bending the legs to any angle; while the lower frame-work, supporting this upper one, rests on a large ball and socket, admitting of movement in all directions, and admitting of being locked fast in any position. . . .

I decided not to take out any protection for the idea: wishing that an appliance which will, as I think, so greatly diminish human suffering, should be sold as cheaply as possible; and I have just been making an agreement with an invalid bed-maker, binding him down to a moderate rate of profit. I hope not long hence to send you photographs of the frame-work in its improved form.

Meanwhile, if you should think well, you might, when occasion offers, inquire for some fit man to undertake the manufacture of it in New York: taking care, however, as I have done, not to disclose the idea until some kind of agreement is made, such as to secure its sale at a moderate price."

Though it is five months later in date, I may most conveniently add here a passage from another letter referring to this matter.

" After long provoking delays, and no end of bother, I have got completed, and brought to London, the improved invalid-bed. Various medical men, Bence Jones, Sharpey, Lockhart-Clark, Marshall, Dunne, Bastian, Hart &c. have been to see it, and very much approve of it."

My decision not to patent the invalid-bed proved to be ill-advised. I hoped to facilitate the use of it, but experience proved that I hindered the use of it. Had I made it a protected invention, I might have induced some one to undertake the manufacture and sale of it; but as it was, no one thought it worth while to invest the necessary capital. As I have not myself had the spare energy requisite to bring it into use, it has remained unused. (For description and illustration see Appendix D.)

Such ease from comfort and from variety of attitude

as was given by the invalid-bed, though in the opinion of the nurse it prolonged life for some months, could of course not do more than this. As spring advanced into summer, more than one sudden summons to Derby indicated that the last days were approaching; and soon after midsummer came the close of a life which had been full of quiet virtues. Here is the announcement of it to my American friend.

"You will infer from the black border what has happened. I am now alone in the world—having no nearer relatives than cousins; with none of whom I have any sympathy.

My mother after her long period of feebleness died on Sunday—having had but a week of positive illness. For these two years her life has been so monotonous and burdensome a one that, sad as the ending of it necessarily seems, it is to be regarded as a cessation of a painful consciousness."

The failure of the faculties which had for years been going on, was fortunately not of a distressing kind; but rather one which tended to mitigate, by obliviousness, the evils to be borne. During this mental decay the ideas and sentiments which had been dominant throughout life, became more dominant by contrast with those which faded. It was pathetic to see how, when there was no longer the power to discharge domestic duties and religious observances, they constantly occupied the mind. Early in the day came directions about household matters; and later in the day came repeated suggestions that it was time to prepare for going to chapel. These alternate thoughts survived to the last; and thus ended a life of monotonous routine, very little relieved by positive pleasures.

I look back upon it regretfully: thinking how small were the sacrifices which I made for her in comparison with the great sacrifices which, as a mother, she made for me in my early days. In human life as we at present know it, one of the saddest traits is the dull sense of filial obligations which exists at the time when it is possible to discharge them with something like fulness, in contrast with the keen sense of them which arises when such discharge is no longer possible.

PART IX.

XL. Re-Casting *First Principles*.
XLI. An Imprudence and its Consequences.
XLII. A Tour in Italy.
XLIII. Developing the *Psychology*.
XLIV. Finishing the *Psychology*.
XLV. An Extra Book.
XLVI. Some Minor Incidents.
XLVII. The *Descriptive Sociology*.

CHAPTER XL.

RE-CASTING *FIRST PRINCIPLES.*

1867. ÆT. 47.

THE house which, from the age of seven to the age of forty-seven, had been my home—practically at some times and nominally at all other times—was now my home no longer. There remained nothing to tie me to it beyond the associations which had clustered in and around it during forty years. And these, some of them pleasurable and some of them otherwise, were not such as to outweigh the motives for permanent residence in London.

To the town, though it was my birthplace, I did not feel any particular attachment. "Here I am again at dull Derby" was the internal exclamation I often made when arriving by train; and the country immediately around it had no such beauties as to compensate for its dulness. Only three families which I cared much about now lived in or near it; so that the social attractions were not great. And then the climate did not suit me: it is anything but invigorating. Thus other feelings than filial were not strong enough to make life at Derby desirable.

Soon after my mother's death I therefore arranged to give up the house. Reserving valued relics and such few pieces of furniture as promised to be useful in London, and distributing the rest among my relations, I surrendered the key to the landlord. Thereafter Derby knew me no more, save in the character of an occasional visitor to friends.

Already in Chapter XXXVI, which tells how, when writing the *Classification of the Sciences* there resulted the discovery that *First Principles* had been organized wrongly, I named the design, thereupon formed, of reorganizing it at the first convenient opportunity. A letter shows that I had intended to do this as soon as Vol. I of the *Biology* was completed. When that time came, however, I found that there was still unsold a large portion of the original edition of *First Principles*. Had my means been considerable, I might have been extravagant enough to sacrifice this; but I could not afford to do so, and had to wait for its gradual disappearance by sale. At the close of March 1867, when the second volume of the *Biology* was finished, this remainder was, I presume, all or nearly all gone; and I eagerly commenced the long-suspended project.

I say eagerly, because during the intervening years there had continually recurred the consciousness that I had left outstanding a seriously imperfect piece of work —a consciousness which I was anxious to get rid of. Some vague dissatisfaction had, indeed, arisen when the book was originally written; and, when, in a chapter entitled " The Conditions Essential to Evolution," there was recognized the fact that Evolution, as I then conceived it, was not universal, but that there were certain aggregates, such as crystals, which did not undergo it. It never occurred to me at that time to put the question—What is that universal process common to these aggregates which do not become more heterogeneous and those aggregates which do become more heterogeneous? Had I put this question I should have seen that the formation of an aggregate necessarily precedes any changes of structure which occur in the aggregate; and that therefore integration is the primary process and differentiation the secondary process.

The impatience I felt to make this rectification of statement, which gave a new aspect to the doctrine and freed it from a now-manifest error in the described order of the phenomena, caused me to lose no time. As soon as the closing number of the *Biology* was issued, I commenced the agreeable task; and such times as I could command throughout the ensuing spring, summer, and early autumn, were devoted to it.

Of incidents during the first part of the interval thus occupied, the following extracts from letters to Prof. Youmans indicate those of chief interest. On March 11, I wrote to him thus:—

"You were saying when over here, that you thought the time was coming when we might recommence the issue of the serial in the U.S. I doubt, however, whether it would be worth while. Our subscription list here has just been gone through for the purpose of giving a peremptory reminder to those in arrear. I find there is not far short of £200 due. Possibly the intimation that has been given, that no further numbers will be sent out to those whose last two subscriptions are unpaid, will have its effect. But I foresee that if things go on as they have been doing, it will be needful to give up the issue in parts by the time the *Psychology* is completed. The trouble and loss will no longer be compensated by the gain."

Until this extract recalled it, the fact that the issue by

subscription in America had been abandoned, had disappeared from my mind. The abandonment had, of course, been caused by the difficulty in obtaining payments of subscriptions. A letter of April 8, contains the passage:—

"This morning I am none the better for a large amount of metaphysical discussion last night with Mill and Grote. It had been specially arranged that Grote and myself were to dine at Mill's together, and the result was a very interesting evening, though one which was a serious tax upon me, as you may suppose. . . .

Tomorrow I shall commence the revision of *First Principles*. I had intended to make one or two replies to criticisms on the first part, but have been dissuaded by the Leweses from doing so. There will only be one or two small verbal alterations."

What I saw of Mr. and Mrs. Grote on this and other such occasions, reminded me of the saying ascribed to Rogers—" Ah! I like the Grotes very much: she is so gentlemanly and he is so ladylike." The saying was unfair to Mr. Grote, however; for his extreme suavity did not prevent his manliness from being manifest. I liked him much, but I did not care about her; and I suppose this fact was displayed in my manner, for I have no power of disguising my feelings. She was a masculine woman, alike in size, aspect, character, and behaviour; and I greatly dislike masculine women. Moreover, she had been accustomed to a good deal of incense, and I, little given to administer it in any case, was in her case deterred by the tacit claim; for when there is assumption without adequate achievement to justify it, I always feel prompted to resent it. Hence, though the relation continued to be civil, and with Mr.

Grote even cordial, the acquaintanceship did not grow into freindship.

Some passages written ten days later are worth quoting:—

"The inclosure contained in your letter was a considerable surprise to me. I had anticipated something very much less. What a wonderful steward you are. I never dreamt, a few years ago, of any such results arising; and had it not been for you it is clear that no such results would ever have arisen. . . .

Your remarks as to the use that is being made of Mill's name, completely fulfil the prophecy I made to him. I told him that I regretted to see the weight of his authority given to a side that is already, to say the least, far too strong; and that the result would be that the Classicists would appropriate all he said in their favour and ignore all he said against them."

The last of these two paragraphs refers to the inaugural address, then recently delivered by Mill as Lord Rector of St. Andrews, in which he urged the claims of Classics, with the apparent implication that they were in danger of being over-ridden by Science. Considering that Science was but just beginning to raise its head, and to obtain a grudging recognition in the high places of learning, it seemed to me that the note of alarm was scarcely called for.

I think I have already named the fact that the Russians took the initiative in translating my books. From the following paragraph written to my American friend on May 3, it appears that M. Nicholas Thieblin, who had undertaken the dangerous task of introducing them to his countrymen, nearly got into serious trouble in consequence.

"A few days ago I had a letter from my Russian translator, giving me the satisfactory intelligence that the prosecution has ended in smoke. It seems that the charge of the minister amounted to a charge of high treason; and this was so grave that the procureur of the court of justice refused to proceed with it; and, one charge having failed, another could not be made. So the poor fellow is out of danger; and we shall have no occasion to make a noise about it in America."

A letter of June 7 contains a paragraph which it seems desirable here to reproduce.

"I have decided, within these few days, to use a specific title for the whole series of volumes that I am issuing. Originally, when drawing up the programme, I contemplated doing so; and was very nearly using the title Deductive Philosophy. But I was dissuaded, and finally fell back upon the indefinite title—'A System of Philosophy.' There are decided evils, however, in the absence of a distinctive name; and I have had these evils just now thrust before me afresh. . . . Another title, therefore, is evidently extremely desirable, and will, I think, in many respects yield positive as well as negative advantages. I have decided upon the title —*Synthetic Philosophy*, which, on the whole, seems the most descriptive. I am intending to make the issue of this second edition of *First Principles* the occasion for introducing it; and propose that each successive volume shall bear this general title on its back in addition to its special title."

The following extract from a letter of June 26, I make more especially for the sake of its second paragraph.

"Mr. Silsbee dropped in upon me quite unexpectedly about ten days ago. He had come over it seems in pursuance of a resolve suddenly taken, intending to spend two or three weeks here before going to Paris. He is looking very well. Mrs. Youmans' friend Dr. —— (I forget his name) came to lunch on the day that Silsbee called; so that I had quite an American party.

We are about to give a public breakfast here to Garrison. Bright is to be in the chair, and the address is to be moved by the Duke of Argyll, and seconded by Earl Russell (probably) and also by John Mill. I am one of the Committee of arrangement."

Had it not been for these records in letters, I should have been able to say nothing about the course of my life during this part of 1867.

And here, indeed, after the above illustration, I may fitly say a few words respecting the biographical materials to be hereafter used.

Unhappily there was no longer any home correspondence. There remained only the correspondence with friends. Of the letters to Lott, large numbers are missing; and hence the fact that in many preceding chapters there are no quotations from them. In 1867 the series of them recommences, and they here and there furnish passages of interest. The letters to my American friend, however, are those on which I have chiefly to depend for filling in the outlines of my life after this date. Besides recalling incidents I had forgotten, their statements give precision to incidents I remember; and they furnish a tolerably full account of everything concerning the writing and publication of my books.

In 1878 I commenced keeping a brief diary. This tells me where I was and what I was doing day by day; and enables me to give to the narrative during eight subsequent years, definiteness if not fulness. Were it compiled from recollections only, the account of these eight years would be bald if not vague; and the account of the preceding seven years would be both vague and bald.

I may add that as, in nine cases out of ten, the quotations made will be from letters to Prof. Youmans, it seems needless always to give his name. Where no name is mentioned it may be inferred that the passage quoted was written to him.

When summer was just passing into autumn I visited my friend Professor Masson, who had taken a house for the season in the Vale of Yarrow, and had asked me to spend a few days with him. They were days of sympathetic talk, carried on during walks and drives—talk which pleasantly and beneficially distracted my thoughts from recent domestic troubles. One of our excursions was to St. Mary's Loch at the head of the vale, and to "Tibbie Shiels" tavern: a place associated with traditions of notabilities of the preceding generation, who gathered there for fishing. Our out-door converse was enlivened by Masson's stories—now concerning the Border raids associated with the locality, of which I remember nothing save the name of some sanguinary ruffian, "Dickie of Dryhope"; and now concerning Dr. Chalmers, whom Masson had known personally and greatly admired. A certain emotional glow which he puts into his narratives, always gives them an interest beyond that which they otherwise have.

After "Yarrow visited" and never "re-visited," I departed for the West, or rather, for the North-west. To fill an unoccupied gap in my holiday, I went as far North as Glenelg; and after a week there spent partly in fishing, partly in rambling, partly in examining the Pictish towers in Glen Beg, I made my way to Ardtornish to have another of those interludes in my life which have formed its chief enjoyment. Here I remained from August 20 to Sept. 10.

RE-CASTING *FIRST PRINCIPLES*

Beneficial as a visit to Ardtornish was always made by its out-door and in-door pleasures, a certain drawback resulted from its relaxing climate. To neutralize this I sometimes on my way South stopped for a time at a bracing place. On one occasion, though in what year I cannot remember, I thus utilized Llandudno; and this year I betook myself to Scarborough. Of incidents during my week's stay I remember but one—a ramble along the coast to a bay some two miles or so to the South, which brought under my notice an extremely exceptional fact. In this bay there crops out on the beach a stratum of clay of medium plasticity; coherent enough for large lumps of it to hold together when tumbled about by the waves, and yet soft enough to be rounded by them. The bay also contains a deposit of shingle, over which the soft clay boulders had in some places been rolled. And here came the strange result. In each rounded mass of clay the pebbles had imbedded themselves, so that its surface was closely studded with them all over. Part of the beach was formed of sand; and it seemed quite possible that one of these clay boulders with its superficial layer of pebbles might be deposited by the waves on some quiet part of the sandy tract, there gradually covered over, and finally left as part of a new stratum. What an incomprehensible phenomenon would it in such case be for the geologist of the future! How incredible it would seem that such a formation should be other than artificial!

This reference to an anomalous process observed on the sea-shore, recalls another scarcely less anomalous, which I may fitly joint with it. Were anyone to assert that Nature gives mankind lessons in describing circles, and furnishes them with the model of an instrument for the purpose, all but a very few would say he was talking nonsense. Yet he would be stating a literal fact. Probably some may conclude that I refer to those arcs of circles occasionally scratched by loose branches of trees trained against walls, and which have been blown backwards and forwards by the wind; and he may say rightly that the curves thus formed—only parts of circles, and, indeed, only approximately circular—are formed under artificial conditions. But I have in mind a case on which no such criticisms can be passed. Where sand-hills are formed along a sea-shore, there grows in them, and serves to hold them together, a species of large grass, having blades that are very long, dry, and stiff. Roots of this occur, not in the sand-hills only, but here and there in the flat interspaces. Hard and wiry though its blades are, they sometimes get broken —perhaps by passing animals. Occasionally may be seen one of which the broken end, longer than the upright part to which it is still attached by some fibres, leans in an inclined position with its point touching the sand. This broken part when blown about by the wind describes part of a circle on the surface of the sand. When the wind changes it describes another part of the circle; and when the fibres by which it is held are few and lax, other changes of wind make it fill in the remaining arc. Eventually this natural pair of compasses may be seen standing in the middle of the circle which it has described.

These instances show how difficult it is to find in all cases a test by which to distinguish the improbable from the impossible.

From Scarborough I departed for Gloucestershire,

and on my way stopped two days at Stourbridge. Why Stourbridge? will probably be asked by any reader who knows how uninviting are the place and its surroundings.

My purpose was to make a genealogical inquiry. As was said at the outset, my maternal grandmother was named Brettell (originally Breteuil); and there were two questions respecting her mother which I wished, if possible, to solve. When, as a boy of 14, I was in London with my parents, I accompanied them to dine with two old gentlemen named Shakespeare, who were cousins of my maternal grandmother. Miss Brettell, a cousin of my mother, had once told me that there was no blood relationship; by which, at the time, I understood her of course to mean no blood relationship of the kind which one might have a motive to establish, were it possible. But I now think she meant that the cousinship of these Shakespeares had arisen not from the marriage of a Mr. Brettell to a Miss Shakespeare, but from a marriage of a Mr. Shakespeare to a Miss Brettell. This was the point which I wanted to determine; and hence my expedition to Wordsley near Stourbridge, where this great-grandfather Brettell had lived. I could not make out anything, however. The name Shakespeare was not infrequent in the register, and, if I remember rightly, occurred on sundry grave-stones. But I could not discover the marriage I sought for.

Another question of this class interested me. As was indicated in a preliminary chapter, the Brettells, resident during a long past in the neighbourhood of Stourbridge, had intermarried with certain de Henezels (or Henzies, as they were eventually called in England)—a refugee family which came over from Lorraine at the time of the religious persecutions: having in earlier times migrated into Lorraine from Bohemia: possibly being Hussites. I gathered in the neighbourhood that there had been two branches of the Brettell family, a richer and a poorer; and I was curious to learn with which of these branches it was that the Henzies had mingled: whether with ours, which I believe was the poorer, or, as I think more probable, with the richer. I failed to learn, however. I knew only that my great-grandmother's Christian name was Sarah; that her marriage with Mr. Brettell must have been about the middle of the last century; and that among the children there were a John, a Jeremiah, and a Jane. Whether it was that these data were insufficient, or whether it was that my search (limited to the registers of Wordsley and Old Swinford) was not wide enough, I cannot say.

The failure was of little moment, however. Were it proved that through this line of ancestry there has descended to me a trace of foreign blood distinguished by such pronounced nonconformity, the fact would have negative significance rather than positive significance. Save certain physical traits, I inherit, so far as I can perceive, scarcely anything from maternal ancestry. Every trait, alike intellectual and moral, which is at all distinctive, is clearly traceable to my father.

After the two days which I spent in this bootless investigation, I continued my journey to Standish; and, at the end of one of my pleasant sojourns with my friends there, returned to London.

The printing of the re-cast edition of *First Principles* had been going on *pari passû* with the revision, and was now nearly complete: the tolerably rapid progress made by the printers having been due to the circumstance that the greater part of the original stereotype plates had, with but trifling alterations, been made to serve afresh.

I name this fact as introductory to some remarks concerning the method of publication I had adopted and have since continued. The system of stereotyping has been objected to by some of my friends as entailing an obstacle to the making of corrections; and it doubtless does this to a serious degree if the corrections are numerous and diffused throughout the work. But it entails no considerable obstacle when the changes are limited to particular parts, or are in chief measure changes of arrangement. In this second edition of *First Principles*, probably for not more than one-third of the work had new plates been required; while the plates of the remaining two-thirds had needed only to be re-paged and to have the sections re-numbered.

Stereotyping of course involves extra loss if a book is unsuccessful; and its profitableness implies something more than temporary success. If an edition consists of but 500 copies or of 750 copies, the cost of setting up the type is the chief cost; and even when the number comprised in the edition is 1000, payment for setting up the type amounts to one-half the sum laid out. If the type has been distributed and a second edition is called for, composition has to be paid for a second time, with the effect of greatly diminishing the net profit. But if stereotype plates have been made, (or rather stereo-moulds, for it is not requisite that the plates should be cast until they are actually wanted) there needs no second composition; and there has to be borne only the outlay for the stereotype plates. If there are many editions this cost of the stereotype plates practically disappears; and leaves nothing to be counted as cost beyond the paper and press-work.

When, some ten years since, I gave evidence before the Copyright Commission, I made a calculation respecting the returns brought by my books. I found that, after making deductions for the usual trade-allowances, the publishers' commission, and the expenses of paper and printing, there remained to me between 30 and 40 per cent. of the advertised price. I say between 30 and 40 per cent. because, so long as the cost of composition and stereotyping entered into the estimate, the per-centage of profit was kept down to something like the lower of these two rates; but, when, after many editions, this element of the cost might be considered as having practically disappeared, the rate of profit approached the higher of the two. That is to say, an edition of 1000 copies of a book advertised at 20 shillings, brought to me nearly £400: an amount which the cost of advertising might reduce to something like £380. No such proportion as this is, I believe, ordinarily obtained by an author who either sells the copyright of an edition or who publishes on the system of half-profits —a system which, on the ordinary publisher's method of estimating profits, is apt to leave the author with a very small sum; if it does not, indeed, vex him by a perpetually retreating mirage of profits—a promise that there will be profits on the next edition.

Of course publication by commission (*i.e.* paying the publisher 10 per cent. on the gross returns for doing the business) accompanied, as in my own case, by direct dealings with the printer, paper-maker, and binder, entails a certain amount of trouble. A friend of mine, who over-estimates this amount, thanks the publisher for undertaking it, and thinks he is not overpaid for going through it. That he is not overpaid when he takes the risk as well as the trouble, is true. The competition of trades keeps the trade of publishing down to the average level of profitableness; and there are bankrupt publishers as well as bankrupt traders of other kinds. But where the publisher does not run any risk—where the author's position is such that his book is sure to more than pay his expenses; then the publisher is greatly overpaid for the work he does on either the half-profit system or the system of copyright purchase, if he gives only what is commonly given. Did he take the course I do, my friend would find that the few hours spent in the needful letter-writing and interviews were paid for by returns at a score times the rate that any hours otherwise spent were paid for: a consideration which may fitly be entertained; since, high as his aims may be, the author must live before he can work.

Of course the penniless author, or one who, though he gains much, is extravagant and lives from hand to mouth, cannot avail himself of this more remunerative mode of publishing. He cannot wait for the ultimate advantages. He has to accept such terms as the capitalist offers; and they are usually hard terms.

Returning from these digressive remarks suggested by the publication of this re-cast edition of *First Principles*, which took place in November, I may here say something concerning the work itself; or rather—concerning the general doctrine now finally embodied in it.

Early in the course of the foregoing narrative, when briefly describing various essays, I indicated the ways in which they severally displayed approaches to the conception eventually reached; and before giving, in its original crude form, the programme of the system in which it was proposed to elaborate this conception, I described the general course of thought by which, as seen in these steps, the conception had been arrived at. Here, while noting the further developments which took place subsequently, it will be well to set down succinctly all the successive steps with their respective dates. They run as follows:—

1850. Recognized the truth that low types of organisms and low types of societies, are alike in the trait that each consists of many like parts severally performing like functions; while high types of organisms and high types of societies, are alike in the trait that each consists of many unlike parts severally performing unlike functions (*Social Statics* pp. 451-3): the tacit implication being that in these cases progress is from the uniform to the multiform.

1851. Made acquaintance with the expression of Milne-Edwards, "the physiological division of labour," as applied to organic life—an expression which, suggesting the thought that in animals as in societies the division of labour increases as organization advances, brought into clearer light the meaning of the "increasing sub-division of functions" on which I had commented in drawing the above parallel, and the meaning of the change from uniformity of structure to multiformity of structure.

1851-2. A disclosure to me, and reception by me, of von Baer's formula;—every organism in the course of its development changes from homogeneity of structure to heterogeneity of structure.

1852. In treating of the development of style there were expressed simultaneously, as being equivalents, the ideas that progress is from a state in which there are many like parts simply aggregated, to a state in which there are many unlike parts mutually dependent, and that it is from homogeneity to heterogeneity.

1853. Alleged that in the course of social development progress is from unity of control to diversity of control—ceremonial, ecclesiastical, and political; and further, that within the ceremonial division itself, progress is similarly from simplicity to complexity.

1854. (Spring.) After enunciating the principle that Education must conform itself to the unfolding mind, it was asserted that mental development is from the simple to the complex and from the indefinite to the definite (a first recognition of the truth that increasing definiteness is a trait of evolution); and concerning scientific development, which is determined by mental development, it was asserted that Science displays an increasing integration, giving it greater coherence, at the same time that by increasing divergence and re-divergence it acquires higher complexity. Though in these cases there was recognized the fact that development is from uniformity to multiformity, or from homogeneity to heterogeneity, these phrases were not used.

1854. (Autumn.) Systematically dealt with as having arisen by evolution, Mind at large, animal and human, was now described as advancing from the homogeneous to the heterogeneous, and from the indefinite to the definite, and as displaying an accompanying integration of its components.

1854-5. These successive extensions in various directions of the idea that progress is from the homogeneous to the heterogeneous, now suddenly led to the perception that this is a universal trait of progress, inorganic, organic, and super-organic; and immediately, in answer to the inquiry how does this happen, there followed the conclusion that the multiplication of effects is everywhere the cause.

[Eighteen months of ill health here intervened.]

1857. Directly after setting forth this theory in the long-delayed essay—" Progress: its Law and Cause " came the perception that there is a further cause of this universal transformation, and, indeed, an antecedent cause—the instability of the homogeneous. At the same time it was pointed out that individual organisms and social organisms are alike in displaying the process of integration.

1857-8. During the last days of the one year or the first days of the other, came the thought that, since the continuous metamorphosis due to these causes is displayed by all orders of existences, it ought to be the guiding conception running through and connecting all the concrete sciences, which severally treat of the different orders of existences; and there was forthwith sketched out a series of volumes in which a presentation of them as thus dealt with should constitute a system of philosophy.

1858 (or else the latter part of 1857). There was now added the perception that increasing heterogeneity cannot go on without limit, but must end with the arrival at a state of equilibrium; and then, or soon after, came the further perception that since the state of equilibrium eventually reached cannot last for ever, there must afterwards come a process of dissolution; and that thus Dissolution is everywhere complementary to Evolution.

1858-9. Partly during the preceding intervals, extending back as far as 1854, and partly during the interval here dated, arose the recognitions of certain simpler facts of existence and action which must in all cases determine the transformations constituting Evolution and Dissolution—the indestructibility of matter, the continuity of motion, the rhythm of motion, and the law of the direction of motion. It became clear that all the changes to be interpreted are consequences of the ceaseless re-distribution of matter and motion everywhere going on; and must conform to those ultimate physical principles which regulate this re-distribution. Finally, it was concluded that the assigned proximate causes of Evolution, as well as these physical principles just named, are all to be affiliated upon the persistence of force; and that the interpretation is complete only when they are all deduced from the persistence of force.

1860-62. The conceptions which had thus been reached, in successive stages, and finally consolidated as just described, were now elaborated in their various applications, as set forth in *First Principles*.

1864. Incidentally, while dealing with the Classification of the Sciences, and asking for the most general form under which all orders of concrete changes may be expressed, there was suddenly disclosed the truth that integration is a primary process and differentiation a secondary process; and that thus, while the formation of a coherent aggregate is the universal trait of Evolution, the increase of heterogeneity, necessarily subsequent, is but an almost universal trait;—the one being unconditional and the other conditional.

1867. Lastly, it was perceived that to the statement

of the mode in which the matter composing an evolving aggregate is re-distributed, should be joined a statement of the mode in which its motion is re-distributed; and the formula was made to include the fact that along with the transformation of the matter from a state of indefinite, incoherent homogeneity to a state of definite, coherent heterogeneity, there goes a parallel transformation of the retained motion.

Thus from the time when there arose the initial thought that organisms and societies are alike in the trait that low types consist of like parts performing like functions, while high types consist of unlike parts performing unlike functions, to the time when there was reached this fully-developed conception of Evolution at large, inorganic, organic, and super-organic, there elapsed a period of 17 years. Of the successive changes which went on during this period, the earlier were incorporations of additional orders of phenomena, and thus exhibited progressive integration—the primary process of Evolution. Simultaneously, sundry of them displayed advance in heterogeneity; since they brought into a coherent whole more and more heterogeneous masses of facts—the secondary process of Evolution. Others, again, by raising the conception into more precise agreement with the reality, gave increased definiteness to it—a further trait of Evolution. And thus, as we saw when it had reached a less advanced stage, the changes passed through by the conception of Evolution themselves conformed to the law of Evolution.

I was about to add that the final phase of Evolution —equilibration—was now illustrated by the arrival at an equilibrium between the conception and the phenomena:

a balance such that the order of the ideas was no longer to be disturbed by the order of the facts. But this is more than I dare to say; seeing that I had before more than once thought that the two were in complete correspondence when they were not.

CHAPTER XLI.

AN IMPRUDENCE AND ITS CONSEQUENCES.

1867. ÆT. 47.

Up to this time I had not felt the need for any assistance beyond that yielded by an ordinary amanuensis. Such materials as were stored up in memory, joined with such further materials as were accessible without much labour, served me while writing *First Principles*.

Though for writing *The Principles of Biology* there was required a far larger amount of information than I possessed, the result proved that I did not miscalculate in believing that I should be able to furnish myself with such detailed facts as were requisite for the setting forth of general conceptions. Nor did *The Principles of Psychology*, partly executed and now to be completed, cause me to seek external aid. The data for the subjective part, which was dealt with after a manner unlike that commonly adopted, were lying ready internally; and the views taken of the objective part were so little akin to those of preceding psychologists, that no extensive study of their writings was necessary. But I had long been conscious that when I came to treat of Sociology, the case would be widely different. There would be required an immense accumulation of facts so classified and arranged as to facilitate generalization. I saw, too, that it would be impossible for me to get through the amount of reading demanded, and that it would be needful for me to read by proxy, and have the collected materials prepared for use. Not, indeed, that this was my first idea. I began by thinking that I must have a secretary who would read to me. I soon became aware, however, that the requirements could not be thus met; and that I must get some one to devote himself, under my superintendence, to the gathering and grouping of data.

There was no time to be lost. The elaboration and completion of the *Psychology* I expected would occupy me some two or three years; and unless, by the end of that time due preparation had been made, I foresaw that I should suddenly have before me the task of building without bricks—or, at any rate, building without any adequate supply of bricks. While staying with Professor Masson in the Vale of Yarrow, I named to him my need, and begged him to let me know if he heard of any one likely to serve my purpose. My friend's aid soon proved to be efficient. Within a month, while still at Ardtornish, I received from him a letter recommending a young Scotchman, Mr. David Duncan, well known to him and to Professor Bain, under whom he had studied. Qualms of conscience had obliged him to relinquish a clerical career, for which he had been intended; and he was seeking something to do. He seemed too good for the place, and I said as much in the correspondence which ensued; but notwithstanding my somewhat dissuasive representations, he decided to accept, and joined me in Town not long after I returned.

Of course preliminary discipline was needed by any one who undertook the work I wanted done; for my conception of the required data was a wider one than he would be likely to frame for himself. Indications of the climate, contour, soil, and minerals, of the region inhabited by each society delineated, seemed to me needful. Some accounts of the *Flora* and *Fauna*, in so far as they affected human life, had to be given. And the characters of the surrounding tribes or nations were factors which could not be overlooked. The characters of the people, individually considered, had also to be described—their physical, moral, and intellectual traits. Then, besides the political, ecclesiastical, industrial, and other institutions of the society—besides the knowledge, beliefs, and sentiments, the language, habits, customs, and tastes of its members—there had to be noticed their clothing, food, arts of life &c. Hence it was necessary that Mr. Duncan and myself should go through some books of travel together, so that he might learn to recognize everything relevant to Sociology.

It resulted that beyond my morning's work, continued, when I was well, from 10 till 1, during which interval Mr. Duncan acted as amanuensis, some work of so light a kind that it hardly seemed worthy the name, now filled an hour or two at the end of the day. Though reading had the same effect on me as dictating, and though half an hour over a book in the evening made my ordinarily bad night decidedly worse, yet I hoped that I might listen when read to without suffering from it. It was a foolish hope. Many experiences might have shown me that the effect would be mischievous.

My nervous affection had been from the beginning of such a nature that disturbance of the cerebral circulation was caused by whatever necessitated persistent mental action, no matter of what kind. Often when at a loss how to pass the time, I have been asked—" Why do you not read a novel?" But the effect of reading a novel is just the same as that of reading a grave book. When at my worst, half a column of a newspaper as surely brings on head-symptoms as do two or three pages of metaphysics. Whatever involves continued attention produces the effect. Dr. Ransom, who had suffered from a similar affection, told me that he brought on a relapse by too persistently watching, through the microscope, the early changes in the fertilised ova of fishes; and he further told me that disorders akin to his own and to mine, were common in Nottingham among the lace-menders—a class of women who, all day long, have the attention strained in looking for, and rectifying, small flaws which have been left by the lace-making machines. Hence I might have known that continuous attention to a reader would have nearly the same result as continuous reading. This presently proved to be the case. My restless nights were very soon made more restless. Without thinking what I was doing I nevertheless persevered; and by and bye found that I had brought about one of my serious relapses.

I have nothing to remind me of the date, but I imagine that this disaster occurred early in December.

In a previous chapter I named the fact that I had recourse to morphia when my nights became much worse than usual; and doubtless on this occasion I sought thus to bring on again the periodicity of sleep, which, once broken through for some time, had to be re-established by artificial means.

And here it occurs to me to describe, for the benefit of those who have not experienced them, some of the effects of morphia on dreams. In me it gives extreme coherence to the ideas evolved. Unlike the actions and events of an ordinary dream, which are linked on by accidental suggestions in such wise that they form a rambling series, the actions and events of a morphia-dream are almost like those of the waking state, in their rationality and orderly connexion. For a long time the thoughts which arise bear a logical relation to some primary thought, and the actions performed continue to be in pursuance of some original intention. Occasionally this trait was so stiking that I next morning recorded the dream illustrating it. Here is an account of one.

"Another peculiarity that has occasionally struck me is the continual occurrence of events or thoughts which, though coherent, are unexpected and do not seem accounted for by any simple process of association. Last night, for example, I happened just to awake at a moment when I was able to lay hold of a portion of a dream presenting these peculiarities. I imagined that I was reading the review of some book which the reviewer brought to a close by condemning the extremely strong language used by the writer, and then proceeded to give an example of it. The example commenced thus:—

'Has this cur the slightest tender-heartedness—is he even hearted at all?'

Immediately on reading this I was startled by the oddity of the word 'hearted' thinking to myself—What made the man use such a word? I supposed he meant to write, 'Has he any heart?' This was a parenthetical thought, and I remember that the paragraph went on to a considerable length; and then that the reviewer wound up by two or three lines, in which he made a quite unexpected parallel, of which, though unexpected, I soon saw the meaning.

In these cases it seems as though there were going on, quite apart from the consciousness which seemed to constitute myself, some process of elaborating coherent thoughts—

as though one part of myself was an independent originator over whose sayings and doings I had no control, and which were nevertheless in great measure consistent; while the other part of myself was a passive spectator or listener, quite unprepared for many of the things that the first part said, and which were nevertheless, though unexpected, not illogical."

When thinking them over I have put different interpretations on these phenomena. At first I ascribed them to a double consciousness. But as in the word tenderheartedness there occurs the fragment " hearted;" and as in such instances as " wrongheadedness " the word " headed," included as a component of the compound word, is also used by itself; it seemed possible that by association in a consciousness active enough to be influenced by it, but not active enough to perceive in time that the word suggested by analogy is not used, the word " hearted " might be evolved; and that then its unfamiliarity might suddenly arouse attention to its strangeness. Afterwards, however, I reverted to the hypothesis of a double consciousness arising from independent action of the two hemispheres of the brain—independent action due to a lack of that complete co-ordination which exists during the waking state.

In ordinary dreams, thoughts which seem valuable or witty, turn out on awaking to be nonsensical or inane; but in morphia-dreams there sometimes arise thoughts which would not discredit the waking state. I have made a memorandum of one which occurred in an imaginary circle of friends, one of whom, referring to a recently-published book, said—" Oh, have you seen the Rev. Mr. So-and-so's story called ' The Lily ': it is the most beautiful moral essay I ever read." Whereupon, in my dream, I remarked—"Ah, I see: a sermon that 'cometh up as a flower'." This happened shortly after the publication of Miss Broughton's first novel; and evidently the title of it partially determined the course which my dream took.

It is an interesting physiological inquiry, what peculiar state of the circulation it is which combines the implied activity of brain with closure of the senses to external impressions.

Various efforts were now made to restore my constitutional equilibrium. In the latter part of December I went to Malvern for some 10 days—not to undergo hydropathic treatment, though I went to a hydropathic establishment. No great advantage resulted. Then, dated London, 2nd January, 1868, a letter to Youmans says:—

"To-morrow I am going off into Glostershire, where, if the frost which has now set in, lasts, I hope to get some skating; and I count upon this for doing a great deal towards setting me right again."

Shortly after I reverted to another form of exercise, previously found beneficial. In reply to an invitation from Lott written on January 25:—

"When I returned from Standish I was considerably better, and recommenced work; and, though I have since been worse again, still I do not think that Derby life, even though joined with the pleasant circle of No. 7, would have been quite the thing for me.

I have resorted to my old remedy of playing rackets, and have to-day derived considerable benefit. By continuing this, and doing a little work, I hope to restore again my easily disturbed balance."

This expectation was disappointed, however. The

state, brought on in December and continued through January, persisted till the end of February; and it then seemed needful to make a thorough change in my life. A letter to Youmans, dated 29 Feb., says:—
" After losing a great deal of time during the last two months, hoping to get into working order by using half-measures, I have been at length compelled to take a more decisive course. I start to-morrow morning for Italy, where I propose to spend some two months—expecting that by the end of April, by the combined effects of desisting from all excitements, intellectual and social, and getting the exhilaration due to so much novelty, I shall regain my ordinary state."

An incident of moment to me, affecting greatly my daily life throughout future years, occurred just before I started. I was elected into the Athenæum Club by the Committee. There are two modes of election: the one by ballot, and the other under what is known to the members as Rule 2—a rule allowing the Committee to select from the list of candidates nine annually who have special claims: the purpose being to maintain the original character of the Club, which, at the outset, brought together the chief representatives of Science, Literature, and Art.

CHAPTER XLII.

A TOUR IN ITALY.

1868. ÆT. 47.

BEYOND the usual interests which attracted me to Italy as a country in which to pass an interval of relaxation, there was an unusual interest: Vesuvius was in eruption. This fact determined not only my choice of Italy as a recruiting ground, but also the route I chose. Already the emission of lava and vomiting of molten fragments had been going on for a month or more; and I feared the eruption might cease before I reached the place if I delayed on the journey. I therefore went to Marseilles and thence took steamer for Naples.

This was during the first days of March; and early in the morning of the 6th, I think it was, the passengers were, in response to a request made over night, called on deck to see the dull red glow of the long lava-stream, then visible at a distance of some 20 miles, amid the scarcely decreased darkness. The sight was impressive; and it was strange to remember it afterwards on observing that by day the lava-stream appeared to emit no light at all.

My first day at Naples, where we arrived before the bustle of the streets had commenced, was passed in an uninteresting way—lying on the bed in a state of exhaustion. I had been rendered fit for nothing, partly by the wear and tear of the journey, and partly by the bad feeding on board the vessel, belonging to the *Messageries Impériales*, which brought us, a vessel which, not subject as others of its class are to competition with the Peninsula and Oriental line, had a very bad *cuisine:* making me, among other things, better acquainted with the large Mediterranean fish called tunny than I wished to be. Only in the evening did I feel sufficiently recruited to walk out, and then I caught a cold which remained with me during the whole of my stay in Italy.

How careless people are in their statements about climate. Thinking that I was going where mildness reigned, I had hesitated about taking my Inverness cape. It was fortunate that I did take it. During the five weeks I passed in Italy I needed it daily, sometimes with a spring overcoat underneath; and at Florence, during the first week in April, I saw many others similarly clad. But it was an exceptional winter, I was told. Yes, it seems always to be an exceptional winter. Friends with whom I afterwards compared notes had the same weather, and heard the same excuse. I may add that my experiences elsewhere in later years have been no less disappointing: so much so, indeed, that I have come to doubt whether a model climate exists anywhere.

Twice during my week in Naples I was led to endanger my life by that trait with which, as I have said at the outset, my father reproached me when a boy—the tendency to become for the moment possessed by a single idea, or, as he phrased it, to think of only one thing at a time.

The first of these occasions was on the day after my arrival. The Hôtel des Etrangers, at which I was staying, is at one angle of a triangular space to which the shore of the bay forms a rude hypothenuse. In the afternoon I was walking across this place to the hotel, unaware that anyone was near me, when my train of thought was broken by a sudden relief from a slight drag on my shoulder, caused by an opera-glass in my coat-pocket. I turned round and a young fellow, some two or three and twenty I should think, rushed away and dropped the opera-glass: probably thinking that I should pick it up and be content with having regained it. He was mistaken, however. I gave chase. Either he must have been a bad runner, or I must have still retained a good deal of that fleetness which distinguished me as a boy. Perceiving that his course would presently bring him to the Chiaja, where there were many persons about, he apparently lost his head, and I came up and seized him by the collar. He went on his knees, kissed my hand, and begged to be let off; and some working-class women who quickly came up interceded for him. But I disregarded what I suppose were entreaties; and when, the moment after, two young Leghornese gentlemen, who had witnessed the pursuit, appeared on the scene, and volunteered to accompany me to give evidence, we moved away into the city: my captive submitting unresistingly. Meeting after a time one of the police, I delivered him over, and, the crowd which accompanied us having dispersed, we went with the policeman and his charge to the station. There the man was recognized as an audacious thief who had been known to pick the pockets of the police! Speaking, as I did, no Italian, and but bad French, the taking down of my statement was a long business. When at length the deposition had been corrected and signed by me, I was both astonished and amused at being asked what punishment I should like inflicted. The reply of course was that I was concerned only to deliver over the culprit into their hands: leaving them to decide on the punishment. And thus the matter ended.

Next day, when I heard how frequently people were stabbed on the Chiaja, I became conscious of the risk I had been running. Most likely, had the young fellow had a knife about him, I should have suffered, perhaps fatally, for my imprudence. Had I not been so exclusively possessed by the thought of bringing him to justice, I should have been content with regaining my opera-glass.

The other incident to which I have referred as illustrating the trait named, or rather, perhaps, in this case the trait of rashness, which I begin to think is somewhat characteristic of me, occurred a few days later, when exploring the area of the eruption on Vesuvius.

For several days during which I was recruiting, I had been content to witness the doings of the mountain as visible from Naples; observing bursts of lava-spray, dark by day and bright by night, and collecting from my window-sill some of the smaller particles of this spray, about the size of coarse gunpowder.* During these days,

---

* I use the phrase lava-spray advisedly. It is clear that in the lower part of the vast volume of molten matter filling the crater of a volcano, there is contained a large amount of matter which, at ordinary temperatures and pressures, would be gaseous: probably carbonic acid and water, which, notwithstanding the high temperature, are, by the immense superincumbent weight, kept either in the liquid state or at the "critical point." As the lower portions of the column are thrust upwards, and the pressure these matters are subject to diminishes, they assume the gaseous state: forming small bubbles distributed through the molten mass. At each stage of the ascent these small bubbles ex-

conversation round the table-d'hôte had enlightened me respecting the impositions practised on all who ascended. I learnt that at the place where the road up to the Observatory diverges from the high road running round the base of the mountain—Resina I think it was—there stood guides and ponies, and that it was imperative to take one of each and pay a prescribed high price. I am intolerant of coercion in such matters, and am always prompted to defeat its aims, if possible. A clergyman, some ten years my senior, who had been a fellow-passenger from Marseilles, had the like feeling; and we consulted how to give effect to it. On examining the map, we found that by diverging to the left from the high road some mile or two short of Resina, we might cut into the road which leads up to the Observatory. Taking a vehicle as far as the bye-way selected, we pursued this for some distance until, to our dismay, it trended off towards the East. But a small gift to some people in a vineyard, purchased the permission to cross it, as well as directions how to proceed, and we presently found ourselves where we intended. Free from the noises of the usual cavalcades, we pursued our ascent; now pausing to contemplate the Bay of Naples below us, and now gathering flowers not seen before. Our arrival at the place where a branch lava-stream had, I suppose some weeks before, obstructed the path, caused, among the guides and others

pand and aggregate: by and bye making large ones, which increase in ascending power as in size. At length, on approaching the top of the molten column, there have resulted vast ones of many feet in diameter—chambers filled with gases which, though no longer of such high tension, are still of a tension like that of the gunpowder-gases in a cannon. And then at some point, perhaps 20 or 30 feet below the top of the molten column, each gigantic bubble as it bursts propels the superincumbent molten lava in portions of all sizes high into the air.

assembled there, much astonishment. How we came unattended was a mystery to them.

Our purpose was, of course, to reach the place at which the lava-stream emerged from the base of the cone, about half a mile off: the intervening space being covered with cooling portions of the stream, which had now taken this course and now that. The guides around proffered their services; but we declined them, and set out over the black rugged tract to be traversed. After some fifty or hundred yards, finding proof that the hardened lava was hotter than he anticipated, my companion turned back. I saw no danger, however, and as the air, though disagreeably warm, was not sulphurous, I went on alone; thinking it would be time to pause when some risk was before me. Half walking, half climbing, I slowly advanced; now passing easily along a tolerably solid and smooth surface, now with difficulty surmounting gnarled masses of lava contorted while moving and semi-solid, now scrambling over heaps of scoria, and now having to cross certain long strange-looking trenches, the sides of which consisted of loose fragments of vesicular lava torn into pieces, looking like a mineral "pulled-beard." Meanwhile Vesuvius was thundering above me, sending high into the air at each explosion a cloud of fragments of all sizes; some of them falling back into the crater, while most fell on the sides of the cone—too far from me, however, to be a source of danger. Presently, as I diminished my distance from the source of the lava-stream, and the blurring effect of the hot and wavy air did not so much obscure distant objects, I discerned a solitary figure near the place towards which I was moving; and after a time he discerned me. As I approached he left his stand, at which, as I found, he had a supply of refreshments, and over the last thirty or forty yards showed me the way. While doing this he drew me aside and pointed out a place where, through a hole broken in the black smooth surface of a seemingly cold lava-stream, I looked down into a red-hot tunnel of some six or eight feet in diameter. Several times in the course of my scrambling walk the sound of my footsteps had suggested hollowness below; and now the cause was manifest. I had passed over some of these tunnels. Further, it was manifest that the trenches I had crossed had resulted from the subsidence of the scoria overlying some of them. Thirty or forty paces more now brought me to the object of my dangerous expedition. It was not, after all, particularly imposing. The stream of molten matter, issuing from a low cavern-mouth at the base of the cone, was, I should think, not more than ten feet wide, and moved at from one to two miles per hour: its surface being so covered with chilled fragments of lava, as in great measure to prevent the emission of light. The heat, however, was great—so great that approach was difficult. I wished to burn the end of my alpenstock in the lava-stream; but, finding that my eyes strongly resented the endeavour to go near enough, I got the man to burn it. This he did by crawling and crouching behind blocks of cooled lava till he was within reach.

And now there came an extremely absurd act. After paying the man for his trouble, and after duly contemplating the sights around, from time to time looking upwards to watch another burst from the cone, I commenced my return. The man proposed to guide me along the usual route, which traversed the chaotic tract I have described, higher up the valley. I declined his guidance, however, and went back by the way I came. That I should have done so is a matter of astonishment to me. Though I had previously passed safely over treacherous places, it by no means followed that on retracing my steps one of these hidden tunnels, crossed at a somewhat different point, would not give way. Had one done so, then, though no longer red-hot internally, it would, by its retained heat, have caused death after terrible torture. How to account for the judicial blindness thus displayed, I do not know; unless by regarding it as an extreme instance of the tendency which I perceive in myself to be enslaved by a plan once formed—a tendency, in this case co-operating with that above illustrated, to become for a time possessed by one thought to the exclusion of others.

My clerical friend had waited for me. We descended unharmed, and returned as the dusk came on: looking over our shoulders occasionally to watch the bursts of lava-spray, which, as the day-light decreased, became gradually more luminous.

To the things of interest in and around Naples I did but scant justice. Of course I saw the Museum, and I ascended to a monastery standing high up behind the city—I forget for what, unless it was for the view. After that came an excursion to Pompeii.

Nothing which I saw in Italy impressed me so much as this dead town. I take but little interest in what are called histories, but am interested only in Sociology, which stands related to these so-called histories much as a vast building stands related to the heaps of stones and bricks around it. Here, however, the life of two thousand years ago was so vividly expressed in the objects on all sides, and in the marks of their daily use visible on them, that they aroused sentiments such as no written record had ever done. The steps of the public buildings worn away by the passage of countless feet; the tracks of wheels deeply cut into the flag-stones with which the streets were paved; the shops with their fronts open from side to side like those still extant at Naples; and the household utensils of all kinds found everywhere; made one easily see in imagination the activities once carried on. While here and there traces of prevalent usages suggested the characters of those who once thronged the streets.

One of the things which interested me was the structure of the Roman house; and this for reasons deeper than the architectural and æsthetic. Its relations to primitive types of habitations and to modern types, serving to link the two, make it a good example of super-organic evolution. From the outset of social life, defence against enemies has been a predominant thought—may we not say *the* predominant thought? Hence when, passing over earlier stages, we come to the stage in which there is a clustering of habitations, or of separate huts forming one habitation, the general method is to arrange them round a small area, presenting their backs to the outer world while their doors open upon the inner space, which has but a single entrance. In a South African kraal the chambers of a chief's wives, the store-houses, and so forth, are thus arranged; as are also the vehicles of a traveller or a migrating Boer. A more complex form of this arrangement was hit upon by the Pueblos of North Mexico, who thus shut out invading tribes less civilized than themselves. The prevalent house throughout the East down to our own day, similarly consults the safety of its inmates by having a blank, or almost blank, outer wall, and a court into which its component rooms open. And a like construction survived with modifications in the Pompeian house, after safety against enemies had ceased to be so imperative a consideration. Throughout times subsequent to the burial of Pompeii, this type persisted, with modifications dictated by the requirements. The feudal castle had its parts thus related. So, too, as we may see in both Italy and France, had the town-hotel of the great noble. The Inn of the middle ages displayed a like arrangement. The bed-rooms opened upon balconies running round the courtyard; and this arrangement survived until recently not only in the Tabard, of poetic fame, but at the Black Bull in Holborn, where, when a boy of fourteen, I once slept in one of such bedrooms. Large town-houses in old Paris, and still more in Italian cities, show us the transition from this type, in which the rooms of the same dwelling open into a central court, to a type in which these rooms have developed into separate dwellings—houses round the court built with their front doors opening into it. And we may readily see how the court as thus composed, is transformed into the narrow passage opening out of a main street, which now bears that name. One of these internal squares with its independent houses, needs but to have its sides brought close together at the same time that it is elongated, to produce one of the modern courts, so-called, such as Dr. Johnson's Court and others opening out of Fleet Street. Evidently there is an interesting chapter of social evolution to be written about these progressive modifications.

Shortly after seeing Pompeii I left Naples. I did not visit Sorrento or Amalfi, nor did I go over to Capri; and, indeed, left unseen many objects and places of interest in the neighbourhood. But the "Eternal City" was in prospect and tempted me away.

A tedious railway-journey took me to Rome. Here the aspect of things, and chiefly of the City itself, impressed me very differently. Especially charming was the colouring, which seemed everywhere harmonious: each turn round a street-corner disclosing a combination of tints such as an artist might have devised. Father Secchi, an astronomer then of some note, to whom I had a letter of introduction, and through whose telescope I saw some star-spectra, ascribed this peculiarity in Rome to the brightness of the light; but as no such peculiarity struck me in Naples, and as I did not see how more light could give harmony to colours which were not otherwise harmonious, I could not accept the interpretation.

Something like a fortnight was spent in Rome with much interest; though probably not with so great an interest as that felt by most. For in me there were very few of the historical associations. What Roman history I had read in my boyhood had left but faint traces in my memory. Even had it left clear images I doubt whether my appreciation of the things seen would have been much enhanced. To me the attractiveness of ancient buildings is almost exclusively that resulting from the general impression of age which they yield, and from the picturesqueness of decay. When I go to see a ruined abbey or the remains of a castle, I do not care to learn when it was built, who lived or died there, or what catastrophes it witnessed. I never yet went to a battle-field, although often near to one: not having the slightest curiosity to see a place where many men were killed and a victory achieved. The gossip of a guide is to me a nuisance; so that, if need were, I would rather pay him for his silence than for his talk: much disliking, as I do, to be disturbed while experiencing the sentiments excited in me by the forms and colours of time-worn walls and arches. It is always the poetry rather than the history of a place that appeals to me. Such being the case, I, of course, looked with uninterested eyes on many things in Italy which are extremely interesting to those familiar with the incidents they are connected with.

I will not weary either the travelled or untravelled reader by detailing my seeings and doings while in Rome. One thing only am I prompted to do—to seize the occasion for venting my heresies concerning the old masters: probably to the satisfaction of a few and the anger of many. I have long wished to do this, and cannot now let pass so convenient an opportunity.

In Kugler's *Hand Book of Painting* I read, in the account of Raphael's death:—" Men regarded his works with religious veneration, as if God had revealed himself through Raphael as in former days through the prophets." A feeling of this kind relative to Raphael, widely diffused I suppose, has co-operated with another feeling, also widely diffused, relative to the old masters at large. Just as the paper and print forming a Bible acquire, in most minds, such sacredness that it is an offence to use the volume for any trivial purpose, such as stopping out a draught; so a picture representing some Scriptural incident is, in most minds, placed above fault-finding by its subject. Average people cannot dissociate the execution from the thing represented; and condemnation of the one implies in their thought disrespect for the other. By these two feelings, criticism of ancient works of art has been profoundly vitiated. The judicial faculty has been mesmerised by the confused halo of piety which surrounds them.

Hence when, in Kugler, I find it remarked concerning Raphael's " Transfiguration " that " it becomes us to offer any approach to criticism with all humility "—when I see the professed critic thus prostrating himself before a reputation; my scepticism respecting the worth of the current applause of the old masters is confirmed. And when those who have " taken exception " to " the twofold action contained in this picture " are called by Kugler " shallow critics," I have not the slightest hesitation in classing myself with them; nor have I the slightest hesitation in rejecting the excuse that this fatal fault " is explained historically " by the circumstances of the depicted incident. As though a fundamental vice in a work of art can be got rid of by learning that it is involved in the scene represented! As though one's eyes, gravitated now to one, now to the other, of the conflicting centres of interest, can be prevented from doing so by any such explanation!

Detailed criticisms cannot be made intelligible when the painting criticised is not before us; otherwise many might be passed on " the Transfiguration." For the same reason it is difficult to deal in any but a general way with Michael Angelo's frescoes in the Sistine Chapel. Were they of recent date, we might marvel that the conception of the Creator is made so little to transcend the conception of the created as in the figures of God and Adam; and might say that the emergence of Eve out of Adam's side is effected by a being more like a magician than a Deity. But when we find the contemporary Protestant Luther saying in his Table Talk that God " could be rich soon and easily if he would be more provident, and would deny us the use of his creatures," and expressing his belief that " it costeth God yearly more to maintain only the sparrows than the yearly revenue of the French King amounteth unto "—when we find ideas so grossly anthropomorphic in a reformer of the faith, we cannot expect from Michael Angelo, holding the faith in its unreformed state, ideas that are other than grossly anthropomorphic. Passing over criticisms of this class, therefore, and admitting that there are many figures and groups finely drawn (though they exhibit too much his tendency to express mental superiority by supernatural bigness of muscles) let me say something concerning the decorations at large. Here the fault in art is of the same kind as that which is common in the reception-rooms of English houses, where the aim is to achieve two ends that are mutually exclusive—to make a fine whole and to include a crowd of fine parts. Continually one sees saloons so filled with paintings or engravings, statuettes, vases, objects of vertu etc., that they have become little else than picture galleries or cabinets of curiosities; and the general impression is lost in the impressions produced by the multitudinous pretty things. But if a room is to be made itself a work of art, as it should be, then the paintings, statuettes and minor ornaments, must be relatively few in number, must be so distributed that they fall into their places as component parts, and must none of them be obtrusive enough to distract attention from the *ensemble*. The like is true of every interior, no matter what its size or purpose, and, among others, of such an interior as the Sistine Chapel. If this be considered as a receptacle for works of art, then it is faulty because it displays them, or at any rate the greater part of them, in the worst possible ways. If it is considered as in itself a work of art, then it is bad because the effects of its decorative parts conflict too much with the effect of the whole. Its fault as a whole is like the fault of one of its chief components—the fresco of the Last Judgment; over which the eye wanders unable to combine its elements.

Were there anything like discrimination in the praises of pictures by the old masters—were they applauded only for certain merits at the same time that their demerits were recognized, I should have no objection to make. Or were each of them more or less approved as being good relatively to the mental culture of its age, which was characterized by crude ideas and sentiments and undisciplined perceptions, I should agree that many of them deserve praise. But the applause given is *absolute* instead of *relative;* and the grossest absurdities in them are habitually passed over without remark. Take, for example, Guido's much admired fresco, "Phœbus and Aurora." That it has beauty as a composition is undeniable. That the figures of the Hours are gracefully drawn and combined is beyond question. Some of its unobtrusive faults may fitly be forgiven. That the movements of the Hours are such as could not enable them to keep pace with the chariot, and that, being attached to figures which are exposed to "the wind of their own speed," some of the draperies could not assume such forms as are given, are defects which may be passed over; since, when the subject is supernatural, there are traits, such as running on clouds, which are not to be tested by congruity with observable facts. But as utter divergence from the natural in the drawing of the figures, etc. would not have been excused by the supernaturalness of the subject; so, neither should utter divergence from the natural in respect of light and shade be thus excused. In the first place, the country over which the chariot is advancing, instead of being shown as dimly lighted by it, is shown as already in broad daylight—a daylight utterly unaccountable. Far more remarkable than this, however, is the next anomaly. The entire group,—the chariot and horses, the hours and their draperies, and even Phœbus himself,—are represented as illuminated from without: are made visible by some unknown source of light—some other sun! Stranger still is the next thing to be noted. The only source of light indicated in the composition—the torch carried by the flying boy—radiates no light whatever. Not even the face of its bearer, immediately behind, is illumined by it! Nay, this is not all. The crowning absurdity is that the non-luminous flames of this torch are themselves illuminated from elsewhere! The lights and shades by which the forms of the flames are shown, are apparently due to that unknown luminary which lights up the group as a whole, as well as the landscape! Thus we have absurdity piled upon absurdity. And further, we have them in place of the splendid effects which might have been produced had Nature not been gratuitously contradicted. If Phœbus himself had been represented as the faintly-outlined source whence radiated the light upon the horses, the hours, the draperies, the clouds, and the dimly-visible Earth, what a magnificent combination of lights and shades might have been produced: not taking away from, but emphasizing, the beauty of the forms!

"You must not criticize the old masters in this way," I hear said by some. "You must consider the ideas and sentiments expressed by their works, and the skilful composition shown in them, and must overlook these technical defects." Space permitting, I might here ask in how many cases the merits thus assumed exist. But without entering any such demurrer, I will limit myself to the defects classed as technical; and I reply that these are *not* to be overlooked. When it is proved to me that, on reading a poem, I should think only of the fineness of the idea it embodies, and should disregard bad grammar, halting versification, jarring rhymes, cacophonous phrases, mixed metaphors, and so on; then I will admit that in contemplating a picture I may properly ignore the fact that the light is shown to come in various directions or from nowhere in particular. After I have been persuaded that while listening to a piece of music I ought to ignore the false notes, the errors in time, the harshness of *timbre*, as well as the lack of distinction between piano and forte passages, and that I should think only of the feeling which the composer intended to convey; then I will agree that it is proper to pay no regard to the fact that the shades in a picture have been all so unnaturally strengthened as to make them everywhere alike in degree of darkness, (a defect which cannot be explained away as being due to the alleged darkening of the shadows by time). Quite admitting, or rather distinctly affirming, as I do, that truthful representation of the physical aspects of things is an element in pictorial art of inferior rank to the truthful representation of emotion, action, and dramatic combination; I nevertheless contend that the first must be achieved before the second can be duly appreciated. Only when the vehicle is good can that which is to be conveyed be fully brought home to the spectator's consciousness. The first thing to be demanded of a picture is that it shall not shock the perceptions of natural appearances—the cultivated perceptions, I mean. If, as in many works of the old masters, a group of figures standing out of doors is represented with in-door lights and shades upon it; and if a spectator who has looked at Nature with such careless eyes that he is unconscious of this incongruity, does not have his attention distracted by it from the composition or the sentiment; this fact is nothing to the point. The standard of judgment must be that of the observant—not that of the unobservant. If we may fitly take the verdicts of those who cannot distinguish between truth and untruth in the physioscopy of a picture, we may fitly go further, and make our æsthetic ideas conform to those of the cottager who puts on his mantel-shelf a gaudily painted cast of a parrot, and sticks against his wall a coloured print of the Prodigal Son in blue-coat and yellow breeches.*

In rejoinder to all this, there will doubtless come from many the question—" How about the experts? how happens it that they, who are the most competent judges, applaud these same works of which you speak so disrespectfully?"

My first reply is that, were the truth known, the question would be less unhesitatingly put; for by no means all experts think what they are supposed to think. As

* I venture the new word just used, because there exists no word expressive of *all* those traits in a picture which concerns the physical appearances of the objects represented. Under "physioscopy" I propose to include the rendering of the phenomena of linear perspective, of aeriel perspective, of light and shade, and of colour in so far as it is determined not by artistic choice, but by natural conditions—*e.g.* that of water as affected by the sky, the clouds, and the bottom. The conception, the sentiment, the composition, the expression, may some or all of them be good in a picture of which the physioscopy, in some or all of its elements, is bad ; and *vice versa*. The characteristics included in the one group are entirely separate from those included in the other; and there needs a word by which the distinction may be conveyed without circumlocution.

there is a religious orthodoxy so is there an æsthetic orthodoxy; and dissent from the last, like dissent from the first, brings on the dissenter the reprobation of the majority, which usually includes all who are in power. Hence it results that many artists—especially when young and afraid of offending the authorities—refrain from saying that which they secretly believe respecting traditional reputations. As I can testify, there are those among them who do not join in the chorus of applause commonly given to the painters of past times, but who know that their æsthetic heterodoxies, if uttered, would make enemies. When, however, they have reason to think that what they say will not bring on them the penalties of heresy, they express opinions quite unlike those they are assumed to hold.

My second reply is that, so long as the professed approval of artists is unaccompanied by adoption of the practices of those approved, it goes for little. Imitation is said to be the sincerest form of flattery—or rather, it should be, not of flattery, but of admiration; and there are many traits of the old masters perfectly easy to imitate, which artists woud imitate if they really admired them. Let us again choose illustrations from light and shade. In the great majority of cases, ancient painters represented shadows by different gradations of black: making a tacit assumption like that made by every boy when he begins to draw. But modern painters do not follow this lead. Though the artist of our day may not have formed for himself the generalization that a place into which the direct light cannot fall, being one into which the indirect and usually diffused, light falls, must have the average colour of this diffused light (often qualified by the special lights reflected from particular objects near at hand), and that therefore a shadow may be of any colour according to circumstances; yet his empirical knowledge of this truth makes him studiously avoid the error which his predecessor commonly fell into. Take another case. An assumption quite naturally made at the outset, is that surfaces which retreat from the light must in retreating become more deeply shaded; and, in conformity with this assumption, we usually see in old paintings that while the outer parts of shadows are comparatively faint, the parts remote from their edges are made very dark—a contrast which must have existed originally, and cannot have resulted from age. But now-a-days only a tiro habitually does this. The instructed man knows that the interior part of a shadow, often no darker than its exterior part, is, under some conditions, even less dark than the part near its edge; and he rarely finds the conditions such as call upon him to represent the interior part of the shadow by an opaque black. Once more there is the kindred mistake, usual in old paintings, that curved surfaces, as of limbs, where they are shown as turning away from the general light, are habitually not shown as having the limiting parts of their retreating surfaces lighted up by radiations from objects behind; as they in most cases are. But in modern paintings these reflected lights are put in; and a true appearance of roundness is given.

Thus, as I say, in respect of some most conspicuous traits, easily imitated, the artist of our time carefully avoids doing as the ancient artist did; and such being the case, his eulogies, if he utters them, do not go for much. When we have to choose between the evidence derived from words and the evidence derived from deeds, we may fitly prefer the evidence derived from deeds.*

Concerning what I did and saw during the rest of my tour, I need say but little. Those who have not seen Italy have read about it. The subject has been so well worn by generations of travellers that it is threadbare.

My journey from Rome to Florence, like my journey from Naples to Rome, of course gave me impressions of Italian scenery. There was much to be admired, joined to something with which to be disappointed. While the colouring of the sky and clouds and the hills on the horizon was more brilliant than any I had before seen, the surfaces near at hand were generally unattractive: being nearly always so ill covered with vegetation that the

* The opinion of several experts to whom I have submitted in proof the foregoing expressions of dissent from current opinion, show that I am not without the sympathy of some who must be regarded as competent judges. An R. A. writes:—"Art amateurs often seem to me quite 'daft' in their worship of old art, simply because it *is* old, without any reference to its merit either of conception or execution. But this worship is so deeply rooted, and so much esteemed 'the right thing' that any reformation in our own time is almost hopeless. Is it not *The Autocrat of the Breakfast table* who says that 'the mind of a bigoted person is like the pupil of the eye, the more light you throw into it, the more it contracts.'" An A.R.A., in whose opinion the works of the old masters should be judged in connexion with the sentiments, ideas, and perceptions, of their respective times, and not from our point of view, proceeds thus:—"Now I have said what I had to say in vindication of the old masters, but I believe that what you have said against them is calculated to do unmixed good, for no subject exists that has hitherto been set forth to the world by persons so ignorant, so affected, or so impotent as the scribbling critics of the last generation." Another A.R.A., who says of certain ancient artists that "with all their faults we can see the hand of genius," also says of what I have written above. that he hopes it "will help to stop some of the nonsense promulgated by the Kuglers and others. As for your criticisms on fact I think all artists will agree."

[While the foregoing note was standing in type there appeared in the

soil was everywhere visible between the leaves of the plants and the blades of grass. I felt inclined to say of Italy, that it is a land of beautiful distances and ugly foregrounds.

Florence I saw very incompletely: staying there, as I did, only a week. From the collections of paintings I derived more pleasure than from those in Rome, which consists so largely of mere rubbish. I observed, however, when going through those of the Pitti Palace and the Uffizj, that some of the works I chiefly admired were by painters whose names were unfamiliar to me: another manifestation, I suppose, of my habitual nonconformity. But, as I say, I gave inadequate attention to the attractions of the place and its neighbourhood—did not even visit Fiesole. I was companionless and impatient. Going alone from church to gallery and from gallery to church, had become wearisome; and, disappointed as I was in the hoped-for benefits to health, I was anxious to get home.

Leaving Florence about the end of the first week in April, while it was still very cold, and spending half a day at Pisa, I went by night steamer from Spezzia to

Magazine of Art for July, 1888, a paper by Sir John Millais called "Thoughts on Our Art of to-day," containing the following significant utterances:—" To say that the old alone is good betrays great lack of judgment and is an ingratitude to the living. Ability and talent are more abundant than ever; but in forming an opinion of them the critic falls into two great errors—the first, in forgetting that the form and demands of Art have changed and expanded with the advance of time; and the second, in failing—unconsciously, of course—to judge of the great works of the past, with which he compares those of the present, in a fair and proper manner. He makes no allowances for the charm of mutilation or the fascination of decay. . . . Time and varnish are two of the greatest of old masters, and their merits and virtues are too often attributed by critics—I do not of course allude to the professional art-critics—to the painters of the pictures they have toned and mellowed."]

Genoa. Two days were agreeably spent there; for the city, like other Italian cities, has an individuality which gives it interest. Thence I proceeded to Turin, which was not attractive enough to detain me more than a day. A railway journey to the Mont Cenis, and a journey by night over the Pass, partly by diligence and partly by sledge (for the tunnel was not yet made), brought me in an exhausted state to Chambery, where I remained a day and a half to recruit. Ending the next day at Medoc and the day after that at Paris, I reached home without further stoppage; having been absent about six weeks.

What I thought and felt about this expedition and its results, may best be told by quoting a letter on the subject written to my American friend on May 3. It ran as follows:—

"I cannot say that my hopes that a journey through Italy would put me into working order were realized. I came back no better than I went: in fact in some respects not so well. I have, however, been improving very considerably during the last week; especially in sleeping, which is my great difficulty. Indeed I now feel pretty sanguine that with tolerable care I shall shortly get into my usual state.

Thanks for your reminder about my visit to America. I fear, however, there is no prospect of my soon responding to your wish. My recent experience has given me very conclusive proof that with my irritable nervous system, I am quite unfit for travelling. I was greatly exhausted by my journey to Marseilles, although I stopped a night at Paris and a night at Lyons. My voyage to Naples did me further damage. Sleep was quite out of the question. What little I got during these nights, I owed to morphia. And during the last three weeks of my stay abroad, a leading subject of thought with me was, how I should get home again with the least amount of injury—which was the shortest route, and how it might best be broken into short stages. After this experience you will see that it is out of the question for me to commit myself to a ten or twelve days voyage, or to such railway journeys as travelling through the U.S. would involve. If I should ever again get into a normal state, which does not seem very probable, I may decide differently; but while I remain as I am I must give up the idea of extensive journeys.

A further reason for thus deciding is that, quite apart from fatigue, I find the penalties of travelling greater than the pleasures. In early days I had a considerable appetite for sight-seeing; but now-a-days my appetite is soon satiated—especially as, not looking at things through the spectacles of authority, I often find but little to admire where the world admires, or professes to admire, a great deal. The chief pleasure I get in travelling I get from fine scenery; and of this there is plenty to be had without leaving Great Britain."

It should be added, however, that in this case, as in many cases, a benefit not appreciable during the journey itself began to be appreciable after it was over. One may figuratively express the results of such experiences by saying that after being hardly used for a time, the system is put upon its good behaviour and goes on better.

CHAPTER XLIII.

DEVELOPING THE *PSYCHOLOGY*.

1867—70. ÆT. 47—50.

My daily efforts for some four months before the Italian tour just narrated, had been expended on the "Data of Psychology"—the first division of the treatise in its developed form. With this I struggled to make some progress notwithstanding my nervous relapse; and to that end, as already described, took Mr. Duncan with me to the racquet court, and alternated between dictation and games.

Some of my friends have expressed surprise that I should be able to carry on my work by dictation; and others have expressed surprise that I should be able to interrupt a course of thought, for the purpose of taking exercise, and then resume it. "I do not think properly until I take pen in hand," said one of them; "and I am at a loss to understand how you can reel off your ideas to an amanuensis." Another described himself as unable to bear interruption when once he got his thoughts bent to a subject.

The solution is much simpler than at first appears. In an early chapter of this volume I described the way in which my conceptions on this or that subject developed themselves. I said that my method was not that of sitting down to a problem, and puzzling over it till I came to some conclusion, but was that of letting my ideas about it slowly take shape. This process usually went on for years. As the time approached when the conception had to be set forth, it was of course more frequently dwelt upon. The divisions of it gradually made themselves clear; and presently a scheme of chapters was arranged. Then each chapter, as I came near to it, fell more or less completely into sections; and eventually, before writing a section, the ideas to be set down in it assumed tolerable distinctness. Thus the essential part of the work—the thinking—was done before-hand; and the process of writing or dictating became simply that of putting into words the thoughts already elaborated. It was therefore easy to take up the thread when broken, and to any idea that had been set down, join the idea already internally arranged to follow it. I felt no such difficulty as is doubtless felt by those who evolve their ideas while writing; and who, if interrupted, lose their hold on thoughts which are just rising into consciousness.

And here, while comparing these two modes of composition, I see that the contrast explains some traits of style respectively accompanying them. Setting forth ideas already reached is accompanied by but little emotion; whereas evolving ideas from moment to moment, while writing, inevitably causes exaltation of feeling. In the one case there is calmness; in the other there is fervour. But calmness is not favourable to strong and vivid forms of expression; whereas fervour prompts picturesque phrases, and vigorous metaphors. The telling expressions used by my friend who says he does not think to purpose until he gets pen in hand, have often raised my envy. It is doubtless true that for purposes of philosophy, clearness rather than strength is the desideratum. But for writing of a not strictly philosophical or scientific kind, one may fitly desire to use those modes of embodying thoughts which result from emotion and are calculated to excite emotion.

Resuming the thread of my narrative, I have to add that when, after partially recovering from the effects of my Italian tour, I recommenced work, I reverted to the alternation of exercise and dictation—substituting rowing for racquets. The part of the Serpentine above the bridge is within 10 minutes walk of Queen's Gardens; and here, on fine mornings in May and June, and again in the Autumn, I passed two or three hours: the shrubbery overhanging the water on the west bank, affording convenient shelters under which to moor the boat while dictating.

My journey to the furthest point South I had hitherto reached, was followed, three months later, by a journey which carried me to the northernmost point of my various excursions. In July I went as far as Sutherlandshire in search of fishing, and stayed for a week at Inverann at the mouth of the Shin. But the long drought of that summer continued, and I came away disappointed.

On my way back I bethought me of Inveroran, a place between Tyndrum and Glencoe, where there was salmon fishing free to all staying at the hotel. Common sense had told me that free salmon fishing must be bad salmon fishing; but common sense had misled me. Common sense, which would reject as monstrously absurd the statement that a whale is more nearly akin to a man than to a shark, always proceeds upon the assumption that the insides of things are just what the outsides might lead you to expect; whereas, not uncommonly, realities are unlike appearances. So it proved at Inveroran; owing to circumstance which no longer exist. A letter to Lott, written thence on Aug. 13, must here be quoted—

"You were quite right in your opinion, given to G. Holme, about my standing for Derby. If they would pay my expenses and give me a salary into the bargain, I would not go into parliament. I could not do my present work and parliamentary work too; and my present work I hold to be by far the most important. Some day, if a constituency should ask me to become a candidate, I mean to give them (and the public) "a bit of my mind," as to the relative values of those who represent public opinion in the House of Commons, and those who mould public opinion by books.

How about our excursion? What do you say to a fortnight in North Yorkshire? It would be new to both of us, and they say there is very fine scenery there. We could meet there conveniently on my way south, and might diverge into the Lake district if we did not like it. . .

As you did not come up to be my guest in London at Xmas or Easter, I propose that you make amends by coming to be my guest in Yorkshire, or wherever else we go.

I have had some capital fishing since the wet weather set in—far better than I looked for."

Many years elapsed before there occurred an opportunity for carrying into effect the intention expressed in the first of the foregoing paragraphs. It did eventually occur, however, and I then fulfilled the intention. My apprehension was that general reprobation would fall on me in consequence; but, to my surprise, there came general approbation. I suspect that a chief cause for this was that the tone of the House of Commons was already undergoing that degradation which has since become so conspicuous.

The proposal made in the second paragraph was presently carried out. My friend and I met at Harrogate, and, taking rail to Ilkley, walked the first day thence to Bolton Abbey, where we lingered till the bats were flying about in the evening. Something more than a week was spent in our subsequent ramble: ascending the valley of the Wharfe to Kettlewell; from there over to Middleham; up Wensleydale to Hawes; down the valley of the Eden to Appleby; over the moors or fells to High Force on the Tees; down the course of that river to Darlington; and thence to York, where we parted for our respective homes.

I have not yet mentioned the fact that, for some years, the Leweses had been residing at The Priory, North Bank. The distance from Queen's Gardens is but a mile; and this proximity conduced to more frequent intercourse. There arose a standing engagement to go and lunch with them whenever I found it convenient. The motive for the arrangement was in part that we might have opportunities for conversations, enjoyed on both sides, which were impracticable during their Sunday-afternoon assemblies.

I am led to name here this established usage because my return from Scotland this year must have been the occasion for one of those witticisms which George Eliot sometimes uttered. I had, as commonly happened after an interval of absence, been giving an account of my doings; and, among other things, had laughingly described the dismay caused in two fishermen at Inveroran by the success of my heterodox flies. This led to an inquiry concerning the nature of my heterodoxy. I explained that I did not believe in the supposed critical powers of salmon and sea-trout, but held that if one of them, being hungry, saw something it took for a fly, it would rise; and that consequently my aim was to make the best average representation of an insect buzzing on the surface of the water. " Yes," she said, " you have such a passion for generalizing, you even fish with a generalization."

This reference to her good things reminds me of one which Lewes told me she had uttered at the expense of Dr. A——, a friend of theirs who was remarkable for his tendency to dissent from whatever opinion another uttered. After a conversation in which he had repeatedly displayed this tendency, she said to him " Dr. A—— how is it that you always take your colour from your company?" "*I* take my colour from my company?" he exclaimed—" What *do* you mean?" "Yes," she replied, " the opposite colour."

Our talk, if not very often enlivened by witticisms, always contained a mixture of the gay with the grave: good stories and a little *badinage* breaking our discussions, which were generally quite harmonious; for there were but few points on which we disagreed. Then after luncheon came a walk, usually in Regent's Park, in which I joined: another hour of interesting conversation being the accompaniment.

Though they were partial adherents of M. Comte my friends did not display much respect for the object which he would have us worship. Reverence for humanity in the abstract seemed, in them, to go along with irreverence for it in the concrete. Few of these occasions I have described, passed without comment from them on the unintelligence daily displayed by men—now in maintaining so absurd a *curriculum* of education (which they reprobated just as much as I did), now in the follies of legislation, which continually repeat, with but small differences, the follies of the past, now in the irrationalities of social habits.

I have myself often startled people by the paradox that mankind go right only when they have tried all possible ways of going wrong—intending it, of course, to be taken not quite literally. Of late, however, I have observed sundry cases in which, instead of going beyond the fact, it falls short of it—cases in which, having found the right, people deliberately desert it for the wrong. They do this even in simple household usages, where a small modicum of sense might have been expected to prevent them. A generation ago salt-cellars were made of convenient shapes—either ellipses or elongated parallelograms: the advantage being that the salt-spoon, placed lengthwise, remained in its place. But, for some time past, fashion has dictated circular salt-cellars, on the edges of which the salt-spoon will not remain without skilful balancing: it falls on the cloth. Table-implements afford another example. In my boyhood a jug was made of a form at once convenient and graceful. The body of the jug had a shape deviating but little from a sphere, and therefore had the advantage that however the jug was inclined the surface of the contained liquid had, for a considerable time, nearly the same area; so that, with increasing inclination, pouring out went on at a tolerably uniform rate. The spout, too, was sufficiently large; and of such shape that it would deliver either a small or a large quantity without waste. And then, within the limits of convenience, the outline of jug and handle admitted of numerous elegant combinations of curves. Now, however, the prevailing—indeed almost universal—form of jug in use, is a frustum of a cone, with a miniature spout. It combines all possible defects. When anything like full, it is impossible to pour out a small quantity without part of the liquid trickling down beneath the spout; and a larger quantity cannot be poured out without exceeding the limits of the spout and running over on each side of it. If the jug is half empty, the tilting must be continued for a long time before any liquid comes; and then, when it does come, it comes with a rush; because its surface has now become so large that a small inclination delivers a great deal. To all which add that the shape is as ugly a one as can well be hit upon. Still more extraordinary is the folly of a change made in another utensil of daily use. Till within these few years, an extinguisher had universally the form of a hollow cone. Nothing could be better. It would fit any candle; it went down upon it until it was arrested by the melted edge of the candle; and it then formed a chamber in which the smoke was shut up and the wick preserved from damage. Now, however, we meet with extinguishers made in the form of a hollow cylinder with a hemispherical end. When one is put on a candle (if it will go over it at all) it descends until the hemispherical end squashes the wick into the melted composition: the result being that when, next day, the extinguisher is taken off, the wick, imbedded in the solidified composition, cannot be lighted without difficulty. Here, then, are three of the commonest household appliances, good forms of which have been deliberately abandoned and bad forms adopted.

One reason why good things thus fail to hold their ground against bad ones, recently came to my knowledge. For twenty years I had used with great satisfaction a kind of inkstand which possesses every desirable trait. It is capacious, stable, checks evaporation, keeps out the dust, and allows the depth of the dip to be adjusted to a nicety. I recommended it to some friends, and tried to buy samples to send them. None of the stationers of whom I inquired knew anything about it. At length I went to the wholesale producer, Perry; and it was only because his people had some old stock remaining that I obtained it even there, for they had ceased to make it. I asked the manager why things which, when they came in, were recognized as eminently good, disappeared again—why the stationers did not keep them. " Oh! Sir," he replied, " when our travellers go round, the stationers, after a short time, will not take them. ' We had some of these last year,' they say: ' show us your novelties.' Always the cry for something fresh." If we go behind this, it is clear that the stationer wants the last new things, because his customers want them; and that they buy them without thinking whether they are better or worse than the old things. Thus articles in every way admirable are actually expelled from the market! And then the insane love of change shown in such cases, we find accompanied by an insane resistance to change in other cases! Where cogent reasons for giving up established usages are manifest to every one, people persist in them; and where there is every reason for adhering to what they have got, they are eager for something else!

But I am getting too discursive. Let me return to an account of my doings in the days which were now passing.

On preparing to do this I suddenly find that I am promising more than I can perform. Of incidents during the remaining part of this year and the early part of the next, my memory contains no traces; and on referring to letters I find scarcely anything to help me. One solitary fact of significance is named in a letter to Youmans dated 19 Sept.; and this is of more interest to me than to the reader—the fact, namely, that another of my books had been taken in hand by a French translator: making three that were simultaneously in progress. Nothing more worth mention occurs before the 15th of March 1869. Then comes a letter containing the following passage:—

"Certainly, the falling off in the American sales of my books last year is somewhat unexpected. The *Biology,* and the second edition of *First Principles,* cannot yet have returned to me the cost of the stereotype plates; so that thus far I am rather out of pocket by the American editions than a gainer by them. It seems odd, too, that with an increased number of volumes on sale, the return should be much less instead of much more. I suppose it must all be taken as proof that the public attention flags when, as you say, nothing has been done to excite it.

"It is, however, a consolatory fact for me that I have no longer any reason to complain that public appreciation here is so much less than it is in America. The relation between the two is now very decisively reversed. Last year my net profit from the sale of books (leaving out the subscriptions for the serial) was considerably more than double that which the account shows to have resulted from the American sales. So you must not in future make any comparisons between the American and English publics to the disadvantage of the latter."

I should have said, however, that the two sums compared did not measure the numbers of books sold; since my profit per copy from sales in England is double that yielded by sales in America. Bearing in mind, too, that the retail price per copy in America is somewhat lower, it would seem that the numbers sold in the two countries respectively did not differ much.

Doubtless the increased sales in England were largely due to the energetic action taken by my friends Mill, Huxley, Tyndall, Lubbock, and Busk, in 1866; and to the consequent attention drawn to my books—an attention which was doubtless increased when statements about the American testimonial were made public here. Let me add that from this time forth I had no adverse circumstances to contend with. The remainder of my life-voyage was through smooth waters.

No memories were raised by coming upon the following sentence in a letter written on 14 April 1869:—
"Though better, I am still not well, and am leaving town to-day for a short ramble in the country." But for a letter written on June 25, I should have failed to identify the occasion as one on which I went first to Oxford (whence, before twenty-four hours had passed, I fled to escape invitations); then walked to Blenheim, where I rambled about the park, and slept at Woodstock; and on subsequent days went through Evesham to Tewkesbury, and into the country beyond. The passage which recalled these incidents was the following:—

"The most striking fact, perhaps, is that which came to my knowledge when at Oxford lately. To my amazement I found that *First Principles* and the *Principles of Biology* are being used as text-books there, and questions for examination papers taken from them. Dr. Rolleston stopped a student and asked him, in my presence, whether he had entered on my books yet. He replied that he was just about to commence them."

This passage I quote not so much for its intrinsic interest as because it introduces the statement of an anomalous fact. University College, London, was founded for the purpose of giving an unsectarian education, free from the ecclesiastical influences which pervade Oxford and Cambridge; and, by implication, it was to be the home of a liberal theology: tinged even with rationalism, if the opinions of its leading spirits indicated anything. Hence there might have been expected a sympathetic reception to books of an advanced kind, embodying what may be called a naturalistic philosophy as distinguished from a super-naturalistic philosophy. But while, in the head-quarters of orthodoxy, my books were being used as text-books, they were not used at the place which, by contrast, might almost be called the head-quarters of heterodoxy. More than this. While at Oxford the authorities put them before the students, at University College they were not even included in the Library. Nay more than this even. Requests made by the students that one of them might be put in the Library received no attention. Two years after the foregoing extract was written, Dr. Bastian shewed me, in the book kept for the purpose, two requisitions for *First Principles;* one of them dated December 1869 and signed by ten students, and the other dated March 1870, also signed by ten students, and marked " third time ": all three, as it seems, having been ignored by the Council; for the book was not in the Library in September 1871.

How many things there are contrary to common sense! I have already named one in this chapter, and here is another.

A letter received during this absence from London recalls an incident which must be here mentioned—the formation of the Metaphysical Society. The letter was from Sir John Lubbock, asking whether I would become a member.

The Society was to have, he said, a somewhat remarkable character; for its members were to be men of the most diverse opinions, from Roman Catholics like Cardinal Manning at the one extreme, to agnostics like Huxley and Tyndall at the other extreme, and everything was to be an open question, even to the existence of a deity: original intentions which were, I believe, fairly well carried out. I declined to join for the reason that too much nervous expenditure would have resulted. Every attendance would have entailed a sleepless night; and I did not think that any benefit to be derived would have been worth purchase by this penalty: involving loss of my small working power next day. After the body was constituted I was again requested to join, and to attend the first meeting; but though Mr. Knowles, the secretary, through whom the request came, named, as a special reason for assenting, the fact that the first paper to be read was one by Mr. Richard Hutton, attacking my theory of the genesis of the moral sentiments, I persisted in my resolution.

Beyond those named above, various distinguished men joined the Society—Mr. Gladstone, Mr. Tennyson (who, with Mr. Knowles, I believe, had started the idea), the Rev. James Martineau, Sir J. F. Stephen, Dean Stanley &c. &c. At each meeting a paper by some member, which had been printed and circulated, was discussed. Several years subsequently, during an after-dinner conversation in which the proceedings were described as remarkably harmonious, a renewed suggestion was made by Mr. Knowles that I should join. After referring to the statement made that many of the members had so little thought in common that they slid by one another without grappling, I remarked that Mr. Knowles had better not press me, since most likely were I one of them I should insist on grappling, and that possibly the proceedings would cease to be so harmonious. A dozen years or so brought the Society to an end. Most of the topics of chief interest had been discussed, and no results produced, save perhaps a certain liberalization in the estimates formed by the members of one another's views. No further results being promised, and the excitement of novelty having ceased, the attendance flagged and the Society dissolved.

I now come upon an incident of which the interest is more than personal—an incident, indeed, of which the impersonal interest is great; since it concerns the correction of a grave error in recent History, and the rectification of international feeling. It may be most conveniently introduced by an extract from a letter three years earlier in date, which I have reserved for quotation here, as being relevant to the transaction which now took place. Writing to Youmans on March 2d 1866, I said:—
"I recently met Mr. [Moncure] Conway, whose papers in the *Fortnightly* have been doing good service here, and have impressed me in his favour much more than when I first saw him. I took the opportunity of suggesting to him to do what I have very much wanted to see done, towards correcting the impressions of Americans respecting the original feeling of the English when the war broke out, and which, as you have heard me say, was quite different from what is supposed in the United States. Mr. Conway's residence in England had, I found, enlightened him on the matter. He

was quite aware that the original feeling here was that which I have described to you; and that it was changed as I told you. He said that he had been thinking of publishing something in America, giving the result of his experience here, towards rectifying American impressions. But he agreed that instead of giving his own impressions, it would be best to take the course I named, namely to give, in the order of their dates, extracts from the leading English periodicals, showing what the feeling originally was and how it gradually changed, and what were the adverse influences that changed it. I hope he will persevere in the intention which he expressed, of issuing in America a pamphlet containing this evidence."

Either Mr. Conway did not carry out his expressed intention, or he did it with but little success; for the ill feeling in the United States not only continued, but became exacerbated. During the early part of 1869, the utterances of the American press against England were violent; and I feared that something more than a war of words might ensue. Knowing that the belief current in America was entirely untrue, I thought it very desirable that some attempt should be made to rectify it; and after talking the matter over with the Leweses, who encouraged me to take the step I contemplated, I drew up a letter for publication in one of the New York papers, giving the indisputable facts. With it I sent the following private letters to Youmans, dated May 22.

" The accompanying long letter, though addressed to you personally, is of course intended for publication. When you have read it, I think you will agree with me that the facts it contains should not any longer remain unknown to your countrymen.

I must leave you to communicate it to such of the New York daily papers as may be the fittest medium. I find the

Tribune referred to as the bitterest of them all against England; and I suppose that some difficulty might hence arise if you took it there. Or else, in other respects, the *Tribune* would seem the most desirable. I suppose simultaneous publication in more than one, would not be practicable.

I do not know what may be the result of the publication of this letter on my personal relations with the American public. But, if it should be injurious, I am content to bear the injury."

In due time there came a reply explaining that the publication had been delayed until he had laid before me the reasons for withdrawing my letter. Among other things he said:—

"I read your letter intended for publication with some surprise and with an unhesitating conviction that it would be unwise to print it. But, as you seemed to think the case both clear and urgent, I at once complied with your request and took it to the *Tribune*. You were quite in error in anticipating difficulty there; when I named to them its subject and author they ordered it to be set up at once. By a singular coincidence, both Fiske and Roberts happened to be in town, and I met them in the evening at the Century Club with Vaux, Holt, and Prompelly—all friends and co-workers. I handed the proof to Fiske, who looked over it and exclaimed 'What does this mean? Surely Mr. Spencer isn't going to publish this!' All the others read it and they were all of the same mind. As for the subject of the letter, they were indifferent and agreed, *first,* that if you had been here at any time when the question was agitating the American mind and had been disposed to enter into the subject, you would not have taken it up in that way; and *second,* if you were here now, you would not dream of touching it at all, as it is a dead subject with us. But their decided expressions of the unwisdom of the publication had reference to your position and influence, which would be damaged by it seriously; and, granting that you had a perfect right to sacrifice them if you thought it best, they were of opinion that you ought not to embarrass your friends in the way that the publication would embarrass them."

Eventually, and with a good deal of reluctance, I assented to the withdrawal; as witness the following extract from a letter dated June 25.

" Taking into consideration all that you tell me, I conclude that it will be best not to publish the letter. It is somewhat vexing to have bestowed so much trouble to no purpose; and I cannot but regret that the facts which the letter contains should continue unknown to the American public. As, however, the occasion which prompted me to write the letter has passed by, and as, indeed, the expressions of your press seem to have misled us here respecting the state of American opinion, I yield to the representations you make. Of course I have no wish to damage my position with the American public, and I should be very sorry to embarrass my American friends. If you have no use for the proof of the letter, you may as well send it to me, as I should like to preserve it."

Though not published at that time, the letter was published some years after, when more pacific sentiments prevailed. Even then, however, the statements contained in it, conclusive though they were, and impossible as it was to invalidate them, were treated with but small respect. How constantly one is misled by the assumption that incontestable proofs will change men's opinions! Where there exists strong prepossessions, no amount of evidence produces any effect.

This letter, as eventually published in the *New York Tribune*, I reproduce in Appendix E; feeling that unless it obtains somewhere a permanent place, the history of our relations with America will be vitiated by a permanent error of a serious kind.

Shortly before the close of the London season, I wrote to John Mill on some matter which I forget, and, referring to my approaching departure for Scotland, suggested, more in jest than in earnest, that if he would join me, I would initiate him in salmon-fishing. The following passage from his reply refers to this offer.

"My murderous propensities are confined to the vegetable world. I take as great a delight in the pursuit of plants as you do in that of salmon, and find it an excellent incentive to exercise. Indeed I attribute the good health I am fortunate enough to have, very much to my great love for exercise, and for what I think the most healthy form of it, walking."

Having in boyhood had little or no experience of the ordinary boyish sports, Mill had a somewhat erroneous conception of them. Hence the inappropriate use of the word "murderous"; as though the gratification were exclusively in killing. But I quite agree in the implied objection he makes to pursuits that inflict pain. Though so fond of fishing as a boy, my dislike to witnessing the struggles of dying fish, becoming stronger as I grew older, had the result that between 21 and 35 I never fished at all. It was only because, on being prompted to try the experiment at the latter age, I found fishing so admirable a sedative, serving so completely to prevent thinking that I took to it again, and afterwards deliberately pursued it with a view to health. Nothing else served so well to rest my brain and fit it for resumption of work.

Of my doings in Scotland during the Autumn, the following letter to Lott, dated Oban, Aug. 11th, says nearly as much as is needful:—

"If you had been at liberty a week or a fortnight ago it would have been all right, but as it happens it is all wrong—along with everything else since I left town.

I have been in Scotland a month last Saturday—chiefly at Inveroran, waiting for fishing which the dry weather would not let me have. I got only two salmon. Last Friday I left in disgust before I had intended; for I meant to stay there till I joined the Smiths, who had left me to fix my own time. They were to leave town at the beginning of this month; and I wrote from Inveroran saying I would be with them on the 11th (to-day). But since my arrival here I learn that they have not reached Ardtornish yet! So here I have to kick my heels again. However they will probably arrive to-day, and I may possibly join them before the end of the week.

After I leave them, sometime early in September, I have promised to join the Busks, who have taken a house at Taynuilt; so you see I am fixed. I am very sorry your holiday was not earlier."

My fishing this year derived a special interest from the trial of a new fishing rod, or rather, a fishing rod with a new kind of joint. Of course it was not in my nature to rest content with that which I found in use, if it had any manifest defects; and both the forms of joint in use were seriously defective: the simple splice-joint entailed much trouble, and the socket-joint was heavy, and had sundry inconveniences. The form of joint which I devised in place of them proved satisfactory; and having borne the tests to which it was submitted, I eventually published an account of it in the *Field* some time in January 1871. The letter is reproduced in Appendix F.

Aird's Bay House, taken by the Busks for the autumn, is on the shore of Loch Etive about a mile from Taynuilt and, leaving Ardtornish towards the middle of September, I there joined them.

Those who have seen Loch Etive only from the railway, or from the high road which skirts it, know little of its beauties. These lie in the part beyond Ben Cruachan, and with the exception of Loch Hourn, Scotland has nothing at once so grand and beautiful. Boating excursions on this secluded portion, with rambles and picnics on its shores, filled a pleasant ten days. An island beyond the ferry was at that time frequented by seals, which it was interesting to watch through an opera glass. Then on the sheltered and smooth water there were sometimes reflections more splendid than I ever saw elsewhere—whole sides of Ben Cruachan and his neighbours being vividly mirrored. An excursion made to Loch Awe is linked to my other memories by a natural-history observation made there. The waters were swarming with the *Volvox globator*, which I had never seen before and have never seen since.

After September 22, when I got back home, the first trace of any break in my daily routine occurs in a letter dated February 25, 1870; and this is but an insignificant trace. Describing myself as "a martyr to indigestion and consequent very bad sleeping," I speak of a forthcoming remedial excursion for a few days with Lewes. We went round the south of the Isle of Wight. How often it happens that extremely small things dwell in one's memory, when great ones disappear. Nothing remains with me of this excursion save two trivialities—the one that we played billiards at Ventnor, the other that, when sitting down to dinner at Freshwater, I made Lewes laugh by exclaiming—" Dear me these are very large chops for such a small island." And here, with this remark about the survival of trivialities in one's memory, I may join the remark that with me any tendency towards facetiousness is the result of temporary elation: either, as in this case, caused by pleasurable health-giving change, or, more commonly by meeting old friends. Habitually I observed that, on seeing the Lotts after a long interval, I was apt to give vent to some witticisms during the first hour or two, and then they became rare.

To Youmans, on March 9, I wrote a letter of which some paragraphs must be quoted:—

"Very unfortunately for me, though perhaps fortunately for himself, Mr. Duncan has been appointed Professor of Logic &c. at Madras; and leaves me for India some six weeks hence. It will be a very difficult thing for me to find anyone to undertake and carry on efficiently the work he has been doing in preparing classified and tabulated materials for the *Principles of Sociology.*

I remember you telling me that in America, there are plenty who would gladly undertake the post which Mr. Duncan fills; and that so far from having to pay a secretary, I might, if I pleased, put up the post to auction, and accept the highest bidder. Without entertaining any such droll notion, I am led to infer from this statement of yours, that I might perhaps be more likely to find with you, than over here, some competent man who would render me the required services in return for the very moderate salary I can afford. . . .

I had a pleasant surprise this morning. It came in the shape of an *Essay on Longevity* by E. Ray Lankester, one of the rising young biologists. It turned out to be an avowed corollary from the *Principles of Biology,* to which, as the author says, it might form an additional chapter. But the pleasant surprise is this, that the prize was offered, and adjudged to this essay of Mr. Lankester, by the University of Oxford. Fancy the Oxford authorities giving a public endorsement to the doctrine of Evolution!"

The loss of Mr. Duncan created great inconvenience. When he joined me, the understanding was that he would continue until the work undertaken by him was finished. But I could not, under the circumstances above indicated, hold him to his bargain. He was engaged; and some little time before this date, had intimated to me his intention of marrying, narrow as his means were. To have let him do so foolish a thing, while also giving up a promising career, was out of the question; and therefore, though he expressed his willingness to abide by our agreement, I released him. He promised to go on with the work in India as fast as his professional duties allowed; and he loyally fulfilled this promise—finishing the division he was engaged upon without further remuneration.

The next passage in the correspondence which seems worth quoting, is dated 26 April:—

"I regretted very much to hear of your having been so unwell. I have long feared that, like many others who are anxious to diffuse a knowledge of the laws of health, you would yourself have to suffer from continuously disregarding them. As I sometimes say jokingly to Huxley, *a propos* of his transgressions, we ought to erase the proverb—"Experience makes fools wise," and write in place of it—"Experience does not even make wise men wise." I hope, at any rate, that henceforth you will not so lavishly expend your energies for the benefit of others, taking no care of yourself. . . .

In the forthcoming number of *The Fortnightly* you will find an article of mine on "The Origin of Animal Worship." You will at first perhaps wonder why I suspended my ordinary work to write it. I did so because it lies in the line of my future work, and because I saw that the matters with which it deals are now being so much studied, that if I waited until I got to the *Sociology* I should probably be forestalled by some one who had meanwhile reached the same conclusion. The article will interest you both as a further illustration of Evolution, and also as, by implication, another heavy blow to current beliefs."

This article was dictated while I was boating on the Regent's Park water; and my amanuensis was a youth whose name I cannot recall, but who, a few years ago, wrote me a letter from the East with the signature Baron ——; telling me how he had prospered, even to the attainment of a title (in what way he did not say), and then reminding me that he had written the above-named essay to my dictation.

Of my life between September 1869 and July 1870, there is nothing more to record than is contained in the above quotations and comments.

An old manor house called The Argoed, about four miles below Monmouth on the banks of the Wye, but high above the stream, had been for some years in the possession of my friend Potter; who had bought it, with the surrounding lands, as a sanatorium for his children: the climate of Standish being relaxing. Here, in July, 1870, I went with him and two of his daughters. During a pleasant ten days there occurred a droll incident. Tintern had to be seen; and one fine day boatmen from Monmouth took the young ladies and myself down the river. The moonlight effects on the ruins of the Abbey are said to be very fine; and, filling the intervening time by going on to the Wyndcliffe, we went to the Abbey in the evening. There we waited and waited, wondering how it was that the moon made no sign, and frequently glancing with impatience towards the grove through which we expected to see its light. Presently the mystery was explained. It rose above the trees in a state of eclipse! There was a laugh at my expense; for it was supposed that I, interested in all science, should of course have known that an eclipse was about to take place. I am reminded of a kindred supposition on the part of the head-waiter at the Athenæum, who sometimes, when the addition of the dinner bill was called in question, smiled at an error made by a mathematical friend of mine: being surprised that a distinguished mathematician should err in his figures. The truth is that wide grasp of the general is not necessarily connected with great aptitude for the special.

After a day at Monmouth, pleasantly varied by a visit to Raglan Castle, a Sunday at Hereford, some of which was passed in the enjoyment of Cathedral music, and days and parts of days at Ludlow, and Shrewsbury, I joined the Lotts at Llanfairfechan, on the north coast of Wales. A fortnight spent there has among its remembrances the rush down to the station every morning to get papers with the last news of the Franco-German war, which had just commenced—a war of which the issues were so immense that one could not but watch its stages with breathless interest. Sir William Gull and Sir James Paget (not at that time bearing the titles they now have) were staying at Penmaenmawr, near at hand; and one of my pleasant recollections is of a drive to the Penrhyn slate quarries, in which they kindly invited me to join them: a good deal of scientific talk being the accompaniment.

I had never seen Ireland; and when my friends left for Derby, I was prompted, partly by this consciousness and partly by the desire for the good salmon-fishing which I heard was to be had at Ballina, to take my departure for Holyhead and Dublin. But as a drought, which then persisted, extended over Ireland; and as the style of living, not very satisfactory even in Dublin, threatened to be unsatisfactory at Ballina; my resolution was abandoned. Taking train to Belfast and steamer to Glasgow, I presently found myself at Inveroran. Thence after a time I returned to London.

This did not end my Autumn holiday however; or rather, there followed it something which was half holiday and half a kind of excitement which tells on me as much as work. The British Association met at Liverpool in September, and Huxley was President. Of course I went there to do what little towards the success of the meeting, might be done by adding one to the assembly. On this, as on other occasions when a member of the X Club presided, the gathering had a concomitant pleasure resulting from the quasi-domestic arrangements made. All members of the X who came, usually bringing their wives, took a suite of rooms at the chief hotel and united their forces: the liveliness of the party being increased by extending hospitalities to distinguished members of the Association not belonging to the group.

Deviating from the ordinary course, which was to give a summary of scientific progress, the presidential address dealt with the subject of spontaneous generation, just then much discussed, and gave an account of the dissipation of the once-universal belief in it. There resulted a controversy which gave special animation to the Biological Section. Strangely enough there were some biologists who thought that their experiments verified the old belief; and further thought that the general doctrine of Evolution received support from them. But, had the alleged facts been established, evolutionists would have been perplexd by them. That microscopic forms as much differentiated in structure as those described, should have been spontaneously generated, would have been at variance with their doctrine; which implies that the earliest living things must have been, if not absolutely structureless, yet with no more structure than is implied by some scarcely appreciable difference between outside and inside. Moreover, it has all along been manifest to the philosophic biologist, that no experiments which, in the materials used, pre-suppose the existence of organic matter, can throw any light on the genesis of organic forms. While believing that such genesis originally took place naturally, under conditions which no longer exist, they find no evidence that it takes place now; and do not believe that it is likely to take place now. And here, let me add, we have an illustration of the truth that the veritably scientific man will not accept evidence which, though plausible, is open to doubt; even when it supports an hypothesis he accepts.

Before the meeting was over, Professor Tyndall and I departed for the lakes. Sunday morning found us rambling along the shore of Windermere on the way to Rydal Mount. Thence we proceeded to Grasmere; and then, after dining, took a boat to the base of Loughrigg. A climb took us to the top and we descended to Ambleside. But a day's walking and talking with Tyndall, who gets me into discussion, proved too much. A wretched night, followed by the fear of more such days, prompted a flight black to Town.

And now the close of the year brought the completion of the first volume of the developed *Psychology*. Commenced at the end of 1867, this volume was published in December 1870. Ill health must, I suppose, be debited with a large part of the delay. Certainly the long time taken over the work could not have arisen from any distaste for it. Contrariwise, several feelings united in making me enjoy the resumption of this topic which I had dealt with in 1854-5.

At that date, as already pointed out, an evolutionary view of Mind was foreign to the ideas of the time, and voted absurd: the result of setting it forth being pecuniary loss and a good deal of reprobation. Naturally, therefore, after the publication of *The Origin of Species* had caused the current of public opinion to set the other way, a more sympathetic reception was to be counted upon for the doctrine of mental evolution in its elaborated form.

Chief, however, was the pleasure of elaborating it—giving completeness to the theory by building its outworks and filling up *lacunæ*. Here, as before, recognition of the fact that the Data and the Inductions had to be set forth before proceeding to the work of construction, led to interesting results. The general views contained in these first and second divisions would never have been reached had it not been for the inquiry—What are the main facts of structure and function which Biology hands on to Psychology; and what are the general truths which mental phenomena present, considered apart from any theory respecting their origin? Then at the close of the volume, in the division entitled "Physical Synthesis," there had to be set forth the theory named in the preface to the first edition as being for several reasons withheld. This was an interesting piece of work; and though it has since been shown me that, under both its physical and its physiological aspects, the theory, in the form there given to it, cannot be sustained, yet, as I hope sometime to prove, the needful qualifications may be made without invalidating the cardinal principle.

I was about to say that the reception of the volume must have been tepid, since it has left no recollection whatever; but on looking through correspondence I find a still better cause for the absence of all recollection. A letter to my publisher, dated 19 December, says:—

"The policy of not issuing copies for review, which we adopted in the case of the second volume of the *Biology,* and the second edition of *First Principles,* answers so well that we will continue it. I find, on examining the accounts, that since the adoption of this policy the sale of my books has about doubled. I do not suppose that the absence of misleading criticisms has had much to do with this; though, as I have learnt from their own lips, some readers have been deterred for years from looking at my books by the erroneous impressions of them they had gathered from reviews. But this large increase of sale may, at any rate, be taken as evidence that the course adopted is not detrimental.

We will therefore establish it as a permanent rule. Do not send out copies of this first volume of the *Principles of Psychology* now published, to any of the periodicals—daily, weekly, monthly or quarterly. And let whatever works I publish hereafter be similarly withheld.

Now, or in time to come, copies for review may occasionally be applied for. To meet such applications, please keep this letter; and let a copy of it be sent by way of answer. This will show that the refusal is not exceptional but general."

Subsequent resumption of the ordinary habit was not due to any change of belief respecting the policy of this course, but was due to a cause which I cannot here indicate without forestalling matters. It will become apparent hereafter.

CHAPTER XLIV.

FINISHING THE *PSYCHOLOGY*.

1870—72. ÆT. 50—52.

WITH the ending of the first volume of the *Psychology* and the beginning of the second, a new kind of mental action was commenced. While the first volume, or, to speak strictly, the constructive part of it, is synthetic, the second volume is analytic. The process of taking to pieces our intellectual fabric and the products of its actions, until the ultimate components are reached, had now to be undertaken; and, among other things, it had to be shown that the structure of Mind, as ascertained in this way, corresponds with its structure as ascertained by tracing up its successive stages of development.

Was this change an agreeable one? I think I may say that it was. Not, indeed, intrinsically, but simply as involving another form of intellectual activity. And here, as being relevant to the question whether I liked best the synthetic or the analytic mode of thought, I may say something about my intellectual tendencies in relation to the two. A few years ago I saw it remarked that there appeared to be in me equal proclivities towards analysis and towards synthesis. Up to that time I had supposed myself to be alone in the recognition of this trait.

It is a trait which will, I think, be manifest to anyone who looks into the evidence furnished by my books. While, on the one hand, they betray a great liking for drawing deductions and building them up into a coherent whole; on the other hand, they betray a great liking for examining the premises on which a set of deductions is raised, for the purpose of seeing what assumptions are involved in them, and what are the deeper truths into which such assumptions are resolvable. There is shown an evident dissatisfaction with proximate principles, and a restlessness until ultimate principles have been reached; at the same time that there is shown a desire to see how the most complex phenomena are to be interpreted as workings out of these ultimate principles. It is, I think, to the balance of these two tendencies that the character of the work done is mainly ascribable.

Much scope for further exercise of the analytic faculty was not afforded by Part VI (Special Analysis). But with arrival at Part VII (General Analysis) there came the occasion for expanding and completing the conception first briefly and crudely set forth in the "Universal Postulate," published in 1853, and further developed in the first edition of the *Principles of Psychology* in 1855. To this division, and the divisions succeeding it, my limited energies were chiefly devoted during the period covered by this chapter.

Already I have hinted that a great change in the routine of my life followed my election into the Athenæum Club; and what there is to say about it I may as well say here.

My place of abode was, in several ways, desirable in

position. Its proximity to Kensington Gardens made more constant than it might else have been, a morning's walk of half an hour before beginning work. Then when, something like an hour after luncheon, came the walk into Town, my route lay over grass and under trees nearly all the way: through Kensington Gardens, Hyde Park, and the Green Park; so that I could reach the Club without more than a quarter of a mile upon pavement. Once at the Club, a miscellaneous process of killing time commenced. Having already glanced through *The Times* after breakfast, the news-room did not detain me; save on Saturdays when some of the weekly periodicals, not found in the other rooms, had to be looked at. Commonly some little time was spent in the drawing room in glancing through the contents of the Monthly Magazines and Quarterly Reviews: skipping most articles and dipping into a few. I rarely read one through. Then came the new books, of which the chief were obtained from Mudie for the convenience of members who wished, some to read them and others to see what they were about. I was usually one of the latter class. Biographies, Histories, and the like, I commonly passed over without opening them. Books of travel had an attraction for me; and I glanced through them with an eye to materials for my work. Passages telling me of the institutions, beliefs, characters, usages &c. of the uncivilized, I not unfrequently copied. Of course all works treating on this or the other branch of Science, as well as those which dealt with philosophical questions, special or general, including those on Theology, were looked into. To observe the current of opinion was one motive; and another motive was to make myself acquainted with the criticisms passed on my own views, which I not unfrequently found objects of attack. Novels were temptations to be resisted; for I dare not expend on them the needful amount of reading power. Once in a year, perhaps, I treated myself to one; and then I had to get through it in a dozen or more instalments.

There was a further occupation which filled a considerable space. Playing billiards became " my custom always of the afternoon." I found it a very desirable way of passing the time: preventing thinking and excluding the temptation to read. Those who confess to billiard-playing commonly make some kind of excuse. Change of occupation is needful, they say; or it is alleged that the game entails a certain amount of beneficial exercise. It must not be supposed that the benefits I have just named are similarly meant as excuses. It suffices for me that I like billiards, and the attainment of the pleasure given I regard as a sufficient motive. I have for a long time deliberately set my face against that asceticism which makes it an offence to do a thing for the pleasure of doing it; and have habitually contended that, so long as no injury is inflicted on others, nor any ulterior injury on self, and so long as the various duties of life have been discharged, the pursuit of pleasure for its own sake is perfectly legitimate and requires no apology. The opposite view is nothing else than a remote sequence of the old devil-worship of the barbarian; who sought to please his god by inflicting pains on himself, and believed his god would be angry if he made himself happy.

Beyond these habitual occupations at the Club there were chattings with my old friends, most of whom were members, and less frequent conversations with friends newly made; for I am slow to make fresh friendships. And then as the evening was approaching there was the walk back to Queen's Gardens, bringing me there in time for dinner at 7; which was followed by such miscellaneous ways of passing the time without excitement as were available. Thus passed my ordinary days.

The close of 1870, and the first four months of 1871, furnish no incidents calling for mention. Such quotable passages as occur in correspondence concern other persons in ways which make it undesirable to reproduce them: one only excepted, which will come more conveniently in a future chapter. The first letter from which I may here fitly extract, is one dated 11th May.

"It is also pleasant news to me that you are likely to come over shortly. What time in June are you likely to come? I shall probably be away for a fortnight during the latter half of June, but shall be in town during July. . .

About a week ago, I received the French translation of *First Principles.* It contains an introduction by Dr. Cazelles which is *admirably done,* and is perfectly fitted to give the uninitiated a general preliminary conception. It is just the thing of which I have long felt the need; and it could not have been better supplied than by a sympathetic Frenchman. *A translation of it would be immensely serviceable;* but I cannot well have it made here. I have ordered a copy from Paris and will forward it to you as soon as it comes."

Of the two foregoing paragraphs the first introduces a matter of considerable general interest. At the time it was written I did not know that which I soon afterwards learned—the motive of my American friend in coming over. He was fertile in useful projects; and the project which now occupied his thoughts was one in pursuance of which English, American, French, German, and other authors, who undertook to write works of a certain class, should, by agreement among the publishers in their respective countries, have certain specified rates of profit secured to them in all these countries. I gladly did all that I was able in furtherance of his scheme. One step taken was to give him a letter of introduction which should serve to facilitate his negotiations with authors and publishers over here. This it will be not amiss to quote in full.

My dear Youmans, "4 *July*, 1871.
I am desirous to do all that is possible to extend and establish the arrangements you are making with English authors—arrangements which practically amount to international copyright.

Having for the last ten years benefited so greatly by the arrangements you have made with the Appletons on my behalf, which have put me on a footing as good as that of the American author, I have the best possible reasons for thinking that the interests of English authors will be subserved in a very important degree by the success of the negociations which you have come over here to carry out. Various of my scientific friends, who have reaped pecuniary and other advantages from the contracts you have made for them, will, I am sure, coincide in this expression of opinion.

From the conversation I had with Mr. Appleton when he was here recently, it was manifest to me that he was anxious to carry out in his relations with other English authors, the same equitable system from which I, and some others, have gained. And now that he has given you full powers to make engagements in pursuance of this system, I think it very desirable that all should co-operate. Standing so high as the Appletons do, alike in respect to the character of the works they publish and in the extent of their business, it appears to me clear that this system which they are adopting needs only to be known and understood by English authors to be at once accepted by them.

Pray make use of this letter in any way that will further your negociations.

Ever yours sincerely,
Herbert Spencer."

The movement thus initiated was one which presently issued in " The International Scientific Series," of which more anon.

I have said nothing of late concerning my social life in these days, and now that I recur to the topic, I find little to say.

I suppose it has been more from inclination than from principle that I have avoided acquaintanceships and cultivated only friendships. There is in me very little of the *besoin de parler;* and hence I do not care to talk with those in whom I feel no interest. Having neither professional interests to push, nor daughters to marry, and not caring to show Mrs. Grundy how many people I know, I have had no motive for multiplying social relations. I have thus avoided the weariness of " the social treadmill." My circle, limited to those whose natures are more or less attractive to me, has ever yielded me pleasure, and brought to me quite as much intercourse as I desired—often too much, in fact.

Of special incidents belonging to social life which dwell in my memory two belong to this year. One of them was a water-party on the anniversary of the marriage of Mr. Leslie Stephen to the younger Miss Thackeray—a party including the elder Miss Thackeray (now Mrs. Ritchie) whose nature, answering to her father's estimate, sometimes expressed its amiabilities in amusing " verbal fireworks," as I once heard a lady call them.

Some of the Huth family were of the party; and also a son and daughter of Sir William Grove. Thames Ditton was our picnicing place; and taking again to our boats, which carried us to Hampton Court, we there of course went the round of the galleries. Although I do not remember it, I doubtless seized the occasion for uttering heresies concerning Raphael's cartoons.

As, in foregoing chapters, I have implied sundry tastes and pursuits incongruous with the popular conception of the philosopher, I shall not, I suppose, surprise the reader by indicating another. In October I went down for some pheasant shooting to Wykehurst —an estate in Sussex not long before purchased by Mr. Henry Huth, and on which a few years later he built the palatial mansion now existing there. Save once, at Ardtornish, when I utterly failed in black-cock shooting, I had not taken a gun in hand since I was 18; and now, though I was to my own extreme surprise, and to the surprise of others, very successful, the sport gave me scarcely any pleasure. I preferred hitting to missing, and that was about all. I suppose it was that the *battue* system, or whatever approaches to it, lacks the chief elements of the sportsman's pleasure. Essentially this, like the pleasures accompanying many other activities, consists in justified self-estimation. Be it in a feat of strength, or a game of physical or mental skill, or a wit combat, the satisfaction of success is caused by proved adequacy to the occasion. Consciousness of efficiency is an accompaniment of every kind of achievement; and, accompanying life-subserving activities of every kind, has roots ramifying everywhere. Hence whatever implies efficiency becomes a source of pleasure: directly and simply if known to self only, and also indirectly and more complexly if known to others too. In such a sport as cover-shooting with beaters, the efficiency is simply that of hitting a moving mark—divested of all those efficiencies which go along with the successful pursuit of scattered birds in a wild state. Hence, except where there is a love of killing for its own sake, it yields but little pleasure.

In the early months of 1871, suddenly passed away my admired and valued friend Mr. Octavius Smith. Though of good age, he was constitutionally vigorous and might have lived many years but for the results of an accident. He exemplified the truth that where great physical vigour and mental resource yield daily experience of efficiency on all occasions there is apt to be generated an excessive degree of courage. Many years before he had suffered serious damage from incaution hence arising; and now, or rather a few years years previously, an accident to which the same trait led, left a slight invisible injury which obviously originated the malady that proved fatal. Among my friends of the preceding generation his death made a great gap—a gap impossible to be filled up.

The autumn of this year was passed in a miscellaneous way. First came a short salmon-fishing expedition to Inveroran. Thence, when the British Association met about its usual date, I migrated to its place of meeting —Edinburgh. This time the prompting motive was not that of being present during the presidency of one of my friends. The motive was that of aiding Prof. Youmans in his project mentioned above. Sundry steps were taken which conduced to its success. Profs. Huxley and Tyndall and myself were formed into a Committee to decide on books which should be admitted into the series; and whether, with this or that author, an engagement should be made to write one. Sundry members of the Association were canvassed with the view of obtaining promises from them to contribute volumes connected with their special subjects: the purpose being that each of such volumes should be one dealing with some part of a science capable of being cut out from the rest, and within the limits of which there had been recent developments of importance. The consultations and negotiations went on favourably, and by the time that the meeting closed the scheme had taken definite shape and organization.

A house at St. Andrews had been taken by the Huxleys for the Autumn, and this led me to go over to an hotel there for two or three days. Two things only I remember—the one that Huxley and I played together a game of golf, the only game I ever played; the other that, while sitting on the cliff watching some boys bathing, we marvelled over the fact, seeming especially strange when they are no longer disguised by clothes, that human beings should dominate over all other creatures and play the wonderful part they do on the Earth.

On leaving St. Andrews I met, in pursuance of an agreement made at Edinburgh, one whom I have not hitherto named—Dr. Hirst, a special friend of Prof. Tyndall since their early days. Originally engaged on the Ordnance Survey, they left it for the purpose of going together to the University of Marburg; whence, after taking their degrees, they went to Queenwood College as professors; and whence, afterwards, they migrated to London: Tyndall to the Royal Institution, as Faraday's assistant and presently his successor, and Hirst to University College as Professor of Mathematics; which post he held until he became Deputy Registrar of the University of London, on the way to his ultimate position as the first Director of Studies at the Royal Naval College, Greenwich.

Our tour into the West Highlands proved in all respects a success. Days were passed at Oban, at Ballachulish, and at Fort William: our stay at this last place being varied by an exploration of Glen Nevis up to its top, where it becomes Swiss-like in character. While at Bannavie a dog-cart took us to Glen Roy, up which we rambled to explore the parallel roads, and to discuss the speculations respecting their origin. On our return south, I remember only the sunny day which gave beauty to our walk along the shore of Loch Linnhe from Ballachulish to Appin. And then there came a junction with our common friends the Busks, who had again taken Aird's Bay House on Loch Etive.

Two breaks in the routine of my ordinary work occurred soon after I resumed it. One of them was entailed by the scheme of my American friend, and the other by a controversy upon which I had to enter.

Arrangements for the proposed "International Scientific Series" had to be made in France; and I agreed to go with Youmans to Paris for the purpose of helping to establish them. He knew no French, and though my French was scrambling enough, it sufficed to give M. Baillière the needful explanations, and to make it manifest to him that it would be worth his while to become the French publisher for the Series. There was also formed a French Committee of judges, who should decide upon such works as Frenchmen might propose; and various other matters were put in train before he went on to Germany and I returned home.

While still in Paris I entered upon the piece of controversial writing which Fate had just then devolved on me: Youmans volunteering as amanuensis. The *Fortnightly Review* for November 1871 contained an article by Prof. Huxley entitled " Administrative Nihilism," in which, criticising a view of mine respecting the limitation of State-functions, he put his objection in the form of a question. I could scarcely avoid giving an answer; for otherwise the implication would apparently have been that the question was unanswerable. Commenced, as above stated, in Paris, and completed after my return to London, my reply appeared in the December number of the *Fortnightly*, under the title of " Specialized Administration."

This passage of arms was carried on in a perfectly amicable spirit, and left the relations between us undisturbed.

Before the close of the year came two occurrences of some interest, one of them leading to the other. The first is explained in the following letter to the Principal of St. Andrews.

DEAR DR. TULLOCH, "*20th Novr.* 1871.

Only on Friday night did I hear, and only on Saturday morning did I see [in the *Times*] that I had been nominated for the office of Rector of St. Andrews.

I regret that some intimation was not given to me beforehand that such a step was contemplated; because some trouble, and possibly some derangement of plans, might thus have been prevented.

To accept such a post, were I elected to it, would entail

on me a loss of time which, though not serious to most, would be serious to me, with my very small amount of working power. My progress with my work, slow enough at the best, is interrupted much more frequently than I like; and I find myself compelled rigorously to negative such interruptions as are not unavoidable. Though, in the position which some of the St. Andrew's students wish me to occupy, I might be of some little service, yet I think I can render better service by devoting the same amount of energy to executing the task before me.

In conveying to those who have put forward my name the request that they will withdraw it from the list, will you be kind enough also to say that I am much gratified by the sympathetic appreciation implied by the course they have taken.

Very truly yours,
HERBERT SPENCER."

I may add that the students, signifying their disappointment at the time, signified it afterwards still more by again asking me in March of the next year: the preceding election having proved invalid. But the reasons given for declining upon the first occasion remained in force, and I again declined.

This incident in November initiated another before the close of December. There came an intimation, conveyed through Professor Flint, that the Senatus contemplated conferring upon me an honorary degree. As my reply contains some general opinions respecting honorary degrees, which I think it desirable to put on record, I here give it in full.

SIR, "*Decr.* 1871.

I cannot but be much gratified by the fact of which you inform me—that "the professors of the United College of St. Andrews have unanimously agreed to recommend to the

Senatus of the University to confer upon" me "the Degree of LL.D." The remembrance of this mark of their consideration will hereafter give me pleasure.

Certain convictions which have been long growing up in me, respecting the effects of honorary titles, will, however, I fear, stand in the way of my acceptance of the degree which the Professors kindly suggest should be conferred upon me. I have come to the conclusion that such honorary titles, while they seem to be encouragements to intellectual achievement, do in reality, by their indirect influences, act as discouragements.

If, supposing due discrimination were possible, men of much promise received from a learned body such marks of distinction as would bespeak attention from the world at large, I can well imagine that such men would be greatly helped, and would oftentimes be saved from sinking in their struggles with adverse circumstances in the midst of a society prepossessed in favour of known men. But there ordinarily comes no such aid until the difficulties have been surmounted—supposing, that is, that they have not proved fatal.

Probably it will be said that because honorary titles do not commonly yield benefits so great as they might yield if given earlier, it does not therefore follow that when given they are otherwise than beneficial. I think, however, that if, instead of considering their direct effects on those older men who have received them, we consider their indirect effects on those younger men who have not received them, we shall see that to these they become, practically, an additional obstacle to success. Always the impediments in the way of one who, without authority, enters the field of intellectual activity, in competition with those having established authorities, are sufficiently great. The probability that he has nothing to say worth listening to, is so strong, that he is almost certain to receive for a long time scarcely any of the attention he may well deserve. But this unavoidable difficulty is made artificially greater when, bearing no stamp of value, he has for competitors those who, to the advantages of known achievements, add the advantage of officially-stamped values. The larger reading world, and the narrower critical world which leads it, are greatly biassed by whatever bespeaks respectful consideration. And if the presence of an honorary title gives this positive advantage to one bearing it, its absence involves a positive disadvantage to one not bearing it.

This conclusion is not one reached *a priori;* but it is one that personal experiences have forced upon me. During a career of more than twenty years, most of which has been passed in writing books that entailed on me successive losses, I have had many opportunities of observing this artificial aid given by honorary titles to those who least needed aid, and the consequent artificial hindrance to those without titles who most needed aid. And it has come to be an established belief with me that the advance of thought will be most furthered, when the only honours to be acquired by authors are those spontaneously yielded to them by a public which is left to estimate their merits as well as it can.

It would be a source of much regret to me if this response to the sympathetic recognition which the Professors of St. Andrew's imply by their proposed step, were interpreted as undervaluing the feeling shown by them. But I hope that what I have said will make it clear that my course is one determined by a general principle, entirely without reference to the particular circumstances."

To save references to them in future chapters, I may add here that on various kindred occasions I took the like course: assigning these and sundry other reasons for declining.

A letter of 8th Jan. 1872, saying " I was better for my excursion to the Isle of Wight," reminds me that the Christmas week of 1871 was spent in company with my friends Busk and Allman in walking and driving round the south coast from St. Helens to Yarmouth. Of incidents during the season of 1872, the following extracts from correspondence give some traces. The first is dated 2nd Feb.

"Haeckel's assistant, of whom he speaks highly, a Dr. Vetter, has undertaken to translate *First Principles,* and proposes afterwards to translate the *Biology* and the *Psychology*. It seems that Brockhaus hesitates about undertaking the publication; but Haeckel speaks as though there will be no difficulty in finding another publisher, if Brockhaus should not shortly agree . . . We had an X dinner last night at which Lowe was our guest. He takes an intelligent interest in scientific matters."

Correspondence also recalls the fact that when over here in 1871, my American publisher, Mr. Appleton, had asked me to sit for a portrait to be painted for him. As he left me to choose the artist, I assented; and some progress was made during the Autumn. A letter of 8th April 1872 says:—

"The portrait has been standing still up to the present time. Since his return from Spain, Burgess has had scarlet fever in his house. I am going to day to give him a sitting " . . .

My reasons for fixing on Mr. J. B. Burgess, were two. One was that he was not a professed portrait painter: my impression being that he would feel more interest, and take more pains, than an artist who had made portrait painting his business. The other was that he had shown a remarkable power of rendering expression. A picture of his, entitled " Bravo Toro," exhibited in the Royal Academy some years before, and representing spectators at a Spanish bull-fight, had greatly struck me by its truthful and varied representations of character and emotion. No picture by an old master which I have seen or heard of, exhibits this kind of success in anything like as great degree. His artist friends told Mr. Burgess that success of this kind was not to be aimed at—was not an element in high art. To me it seems, contrariwise, that such success is the highest. I know a novelist, skilful in devising plots, who holds that a good story is the thing, if not of sole importance, still of chief importance, in fiction; and who accords small praise to characterization, and the delineation of those lights and shades of thought and feeling which give individuality: components that are, in fact, the flowers to which the story is but the stem. I would as soon believe him as I would believe these artists who pooh-pooh the vivid pourtrayal of moral natures and states of mind in the faces of the personages they represent.

"I have been away at Boulogne," says a letter of June 12; and now that I meet with this sentence, I remember that my old engineering friend, Loch, whose name has for a long time disappeared from the record, was staying there with his wife and family, and that to join him was the motive for going. He and I renewed our habit of early years, and took country rambles inland and along the coast. One of them left a permanent impression. We passed a wayside shrine, at the foot of which were numerous offerings, each formed of two bits of lath nailed one across the other. The sight suggested to me the behaviour of an intelligent and amiable retriever, a great pet at Ardtornish. On coming up to salute one after a few hours' or a day's absence, wagging her tail and drawing back her lips so as to simulate a grinning smile, she would seek around to find a stick, or a bit of paper, or a dead leaf, and bring it in her mouth: so expressing her desire to propitiate. The dead leaf or bit of paper was symbolic, in much the same way as was the valueless cross. Probably, in respect of sincerity of feeling, the advantage was on the side of the retriever.

Though I had arranged to go abroad with friends for my autumn holiday, yet my habit of visiting Scotland annually was too strong to be resisted. The beginning of August found me at Taynuilt, where I went for some salmon fishing in the Awe. But the weather was dry, the river low, the days bright, and after a week of disappointments I returned.

An excursion to Switzerland with Mr. and Mrs. Busk and their daughters shortly followed. After brief pauses at Cologne, Heidelberg, and Berne, we made our way to Mürren, where a week or perhaps more was spent in face of the Jungfrau and the Silberhorn. No more on this occasion than on the first, did I find Switzerland physically beneficial. On neither occasion did I experience the invigoration which many feel; and Mürren was positively enervating.

There is much yet to be learnt respecting the effects of atmospheric conditions. It seems to me that it is with these as, according to a physician I quoted some distance back, it is with drugs: cases prove that under different conditions they may produce opposite effects. Certainly, the air of great altitudes, which is exhilarating to some, is depressing to others. I was not alone in feeling the ill effects of Mürren. Two of the ladies furnished clear proofs of enfeeblement. Evidently that state of exhaustion which the rarified air of very high mountains causes in all, begins to be felt by a few on lower mountains. The decrease of atmospheric pressure accompanying an ascent of 6000 feet, produces on the respiratory process effects which, not manifest in some are conspicuous in others. May it not be that two factors which come into play, work, by their joint actions, diverse results in diverse constitutions? Diminished atmospheric pressure causes augmented exhalation from the skin and lungs: water turns into vapour more rapidly. One of the consequences is that the currents of liquids through the tissues are accelerated; change of matter is furthered; and exaltation of energy results. At the same time the charge of oxygen which the blood contains is lessened, and greater action of the lungs is required to compensate for this. If the lungs are well developed, a small amount of extra activity enables them to meet the requirement, and then the benefit of a more rapid evaporation of water is felt. If, contrariwise, the respiratory system is below par, then more is lost by decreased oxygenation than is gained by increased evaporation.

While the heights of Switzerland were not favourable to me, neither were the depths. Our descent to Grindelwald was not followed by any improvement, but rather the contrary. After a few days it became evident that I must escape into the open country. Bidding good-bye to my friends, I made my way to Vevay; and after a few days at St. Evian les Bains, and a few others at Geneva, I reached home a week before the end of September.

Not long after my return was published Mr. Darwin's

work on *The Expression of the Emotions*. As my acknowledgment of the copy he was good enough to send me contains some expressions of opinion concerning a point on which we differed, it may be not amiss to quote it here.

DEAR DARWIN, "*Nov. 16th, 1872.*

I have delayed, somewhat longer than I intended, acknowledging the copy of your new volume, which you have been kind enough to send me. I delayed partly in the hope of being able to read more of it before writing to you; but my reading powers are so small, and they are at present so much employed in getting up materials for work in hand, that I have been unable to get on far with it. I have, however, read quite enough to see what an immense mass of evidence you have brought to bear in proof of your propositions.

I will comment only on one point on which I see you differ from me; namely the explanation of musical expression, in respect of which you quote Mr. Litchfield. I think if you would trace up the genesis of melody, beginning with the cadences of slightly emotional speech and passing through recitative, you would see that melody is quite comprehensible on the principles I have pointed out. The fact that melody proper, has been *evolved* in comparatively recent times, is strong evidence of this. That recitative is a natural expression of emotion is abundantly proved. I remember having read of Australians who used a kind of recitative in talking to themselves when walking along, about things that interested them; and I have heard children, when engaged in any play that interested them, or such occupations as gathering flowers, talk to themselves in recitative. Join this with the fact that many inferior races have never risen above recitative (as the Chinese and Hindoos) and that there is reason for believing that even among the Greeks, melody had not become so markedly different from recitative as now,—

add, too, the fact that even now in the Highlands you may hear Gaelic songs that retain very much of the recitative character; and I think you will see that melody is, as I have contended, an idealized form of the natural cadences of emotion. Indeed I could point out musical phrases which would, I think, clearly prove this to you. Ask your daughter to play to you "*Robert toi que j'aime*," and you will I think see this. I do not mean to say that this is *all;* for there are other elements of effect in melody. But this is, I think, the cardinal element.

Yours very truly,
Herbert Spencer."

I have long intended to add to the essay on the *Origin and Function of Music*, a postscript dealing with objections: its chief purposes being, first, to dissipate the misapprehensions of Mr. Edmund Gurney, and second, to criticize the hypothesis of Mr. Darwin. But I do not suppose that I shall now ever be able to fulfil my intention.

Shortly before the date of the above letter (which I have transposed for convenience) came the completion and publication of the volume to which this chapter owes its title. I have not very much to say concerning it.

Beyond the verbal improvements made on nearly all the pages throughout part VI, "Special Analysis," not many changes were made. Only one of them calls for mention here, namely, the enunciation of the paradox that Logic is a science of objective phenomena, and not a science of subjective phenomena, as hitherto assumed. The proof as given in § 302, still appears to me conclusive. Save one writer in *Mind*, who expressed his surprise that no attention had been given to it, everybody has, so far as I know, passed by this revolutionary doctrine without remark. It should, I think, be either disproved or admitted; for clearly the issues involved are of some philosophical importance. Does not one of them touch fundamentally the entire system of Hegel? I express the thought interrogatively, because I know so little of the Hegelian philosophy. My impression is that it sets out with a proposition impossible to conceive. If this proceeding is legitimate, it is no less legitimate to make each step in the reasoning that follows, of like nature; and to assert that though a particular conclusion appears necessary, and the opposite conclusion impossible to conceive, yet the opposite conclusion is true. As this course, actual and potential, is one against which I feel an obstinate prejudice, I never read further any work in which it is displayed. But I wish some one would put the proposition that Logic is an objective science, side by side with the Hegelian philosophy, and see whether the two can co-exist.

Concerning Part VII, I may here remark that the elaboration of it illustrated in an extreme degree a habit of thought which I have before described. The germ was contained in the essay on the "Universal Postulate," published in the *Westminster Review* for October 1853. In the first edition of *The Principles of Psychology*, this essay grew into four chapters; and now, in the second edition, its thoughts had so developed in various ways that nineteen chapters were required properly to set them forth. How to arrange these chapters long remained a perplexity. For some two or three years, I think, I occasionally thought over the general argument in my morning walks or at other times, and tried to find the right order for its parts, but without success. Only after this long period did they slowly gravitate into their respective places, and form a coherent whole.

How happened it that the volume was so long in hand: commenced, as it was, in 1870, and not completed till October 1872? I find in correspondence various references to ill-health—being obliged to work only at "half-speed," or to be "very careful of my head." While the delays hence arising partly account for the long time taken, it is also in part accounted for by the fact that the work was interrupted by the execution of other work presently to be mentioned. But I was nearly forgetting a further cause. The volume ended with an additional part (Part IX "Corollaries"). Psychology underlies Sociology; and there had to be specified a number of those more special truths in Psychology which have to be handed on to Sociology as part of its data. The deduction of these special truths from the general truths set forth in the preceding parts of the work, was an interesting task.

CHAPTER XLV.

AN EXTRA BOOK.

1872—73. ÆT. 52—53.

ANOTHER overlap in the narrative, like two already made, has to be made here. Without causing some confusion, I could not, until now, give any account of work which was undertaken before the second volume of the *Psychology* was finished; and which, as lately implied, was one cause of its long-postponed publication. Going back some six months, I must here say something about an extra book then commenced.

"Why an extra book?" thinks the reader. "Surely the remaining volumes of the Synthetic Philosophy formed a sufficiently large task, and to attempt more was unwise, if not, indeed, absurd." This reflection is perfectly just, and I have nothing to say in mitigation of censure save that, though very reluctant, I was in a manner forced to commit myself to this extra book.

I have already described the scheme of Prof. Youmans which resulted in "The International Scientific Series"; and I have noted some efforts I made in aid of it. In the course of his negotiations with one or other author, he urged me to contribute a volume to the series. I felt, as the reader above imagined feels, that I had quite enough on my hands, and for some time resisted the suggestion. But my friend was pressing; and, being under great obligations to him for all that he had done on my behalf in America, I could not utter that decided "No" which I should have uttered to any one else. Eventually I yielded; not, however, without making such modification of the engagement as would, I thought, enable me to do what was asked without seriously retarding more important work. It occurred to me that I might obtain a fit *collaborateur,* who should give literary form to the ideas with which I furnished him. It was a wild notion, to be excused only by the pressure and hurry which prevented deliberation. Had I reflected, I should have seen that no one could be found who would prove adequately subordinate at the same time that he had sufficient vigour of thought and style to satisfy me. During the time in which this idea was entertained, Mr. C. E. Appleton, founder and editor of *The Academy,* came to me proposing himself as joint author; and it was his proposal more than anything else which opened my eyes to the impracticability of the scheme. I foresaw that we should disagree and part over the first chapter; and it became clear that neither anyone else's version of my thoughts nor anyone else's expression of them would satisfy me.

Very shortly, therefore, the notion of collaboration was abandoned, and I undertook to do the entire work myself.

Before he left England my American friend volunteered to arrange for the carrying out of a suggestion which had arisen, I do not remember how, that the successive chapters of *The Study of Sociology*—the extra book in question—should be first published serially, in England and America at the same time. Here the *Con-*

temporary Review, then owned by Mr. Strahan and edited by Mr. Knowles, was the contemplated medium; and a fit medium in the United States, Prof. Youmans proposed to negotiate with as soon as possible after his return. With this explanation the meanings of the following extracts from correspondence will be clear. The first is dated 8th Jany. 1872.

"I have, as I proposed before you left, arranged with Knowles for publication of the *Study of Sociology* in the *Contemporary,* in successive instalments. He, and the publisher, Strahan, express themselves as rejoicing to make the arrangement. No difficulty appears to arise respecting the simultaneous publication in America. . . . I was the better for my excursion to the Isle of Wight, but am not well, and am obliged to be careful as to work."

I may remark in passing, that the last sentence gives me the date of an excursion which otherwise I should have been puzzled to fix—an excursion made, partly driving partly walking, in company with Huxley, Tyndall, and Hooker, round the south of the Island and then from Freshwater across the hills to Newport. The next letter which I extract from is dated 16 February, 1872.

"I have just completed No. 32 of my Serial, and am about to commence the first chapter for the *Contemporary.* It will appear on the 1st April. . . .

The successive chapters will be in great measure independent, and will be popular both in manner and matter. I find that I have got a large amount of interesting and piquant illustration that can be worked up in them."

And now there arose an unlooked-for result from the understanding that had been made for simultaneous publication in America. Negotiations which Youmans had carried on with one or other periodical in the United States had all failed; and at the time when the first chapter had been put in type, neither he nor I saw how our plan was to be carried out. When the proof of this first chapter reached him it caused prompt and surprising action, as witness the following extract from a letter of his dated April 3, 1872:—

"A thousand thanks for your favour of March 13th, with article on *Study of Sociology* enclosed. I was beginning to be worried about it, and was on the point of telegraphing you to telegraph me as to what you would do. You did wisely in sending it, and I decided upon our course in ten minutes after getting it. I determined to have a monthly at once, and in time to open with this article . . . I received your article less than a week ago. We have started a monthly of 128 pages. The first part of it is now printing; the last pages will be closed up tomorrow, and we will have it out in a few days more. Of course we had to go in on selected articles here. With yours for original, and a translation by my sister from the French, a short article by myself, and fragments by my brother, we shall make a very fair show. . . . Nothing happens as expected, but often the unexpected is best. I am utterly glad that things have taken the course they have. I have wanted a medium of speech that I can control, and now I shall have it."

The magazine thus suddenly started was *The Popular Science Monthly;* which, under the editorship of my friend, has had a prosperous career and done very good work. His brother, Dr. W. J. Youmans, for many years his assistant, is now the Editor. The next extract is from a letter of mine dated 29th April:—

"Thanks for the cheque, which is ample. I had intended, before receiving it, to write and ask whether this magazine is *pecuniarily* a speculation of *your own;* or whether the Appletons run the risk. If it is your own, then I propose that you shall have these articles of mine *gratis.*"

It turned out, however, that the magazine was to be the property of the Appletons. I consequently accepted the cheque, and continued to receive payments from America equal to those which publication here brought me.

A digression, within the digression constituted by the *Study of Sociology,* occurred after the issue of some chapters. I then wrote, and published in the *Contemporary,* an article entitled " Mr. Martineau on Evolution," which was called forth by some strictures of his made in a lecture uttered and printed not long before. A reference to it had, I see, been made in a letter to Youmans on 8th April 1872.

" Martineau has published in the *Contemporary* that essay of which you sent me a report. Its concessions are large, and its criticisms feeble. It illustrates what continually happens with all parties who stand by the old. If they do nothing, things go against them; if they stir, things go against them still more."

As is implied by this extract, the attack did not seem to me to call for any notice. Afterwards, however, I was prompted to reply. Mr. Knowles is well known for his editorial tact, and it did not in this case fail him. In the course of an after-dinner conversation at Prof. Huxley's, Mr. Martineau's criticisms were referred to, and a remark made by Mr. Knowles:—" The general opinion is that you gentlemen are getting the worst of it,"—served its purpose effectually. I forthwith took up Mr. Martineau's gauntlet and suspended other work for an interval.

The refutation of his arguments was an easy task. Within the limits of the abstract and higher sciences

—logic, metaphysics, and psychology,—his competence was undoubted; but his knowledge of molecular physics, chemistry, and biology, was not such as fitted him for dealing with the general question of Evolution, and he had consequently laid himself open in fatal ways.

The absence of a rejoinder from him was, I believe, caused by an illness from which he did not recover till the matter had drifted by. Otherwise I dare say he would have attempted a defence. A capable man can always find something to say; and the majority of readers, never referring back to see whether the main points have been dealt with, accept what he says as adequate. "Oh, that has been answered," is the subsequent remark; and the answer is assumed to be, as a matter of course, a sufficient answer.

Such small incidents as the remainder of 1872 brought, have been already narrated in the last chapter, which this chapter in part overlaps. There do not occur in letters any passages worth quoting until the beginning of 1873. The first of them, dated 8th February, runs thus:—

"It turns out to have been in all respects a lucky thing that I yielded to your pressure, and undertook to write this *Study of Sociology.* The successive chapters in the *Contemporary* are having a great effect on the sale of my books. Strange to say, I am getting quite popular with women."

The second of them bears date the 7th March, and is as follows:—

"Tyndall was saying last night at the X that religious liberality is now greater here than with you. And many facts imply it. While, as you tell me, your papers are shrinking from saying anything about the chapter on the *Educational Bias,* here it has met with more open approval than any. An extremely astonishing illustration of the rapid theological thaw, you will find in the copy of the *Nonconformist* I send by this post, or the next. In a review of a late metaphysical book—Graham's Idealism—you will find a passage expressing sympathy with the doctrine of the Unknowable, as probably the theology of the future. Think of that for the leading organ of the Dissenters!"

Doubtless the theological liberalization was then, and is still, progressing at an unexpected rate; but it is accompanied by great energy and activity in upholding and propagating the old beliefs. Though in many circles it is now possible to say, without producing great astonishment, all that one thinks, I hear of other circles in which the reactionary feeling is carried so far that even ordinary liberality is inadmissible. I do not regret this. The change is quite as rapid as is desirable—perhaps even more rapid than is safe.

Another two months brought me a serious deprivation. An intimacy which had, within a few preceding years, become well established, and from which I expected pleasure and profit during years to come, was suddenly brought to an end. On May 10, 1873, there came from Avignon the news of the death of John Stuart Mill the day before. Erysipelas, consequent apparently upon a little over-exertion and exposure, carried him off quite suddenly, while yet he was still active in body and mind.

During a considerable period his had been the one conspicuous figure in the higher regions of thought. So great, indeed, was his influence that during the interval between, say 1840 and 1860, few dared to call his views in question. Beyond the intrinsic causes for this predominance there were two extrinsic causes. The time was one in which the deductive method had fallen into such disrepute, that in the concrete sciences nothing beyond the accumulation and colligation of facts was tolerated. Hence the *System of Logic,* which, though it did not ignore deductive reasoning, was mainly occupied with the methods of inductive reasoning, served as an authoritative embodiment and justification of the beliefs and practices of most cultivated men. The time was also one in which the Free-trade agitation had imparted to politico-economical discussions an interest much greater than they ever had before. This, of course, gave to his work on Political Economy, which furnished weapons to the Free-traders, an unusual currency. A yet further cause possibly was that the Experiential Philosophy, of which he was the leading exponent, did not, at that time, meet with much criticism from the Transcendentalists, who have since become active antagonists.

To the extent of attending some meetings, I had taken a small part in his election as Member of Parliament for Westminster: being desirous that his views should find expression in the House of Commons. There was, I suspect, on my part and on the part of others, too high an expectation of the results. One who has produced by his books a strong impersonal impression rarely produces a personal impression to correspond. The faculties which have caused his superiority as a writer are not, in all cases, accompanied by the faculties which give superiority in personal intercourse or in debate; and this is especially the case when he has to address those with whom he is so little in sympathy as Mill was with the humdrum rank and file of our legislators. When, on a subsequent election, he lost his seat, I happened, while writing to him on some other matter, to express my belief that on the whole he was better out of the House of Commons than in it; and he replied that he was inclined to think so himself.

Had he lived longer there would doubtless have been, beyond further writings of importance, further efforts to advance social welfare; for Mill was not content to do this by word only: he sought to do it by deed also. I wish some one would compare him as a typical utilitarian with Carlyle as a typical anti-utilitarian. As measured, alike by his domestic relations and his public activities, the utilitarian would have much the best of the comparison; and his conduct as husband and citizen would constitute a sarcastic comment on his competitor's denunciations of his ethical creed.

In a letter to Youmans, dated 16th May, I find the passage:—" In a day or two I shall send you a copy of the *Examiner*, in which, along with other accounts of John Mill's life and works, you will see something from me." In Appendix G, I have resuscitated this long-buried sketch.

If not about this time, then a year or two earlier, I was compelled to restrict the hindrances to work caused by correspondence. To do this I drew up a circular which I had lithographed, and copies of which I used in as many cases as possible. It ran as follows:—

"Mr. Herbert Spencer regrets that he must take measures for diminishing the amount of his correspondence.

Being prevented by his state of health from writing more than a short time daily, he progresses but slowly with the work he has undertaken, and his progress is made slower by absorption of his time in answering those who write to him. Letters inviting him to join Committees, to attend Meetings, or otherwise to further some public object; letters requesting interviews and autographs; letters asking opinions and explanations—these, together with acknowledgments of presentation copies of books, entail hindrances which, though trivial individually, are collectively serious—serious, at least, to one whose hours of work are so narrowly limited.

As these hindrances increase Mr. Spencer is compelled to do something to prevent them. After long hesitation he has decided to cut himself off from every engagement that is likely to occupy attention, however slight, and to decline all correspondence not involved by his immediate work.

To explain the absence of a special reply to each communication, he sends this lithographed general reply, and he hopes that the reasons given will sufficiently excuse him for not answering in a more direct way the letter of Mr. ——."

The mention of correspondence which had to be thus abridged, reminds me that from time to time I received letters of startling kinds—now vituperating me for my opinions and now going to extremes of laudation. A few have been astonishing, and even amusing, as exhibitions of vanity. One of these seems worth reproducing here. I suppress not the name only, but the place and date, lest the writer should be identified.

" Dear Sir,—As the head of my own school of thought and effort, I take the liberty of forwarding you for publication or any other use you think desirable, three copies of a paper read by myself before the Philosophical Society here on the 11th inst. You will see its nature by its title: " The Theory of Gravitation ", " The Neb. Hypothesis ", the " Tidal theory of Evolution and the Dynamics of Elliptic motion," all stand disproved.

The apparatus was too cumbersome to forward, but I think there will be no difficulty in constructing another: should you consider that I should be at the expense myself, I am willing to be so. For my trustworthiness I can refer you to . . . . but I do not think you will consider references necessary.

I am not by any means monied; a few hundreds, (some six or so) recently inherited, being the sum of my possessions. Between an inebriate father, and dyspepsia, and neglect, and want of opportunities at home, plus hard work, poverty, religious and sexual troubles out here, my life has not been altogether sunshine.

I am now an atheist of a fairly contented mind, but resolved, (for no selfish reasons) that for every inch I have been thrust down, I will go up a mile.

I am only fairly read, but have a good grasp of the Universe that is daily improving. I have also a pretty good knowledge of the world; and having seen some vicissitudes and mixed with some variety of men, and foreigners, and travellers, though comparatively untravelled myself, I have few prejudices and an enlarged understanding. I must ask your pardon for thus introducing myself, but I know you will grant it when I tell you that I have labored most diligently these last four or five years entirely with the object of benefiting my fellow-man—though the practical turns one sometimes takes, make one feel as if laboring for an undeserving and unworthy being. . . . . .

In my endeavours to win for myself a name, I have made sallies into military, political (have written a little) and other matters where I thought my powers of origination would serve me. I believe if I had means and appliances I could bring aerial navigation and one or two useful inventions to useful issue. I have been a hard thinker for seven or eight years, and have not been young since 16 years of age,—when I became dyspeptic.

I suppose if the Theory of Gravitation falls, some theologians will again plead for direct divine interference: their day is drawing to a close.

One object I had in view in making the investigation, was to silence the argument I have often heard and that has been used against myself in religious controversy, that the greatest scientist that ever was or ever would be, was a Christian! The hammer of the Iconoclast has fallen, and behold their fetish! I was once told that Newton "ought to be worshipped as a fetish"!

I will trespass on you no longer, but hoping you will derive pleasure and our cause will benefit by my work, and that I am not but asking an agreeable favor of you in entrusting my paper to your hands and pilotage,—Believe me, a worker for truth, and yours sincerely, —— ——."

Perhaps it will be thought that the writer was insane; but the photograph which he inclosed betrayed no mark of insanity, technically so called. He was insane only as being swayed by an enormously disproportionate self-esteem.

There needs a local meteorology which shall take account not only of the modifying effects which the surface of each considerable area produces on the weather, but also of the modifying effects produced by adjacent surfaces. The climate of a region is in no small degree determined by its position in relation to regions around, unlike in character. A striking illustration occurs in Strath Spey. Between it and the western seas lies a mountainous tract some 50 miles wide; and, coming over its chilly high lands, which form good condensers, the westerly winds deposit much of their contained water. Hence, when they reach Strath Spey, which is a broad open space, they have comparatively little water to deposit, and cease to send down rain. It results that there the westerly winds are not rainy winds, and the climate is comparatively dry.

Why do I make this remark here? Well, the reason is that this year, at the end of July, I made acquaintance with Strath Spey, and heard of its peculiarity. The daughters of my friend Potter, all of whom I had seen grow up from infancy, were now, several of them, mothers of families. The eldest had married Mr. Robert Holt of Liverpool, who rented the Dell of Abernethy and the extensive moor appended to it, which includes Cairn Gorm, one of the four peaks of the Grampians. Here I had been invited to visit them: one of the offered temptations being that the Spey, which borders part of the estate, affords good salmon-fishing. To fix the dates of my several visits, respecting which I was uncertain, Mrs. Holt has furnished me with some entries from their record; of which here is one dated 2nd August:—

"Mr. Spencer, Mr. Potter, and Robert, went to Advie by early train and after a pleasant, cloudy but fine day, returned with seven salmon and grilse."

Another entry, dated the 6th, has a little more interest. Some 8 or 10 miles from the Dell there is a loch containing an island on which exist the ruins of a castle, said to have been one of the strongholds of "The Wolf of Badenoch"—a name with which my acquaintance, now made, served me in future years as illustrating the genesis of certain superstitions. The entry referred to runs:—

"Drove over in two carriages to Loch an Eilan. Mr. Spencer, Kate, and Robert went by train to Aviemore and walked thence. The Martineaus joined us at lunch."

For the recovery of his health Mr. Martineau had taken a house near Aviemore, where he has since spent his summers. The recent passage of arms between us did not interfere with friendly intercourse during our picnic.

I had never seen anything of the East coast, and decided to return south by that route. A day was spent with Bain, who played the guide to Aberdeen and its surroundings. Thence I journeyed to Inveroran, where I followed my usual occupation for a short time only, as the dates imply; for I was in London again early in September.

Before I had got two-thirds through *The Study of Sociology*, I became conscious that, for more reasons than the one above named, it was well that I had undertaken to write it.

One reason of undeniable validity was that the accumulation of materials for the *Principles of Sociology*, which I was carrying on by proxy, though it had been progressing for four years, was not yet advanced far enough to meet with my requirements; and it became clear that a delay of a year and a half or so, before entering on this larger undertaking, would give me a better equipment.

Another reason disclosed itself. Sundry general considerations touching Sociology which I had seen would be needful as preliminaries to a scientific discussion, and which yet could not be included in the *Principles of Sociology*, or if prefixed would make it too voluminous, could now be treated of with advantage. There was furnished for them a fit place in the *Study of Sociology*, which stood in some sort as an introduction.

A further reason was that but few persons had any conception of a Social Science; and that the diffusion of such a conception would usefully precede the publication of the *Principles*. The possibility of Sociology was not only not conceived by historians, but when alleged was denied. Occupied as they had all along been in narrating the *events* in the lives of societies, they had paid little or no attention to the evolution of their organizations. If a biographer, seeing that the incidents of his hero's life did not admit of scientific prevision, therefore said that there is no science of Man, ignoring all the phenomena of bodily formation and function; he would parallel the ordinary historian who, thinking of little else but the doings of kings, court-intrigues, international quarrels, victories and defeats, concerning all which no definite forecasts are possible, asserts that there is no social science: overlooking the mutually-dependent structures which have been quietly unfolding while the transactions he writes about have been taking place. The mere fact that during all these centuries he, in common with his readers, has been in nearly every case unconscious of that increasing division of labour which characterizes social evolution everywhere, shows how much need there was to explain the scope and nature of the social science.

A still more cogent reason presently became manifest to me. While describing and illustrating the various forms of bias which a student of Sociology must guard against, I became conscious that I myself needed the warnings I was giving. The result was that, while retaining my social ideals, I gained a greater readiness to recognize the relative goodness of forms which have passed away, and a greater preparedness for looking at the various factors of social development in an unprejudiced manner. Without losing my aversion to certain barbaric institutions, sentiments, and beliefs, considered in the abstract, I became more impressed with the necessity of contemplating them calmly, as having been in their times and places the best that were possible, and as unavoidably to be passed through in the course of social evolution.

The last chapter of *The Study of Sociology* was published in the *Contemporary* on the 1st October, and the volume was issued on the 1st November. Respecting its reception I remember nothing; and all I find in correspondence about it is the second paragraph of the following extract from a letter dated 2nd December, 1873:—

"Mr. Gladstone, a little nettled, I suppose, by my criticism upon him as a type of the anti-scientific public, has published an explanatory letter in this month's *Contemporary*. I am appending his letter to the end of the volume, with some comments. I will send you a proof in a few days.

Inclosed is a notice of the *Study* from this week's *Saturday Review*, quite sympathetic in tone. If the reviewer is right, you will see that you have a good deal to answer for in tempting me to misemploy my time! However, I think the book is desirable, as preparing the way for what is to come. Moreover, had it not been for the large returns it has brought me, I should have been unable to go on with the *Descriptive Sociology*."

The closing sentence of this extract prompts me to remark that *The Study of Sociology* has been, pecuniarily considered, unusually successful for a book of its kind. When, to the sums received from England and America for the separate chapters as they appeared serially, there are added the sums since received as royalties on the successive editions of the volume, the amount reaches between £1300 and £1400; and, as editions are still called for with tolerable regularity, I suppose the total will eventually be £1500 or more. For a five-shilling book on a grave subject, such a result was hardly to be expected. A further amount, indirectly accruing, has to be named. As already intimated, the publication of the chapters in the *Contemporary Review* greatly increased the demand for my books; and the increased demand proved to be a permanent one.

Referring back to the first paragraph of the above extract, I may say here that this brief controversy between Mr. Gladstone and myself led to a private correspondence which ended quite amicably, and established between us social relations of a pleasant kind.

CHAPTER XLVI.

SOME MINOR INCIDENTS.

1873. ÆT. 53.

ESSAYS from time to time published after the issue of the second series of *Essays* in 1864, had now become sufficiently numerous to fill another volume. Written, like preceding ones, not about matters of temporary interest, and originally designed to have eventually a permanent form, these essays I now decided to re-publish. Not unfrequently one who thus reproduces articles contributed to periodicals is reprobated; but I suppose that in my case sufficient justification has been yielded by the demand for successive editions of this volume, as of the preceding volumes.

Partly because I wished to include it in this third series of essays, and partly because the interval between the ending of the *Study of Sociology* and the commencement of the *Principles of Sociology* afforded a convenient opportunity, I devoted myself, after my return to town, to an episodic work which I had long contemplated. This was a piece of polemical writing, which, after so many years occupied almost exclusively in producing books of a purely expository kind, I entered upon with some zest. As the reader has probably already inferred, argumentative contests are not wholly disagreeable to me.

Since the publication of *First Principles* in 1862, nu-

SOME MINOR INCIDENTS

merous criticisms of that work and of subsequent works had from time to time appeared: most of them not worthy of notice; either because of their triviality or because they were anonymous or by writers of no mark. But there had been some which asked attention; either because of their seeming validity or because they came from men of acknowledged weight—the Rev. H. L. Mansel (afterwards Dean of St. Paul's), Principal Caird, the Rev. James Martineau, Mr. H. Sidgwick, Mr. Shadworth Hodgson. The objections raised by these I undertook to answer; and I published the answers in the November and December numbers of the *Fortnightly Review* under the title of "Replies to Criticisms".

This article, or rather these two articles, had an unexpected sequence, which entailed on me much trouble and some annoyance. Before they were out of hand there appeared two lengthy criticisms upon *First Principles* and other books of mine—one in the *Quarterly Review* and the other in the *British Quarterly Review*. The first of these, though partly dissentient, was civil in manner and not unappreciative; but the second, making much of some small flaws which did not in the least affect the general conclusions, was written with evident animosity and in an intemperate manner. Under ordinary circumstances I should have let both pass without remark; but, as I was then publishing replies to criticisms, I could not well keep silence respecting these without making the tacit admission that the objections they urged were valid. I therefore added some pages dealing with them—with the first briefly and with the second at greater length.

In the next number of the *British Quarterly Review* there appeared a rejoinder from my critic (a senior wrangler, as it turned out) in which he sought to justify his assertions. As some of these, touching the natures of our mathematico-physical cognitions, tacitly called in question the philosophical method pursued by me, I thought it needful to go further into the matter: defending my own positions and making assaults on those of the reviewer. The result was the publication of a pamphlet which I distributed widely among leading men in the scientific world.

This pamphlet, which was issued early in 1874, would, I supposed, end the matter; but it did not. It initiated a controversy in the pages of *Nature* (chiefly concerning the bases of the mechanical axioms), into which other combatants rushed; and, broadening out as all controversies do, this continued during the spring. As left standing in *Nature*, the results were unsatisfactory. Determined as I was that the main question, obscured in the dust raised, should not be lost sight of, I drew up a second pamphlet, consisting chiefly of the letters published in *Nature* with explanatory notes, and ending with a summary of the results: pointing out that my several theses, which I prefixed to the summary, remained outstanding. Of this pamphlet, too, I sent copies to numerous competent men who might feel interested. The final result was not unsatisfactory; as witness the second paragraph of the following extract from a letter to Youmans.

"On Tuesday I had a little dinner to bring together the publishers and the Committee of the International Series. The Kings and the Appletons seemed on very friendly terms —there was no sign of any misunderstanding, as you seemed to imply.

Last night Hirst gave me the satisfactory information that

SOME MINOR INCIDENTS

Cayley, who is A1 among mathematicians, entirely agrees with me in the controversy with M——, and thought M—— deserved all he got."

As I had also the suffrages of Prof. Sylvester (who, if Prof. Cayley is A1 among mathematicians, may be distinguished as A2) as well as of Prof. Tyndall and Dr. Hirst (the last of whom was at that time president of the Mathematical Society), I was content with the result.

Another incident, dating back to this time, I should probably have omitted had I not been reminded of it by the following note from Mr. Edward Miall; whom I have, in some of the earlier chapters, referred to as proprietor and editor of the *Nonconformist*, and originator of the Anti-State-Church movement. Dated Oct. 29, 1873, the note runs:—

"On Friday next, at three o'clock p.m. I will hope to meet you and Mr. Morley, to whom I have written, for some preliminary conversation on the question of Disendowment."

At that time it seemed not impossible that the question of disestablishment might suddenly come to the front, in the form of a proposal for separating the Church from the State, and assigning to it all the property it now holds in trust; and that those who were opposed to any scheme of the kind might find themselves taken unawares unless they were ready with specific plans for disendowment. Already Mr. Miall and I had talked over the matter; and I had spoken to Mr. John Morley and Mr. Frederic Harrison. The meeting took place as arranged, and a general understanding was come to. It was thought that it would be a fit division of labour if the agitation for disestablishment on religious grounds were left to dissenters, while those who regarded the matter mainly as a secular one should deal with the disendowment problem. Respecting the measures to be proposed, too, common views were arrived at. It was agreed that disendowment should be effected by the dying out of life-interests in the mass of cases; by the compensation of lay patrons; by the making over of parish churches to parishioners, to be used at their discretion for religious purposes; and, after the satisfaction of all equitable claims, by the appropriation of the remaining funds towards the liquidation of the National Debt. And it was also agreed that the property which has accrued to the Church from voluntary sources since the Reformation, should be dealt with by the State exclusively in its judicial capacity; that is to say, the State should, in each case, decide in what way the property should be settled so as best to fulfil the intentions of the donors.

Some little time afterwards we had a dinner at the Westminster Palace Hotel, to which, besides those already named, there came sundry others interested in the matter; among whom, I remember, was Mr. Joseph Chamberlain, at that time known only as a Birmingham notable. It was decided that a draft Bill should be prepared, embodying in specific shapes something like the general proposals above indicated. This was done; and I suppose this draft Bill somewhere exists in a state—I was going to say, of suspended animation; but, as it was never born, the phrase would be inapplicable.

What happened subsequently I do not remember.

CHAPTER XLVII.

THE *DESCRIPTIVE SOCIOLOGY.*

1867—74. ÆT. 47—54.

In the last chapter but one I had to make an overlap in the narrative, and here I have to make a double overlap. For not only while there were occurring the incidents set down in many preceding chapters, but also while there were occurring those set down in the chapter described as an overlap, there was being carried on an undertaking, the progress of which I could not continually refer to without confusing the accounts of doings which mainly occupied me.

In Chapter XLI I briefly described certain preparations, then commenced, for the *Principles of Sociology:* saying how I had arranged to have collected for me, and put in fitly classified groups and tables, facts of all kinds, presented by numerous races, which illustrate social evolution under its various aspects. Though this classified compilation of materials was entered upon solely to facilitate my own work, yet, after having brought the mode of classification to a satisfactory form, and after having had some of the tables filled up, I decided to have the scheme executed with a view to publication: the facts being so presented, apart from hypotheses, as to aid all students of Social Science in testing such conclusions as they have drawn and in drawing others.

This undertaking, commenced at the close of 1867, had been quietly progressing from that time to the time now reached—1874. The chief occurrences connected with the prosecution of it down to the latter date, must here be set down.

The loss of Mr. Duncan's services was followed by a considerable interval during which the work stood still: no successor being discoverable. As already shown by an extract from a letter dated 9 March 1870, I sought for aid in the United States as well as in Great Britain. A passage preceding the one quoted, which I had reserved for use here, runs as follows:—

"The accounts of the uncivilized races have been in a great measure digested, and the facts they present duly arranged; and Mr. Duncan will, I hope, be able to complete them within a moderate period after he reaches India. We have agreed, too, that he shall, while in India, carry on the second part of the work, dealing with the extinct and decayed historic races. But I see that it will be needful, with a view to the completion of the undertaking in such time as to render it available for me, that the modern historic races should be undertaken by some one else."

Of course the required qualifications, which were high, excluded the mass of applicants. At length there came to me, on recommendation, a young Scotchman, clerical by education and ambition, but who was, I suspect, "a stickit minister." He had not abandoned his ambition, however; for I afterwards learned that during his engagement with me he occasionally preached: an anomalous combination of functions. He was a dull fellow. So wanting in ability to do anything requiring more than mechanical intelligence did he prove, that I had shortly to dismiss him.

And here I seize the occasion for expressing my belief that not only does education, as at present carried on, fail to increase the power of independent thought, in those who have little, but it tends to diminish such power of independent thought as they naturally have. Of sundry instances which have fallen under my observation, I will name only the most striking—that of a University graduate who had recently taken his degree with honours, though not high ones. Along with the knowledge thus implied there went almost incredible ignorance. He asked me whether the disappearance of a distant vessel at sea was due to failure of vision, or whether, as some said, it was consequent on the curvature of the Earth. On a reference being made to the increase of the population in England, he proved to be unaware of the fact that our population is increasing. He spoke of the gizzard of a dog; and was surprised on being told that mammals have no gizzards. But the most astonishing example disclosed itself the moment he began to write to my dictation. He did not know that the commencement of a paragraph is invariably shown by the setting back of the initial word! He began the first line of each paragraph level with the other lines; and, until I explained it to him, did not see that when the preceding paragraph happens to fill out completely its last line, a new paragraph cannot be marked at all unless its first word is thus set back. Here was one who, during his school career and college career, had been daily occupied with books for many hours, and who was so unobservant that he had never remarked this uniform trait in them; much less had perceived how such a trait arises!

Everybody nowadays hears of the mischiefs of "cram"; and yet insistence upon them seems to produce no effect whatever. Though it has become manifest that the accumulation of knowledge in excess of power to use it, is not only no aid to efficiency, but is an impediment to efficiency; yet the quantity of knowledge accumulated continues to be used as the measure of efficiency. In pursuance of the law-established conceptions of education the system has practically become unalterable; and the minds of the young, overburdened with useless knowledge, will presently exhibit the effects of measures which might fitly be called measures for the increase of stupidity.

It was not until after many months had passed that I succeeded in finding, in the person of Mr. James Collier, a capable successor to Mr. Duncan. Educated partly at St. Andrews and partly at Edinburgh, Mr. Collier, though he had not taken his degree, possessed in full measure the qualifications requisite for the compilation and tabulation of the *Descriptive Sociology;* and the third division of the work, dealing with the existing civilized races, progressed satisfactorily in his hands.

Thereafter, correspondence yields no trace of the progress of the work until 27 April 1871, when I find in a letter to Youmans the following passage:—

" In so far as immediate personal results are concerned, this [product of American sales of my books] is a matter of comparative indifference to me. Now, and for the future, the realization of profits interests me mainly as facilitating this large expensive undertaking which, as you know, I am having carried on by proxy; partly with a view to the facilitation of my own work when I come to the Sociological division of it, but still more with a view to wide and permanent use. It is now nearly a year since the printing of the first volume (that is, the preparation of the stereotype-moulds) was commenced. On a rough estimate, something like £600 will have to be laid out before any returns can begin to come in; and the rate at which the work can be carried on, is limited by the rate at which the surplus returns from the sale of my books enable me to pay printers' bills. With a view to more rapid progress with this work, I am therefore interested in the advance of the American sales."

Evidently the prosecution of the scheme, irrespective of the immediate needs of my own work, had come to interest me greatly.

The undertaking had now so far advanced that the tables embodying the classified facts presented by some of the uncivilized societies, were in type; and when my friend Youmans came over in July 1871, he saw a number of the proofs. Unlike those who have not dropped their educational blinkers, he was in all cases quick to recognize things lying off the beaten track, and to see their relative importance. It became at once manifest to him that exhibiting sociological phenomena in such wise that comparisons of them in their coexistences and sequences, as occurring among various peoples in different stages, were made easy, would immensely facilitate the discovery of sociological truths. To have before us, in manageable form, evidence proving the correlations which everywhere exist between great militant activity and the degradation of women, between a despotic form of government and elaborate ceremonial in social intercourse, between relatively peaceful social activities and the relaxation of coercive institutions, promises furtherance of human welfare in a much greater degree than does learning whether the story of Alfred and the cakes is a fact or a myth, whether Queen Elizabeth intrigued with Essex or not, where Prince Charles hid himself, and what were the details of this battle or the other siege —pieces of historical gossip which cannot in the least affect men's conceptions of the ways in which social phenomena hang together, or aid them in shaping their public conduct. Without recognizing such sociological correlations as those just instanced, which, indeed, at that time did not "jump to the eyes," as they did when a large number of tables had been prepared, my friend anticipated much help in rationalizing men's conceptions of civilization and guiding their actions in politics.

It resulted that he became anxious to have the undertaking pushed forward with greater rapidity. The first division, dealing with the uncivilized races, was in progress; as was also the third division, dealing with the existing civilized races; but nothing had been done, or was about to be done, towards executing the second division, dealing with the extinct and decayed civilized races. On learning this he urged me to put this division also in hand. I explained that already my resources were taxed to the uttermost by payments for compilation and printing, and that more rapid progress was impossible. Eager to have useful things done, as he always was, he presently made me a remarkable proposal. If I would superintend the execution of the second division, he undertook, on behalf of the Americans, that they would furnish funds for paying the compiler and the printer. In what way I received this proposal I cannot remember. Indeed, until correspondence recalled it to me, I had forgotten it. Evidently, however, as shown by subsequent occurrences, I finally assented. For when, after making arrangements with M. Baillière for the publication of the "International Scientific Series" in France, we parted, I for home and he for Germany, it was with the understanding that he should advertise in German newspapers for a fit compiler.

In most cases the answers to advertisements are anything but satisfactory. Ordinarily there come many blanks and no prize; but in this case there came one prize and no blanks. The solitary respondent was Dr. Richard Scheppig, at that time a teacher at Hoffwill school. He accepted the engagement, and joined me at the end of the year. Writing to Youmans on Feb. 2, 1872, I said of him:—" Scheppig is beginning to get into his work, and, as I gather, likes it. He seems to me a clear-headed fellow, and is, I think, likely to succeed." This expectation was fully verified. He turned out to be admirably adapted for the work he had undertaken.

The financial arrangement made with Youmans, however, was not carried out. Mis-statements which had become current in America respecting the continuance of my work, which was represented as having been made possible exclusively by the American testimonial, increased the reluctance I originally felt. The following letter refers to the erroneous impressions that prevailed and to the course consequently taken by me. It is dated 4 May, 1872.

" I heard lately of certain absurd statements that are current in America respecting the aid rendered to me by Americans, and the difficulties from which I was rescued by them. The copy of the *New York Evening Mail* of April 15, which I received from you this morning, serves indirectly to verify the report that had reached me respecting these statements; since it makes statements, nearly akin to them, that are no less erroneous.

It is needful, that this propagation of misconceptions

should be checked. I at first thought, on reading the article, of writing a letter myself to the *New York Evening Mail* on the matter. But on second thoughts I see that the statement will come better from you. Inclosed I give you an outline of the facts, sufficient to dissipate the erroneous beliefs that have been spread among you, and are likely to become exaggerated as well as confirmed if they pass uncontradicted. . . .

Under the circumstances I must cancel the arrangement made with regard to the payment of Scheppig, and the American publication of the second division of the *Descriptive Sociology*. I see that whatever precaution may be taken it is sure to be misapprehended and mis-stated. I see that I shall be able to pay Scheppig myself—especially now that the proceeds of these sociological articles have come to help."

Writing on the 10th August, I said:—" Your letter was just the thing needed, and the circulation of it through the *Tribune* will be quite sufficient." Most of the facts contained in this letter are already known to the reader; but as there are joined with them some not before stated, I have decided to reproduce it in Appendix H.

The work proceeded without incident until the succeeding midsummer, when a letter of July 31, 1873, says:—" The first number of *Descriptive Sociology* was published yesterday." On the 27th September, time having been given to contemplate my position, I sent my friend a discouraging report:—

" I have just been going through my bills, and I find that this first number has cost me for the—

Composition, Correction, Stereotyping, Duplicate Plates and Printing One Thousand Copies £351 15 10
Cost of authorship [*i.e.* payments to compiler].. 296 7 2

£648 3 0

You will see at once that to reimburse myself for this large outlay (which would reach £700 were I to add loss of interest) will require either an extensive sale or a pretty high rate of profit on a small sale; and I see little chance of being able to go on with such returns from America as even your last letter seems to imply." . . .

"I am quite content to give my labour for nothing. I am content even to lose something by unrepaid costs of authorship. But it is clear that I shall not be able to bear the loss that now appears likely. In addition to the sum of £648 named above, I have already spent on the first division of Duncan, "Uncivilized Races," in printing and authorship, about £400; and on the second division about £280. So that you see I am more than £1300 out of pocket without getting a penny back. I must now, being in the middle of it, complete the first part of the "Extinct Civilized Races" and the first part of the "Savage Races," by which time I shall have laid out more than £2000. It will then be time to stop; for, as I now infer, there is but little probability of getting a return that will approximately meet my outlay."

At the close of the subsequent March, I find a passage implying further discouragement:—

"No. 2 of the *Des. Soc.* is out, and I have ordered a copy to be sent to you. It will be a very valuable instalment for all people sufficiently rational to appreciate it; of which, however, there are unfortunately but few. The third volume of Forster's *Life of Dickens* sold 10,000 copies in ten days. The first part of *Descriptive Sociology* has been asked for by the public to the extent of not quite 200 copies in eight months."

It was thus becoming clear that I had greatly overestimated the amount of desire which existed in the public mind for social facts of an instructive kind. They greatly preferred those of an uninstructive kind.

My American friend had, I suppose, been naming to some of those likely to be interested, these adverse results, and the consequent probability that I should shortly bring the undertaking to a close; for, early in the autumn, he transmitted to me a letter from Mr. Edwin W. Bryant, an actuary of St. Louis, showing something more than ordinary sympathy. This letter, dated 27 June, setting out with remarks of a complimentary kind concerning the importance of the undertaking, went on to say:—

"But, leaving to you all this argument, to amplify, supplement, or suppress, as you may think best, I propose this: that we try to get £1000 (or more if we can) to send to Mr. Spencer, to be used by him as he chooses, in aid of the work —to pay for assistance, printing or whatever else there may be to pay for. Of this amount, you may count on me for one half—five hundred pounds—any time at call, and without reference to what you may get or fail to get from any one else."

This drew from me the following response in a letter dated 23 Sept. 1874:—

"Bryant's proposal is a very noble one, and the more noble because he is not, I suppose, a man of very extensive means. I suspected that there was behind the question in your previous letter, some scheme of the kind; as I concluded that it was not likely to come from the Appletons.

While fully appreciating the feeling with which Mr. Bryant's proposal is made, and that which has previously prompted others to offer to bear part of the expenses, I still cannot yield to such an arrangement as that proposed. There is, however, a plan which it occurs to me might possibly be practicable, and which would, I think, serve the several ends aimed at, in an unobjectionable way. Mr. Bryant and other Americans, while anxious to insure the continuance of the *Descriptive Sociology,* are also anxious that local institutions should have copies. Both ends would be subserved if they were to purchase from me, and were to distribute to these institutions; and this arrangement might be made in such a way as to divide the advantages. It would yield me an ample return were I to supply copies at half the retail price. Instead of absolutely giving copies to American libraries, schools, &c., my American friends might offer them to such buyers at, say, 1-3rd the retail price. In this case they would themselves have to lose on each copy only 1-6th of the retail price; and thus a moderate sum would go a long way. Even if they offered copies to these institutions at 1-4th the retail price, themselves paying the other 1-4th the distribution of, say, 300 copies, would go far towards covering the printing expenses, and would leave the English sales to do something towards returning cost of authorship [*i.e.* payments to compilers]."

Three weeks later, however, I wrote withdrawing this qualified assent, as follows:—

"After several times thinking over again the reply I made in my last to the generous proposal made by Mr. Bryant, I have decided to decline even that modified mode of aid which I described as one that might perhaps be adopted. On considering my accounts and probable resources, I conclude that the amount of loss entailed on me will not be greater than I can bear. Manifestly, the undertaking will become easier as it goes on; since, besides the proceeds of my books at large, which seem likely to go on increasing, I shall have the proceeds from the *Descriptive Sociology* itself, which, inadequate as they may be, will go some way towards defraying the cost of each succeeding number. As I have been able to meet the expenditure up to the present time (for I have now settled my printer's account) I may fairly calculate upon being able to do so in future—especially as the parts are not likely to be issued so near together as the two in last half year. Concluding, thus, that I shall be able to do the work myself by devoting to it such part of my income as remains after defraying personal expenses, I prefer to do this. I have no motive for accumulating."

Nothing further passed; and thus ended all plans for lightening the burden I had taken upon myself.

A foregoing extract, dated 27th Sept. 1873, intimates my intention of stopping as soon as I had printed and published the first part of the " Extinct Civilized Races " and the first part of the " Savage Races." This intention, however, I abandoned for more reasons than one.

The understanding in pursuance of which the compilers were working, stood in the way of so prompt a cessation. To each of them I had given a double incentive beyond the direct payment for work done which he received. One was the publication of his name as compiler and abstracter, and consequent obtainment of credit for such skill and labour as were implied. The other was a promise that, as soon as the sales repaid me for printing expenses, I would give him half the net returns, without waiting to repay myself for the cost of compilation. This undertaking I felt bound to carry out in respect not only of those parts which were completed or far advanced, but also in respect of those which were commenced. Of the " Uncivilized Races," compiled by Prof. Duncan, such parts as were not wholly or partially through the press were in manuscript. Dr. Scheppig had already made considerable progress with the " Hebrews and Phœnicians." And Mr. Collier had been for some time at work on the " French." To have stopped at the point above named would, of course, have been to break, if not wholly still in part, the engagement I had made; so that I was obliged to continue.

A further reason for continuing was that if I did not do so, a large amount of collected, classified, and digested information, extremely valuable to the sociological student, would be thrown away. That I was leaving in a useless state the products of years of labour, would have been a thought scarcely tolerable to me. I should have been restive under the consciousness of what would have seemed a serious loss to social science.

Thus I found myself committed to more than I at first foresaw. I accepted the situation; and, disastrous as was the undertaking pecuniarily considered, I persisted in it through the seven following years.

PART X.

XLVIII. A Retrospective Glance.
XLIX. Vol. I of the *Sociology*.
L. A Series of Articles.
LI. *The Data of Ethics*.
LII. *Ceremonial Institutions*.

CHAPTER XLVIII.

A RETROSPECTIVE GLANCE.

1874. ÆT. 54.

BEFORE saying anything about my next book, or rather about my life during the time it was in hand, it will be well to look back from this advanced stage of my undertaking to the earlier stages. This retrospective glance discloses a certain trait not hitherto named.

For now I had come round a second time to the topic with which I commenced my career as a writer; after having made, first a narrower, and then a wider, circuit of exploration. In 1842, while but two and twenty, the predominant interest I displayed, apart from interests in subjects bearing on civil engineering, was an interest in the politico-ethical question—" What are the duties of the State, and what are not its duties". There resulted the letters, and subsequently the pamphlet, on *The Proper Sphere of Government*. In the interval between 1842 and 1848, a consciousness that the conceptions set forth in this pamphlet were crude and incomplete, prompted me to enter on new fields of thought and inquiry. Various readings in politics and ethics, joined with some excursions into biology and psychology, gave to these conceptions more developed forms and more satisfactory foundations. A desire to set forth the ethical principles reached, and the derived conclusions respecting the right limits of governmental action, led, in 1848, to the commencement of *Social Statics*. At the close of 1850 the results of this widened range of inquiry, as embodied in that work, were published: the completion of the first circuit having brought me round, in the latter chapters, to my original topic.

In the subsequent seven years, less from intention than from unconscious proclivity, this process was repeated. Not only subjects nearly allied to the politico-ethical, but also subjects remotely allied to it, occupied my attention and were dealt with in various essays. This extension of the range of inquiry, leading to more general conclusions, ended in those most general conclusions set forth in the programme of the Synthetic Philosophy, written out in the first days of 1858. In this the doctrines concerning social organization, and after them the ethical doctrines, were, by their positions in the series of volumes described, represented as the outcome of the doctrines included in the volumes on Biology and Psychology, as well as of those included in *First Principles*. That is to say, the politico-ethical conclusions held, had come to form the terminal part of a system the earlier parts of which prepared the way for it. From that date, 1858, down to the time now arrived at, the years had been spent in writing the volumes in which the simpler sciences, forming the true bases of the most complex sciences, were dealt with. At length, in 1874, the second circuit, immensely wider than the first, had been traversed; and I had come round once more, not immediately to the topic with which I set out, but to the science of Sociology at large, which eventually rises to this topic.

Beyond this long and elaborate preparation, which, at

first pursued without conscious reference to an end, was, during the preceding 16 years, consciously pursued with such reference, there had been a preparation not contemplated. The *Descriptive Sociology* had been for seven years in progress; making me gradually acquainted with more numerous and varied groups of social phenomena, disclosing truths of unexpected kinds, and occasionally obliging me to abandon some of my pre-conceptions. And then, lastly, I had been incidentally led into writing a book which, ostensibly for the instruction of others, served at the same time for self-instruction—*The Study of Sociology*. In setting forth the difficulties to be encountered and the varieties of bias to be guarded against, I became myself better disciplined for the task I was about to undertake.

This second recommencement, forming a new departure in my work, seems to call for some definite division in the narrative; and I have therefore thought it well here to commence Part X.

CHAPTER XLIX.

VOL. I. OF THE *SOCIOLOGY*.

1874—77. ÆT. 54—57.

WITH the entry on this new division of my work, the marshalling of evidence became a much more extensive and complicated business than it had hitherto been. The facts, so multitudinous in their numbers, so different in their kinds, so varied in their sources, formed a heterogeneous aggregate difficult to bring into the clear and effective order required for carrying on an argument; so that I felt much as might a general of division who had become commander-in-chief; or rather, as one who had to undertake this highest function in addition to the lower functions of all his subordinates of the first, second and third grades. Only by deliberate method persistently followed, was it possible to avoid confusion. A few words may fitly be said here concerning my materials, and the ways in which I dealt with them.

During the five and twenty preceding years there had been in course of accumulation, extracts and memoranda from time to time made. My reading, though not extensive, and though chiefly devoted to the subjects which occupied me during this long interval, frequently brought under my eyes noteworthy facts bearing on this or that division of Sociology. These, along with the suggested ideas, were jotted down and put away. The resulting mass of manuscript materials remained for years unclassified; but every now and then I took out the contents of the drawer which received these miscellaneous contributions and put them in some degree of order—grouping together the ecclesiastical, the political, the industrial &c.; so that, by the time I began to build, there had been formed several considerable heaps of undressed stones and bricks.

But now I had to utilize the relatively large masses of materials gathered together in the *Descriptive Sociology*. For economization of labour, it was needful still further to classify these; and to save time, as well as to avoid errors in re-transcription, my habit was, with such parts of the work as were printed, to cut up two copies. Suppose the general topic to be dealt with was " Primitive Ideas." Then the process was that of reading through all the groups of extracts concerning the uncivilized and semi-civilized races under the head of " Superstitions," as well as those under other heads that were likely to contain allied evidence—" Knowledge", " Ecclesiastical " &c. As I read I marked each statement that had any significant bearing; and these marked statements were cut out by my secretary after he had supplied any references which excision would destroy. The large heap resulting was joined with the kindred heap of materials previously accumulated; and there now came the business of re-classifying them all in preparation for writing. During a considerable preceding period the subdivisions of the topic of " Primitive Ideas " had been thought about; and various heads of chapters had been settled—" Ideas of Sleep and Dreams," " Ideas of Death and Resurrection," " Ideas of Another Life," " Ideas of Another World" &c. &c. Taking a number of sheets of double foolscap, severally fitted to contain between their two leaves numerous memoranda, I placed these in a semi-circle on the floor round my chair: having indorsed each with the title of a chapter, and having arranged them in something like proper sequence. Then, putting before me the heap of extracts and memoranda, I assigned each as I read it to its appropriate chapter. Occasionally I came upon a fact which indicated to me the need for a chapter I had not thought of. An additional sheet for this was introduced, and other kindred facts were from time to time placed with this initial one. Several sittings were usually required to thus sort the entire heap. Mostly, too, as this process was gone through some time in advance of need, there came a repetition, or several repetitions, before the series of chapters had assumed its final order, and the materials had all been distributed.

When about to begin a chapter, I made a further rough classification. On a small table before me I had a large rude desk—a hinged board, covered with green baize, which was capable of being inclined at different angles by a moveable prop behind. Here I grouped the collected materials appropriated to the successive sections of the chapter; and those which were to be contained in each section were put into the most convenient sequence. Then, as I dictated, I from time to time handed to my secretary an extract to be incorporated.

Concerning the start made with this division of my work, the only information I have is contained in the following extract dated 5 March 1874:—

"But for various minor bothers, and chiefly these replies to criticisms, I should have been by this time pretty far advanced with the first number of the *Principles of Sociology*. As it is, about 50 pp. of MS. are ready; and I shall give the first two chapters to the printer immediately. . .

I received this morning from the Prof. of Philosophy at Messina, a proposal to translate my books into Italian in conjunction with his brother. He seems a fit translator, and I have assented. . .

I suppose I shall hear of the Appletons soon after their arrival. I must ask them to meet Huxley, Tyndall and King at dinner. To night I expect to meet President Eliot of Harvard, who is coming to dine at the X."

Respecting the second of the foregoing paragraphs, I may remark that the proposal to translate into Italian did not then take effect, because the translators were unable to find a publisher who would run the risk.

On turning over my papers I find that in 1874 I made an abortive attempt to keep a diary. I say abortive, because the entries, irregular while they continued, ceased altogether in March. The diary sets out with mention of the usual New Year's Day dinner at Huxley's: the joining in which, commenced in 1856, still continued. On Jan. 24 occurs the entry:—

"Went to the Burrs at Aldermaston. Met there Reeve of the *Edinburgh Rev.*, Lord Aberdare, Lord A. Russell, Miss Thackeray &c."

This was not the first, but the second or third, of my visits to Aldermaston Court, the seat of Mr. Higford Burr— or rather, one might almost say, of Mrs. Higford Burr; who took the lead and who habitually gathered together on such occasions circles of agreeable people. The place has attractive surroundings: notably the "Chase," which is said to date back to the time of Doomsday Book. On two occasions when I was there, visits were paid to

Silchester, an adjacent old Roman town of which the remains are very striking. It must have been nearly as large as Pompeii: the surrounding walls, which are still almost if not quite complete, showing its dimensions. After contemplating the uncovered basements of public buildings, baths &c., and seeing the entrance-steps deeply worn by passing feet, and noting, too, the remains of an amphitheatre, I conceived far more vividly than before the hold which Roman civilization had obtained in England.

While mentioning these visits into the country, I am reminded that Spottiswoode (one of our X Club) had, before this time, purchased Coombe Bank near Sevenoaks. Here I occasionally spent the time from Saturday to Monday: usually in company with others of our common friends. After his mathematics, Spottiswoode especially devoted himself to researches in electricity; and, as a natural consequence, he early made domestic use of electric lighting. I believe he was the first to have his dinner table lighted by the Swan-lamps.

I may here add the fact, recalled by letters of this date, that I avoided social gatherings of a public kind. The last public dinner I attended was in 1865; and several motives then prompted a resolution never to attend another. In pursuance of this resolve I invariably declined not only such dinners as those given in the City but more select dinners; even including those of the Royal Academy, which are, with good reason I believe, regarded as particularly enjoyable. Though not from deliberate resolution, I also fell into the habit of neglecting invitations to public *soirées*. Those of the Royal Academy were the only ones which I went to a few times during more than twenty years. Even when I decided to go, which occasionally happened, my intention melted away when the hour for dressing came.

In May of this year I was elected a member of the Committee of the Athenæum, and for a long subsequent period continued to take an active part in the administration of the Club. I say an active part, because I attended the committee-meetings with regularity. Save when I was away from town, I believe I missed only one, and then forgetfulness was the cause.

Certain traits of nature, made manifest to me by experiences of myself as a committee-man, I may here set down. The most conspicuous is want of tact. This is an inherited deficiency. The Spencers of the preceding generation were all characterized by lack of reticence. Things thought were habitually said; and there was little prudence in the expression of them. My mother was distinguished by extreme simple-mindedness: so much so that, unlike women in general, she was without the thought of policy in her dealings with other persons. In me these traits were united. I tended habitually to undisguised utterance of ideas and feelings: the results being that while I often excited opposition from not remembering what others were likely to feel, I, at the same time, disclosed my own intentions in cases where concealment of them was needful as a means to success.

On one occasion my attention was irresistibly drawn to this trait and its effects. Some proposal—I do not remember what—which I had made in committee, I had urged with my usual bluntness; with the result that those whose prejudices I had not duly respected, voted against me and the proposal was lost. A week or so afterwards, the late Sir Frederick Elliot, a man whose official life had disciplined him in cautiousness of expression, and who, judged by his manner, was also diplomatic by nature, brought forward substantially the same proposal; and, taking care not to tread upon anybody's toes, he carried it without difficulty. But though I recognized the lesson, it wrought, I fancy, little or no alteration. We say that experience teaches; but experience is practically powerless to change by its teaching any marked organic tendencies. Let me add that, though I sometimes failed in my aims from want of tact, I frequently succeeded by persistence.

The term of service on the committee is three years, and a rule provides that one who has served is not again eligible until after the lapse of a year. During the year which intervened between my two terms of service, I was one of a special committee appointed at the annual general meeting to investigate a matter respecting which the committee and the Club at large differed. Hence resulted the anomaly that I was concerned with Club-business for seven consecutive years.

While speaking of committees I may name the fact that I had been, for some time before this date, and for long afterwards continued to be, a member of the London Library committee. At this my attendances were far less regular: I suppose, in part, because the administrative business, neither so extensive nor so complex, attracted me less.

This autumn I made an observation that interested me much, as demonstrating a physical truth which is difficult to believe.

While I was at the Dell of Abernethy we had a picnic

on the shore of Loch Garten, some four or five miles off. This loch is from half a mile to a mile long, and perhaps a quarter of a mile broad. A breeze of moderate strength was blowing; so that, on the sandy beach next to us, there broke small waves, say of eighteen inches wide and three inches high. After our picnic we rowed towards the other end of the loch. As we approached it the waves diminished in size, gradually becoming ripples; and finally we came to still water. On arriving at this glassy surface I saw, to my great surprise, feeble undulations, discernible only by the aid of reflections, moving in a direction opposite to the wind. No other origin for these could be assigned than the recoil-waves from the sandy beach at the opposite end, which had persisted through all the intervening rough water, and finally made their reappearance in this remote smooth water. Many must have occasionally observed how, when a breaker bursts against a sea-wall, the recoil-wave rushes out seawards; and some have learned that this wave continues its progress out to sea, invisibly modifying the forms of the incoming waves, until at a great distance it is dissipated by fluid friction. Though theoretically accepted by me, this truth had been but vaguely conceived. Now it was brought home very clearly.

My stay at Ardtornish this year was abridged to little more than a fortnight; for I was due at Belfast on the 19th of August. The British Association met there. Tyndall was president; and I felt bound to be present. As on the occasion of the meeting at Liverpool, the members of the X Club, with their wives, made a family party at the chief hotel; and this of course gave an enjoyable character to our sojourn. Many will remember that Prof. Tyndall's address, dealing with those aspects of

Science which bring it into relation with Theology, was a very bold one, and produced a strong sensation followed by a good deal of controversy. My remembrance of the address is further strengthened by a personal interest it had for me. Some passages in it referred to the evolutionary character of the *Principles of Psychology*, and aimed at correcting current misapprehensions respecting the origin of the evolutionary doctrine, in so far as it applies to Mind. I have before exemplified Prof. Tyndall's chivalrous desire to see justice done where he thinks it is not done, and it was here manifested on my behalf. Not much effect was produced, however. The public mind, difficult to impress, having once taken an impression, retains it right or wrong, and resents any effort to change it.

The pleasures of my stay at Belfast were increased by the presence of my friend Lott. At its close he and I had a further week or ten days of companionship at Llandudno on our way south. Departing thence, I sojourned for a while at Standish before returning to London.

Neither correspondence nor memory furnishes me with anything to set down until the close of the year. A letter of 8. December says:—
"I am dreadfully bothered with an increasing business-correspondence, and with increasing private correspondence, and with presentation copies of books. I am now deciding to do the replying and acknowledging by deputy, whenever it can possibly be done. One-third to one-half of my morning has been of late cut off by these distractions.

Otherwise things are going on remarkably well. The second volume of the French translation of the *Psychology* is out; and I have also recently got the German translation of the *Education,* and am expecting shortly to have their translation of *First Principles.*"

Winter passed and the early spring passed without incident. Here is a passage written to Youmans on April 10, 1875:—

"Thanks for your untiring advocacy, and for your defence in the last number of the Monthly. It is droll to find myself described by some as not being inductive, while by others I am blamed for overburdening my arguments with illustrative facts."

And here is another from a letter dated April 14:—

"Though I wrote to you a few days ago, I write again on receiving your letter of the 3rd, to say how glad I shall be to see you. Irrespective of other ends, I doubt not you will derive physical and mental benefits from the change of scene and from the enforced rest of the voyage. I shall be in town till towards the end of July; after which date I shall probably be away for some six weeks, so that if you come in May there will be some six weeks during which we may be together (for of course I shall expect you to come and stay at Queen's Gardens as my guest) and there will be a further interval after my return to town."

This programme was partially carried out: he arrived on July 14, and joined me as proposed.

Very little more has to be said concerning the incidents of the season. There were the usual perturbations of health, and short absences of a week or so to obtain, partly by fresh air and partly by quiet, better nights and restored power of working. Letters show that during two such absences in February and May I was at Brighton; and at Easter I was at Clifton, where I was joined by Lott.

But the fact perhaps most worth mentioning is that in

May I commenced dictating the rough draft of this autobiography. How came I to take such a step at so relatively early a period? may be asked. The cause was this. Not long before, a friend referred to a not unimportant scheme I had several years previously suggested to him, for furthering a public movement then in progress. By the help of his reminder I recalled the incident; but it was clear to me that, had it not been for his reminder, it would have disappeared absolutely from my memory. There afterwards resulted the reflection that if a biography was to be written, either by myself or any one else, the materials for it should be collected at once; otherwise there would probably be serious omissions.

"But why a biography at all?" will perhaps be asked. The question is reasonable enough, considering how often I have uttered unfavourable opinions concerning biography at large. The reply is that in these days of active book-manufacture, when there are so many men each of whom, having completed and sold one work, forthwith casts about for the subject-matter of another, no one whose name has been much before the public can escape having his life written: if he does not do it himself some one else will do it for him. This induction from current experience brought with it the conclusion that in either case it was desirble that a connected narrative of events, such as I alone could furnish with anything like completeness, should be written; and that the verifying and illustrative materials should be put in order along with it.

How to execute this task remained for some time a problem. I could not think of suspending my ordinary work for the purpose—sacrificing the important for the relatively unimportant. And yet, if I postponed setting down these biographical memoranda until after the completion of the Synthetic Philosophy, it was pretty clear that they would never be set down at all. At length I hit upon a compromise. Each successive week I prepared myself by looking through the correspondence and documents referring to the period to be dealt with, and then, for an hour on Saturday afternoon, I dictated to a shorthand writer: narrating in brief form the chief events, with my comments upon them, without regard to literary form or even correctness of expression. The transcribed notes, which the shorthand writer handed to me the next week in the shape of a large-sized copy book of twenty or thirty pages, I took from him, and inserted between the leaves in their respective places all the relevant letters and other papers. How long this process continued I cannot remember: for something like a year I think. Eventually the narrative was brought up to date and the process ceased.

This rough draft, with its incorporated materials, remained for many years in the same state; changed only by an occasional addition, and in a few places by redictating portions in somewhat more complete forms. It would have remained in this state to the present time had it not been for the utter breakdown of health which made it impossible to do any but the lightest work, and limited me to extremely little even of that.

In the middle of July, as already indicated, arrived my friend Youmans with his sister and nephew; and a week afterwards, leaving them in possession, I departed for the North.

Little needs be said concerning my month at Ardtornish. I may set down, however, an interesting elucidation of a truth in optics I noted while there.

Along the shore of Loch Aline, between the new house and the ferry, there is a tract of shelving beach on which grows a zone of bladder-weed, covered at high tide, dry at low tide, and at mid-tide partially floating, in such wise that the upper fronds of each plant lie on the surface. As we drove by one day, when a fresh breeze was blowing from the other side of the loch, producing waves of moderate size, the surfaces of which were of course covered by wavelets and ripples, my attention was drawn to the fact that all the wavelets and ripples were stopped by this belt formed of the patches of partially-floating bladder-weed, while the larger undulations passed through this belt, and, traversing the smooth water inside of it, reached the beach. This struck me as illustrating that which is said to happen with luminiferous undulations. Passing through air containing impurities—dust, smoke or thick vapour—the shorter among these are stopped, while the longer pass through. The result is that under such circumstances the Sun appears red: the red rays being those formed of the longer undulations. Doubtless the waves are of utterly different natures, so that nothing more than analogy may be alleged; but it is an interesting analogy.

The transition from the scientific to the comic is a violent one; but I am led to make it here by remembering that during my stay I verified a rather amusing story which dated back some dozen years or more. The head gamekeeper's son, a young man of twenty, was quizzed by me one day when we were out fishing, concerning this story of his boyhood; and, as he looked sheepish and did not deny it, I presume it was true. At the time in question Lord Kirkcaldy—a very unimposing sample of humanity, which added somewhat to the point of the incident—was staying at Ardtornish for a little salmon-fishing. One day during his stay this gamekeeper's son, then perhaps some six or seven years of age, ran in to his mother exclaiming—" O mither, mither, I've seen the Lord, and he's just like a man!"

Leaving Ardtornish towards the close of August I broke my journey south by a week at Llandudno and reached London early in September. When I add that the latter part of October and beginning of November were spent at Standish, I have sufficiently indicated my autumn doings.

Late in the autumn my friend Youmans, after returning to America, sent me a discouraging account of himself. Already extracts from my letters have from time to time shown that I expostulated with him for his disregard alike of health and of personal interests while pursuing his aims—aims largely directed to the propagation of Evolution-doctrines and diffusion of my works. He had now illustrated afresh this tendency to undue self-sacrifice, and I wrote to him strongly on the subject. My letter, dated 18. Dec., while it may serve as a general lesson, I quote here partly because it illustrates this trait of his nature, and partly because it illustrates a trait of my nature—a somewhat too candid expression of opinions.

" Turning to your letter, let me say first that I have regretted greatly to have an account of your state that is so unsatisfactory, alike by what it says and by what it implies. To think that you should have come over here mainly to recruit, and now that you should be apparently no better than when you left; and all because you would go on working and worrying instead of resting! Your intention to be careful now amounts to nothing—you have all along been intending that and doing the contrary. That you will either cut short your life, or incapacitate yourself, is an inference one cannot avoid drawing; seeing that in your case, as in a host of other cases, experience seems to have not the slightest effect. It is a kind of work-drunkenness; and you seem to be no more able to resist the temptation than the dypsomaniac resists alcohol. Excuse my strong expressions. I use them in the hope that they may do some good, though it is a very faint hope. The only course which could give me any confidence that you will not bring your career of usefulness to a premature close, would be to learn that you had put yourself under the despotic control of your sister; and even if you did this, I suspect you would quickly break the agreement under the pressure of some fancied necessity. As though fulfilment of some passing purpose was necessary and maintenance of life unnecessary! What is the use of all this propagation of knowledge, if it is to end in such results?"

Unhappily the opinion above expressed that he would bring his life to a premature close was verified. Though he reached the age of sixty-six, yet that his death at that age was premature is shown by the fact that both his parents were then alive.

In a letter to him written ten days later, I find the following passage about another matter:—
" Since I wrote I received some news from Russia which will interest you. A professor at Kiev proposes, in conjunction with his colleagues and pupils, to translate the *Descriptive Sociology*. He tells me, to my surprise, that all my books have now been translated into Russian with the exception of the *Descriptive Sociology,* which will thus soon be added to the list. Further, he tells me that he has proposed to the Historical Society of Kiev to make a like classification and tabulation of Russian history. The name of this Russian is Soutchitzici (?)".

Whether this project was carried out I could not at first remember, but I have since found proof that it was.

While I am quoting from letters I may as well add a passage from one to my friend Lott dated a week after, namely Jan. 5, 1876. This I give chiefly for the sake of its second paragraph:—

"I am sorry to hear your plans are interfered with. However, next week will suit me just as well. If Mr. Earp is sufficiently recovered you might come on Saturday. You would not, indeed, find me at home in the evening; for we shall be celebrating our hundredth meeting of the X club; but Miss Shickle will take care of you until my return.

I am glad you like No. 40. It is surprising what an effect is produced on one by this tracing out the natural history of beliefs. I feel, even myself, more completely out of the wood now that the whole thing is accounted for: not having been conscious that I remained at all in the shade of the wood, until now that I have got into broad daylight."

The process here described as at length ended had been a long one, for it commenced when I was in my teens.

The first volume of the *Principles of Sociology* might have been issued before Midsummer 1876, had it not been for the discovery of a serious *lacuna* in my original scheme. Up to this time the programme of the Synthetic Philosophy, issued in 1860, had been in all respects adhered to; but now it became clear that an addition must be made. I had, as most do, approached the subject of Sociology on its political side; and though, when its divisions were set down, there was a clear recognition of sundry other sides—the Ecclesiastical, the Industrial, and so forth,—yet all of these were what may be distinguished as the public sides of the subject. Sociology in fact, as we ordinarily conceive it, is concerned exclusively with the phenomena resulting from the co-operation of citizens. But now, when about to deal with institutions of this or that kind, I suddenly became aware that domestic institutions had to be dealt with. It was not that I accepted in full the views of Sir Henry Maine; for my studies of primitive societies had familiarized me with the truths that the patriarchal form of family is not the earliest, and that the relations of parents to one another and to children have sundry more archaic forms. But I became conscious that these more archaic forms, as well as the more developed form supposed by him to be universal, influence deeply the type of social organization assumed. Further, reflection made it clear that intrinsically as well as extrinsically, the traits of its family-life form an important group in the traits presented by each society; and that a great omission had been made in ignoring them.

The result was that in the spring of 1876 I began to prepare myself for treating this topic; and a further result was that I delayed the publication of Vol. 1 of the *Sociology* for the purpose of adding to it the new division required: a course which I have since regretted; for it is now manifest to me that the first volume ought to have included the Data and the Inductions only.

Neither letters nor documents recall anything worthy of record during the season of 1876; and I pass at once to the latter part of July, when I left for the North.

I had been told of good fishing in the Morar, and while staying with my friends at the Dell of Abernethy this information had its effect. I opened negotiations with the factor of Lord Lovat, to whom the north bank of the river belonged, and eventually agreed to take the fishing. Ten days later I started for the west. The drive from Banavie to Arisaig was new to me; and though I internally grumbled at having to post all the way (more than forty miles I think), yet I felt before the day was over that I was amply repaid by the scenery. A letter describes the drive as "the most beautiful drive in the kingdom so far as I have seen." As I approached Arisaig I heard that Lord Lovat was in advance of me; and, on my arrival, found the hotel occupied by him and his suite. The factor, coming afterwards, explained that Lord Lovat, somewhat taken aback that his fishing had been let, suggested that I might like to try the river for a few days before finally agreeing to rent it, and that meanwhile he would take a cast himself. Of course I assented; and next day, not wishing to interfere with the owner's amusement, I postponed going over to the Morar, which is some miles off, till the evening after his return. Here I found myself a good deal deceived—not by the untruth of statements made but by the omission of something equally true. Success quickly proved the presence of numerous sea-trout; and then, just below the falls, which could not be leapt by fish for want of water, I had remarkable ocular proof of the presence of salmon. There, in a smooth back water, were lying, unconcealed and unalarmed, half a dozen salmon and a score of sea-trout. While sitting on an overhanging rock with feet dangling above the water, one could see these large and small fish quietly sailing about so close that even the opening and shutting of their gills was visible. The place was a kind of natural aquarium, the like of which I have neither seen nor heard of elsewhere. But now the *per contra* facts were that the fishable part of the river, extending from the falls to the sea, was less than two hundred yards in length, and that out of some four salmon-casts in that distance there was but one at which there seemed a fair chance of landing a fish when hooked. Joining these facts with the fact that after three days' stay there came no rain, nor at the end of that time any sign of rain, I decided to relinquish the agreement and leave Lord Lovat uninterfered with.

But how to get away? I discovered that next day a steamer coming south would touch at Armadale in Skye —a place on the other side of the Sleat Sound about a dozen miles higher up. Here was an escape. Next morning a fishing boat which I hired took me, partly sailing and partly rowing, to Armadale bay in good time. Here occurred an instructive incident which must be my excuse for the foregoing details. " Shall we land, sir? " asked the boatmen. " No," I replied. " See, there is the steamer coming; she will be here in less than half an hour." So the men rested on their oars in the midst of the bay. As the steamer approached they rowed me out to meet her, and my ascent up her side was watched by two friends who saluted me as I stepped on deck—a daughter of Prof. Sellar and an uncle of hers.

Suppose there had arisen some question the decision of which turned on my presence in or absence from Skye that year. My oath or affirmation that I had not been in Skye might have been met by two witnesses who swore that they saw me come out of Armadale bay in Skye and get on board the steamer: the visible fact testified to by them being identified with the inference that I had come from the shore. In face of their testimony the explanation given by me would have been taken by all as an audacious fiction.

Three days later I was at Laidlawstiel, the residence, or rather one of the residences, on the estate of Mrs. Mitchell (now Lady Reay)—a lady whose scientific proclivities were shown by the establishment of a laboratory, and for whom Prof. Piazzi Smyth had set up a reflecting telescope. The place stands high above the Tweed nearly opposite Ashestiel, the residence of Scott at one time. Here, in a pleasant circle, a week passed away, partly filled with some lawn-tennis playing and a great deal of talking—far too much indeed for my welfare.

Before I returned to town a few days were spent at Derby with my friend George Holme, who, as narrated in an early chapter, saved me from drowning when I was a boy. Other few days were spent with Lott at Quorndon, or Quorn as it is commonly called,—a place about four miles off, which serves as a sanatorium for Derby, and where my friend had now taken a house, in which he continued to reside during the rest of his life. Home was reached early in September.

Immediately after my return I made a change in working arrangements; consequent, partly, on the desire to relieve Mr. Collier from a daily task too mechanical to be properly assigned to him. As explained in a preceding chapter, I had, in earlier years, employed a youth as amanuensis; and then, after 1867, when Mr. Duncan came to me as secretary, he was occupied every morning in writing to my dictation from 10 till 1, and devoted the rest of the day to the *Descriptive Sociology*. This routine had continued: Mr. Collier fulfilling the same divided functions. For some time he had been occupied with the French Civilization; and it now seemed to me undesirable, alike on his own account and on mine, that he should any longer be prevented from spending all his energies on the work for which his powers and culture fitted him. Having become able to pay for more help, I therefore decided to emancipate him from his morning's clerk-like duties, and to employ some one else to discharge them.

The experience I had recently had while dictating to a shorthand-writer the rough draft of the autobiography, opened my eyes to the fact that I might effect some further economy of brain-power by having an amanuensis who could write shorthand. On trial I found that my anticipations were fulfilled; and thereafter continued to benefit by the discovery. For letter-writing the advantages proved great. Choice of the best expressions not being of moment, a marked saving of time and effort was achieved. For book-writing the advantage was by no means so great, but still appreciable. Forms of sentences having to be as carefully weighed as before, the required pauses remained unabridged; and I habitually kept my shorthand-writer waiting, sometimes for long intervals, while I decided on the way in which a thought should be framed. But, though thus far there was no gain of time or of effort, there was a gain in the rapidity with which a sentence, or part of a sentence, once fixed upon, could be disposed of. With a longhand-writer as amanuensis, a few words only could be uttered at a time; and if a whole sentence, or large part of a sentence, had been mentally prepared, it had to be kept before the mind while the successive instalments forming it were written down. When, however, the amanuensis was a shorthand-writer, the whole sentence, or such part of the sentence as was ready, could be uttered right off, and the attention forthwith occupied with the next. A little time was thus saved and a great deal of attention economized.

Hereafter, if the employment of shorthand-writers increases, this proceeding will seem an ordinary one. At the time of which I speak it was quite exceptional for an author, though not for a lawyer or merchant.

During the subsequent two months at home, considerable progress was made with " Domestic Institutions," by the completion of which I hoped shortly to end the volume. But either because of my unsatisfactory autumn-holiday in the course of which an injury to my foot negatived the usual amount of walking, or because I applied myself too strenuously to work, there came, before the middle of November, a collapse, and I had to desist. My friends at Standish had recently invited me, and I had postponed acceptance. Now, however, I revoked my decision and went: not with a beneficial result, as is shown by the following extract:—
" Unfortunately it happened that my friends in the country had their house full of guests, and that there were large and elaborate dinner parties nearly every night of my stay; so that, so far from leading a quiet life as I had anticipated, I did the reverse, and ended by making myself worse than when I went. The climax of the mischief was brought about by the Bishop of Gloucester, who would get me into metaphysical controversy."

To this last sentence there hangs a tale, or rather there hang two tales, not altogether unamusing. On my arrival I found that some of the family and guests had taken tickets for an amateur concert, about to be given at the Bishop's Palace at Gloucester. I willingly followed their example (by doing which, however, I afterwards found that I had subscribed half-a-guinea to the funds of a Church School!) When, on the appointed day, we had taken our seats, and were glancing through the programme, I was alike pleased and amused to find among the pieces " Mynheer van Dunck "—pleased because the music is fine, amused because of the incongruity suggested by the words of the glee, which I here give for the benefit of those who do not know them. If I recollect rightly, they run thus:—

"Mynheer van Dunck, tho' he never was drunk, sipped brandy-and-water gaily; and he quenched his thirst with two quarts of the first, to a pint of the latter daily; singing ' Oh that a Dutchman's draught might be, as deep as the rolling Zuyder Zee.' "

It struck me that it would be droll to hear these words amid the ecclesiastical surroundings, sung by a Cathedral Choir aided by the Bishop's wife, who was one of the performers. I was disappointed, however. When the time came there was a good deal of hesitation and moving about on the platform, and another glee was sung instead. A few days later, the Bishop and Mrs. Ellicott were among the guests at one of the county dinner-parties at Standish; and, being seated next to Mrs. Ellicott at dinner, I took occasion to express my regret at the substitution: saying that I supposed their courage had failed them at the last moment. " Oh, not at all " she replied. " It was simply that we had lost the music." I suspect, however, that the loss was not accidental; but that the Bishop, having seen the programme at the last moment, had "put his foot down," as the Americans say, and caused the abstraction of the music.

The other incident concerned the Bishop himself. Being fond of walking, he had, on the day of the dinner-party, come to Standish on foot in the course of the afternoon. During a conversation in the billiard-room, reference was made to the fact that I had come down from London to recruit: finding myself unable to work. "Ah," remarked the Bishop to our host, "perhaps it's quite as well; because otherwise he would have been promulgating some mischievous doctrine or other." I replied that, as the Bishop supposed the doctrine I was setting forth was mischievous, he would, of course, be prepared to defend the opposite doctrine. His assent to this I followed up by saying that, as I was then engaged in writing a chapter showing the great superiority of monogamy, he was bound to take up the defence of polygamy. Finding himself thus fixed, the Bishop jestingly accepted the situation, and pointed out that at any rate he would be able to cite the example of the patriarchs in justification.

The close of the year was reached without much improvement in health, and Christmas week, spent with my friend Lott at Quorn, did not much aid recovery. Throughout the early spring, too, I struggled with my work to small purpose. In March, matters were made considerably worse by an imprudence. I unwisely yielded to a suggestion to give evidence before the Copyright Commission, then sitting. Partly by the trouble taken in preparing my evidence, and partly by the excitement attendant on giving it (which I did in great fear of the consequences, and rushed down to Brighton by the next train), my nervous symptoms were exacerbated; and, as may be supposed, they were not much improved by attending a second time to give further evidence. At Easter another sojourn at Quorn did but little towards setting me right. A more drastic measure was now taken.

My friend's partner, a keen fisherman, usually paid one or two visits to Killin every spring for the purpose of salmon-trolling on Loch Tay. I was pressed to accompany him. Being unable to work, and hoping for benefit, I agreed. But the weather was unpropitious. Even my companion, enthusiast though he was, declined to sit out in a boat in the midst of bitter East winds with occasional snow-showers. Three days of this weather sent me south in disgust; and, as the following letter to Lott, dated 16th April, shows, I had no reason to regret that I was thus driven away:—

"Thanks to Quorn, thanks possibly in some degree to the few days in Scotland, and thanks to some unknown causes which I cannot understand, I am considerably better since my return to town. From time to time one gets rather shaken in one's determination to be careful in diet &c., by finding the benefits of carelessness. I continued to be troubled by indigestion while in Scotland, and even on my way back to town. Next day was the X. dinner; and, contrary to my habit for a month or six weeks previously, I took a substantial miscellaneous late meal, with several kinds of wine. I had no indigestion after it, and have been exceptionally well since. This is one of the many illustrations of the great effect of mental exhilaration. I know no other cause for this odd change.

It was well I was driven back to town by the weather when I was; for, quite contrary to my anticipation, the committee-meeting for selecting new committee-men was fixed *before* instead of *after* the Rule II election, namely yesterday; and, had I stayed in Scotland as long as I intended, my plans would have been thwarted. As it was, they have answered pretty well. We carried eight good men: none of them being of the public-service class, and four of them being among those I had fixed upon;—the others equally good.

There was a still further reason why I was glad that I returned when I did; for, on going to the Athenæum on Thursday, I found lying there a note from Mr. Gladstone, asking me to meet Dr. Schliemann at dinner on Saturday. As you may suppose, I should not have liked to miss it. The party was a pleasant one. Beyond the guest of the evening there were present, Lowe, Lubbock, Forsyth (the member for Marylebone), the Duke of Argyll, Hayward &c."

The second of the above paragraphs refers to measures for reinforcing the representatives of Science, Literature, and Art on the committee, with a view of preventing the Rule II. elections from going so largely in favour of those whose merit was " distinguished public service " —a merit which had come to be chiefly found among retired Anglo-Indian officials. Persisted in for several years, the course taken completely succeeded, and the original purpose of the elections under Rule II. was, for a time at least, fulfilled.

The only further incident of the season to which I may refer, was my attendance at some of the Wagner concerts, given in illustration of his musical dramas, at the Albert Hall. One of my attendances was in company with some friends who had a box; and, as we came down stairs, the lady of the party was accosted by an acquaintance with the question—" Well, how did you like it?" to which her reply was—" Oh, I bore it pretty well "—a reply which went far to express my own feeling.

Now-a-days it is the fashion to admire Wagner, and those who care to be in the fashion dare not, I suppose, say anything in disparagement of him. As the reader must have pretty clearly seen, it is my habit to say what I think, though I may so show myself one of a very small minority, or even a minority of one. In this case, however, the dissentients from the fashion are tolerably numerous. I discussed the question with the Leweses, who had been to these same performances; and though George Eliot, herself a good musician and a cultivated judge, said that the music pleased her, yet she confessed it was lacking in that dramatic character which it especially aims at—did not give musical form to the feelings which the words expressed. I remember observing of two songs, quite different in the sentiments verbally embodied, that the melodies might just as well have been exchanged. Moreover, I observed that the musical phrases were very generally of kinds to be anticipated. They were not like those of true musical inspiration, which suddenly discloses beautiful combinations one would never have conceived, but they were of familiar types.

On this occasion, as on previous occasions when I listened to Wagner's music, I came to the conclusion that he was a great artist but not a great musician: a great artist in the respect that he understood better than other composers how to marshal his effects. To make a fine work of art it is requisite that its components shall be arranged in such ways as to yield adequate contrasts of all orders: large for the great divisions and smaller for the sub-divisions and sub-sub-divisions; and that there shall be contrast not of one kind only but of many kinds. Wagner, I think, saw this more clearly than his predecessors. Complex music as ordinarily written is not sufficiently differentiated. Composers for the orchestra habitually use in combination instruments of all kinds, having tones with *timbres* quite unlike in their characters, and tones which are not sufficiently congruous to make good harmonies. Further, by constantly employing them together, they produce a monotony of general effect, which would be avoided if there was a more distinct predominance now of tones having this quality, now of tones having that. Wagner—certainly in some cases, but in how many I cannot say—specialized the uses of his instruments more than most; and so gave more marked kinds of effects, each having its distinctive character, and all of them together constituting a more heterogeneous whole. I hope that his example will be followed and bettered.

And now, to my great satisfaction, there came, at the end of May and beginning of June, the completion and publication of the first volume of *The Principles of Sociology*. It had been more than three years in hand: its progress having been hindered in large measure by ill-health, and in some measure by digressions. There had, indeed, been a first issue of the volume early in December 1873; but the final chapters, which formed a somewhat independent portion, were not contained in it. What prompted the premature issue I cannot now remember.

This long incubation was in part due to the fact that the volume was much larger than any of its predecessors. It extended to nearly eight hundred pages, and contained an immense accumulation of facts, the incorporation of which had been a laborious business. Mr. Tedder, librarian of the Athenæum Club, who, when the third edition was in preparation, verified for me all the quotations with their references, found that in this first edition " there were 2192 references to the 379 works quoted " (in the new edition there were " about 2500 references to 455 works "). And here I may note, in passing, the great aid rendered me by the *Descriptive Sociology*. Evidently, had it not been for that compilation, the gathering together of so great a mass of evidence would have been impracticable.

With the ending of this volume came a decision to change my mode of publication. Forty-four numbers of the serial had now been issued; making, with certain occasional extra portions which were included, about three thousand six hundred pages thus covered: a longer continuance than might have been anticipated. But the motive for this mode of publication had now become relatively weak. It is true that, by giving up the distribution to subscribers, I sacrificed perhaps some fifty pounds a year. This sacrifice was, however, of less moment to me than was the economy of time and attention. Each number of the serial had entailed a set of transactions with printer, binder, and publisher; and there were other small worries attendant on the frequently recurring issues. To avoid all these evils I willingly submitted to some pecuniary loss. With No. 44 was therefore sent round a notice of discontinuance.

As intimated in a preceding chapter, I eventually resumed the practice of distributing copies of books to the press, and did this with the first volume of *The Principles of Sociology*. The reasons, which I could not then give without forestalling the narrative, I am able to give now. The first was that *The Study of Sociology,* of which a qualified copyright was in the hands of the publishers, was of course sent out by them after their ordinary habit. The second was that the successive numbers of the *Descriptive Sociology* had also to be sent out; since the interests of the compilers apparently dictated a pursuance of the usual course. To have withheld volumes belonging to my series while these other volumes were subjected to criticism, would inevitably have caused misinterpretations. Hence I was in a manner compelled again to do as others do.

CHAPTER L.

A SERIES OF ARTICLES.

1877—78. ÆT. 57—58.

WHILE words are necessary aids to all thoughts save very simple ones, they are impediments to correct thinking. Every word carries with it a cluster of associations determined by its most familiar uses, and these associations, often inappropriate to the particular case in which the word is being used, distort more or less the image it calls up. An instance of this is furnished to me by an incident which occurred when about to commence my next volume.

Government, conceived apart from any particular species of it, is a form of control. But, when we think of government, we instantly think of a ministry, a legislature, laws, and police—we think of that particular kind of government made dominant in consciousness by the reading of newspapers and by conversation over dinner-tables. If, on occasion, we extend the conception of government so as to include the control exercised over men by clergy, creeds, and religious observances, it is rather by deliberate analysis than by spontaneous association that we are led to do this. And neither spontaneously nor after consideration do we habitually include in our conception of government the regulative influence of usages, manners, ceremonies; though, as measured by its effects on men's conduct from hour to hour, this kind of government is more powerful than any other. While I was not so swayed by current ideas as to ignore the governmental nature of ceremonies, I was swayed to the extent of under-estimating its relative importance. Hence, in the programme of the Synthetic Philosophy, the divisions III, IV, and V, of the *Principles of Sociology*, stood in the order Political, Ecclesiastical, Ceremonial; and in this order I was about to write them.

But the process of reading and arranging my memoranda brought with it a revelation. There dawned upon me the truth that political government is neither the earliest nor the most general; but that, in order of evolution, and in order of generality, ceremonial government precedes it. There are small social groups without any kind of political control; but there are none without that control which is exercised by established modes of behaviour between man and man. Even among the rudest savages there are peremptory rules of intercourse—rules more peremptory, indeed, than those existing among the civilized. Thus it became manifest to me that Ceremonial Institutions stand first; and there was a resulting change in the order of my work.

In what manner to publish was a question which now arose. No longer tied to a serial issue, but proposing to issue the remaining divisions of the Synthetic Philosophy in volumes, I still had to choose between certain alternatives. I might continue writing, and make no sign until the second volume was completed; or I might publish instalments of it in the shape of magazine-articles.

This last course was one which I should probably not

have thought of, had not a preceding experience suggested it. *The Study of Sociology* made its first appearance as a series of articles in the *Contemporary Review*. Why should I not in like manner bring out *Ceremonial Institutions* chapter by chapter? In a letter to Youmans, dated May 26, 1877, I find the following passage referring to the matter:—

"I think of beginning with the division treating of Ceremonial Institutions, and, in connexion with this, am entertaining the thought of preliminary publication in chapters. The subjects will be popular and novel, as well as instructive, and will bear detachment in the shape of magazine-articles, under the titles of "Mutilations," "Presents," "Obeisances," "Salutations," "Titles," "Badges," "Dresses" &c. I shall probably propose them to Morley for the *Fortnightly,* and they would probably suit you also."

Before anything was settled there presented itself the further question—Why should the serial publication be limited to England and America? Why not publish at the same time in periodicals on the Continent? Translations of my books had made my name known abroad; and it occurred to me as possible that editors would like to have early proofs of the articles sent them in time for translation, so that they might be issued in their respective magazines when they were issued here. My anticipation proved not ill-founded; and arrangements were accordingly made such that, as the successive chapters were published in England and America, they were simultaneously published in France, Germany, Italy, Hungary, and Russia.

None of these chapters were, however, as yet written; and it was only after the lapse of some six months, occupied in preparing them, that the publication thus described commenced.

During this summer, as during the preceding summer, several picnic water-parties had been given by my friends the Potters on the Thames above Taplow—chiefly in the grounds of the Duke of Sutherland, where a picturesque cottage by the water-side has been provided for those who, on such occasions, obtain permission to use it. Picnics are about the most enjoyable of social gatherings, and these had been very pleasant.

Why should not I give a picnic? was a question that resulted. Entertainments of friends had, up to this time, been limited, first of all to occasional dinners given at an hotel; afterwards to dinners given at the Athenæum, which were necessarily restricted to members; and only in more recent years, when I had come to have adequate facilities, at Queen's Gardens. Of course, among the friends who came to these parties, there were no ladies. But to a picnic ladies in due proportion might be invited. This consideration furnished a motive enforcing others that arose; and a picnic was decided upon.

St. George's Hill, Weybridge, was the place I fixed upon; and, having obtained permission from Admiral Egerton to do so, I there, in July, assembled a number of friends—between a dozen and twenty I think. The experiment was a success, but it created considerable surprise. One of the ladies, I remember, could not refrain from expressing her astonishment—"A philosopher, and give a picnic!" She exhibited afresh what I have before remarked on: she identified philosophy with disregard of pains and contempt for pleasures.

Picnics generally drag a little towards the close; and to avoid the dragging I adopted the device of changing the scene. The carriages were ordered to fetch us between five and six, and in them we drove to the Oatlands-Park Hotel. After an hour or so spent by some in playing a game of one or other kind, and by some in rambling about the grounds, we went indoors for a "high tea". The animation was thus kept up to the last. A like routine was followed on subsequent occasions, which recurred annually until my bad health compelled desistance.

A few weeks earlier than this first picnic, I had passed by Weybridge on my way to Godalming and Witley, where the Leweses had just bought a country house. They presently derived much benefit in health from it: not wholly from the fresh air, but partly from taking to an outdoor game. Often when at the Priory, I had urged them not to spend their evenings in reading aloud, but to find some indoor amusement; and I suggested a billiard-table as a resource. They were deaf to my arguments. Soon after they bought the house at Witley, however, a letter from Lewes told me that they had been following, if not the letter, yet the spirit of my advice, and had taken to lawn-tennis, with the effect of improving their physical state. It is a great mistake for adults, and especially for adults who work their brains much, to give up sports and games. The maxim on which I have acted, and the maxim which I have often commended to my friends is—Be a boy as long as you can.

This mention of a letter from Lewes calls to mind an earlier one in which he gave me a fact that bears upon a question recently discussed—the question whether writers of fiction feel much sympathy with their characters: the *consensus* of opinion appearing to be that they do. Certainly George Eliot did. Clear proof was given to me by a passage in the letter I have referred to, which ran:—" Marian is in the next room crying over the distresses of her young people."

Two or three incidents of interest dating in the autumn of this year, sufficiently justify an account of my doings during it.

Rheumatism, which had been troublesome for some time, prompted me to visit Buxton on my way North. In the train which took me there about the middle of July, were Prof. Goldwin Smith and his wife, who were bound for the same place with a view to benefiting Mrs. Smith's health. It happened that we went to the same hotel. The result was that I saw a good deal of them, and had many pleasant talks during my ten days' stay. I have never been able to understand him: the manifestations of nature on different occasions having been so widely unlike. When, in 1861, a relapse obliged me to issue a notice that the next number of my serial must be postponed, and that subsequent numbers would appear at irregular intervals, Prof. Goldwin Smith wrote me a letter of condolence. From him alone, out of 450 subscribers, there came this mark of sympathy—a mark of sympathy the more surprising, because we were but slightly acquainted and he was theologically an antagonist. On the other hand, when, after the *Data of Ethics* was published, he commented upon it in the *Contemporary Review*, he made misrepresentations so grave, and, it seemed to me, so inexcusable, that I had to expose them in a subsequent number of that periodical. How to reconcile the two traits of character thus implied has always been a puzzle to me. I can only suppose that he does not perceive the gravity of the statements he makes.

From Buxton I betook myself to Whitby: being prompted by the prospect of companionship with the Huxleys, who were about to spend their autumn there. Unfortunately the greater part of my stay passed before they arrived; and the search for ammonites, for which the place is famed, did not much console me. One incident has remained in my memory, and is worth recording. Seating himself at the same table at the hotel one day, a clergyman of advanced years entered into conversation with me over our dinner. It turned out that he had, when young, resided in or near Derby, and had known my father. This disclosure led to friendly talk, in the course of which he remarked on the great change which had taken place in the general state of men's minds during his life. He said that, whereas in his early days indifference was the rule, nowadays everybody is in earnest about something or other. The contrast struck me as one of great significance.

An excursion-steamer by-and-by took me to Scarborough; whence, after a time, I departed for the North: staying a day at Edinburgh to see Masson, and then, after a short pause at Innellan, proceeding to Ardtornish, where the record shows I arrived on August 15.

Have I, or have I not, named the fact that yachting had become one of the recreations at Ardtornish. Mr. Valentine Smith, to whom the estates had descended on his father's death, had built himself a fine steam-yacht of 450 tons burthen, the "Dobhran" (pronounced Doran, the Gaelic name for a sea-otter); and excursions in this varied the routine of fishing, grouse-shooting, and deer-stalking. Two extensive ones were made this season, the last of which ended in a catastrophe. Taking our course up the Sleat Sound, we had coasted the western side of Skye as far as Dunvegan; and, anchoring in the loch for the night, had visited the ancient castle, where the honours were done by Miss McLeod—a polished old lady whose presence in so wild and remote a region seemed anomalous. Next day we steamed along the northern coast of the island, and onwards to Gairloch; and then, taking to a wagonette provided by our host, we drove along the shore of Loch Maree and through Glen Torridon: going on board the yacht in Loch Torridon, where it had been sent round to meet us. The following morning saw us going South between the island of Raasay and the mainland; and now came the disaster. Mr. Smith and the captain had gone below to consult the charts before entering Loch Carron: leaving the vessel in the charge of the mate, with directions respecting his course. But the mate, thinking he could make a short cut, quickly put an end to our cruise. The following letter to Lott, dated 9 Sept. 1877, tells what happened:—

"In the papers of about a week ago, you might have seen the brief account of the wreck of the steam-yacht Dobhran on a sunken rock near the shore of Applecross. This was the yacht of my friend here, Valentine Smith. There were eight of us, besides a crew of 21. We had been cruising about Skye, Dunvegan, Gairloch, Torridon, and were coming south to Loch Carron, when the mate brought us to grief. The vessel struck and heeled over to about 45° forthwith, and her stern began to sink. We all got into the boats safely in about five minutes. She is still on the rocks, and the insurers are trying to raise her and will probably succeed. She cost about £20,000 and is insured for £15,000."

Having all got safely into the boats, we hung around for some time to see what would happen: some of the sailors fearing that the vessel, which was continuing to blow off steam, would explode (but with what reason I could not understand), and others fearing that she would slip off the rock and go down. Spite of all protests, Mr. Smith, with the daring characteristic of the family, insisted on going on board again to get the ship's papers and other valuables; and presently returned, bringing, among other things, a quantity of wraps for the ladies. After a time we were taken on to Strome Ferry by another yacht, and, our host and his cousin remaining behind to look after the wrecked vessel, the rest of us made the best of our way back to Ardtornish. Eventually the insurers succeeding in getting off the "Dobhran". She was duly repaired and has since led an active life every season.

The record kept at Ardtornish shows that I left that place on Sept. 13, and, I suppose, returned straight to town.

During the remainder of the year little occurred calling for mention. My daily routine was broken by a short stay at Wykehurst, and a longer one at Standish, and there also occurred a visit from my friend Youmans. A letter to him written on Dec. 17, after his return to America, contains a quotable passage:—

"About ten days ago I received from Russia a copy of a Russian translation of No. I. of the *Descriptive Sociology*— "English". I was at first puzzled to make out what it was— whether it was the Descriptive Sociology for Russia which they proposed to undertake, or whether it was a translation; but comparison of dates, divisions and names, finally made it clear that it was a translation. What a go-a-head people they are!"

This was the translation referred to in an extract some

time since given, which indicated that the professors of the University of Kiev were about to undertake it. Commenting on the mental inertness of most people here, a Russian once told me that in his country the young men starve themselves to buy books: a fact which seems related to that great receptivity which these professors exemplified. Certainly their proceeding implies a strange contrast between the appreciation of the *Descriptive Sociology* in Russia and its non-appreciation in Britain.

Whether it was during this autumn, or whether it was at an earlier period, that I decided to have a set of my books permanently bound, I cannot now remember; but the incident resulting from the decision remains the same in either case. "Why should I not treat myself to copies in handsome bindings?" I asked. So I went to the binders to consult and order. Various samples of leather were shown to me. Some I objected to as unfit in colour—too gay perhaps, or too sombre; while this was too dark, and that too light. At length the manager, seeing the kind of thing I wanted, put his mouth to the speaking tube and called—"Mr. Jones, send me some light divinity calf". The sample brought down proved to be just the thing I wanted; and, accordingly, in "light divinity calf" my books were bound.

The year 1878 opened for me with a serious illness. A letter dated Feb. 16, concerning it, I quote chiefly because it serves to explain the step I took the winter after:—

"Perhaps I am the more apt to put this construction on the matter [inferring Youmans' illness from his silence] because I have myself been seriously unwell since I wrote last. More than a month ago, I got one chill upon another, and, mismanaging things, got into a state of pyrexia—pulse high, temperature over 100—and passed eleven days indoors: the most miserable eleven days I remember; for, upon the whole, my life thus far has been tolerably free from illnesses that have kept me within doors. . . .

As I was saying to the doctor, who has just now left me, I begin to find more and more difficulty in reconciling the physical, intellectual, and moral requirements of my life. More and more each winter there is forced upon me the experience that five months of bad weather,—cold, wet, gloomy, relaxing, by turns—is trying to my system, and that I profit greatly by getting away to some sunnier and drier region on the South Coast of England, and perhaps should do the like still better on the South Coast of Europe. But the difficulty of meeting the mental requirements is insuperable. I cannot take my friends with me; and in the absence of ability to pass the time in reading to any extent, I get dreadfully bored; so that when I go away for a week, and have profited by the better sleeping and other physical advantages, I always rejoice greatly when the last days come, enabling me to return to town from my wearisome banishment. I really cannot see how I am to manage matters; having to choose, on the one hand, between the physical mischiefs of a winter in London, and, on the other hand, the delay of work and moral depression resulting from a winter spent elsewhere, in the absence of friends about me I care for, and in the absence of those occupations which enable me to kill time."

The sequence of this illness was a ten-days stay at Brighton to recruit. Entries in my diary show that a fortnight after my return came another week indoors, implying that my state was still unsatisfactory.

Two extracts from letters dated respectively May 10 and May 15, may fitly be given here. The first shows the commencement of a task which was slowly completed in the course of some years:—

"Talking of occupying greater space, I took up a while since the first volume of the *Sociology,* and, on beginning to re-read the earlier part, found that there was much that could be condensed; not by omitting anything, but by cutting out superfluous qualifications and clauses that were entirely unimportant. I have gone through several chapters, and on averaging them I conclude that I can economize to something like the extent of three lines a page; and this will, I think, effect an abridgment of some 60 or 70 pages on the whole volume. I feel alike pleased and disgusted with this result—pleased that there is so much room for improvement, and disgusted that the improvement is called for."

The second extract concerns a matter of more interest: to me at least, if not to others:—

"I think you take in the *Revue Scientifique.* Just look at No. 45, for 11 May, 1878, which I have just received. You will find in it an Essay by M. Paulhan, entitled " Le Progres, d'apres M. Herbert Spencer ", which is a review based upon the translation of the Essay by M. Burdeau. It has for me, and possibly will have for you, a certain interest as pointing out what I had forgotten—the extent to which the general theory of Evolution, as set forth in *First Principles,* is indicated in " Progress its Law and Cause ", in other directions beyond the transformation of the homogeneous into the heterogeneous: how segregation and integration and coherence are incidentally and vaguely implied; and how also what he calls the metaphysical defect is similarly implied. I had not been conscious, until thus pointed out by this French critic, that the rudiments of the other parts of this theory of Evolution were lying there in germ; and the fact is interesting to note."

Certainly it seems strange I should have needed a critic to reveal to me the extent to which, in 1857, I had expressed ideas which I thought were reached in subsequent years.

Of occurrences during the season, only one calls for notice—a visit to Paris, extending from May 18 to May 27, in company with my friend Lott, to see the International Exhibition, then just opened.

Paris was unseen by him save through such glances as he got during a few hours when on his way to join me in Switzerland in 1853; and it was pleasant to play the guide and participate in his interest. Of course, joining the chief sights with the contents of the Exhibition, and with the display in the *Salon*, which opened while we were there, gave us so much to look at that our time was overfilled.

I see by my diary that I did not, during our stay, desist entirely from such work as might be done in the shape of revising. Being able to do so little each day, I was always reluctant to sacrifice wholly the working power which each day gave me. I remember correcting some MS. when seated in the garden of the Trocadero, while Lott pursued his researches in the annexed Exhibition Building.

The chief incident which this visit brought forth, may be conveniently described in the words of a letter dated May 30:—

"I am just back from Paris not the better, but rather the worse for my excursion. Too much sight-seeing and too many excitements of one kind or other, have rather knocked me over, so that I am by no means in working order. I am, however, better this morning and hope to be able to do something to-morrow. I send you by this same post a French paper, *Le Temps*, from which you will see that I did not escape, as I had intended to do, from seeing some of my Parisian friends. Anxious to avoid all social excitements, I postponed calling on Baillière until I had been in Paris for a week, and only two days before starting back: thinking that I should so render impossible the making of any engagements. However, I was deluded. Within twenty-four hours he got up the dinner you see noticed, and I had no escape from it."

Failure of the reporter to understand my English speech, made in response to the compliment paid me, led three French papers to represent me as having proposed "Fraternity" as a toast. The statement was repeated in the English papers; and, being at once ludicrous and annoying, I had to publish a letter correcting it.

I regretted that the non-intimation of my presence in Paris prevented me from seeing Dr. Cazelles—my first and chief French translator—who had been drawn from his home in the South by the International Exhibition; and to whom I should have liked to express personally my thanks for his conscientious labours.

The successive articles agreed on as above described, had been coming out in the *Fortnightly Review* and other periodicals during the half-year: the first having appeared in January, and the last in July. Not, indeed, that the series of chapters proposed to be thus issued was so concluded; for there were others which remained. But no more had a periodical publication.

The reason for the cessation was that the articles had not proved as attractive as I expected. I thought that the genesis of ceremonies of all kinds would be found not uninteresting, and that, as the illustrations were many of them curious, and many of them *piquant*, people would be led to give attention. To judge from the Press-notices, however, this was not so. There was, indeed, along with the facts cited, now strange and now amusing, a doctrine set forth—a theory which served to link them together. I suppose this element proved repugnant. It seemed as if the mass of readers preferred to have their amusement unadulterated by thought. The result is shown in the following letter, dated May 15, 1878; which, after describing this lack of interest displayed, continues—

"Thinking that Morley might be led to regret that he had undertaken to publish the whole series of chapters, I wrote to him the other day saying that I thought, from what I saw, that the series was not successful in respect of popularity; and that I did not wish that he should feel himself bound to fulfil our engagement by occupying his pages with matter that turned out not to be advantageous; and that consequently we would, if he pleased, publish no more. Though himself apparently surprised at the result, he recognizes the fact to which I drew his attention; and, thanking me for making the proposal, which he says he hardly likes to entertain, yet yields to it if I wish: suggesting, however, the desirability of publishing the next instalment in his June number—that is, the chapter on 'Forms of Address'."

Five chapters were in consequence of this decision withheld: some of them already written, and the closing ones unwritten. The entries in my diary appear to imply that I completed them before doing anything else; or, at any rate, before devoting myself entirely to the task I proposed next to undertake.

CHAPTER LI.

THE DATA OF ETHICS.

1878—79. ÆT. 58—59.

An unusual amount of ill-health experienced during the winter months of 1877—78, had, even before the illness described in the last chapter, led to serious thoughts respecting my future; and these had prompted a precautionary step. On the 9th January, while lying in bed with a bad cold, I sent for my secretary, and, after disposing of a small matter, began dictating memoranda for the *Data of Ethics.* My reasons for doing this are given in a letter dated Feb. 16, 1878, as follows:—
"When I have got through the chapters on Ceremonial Government, and have also got through those on Ecclesiastical Government, which I propose to deal with next (not, however, publishing them in the same way), I have some idea of writing, and publishing as I am now doing in the *Fortnightly,* the first division of the *Principles of Morality:* showing how morality is to be dealt with from the Evolution point of view, as the outcome of all preceding investigations. I begin to feel that it is quite a possible thing that I may never get through both the other volumes of the *Principles of Sociology,* and that, if I go on writing them, and not doing anything towards the *Principles of Morality* till they are done, it may result in this last subject remaining untreated altogether; and since the whole system was at the outset, and has ever continued to be, a basis for a right rule

of life, individual and social, it would be a great misfortune if this, which is the outcome of it all, should remain undone. So that I think of putting together some ten chapters under the title of the "Data of Morality", in which the evolutionary conception of the subject will be so far clearly set forth, that the development may safely be left to others, if I cannot achieve it myself."

Of course this dictating of memoranda for *The Data of Ethics* I was able to carry on only at intervals; for as I had committed myself to the series of articles described in the last chapter, my time was chiefly occupied in writing them. But the ideas to be set forth were gradually being arranged and developed, as is implied by the following extract dated March 13:—

"I have quite decided upon the course I named with regard to the first division of the *Principles of Morality,* and, indeed, am getting a little anxious to undertake it; for now that I have for some time been thinking it over, and putting the ideas into shape, it is taking so satisfactory a form, and so much more complete a development than I anticipated, that I shall be glad to set it forth: even apart from the precaution of avoiding any possible ultimate failure in publication of it. It will, however, as I think I indicated, be postponed for some time; inasmuch as I have committed myself to writing the Ecclesiastical division as soon as I have done the Ceremonial. But when that is done I shall take up the Ethical forthwith."

Continued during the remainder of the spring, this elaboration of ideas had the result that when, towards the close of June, the chapters on Ceremonial Institutions were completed, I was ready to begin putting into shape this new division of my undertaking: the intention of previously executing the Ecclesiastical division, having been abandoned.

The latter part of June 1878 was extremely hot: making one long for a shady place out of doors. Kensington Gardens, only three minutes walk off, fulfilled the *desideratum;* and thither I betook myself with my shorthand secretary. Hiring two chairs, we seated ourselves under the trees, and I dictated for half an hour. Then we walked about awhile; after doing which came more dictating; and so on alternately throughout the morning. In the course of a week the rough drafts of sundry chapters were thus prepared.

I say " rough drafts "; for I had been led into a mode of composition unlike that hitherto pursued by me. Usually my first MS. was also the last, and went to the printers with my erasures and inter-lineations upon it. But having in this case commenced by jotting down memoranda, and having from time to time during the spring continued this process, I now persisted in it under a modified form: the memoranda taking a coherent shape, so as to become a full presentation of the argument. Hence resulted the practice of devoting a "copy-book" to each chapter, and putting it aside with the intention of using it as a basis for the final dictation.

I name this fact because of a certain accidental sequence worth mentioning. One of the "copy-books" was mislaid; and when I came to the chapter sketched out in it, I had to re-dictate this without reference to what I had before said. Some time after the book was published, I found this missing rough draft. A perusal showed that, besides a different presentation of the argument, it contained some illustrations which the chapter in its finished form did not contain; and the perusal also showed that, though the ideas had been given forth in an off-hand way, the expression of them was sufficiently good to make the chapter readable. When preparing the second edition, I therefore decided to append this rough-draft chapter just as it stood: merely punctuating it, and substituting the right words in some few places where the shorthand writer had put wrong ones by mistake. It serves to exemplify my mode of expression when unstudied and unrevised.

Of late years, since the need for economy of time and labour has become so manifest, there has sometimes occurred to me the question—Why not do the rest of my books in this easy and rapid way; so as to get the ideas set forth in some shape, if not in the best shape? More than once I have tried to dictate permanent work after the suggested manner, but have completely failed. The rough drafts above described were dictated in the belief that they *were* rough drafts—were not to be printed; and the facility resulted from this belief. As soon as I begin to dictate in the same manner with the consciousness that what I am doing is to be final, I am hindered by self-criticism. Flowingly as I may commence, I quickly find the current of my composition checked by pausing to weigh this sentence or that expression, until presently I drop down to my ordinary rate. It is a provoking difficulty, which I see no way of surmounting.

Neither anecdote, nor adventure, nor scientific observation, affords a reason for giving much space to details of my life in the North this autumn.

Leaving town on the 25th July, I passed a few days at Liverpool with the Holts. My chief recollection of the visit is that I spent the mornings in wandering about Sefton Park (on the border of which Mr. Holt's house stands), carrying Bain's *Mental and Moral Science* under my arm, and occasionally sitting down to read portions of it. The motive for this is implied in the following extract from a letter written on July 5:—

"At intervals during the Spring, and more especially of late, I have been sketching out in the rough the division which I named to you—the *Data of Ethics,* which I am, as I said, intending to write and publish before I go further with the Sociology. This rough outline is now mainly done: being complete in chapters and sections of chapters, each of which is sketched out. I shall finish it before leaving Town, and then, taking it with me, along with sundry books to be consulted, I shall devote myself while away to the re-elaboration of it before proceeding finally to write".

From Liverpool I departed for Inveroran, where three weeks were spent with but moderate success in catching salmon, and considerable success, I suppose, in reading and revising, if I may judge by the time devoted to it; for my diary shows that there was but little fishing weather. Why I left for the South on the 19th I do not understand, for an entry on the 17th tells me that I hooked and lost four salmon in succession; proving that there was no lack of fish in the river. Nor do I understand what prompted me to make a *detour* into the Island of Arran on my way South. Two days were spent at Brodick; and, that time having sufficed me, I returned to London, which I reached on the 23rd August. Perhaps a desire to get to work again chiefly moved me thus to abridge my absence to less than a month.

But it seems I was not satisfied with this half-holiday. There shortly came a supplementary one, as shown by the following extract dated Sept. 27:—

"Your letter of Sept. 3 reached me at Lyme Regis, where I have been spending the last ten days with the Busks. I had, as you suppose, returned to Town, and indeed had been three weeks here before going away again; so that I was able to take away a sufficiency of MS. to occupy me in revision. I arrived back last night and am now setting to work again."

One of the incidents of my stay at Lyme Regis was a visit to the remarkable landslip, about six miles to the west, where a tract some quarter of a mile long and many acres in area, bearing a house, slid bodily forward over the shore into the water; leaving inland a vast chasm of perhaps fifty yards wide and thirty or forty feet deep.

As my beliefs are at variance with those expressed in burial-services, I do not like attending funerals, and giving a kind of tacit adhesion to all that is said. But I am compelled to make exceptions, and made one towards the close of this year; partly because my absence would have been generally misinterpreted, and partly because it might have given pain to one whose feelings I should have been very reluctant to hurt, though probably she would have understood my motive. The funeral I refer to was that of my friend Lewes, which occurred on the 4th of December.

His death ended a domestic union of nearly twenty-five years' duration. One might have expected that the expressions used in the dedications of George Eliot's MSS. to him, would have sufficed as proofs of his devotedness. But there are not a few who, in such cases, gladly find occasion for unfavourable comment, or assume occasion if they cannot find it; and most people have no scruples in circulating adverse statements without asking for evidence. So far as I saw (and I had many opportunities of seeing) they exceeded any married pair I have known in the constancy of their companionship; and his studious care of her was manifest. I remember that on one occasion when, perhaps during a temporary mood, I had been saying that though possessed of so many advantages I valued life but little, save for the purpose of finishing my work, they both of them ascribed my state of feeling to lack of the domestic affections, and simultaneously exclaimed that their great sorrow was that the time would soon come when death would part them.

In the brief characterization of Lewes which I gave in an early chapter of this volume, I omitted two allied traits which ought to be mentioned. One of them was that he was studiously fair in his criticisms, alike of friends and of foes. Bias in another's favour did not prevent him from indicating such faults as he recognized; and antagonism did not prevent him from according praise for merit, where it existed. The other was that in controversy he was exceptionally open-minded. Of all those with whom I have had discussions, I cannot remember one who, when he saw that a position was untenable, would with such entire candour avowedly surrender it. Though he had plenty of *amour propre*, it did not prevent him from yielding to a conclusive argument—did not induce him to go on fighting, as most men do, after they are conscious that they are wrong.

Later in December came the preparations for a change foreshadowed in the last chapter. Already to a letter I have quoted concerning my health, there came from Youmans a response the nature of which is implied in the rejoinder I made on March 13:—

"I wish I could follow out your advice with regard to wintering in Algiers, but I do not find it practicable to get a friend about whom I care anything to join me; and it is quite out of the question to go alone. That you should propose to make a sacrifice of the kind you so generously indicate, is quite in harmony with your nature, and your interest in the end to be achieved; but you must not suppose that there are many others who have like feelings, and would be ready to do like things. However I shall make an effort next year, if I can manage to conform such an arrangement with the progress of my work, to carry out this scheme."

On July 5, in a letter partially quoted already, I wrote:—

"I have pretty well decided to spend my next winter in the South of Europe. My experiences year after year, and especially this year, have impressed me more and more with the fact that our winter is very injurious to me; and is injurious because my powers of making vital heat, naturally not high, have fallen so much below par. One of the evidences of how much I fail in maintaining my vital heat, which has long struck me, has been that, far from finding a hot bath enervating, as many people do, it always gives me a better appetite: showing that the exaltation of the functions due to a gratis supply of heat, enables me to carry on my physiological business better. Quite recently I have had still clearer evidence of this; for a fit of hot weather which we had lately, did me very great good—increased my appetite and improved my digestion, and in all respects made me better. So that I see that my health and power of working for the future, will depend very much on avoiding the evils which the winter's cold entails upon me."

A passage from a letter dated Sept. 27, shows what was about to happen:—

"I was delighted to find that my suggested intention of going to the South of Europe to spend some of the winter months, raised in you the thought of accompanying me; and I strongly urge you to carry out that thought."

Accordingly, on Dec. 17, my American friend arrived in London. Starting on the 20th for Paris; spending two days there to arrange for the translation of *The Data of Ethics;* and halting for a day at Lyons to rest; we reached Hyères on Christmas eve.

After leaving the gloom and inclemency of a London December, it was delightful, on Christmas morning, to saunter about the garden of the Hôtel des Iles d'Or, and hear the buzzing of the flies in the sunshine—a sound so strongly associated with the glow of a summer's day. It was pleasant, too, to pass from trees black and bare, to trees and plants in full leaf, native and introduced—the eucalyptus, the palms, the aloes, which are becoming so abundant along the Riviera as greatly to mask the indigenous vegetation.

Speaking of aloes reminds me that I observed one which, having lately sent up its vast flower-stalk, had drooping and shrunken leaves; and this suggested a good question that might be put to those who are studying plant-life after a rational manner: the question, namely—What are the conditions which make it profitable to the aloe-species to postpone flowering so long? Young people should always have in their minds problems to be solved concerning the phenomena of the surrounding world, and of human life. A boy or girl rising in the teens, might with advantage be asked—How happens it that in hilly counties, such as Devonshire, the lanes are deep down below the surfaces of the adjacent fields; whereas in flat countries the surfaces of the lanes and of the fields are on the same level? What is the definite and unmistakable distinction between running and walking? Why do horses and cows drink as human beings do, by sucking in the water; whereas dogs and cats drink by lapping? What is that adjustment of the parts of the eye which gives the infantine stare, as contrasted with that adjustment which gives the calm gaze of the adult? What advantage does a plant get from having a hollow stem or stem filled with pith? and why is this advantage, which many short-lived plants avail themselves of, unavailable by trees, save when young and afterwards in their shoots? Why, in a river, is the water next a convex shore usually shallow, and the bottom often sandy?

A teacher who understood his business would be continually devising questions of these and countless other kinds, to which no answers could be found in books, and would persistently refuse to give the answers: leaving the questions to be puzzled over for years if need were. The mental exercise which solving one such question implies, is of more value than that implied by a dozen rote-learnt lessons.

Details of our seven-weeks' sojourn on the Riviera are not called for. I had left a quantity of MS. with the printer, and had taken a further quantity with me to revise. My mornings up to the time of the *dejeuner* I devoted to correcting MS. and proofs; while the afternoons were spent, weather permitting, in saunterings and explorations.

On New Year's day we left Hyères for Cannes; and, after a pleasant week there we passed on to Nice, or rather to Cimiez—a little place on the high ground some three miles inland. A post-card to Lott written thence on Jan 15, says something about our experiences:—

" This is the region of extremes—winter and summer mixed.

Now sitting crouching over the fire with great coat and cap on, and piling rugs on the bed at night, and now walking in bright warm sunshine, seeing butterflies about and peas six feet high in blossom, and being obliged to use mosquito cutrains!

We have been at Hyères and Cannes for a week each, and on Friday shall go on to Mentone, to which place I went yesterday "prospecting" and was delighted with it."

On the 17th a charming drive along that beautiful part of the Corniche road lying East of Nice, took us to Mentone; and there we settled: both of us preferring the place to any of the others, chiefly because of its surprizing number of picturesque walks. Of course we made expeditions. There was a trip to Monaco and Monte Carlo to see the gambling-tables, where the faces of the players were less repulsive than I had expected. A day was spent at Ventimiglia. During an absence of two days we visited Bordighera and San Remo. And there were smaller excursions to places near at hand—Roquebrune and Eza.

Concerning this last place, to which I went alone (for Youmans was not equal to much exertion), something may be said. Already from the Corniche road we had looked down upon its truncated peak of rock, and cluster of habitations on the top; and now I climbed up to it from the railway-station near the sea-side. The climb occupied me more than an hour; for I sat down occasionally to rest and do a little revising. But the sight of its curious interior well repaid me for the climb. With its irregular dwellings huddled together chaotically around narrow streets and passages and archways like tunnels, it may be compared to the oldest part of one of our oldest provincial towns, in course of being changed into a magnified rabbit-warren. At the highest part there is a ruined stronghold, in which I sat down. After contemplating awhile the magnificent panoramic view, I took out a portion of *The Data of Ethics*, and spent half an hour upon it; and, remembering what the place had witnessed during the times when it was a refuge for the people of the district, and during other times when it was held by the invading Saracens, I was struck by the odd contrast between the purposes to which it was then put, and the purpose to which I was putting it.

By the middle of February my friend and I found reasons for returning: I, because I had got through all the MS. I had brought with me, and he, because he longed for home. We reached London on the 17th; and, after remaining with me a fortnight he departed for America. Writing on Feb. 19 to Lott I said:—

" The excursion was a success as being an escape from the terrible winter you have had here, though not so satisfactory absolutely. One-third rainy days, one-third dull days, one-third bright days, describes the weather approximately. Still, the change was beneficial in some respects and enjoyable; and as I did my full stint of work or rather more, and have come back perhaps a little better than I went, I am content."

This description of the unsatisfactory weather is, I find, an over-statement. My diary shows that the fine days were slightly in excess of the rest.

Save a week's visit to Quorn at Easter, nothing occurred to vary the even tenor of my life until the beginning of June; on the 7th of which month I find the entry " Finished the *Data of Ethics* ". The printers had been at my heels all through the Spring; so that now, when I put the final portion of MS. into their hands, there remained only to pass the last sheets through the press.

This small task was not, however, completed in London, but near Salisbury; where I had been invited to spend a few days at Wilton House, with the kind intention of benefiting my health. Had I thought of it, I might have corrected the closing pages of *The Data of Ethics* in the groves where Sir Philip Sidney is said to have composed his *Arcadia;* but attractive though the grounds are, it did not then occur to me to take my work out of doors. A little time only being occupied in looking through proofs, the rest was spent partly in drives and walks accompanied by somewhat too much conversation for my welfare, and partly amidst an agreeable circle of Whitsuntide guests. I have often regretted that the health of our host has not allowed him to take a more prominent part in public life; where the philanthropic nature he inherits, joined with a clear intelligence, might have done conspicuous service.

Shortly after my return to town *The Data of Ethics* was issued, and met with a more favourable reception than I had been accustomed to. More endeavour was made than usual to give some idea of the contents of the work; and especially in one instance, a clear and succinct account of its argument was set forth. A curious commentary on current criticism is supplied by the fact that I was, after nearly thirty years experience of it, surprised to meet with a case in which the reviewer did that which every reviewer ought to do.

CHAPTER LII.

CEREMONIAL INSTITUTIONS.

1879. ÆT. 59.

As the articles named in the last chapter but one were all nearly completed, though not all published, before *The Data of Ethics* was seriously commenced, why was not the volume on *Ceremonial Institutions,* constituted by these articles, published first? Was I so anxious to write *The Data of Ethics* that I could not even delay to pass *Ceremonial Institutions* through the press? These questions at first puzzled me; and it was only after some consideration that I saw what had happened.

At the time when I made the resolve to write *The Data of Ethics* forthwith, lest it should never be written at all, my intention was to publish the second volume of *The Principles of Sociology* as a whole, according to programme. As the chapters dealing with Ceremonial Institutions formed but the first division of it, they were consequently laid aside until the other divisions should be written. On returning to the subject, however, I reflected that as the volume was to contain five divisions, treating respectively of Ceremonial, Political, Ecclesiastical, Professional, and Industrial Institutions, it would be very bulky, and would be a long time in hand—certainly several years. Hence there arose the thought—Why not publish each division separately? Though organically connected with the rest, each division has a sufficient degree of independence to admit of separate treatment; each division will form a volume of sufficient size; and, further, each division will have more chance of being bought and read than did it form a part of one large expensive volume. Moreover, if the paging was made to run consecutively through these successive divisions, they could be bound into one volume when all were issued.

Once entertained, the thought of making this change of plan quickly ended in action; and, soon after *The Data of Ethics* was through the press, I took the requisite steps.

The season, verging towards its close when this happened, brought no further incident worthy of mention. A letter, however, dated 26 June, names a fact which, I suppose, ought not to be omitted:—

" You will, I daresay, be somewhat surprised so soon again to have a letter from me; but I have just received a piece of news of a satisfactory kind which you will be glad to have. . . . It is contained in a letter just received from Ribot.

'I have the pleasure of informing you that, by official resolution of the Minister of Public Instruction, your principal works (*First Principles, Principles of Biology, &c.*) are henceforth to be placed at the disposal of the pupils of the Lyceums, and may be given to them as prizes. This resolution is the result of efforts to this end which I have long made in company with some friends (MM. Marion, Maspero, &c.) who are, like me, members of the Ministerial Commission which selects books. There were animated discussions over each of your works. We have nevertheless had a majority (the Commission is composed of about forty members), excepting the work on Education, which has been excluded " as being likely to make the students conceive a dislike for classical studies ". At the same time it has been decided that this book may be given to students who are about to leave the Lyceum. These resolutions apply to the whole of France.' "

I feel that the quoting of this passage is in somewhat questionable taste; and yet to say nothing about the endorsement it describes would be to leave out an occurrence of some significance.

A biographer, or autobiographer, is obliged to omit from his narrative the common-places of daily life, and to limit himself almost exclusively to salient events, actions, and traits. The writing and reading of the bulky volumes otherwise required, would be alike impossible. But by leaving out the humdrum part of the life, forming that immensely larger part which it had in common with other lives, and by setting forth only the striking things, he produces the impression that it differed from other lives more than it really did. This defect is inevitable.

Consciousness of it, and the desire to diminish it, have helped to make me persist in noting my various absences from town, and in many cases giving accounts of their doings; since, being parts of the life which might as well have belonged to other lives, they tend to assimilate it to other lives. Not, indeed, that I have done this exhaustively. Partly by intention, and partly because there was no diary to bring them before me, nor references in correspondence to remind me of them, I have left out many of the least important of my relaxations—short sojourns at Brighton, and others at Eastbourne, Hastings, Folkestone, Tunbridge Wells, Sevenoaks; as well as various short visits to High Elms, Coombe Bank,

Wykehurst, Aldermaston, and longer ones to Standish and Quorn. But if the reader will conceive that the breaks in my London routine, already shown to be frequent, were still more frequent, it will suffice.

Instead of indicating in the same way as heretofore my doings in the autumn of this year, I may copy verbatim my diary during the period, or, at any rate, during the greater part of it: so giving the reader a clearer idea how my holidays were spent than any description would do.

"*July* 30th. Left Euston Station by the 8.50 limited mail for Stirling.   31st. Stirling at 7.50.   Inveroran about 3. *Aug.* 1st. Began fishing at 11, ended at 5. Got 3 salmon—one 17 lb., one of 15 lb. and one 10 lb.—all in the Island-pool. 2nd. Revising Ceremonial Government in morning.   Afternoon fishing; river gone down; no sport.   3rd. Revising Ceremonial Government most of the day—foot blistered and could not walk much.   4th. Revising Ceremonial Government; short walks.   5th. Revising and short walks.   6th. Revising; some rain; river higher; fished from 12 to 5—one salmon 16 lb.   7th. River low—reading, revising, and walking.   8th. Reading, revising, and walking.   9th. Reading, revising, and walking.   10th. Reading, revising, and walking.   11th. Left at $10\frac{1}{2}$; Tyndrum at $12\frac{1}{2}$; left at 1; got to Oban at $6\frac{1}{2}$—Craigard Hotel; met Lingards.   12th. Left at 7 by Skye-boat; Loch Aline at $8\frac{1}{2}$; and Ardtornish at $9\frac{1}{2}$; afternoon, netting in Loch Arienas and picnic with the ladies there.   13th. Revising, walking, and drive to old Ardtornish in afternoon.   14th. In the yacht Dobhran up Loch Sunart to Strontian; back by 9 o'clock.   15th. Started at 8 in the Dobhran to Staffa; fine day; explored cave; back by $6\frac{1}{2}$.   16th. Walking, and revising, and reading.   17th. Walking, revising, and reading.   18th. Started in Dobhran up Loch Linnhe; saw two stags stalked and shot by V. Smith; on to Loch Corrie and Loch Leven; back at 8.   19th. Fishing on Loch Arienas; 14 sea-trout and 12 loch-trout in 5 hours. 20th. Revising, reading, and walking. 21st. Fishing on Loch Arienas; no sport. 22nd. Revising, walking, and playing lawn-tennis. 23rd. Excursion in the Dobhran to Loch-na-Kiel, in Mull. In the sound saw a whale about 50 ft. long [which accompanied us for a mile or more]. 24th. Revising, billiards, and walking; went to Old Ardtornish in afternoon. 25th. Fishing from 11 to 5 in river; 6 sea trout—one 5 lb. one 2 lbs.; missed 4 salmon. 26th. Fishing in river 11 to 5; got 2 salmon—one 7 lb., one 6 lb.; and lost a third. 27th. Revising and walking. 28th. Fishing from 11 to 3; 3 sea-trout—one of 2 lbs. 29th. Revising and walking; afternoon to Acharn with the ladies. 30th. Revising and walking. 31st. Revising and walking to Old Ardtornish in afternoon. *Sept.* 1st. Revising, very wet; in all day. 2nd. Ditto. 3rd. Ditto; packing up. 4th. Left for Oban by the Plover at 2; Oban at 4; met E. Lott and Phy at the Craigard; evening with them. 5th. At 8 left by Chevalier; reached Glasgow 7.40. 6th. At 10.20 left for Edinburgh; there at 11.50; left at 2.30; Galashiels at 3.30; Laidlawstiel at 4.30."

Here follows a week's record; chiefly of walks and drives with host or hostess. Then there is a journey to Rusland near Windermere, to join the Potters; where another week was spent—now in some unsuccessful fishing in the Leven, now in excursions to Barrow and Carpmel, and now in climbing hills and rambling over moors. After which, on the 20th September, comes the journey home.

Perhaps I should explain that there had been no permanent migration from Standish. The timber-importing firm, of which my friend was the leading partner, in addition to their place of business at Gloucester, had established branches at Great Grimsby and Barrow; and finding it needful to be near Barrow for some months in the autumn, he had taken Rusland Hall furnished.

The foregoing extracts from my diary imply that a good deal had been done during my vacation; and the following passage from a letter dated Laidlawstiel shows the result:—

"I have been revising the chaps. on *Ceremonial Institutions,* and shall go to press as soon as I get back. Probably I shall publish by the end of November."

Some extracts from letters written shortly after, which have interests of several kinds, may be added. The first is dated October 1.

"I heard yesterday from John Evans some lines [of his own] which have become current, summing up the moral of Allman's address at the Association. They are as follows:

> " 'Twixt life and consciousness the chasm,
> Cannot be bridged by protoplasm;
> All flesh is grass, yet chlorophyl
> Can All man's duties not fulfil.' "

It rarely happens that a pun has the peculiarity that it is not only true either way, but has the same kind of truth both ways. The next extract is from a letter written on Oct. 8.

"Mrs. Lewes, in writing to me about the *Data of Ethics,* expressed her anxiety that I should forthwith finish the Ethics, rather than return to the Sociology; but, though it would be important to do this, I feel that there is still greater importance in forthwith dealing with Social Evolution under its political aspect, even if under no other."

In a letter two days later in date there is a passage of which the significance will appear hereafter.

"While away in the country this time, I have been so frequently thinking of the question of Militancy *v.* Industrialism, and the profound antagonism between the two which comes out more and more at every step in my Sociological inquiries, and I have been so strongly impressed with the rebarbarization that is going on in consequence of the return to militant activities, that I have come to the conclusion that it is worth while to try and do something towards organizing an antagonistic agitation. We have, lying diffused throughout English society, various bodies and classes very decidedly opposed to it, which I think merely want bringing together to produce a powerful agency, which may do eventually a good deal in a civilizing direction. The Nonconformist body as a whole, through its ministers, has been manifesting anti-war feelings very strongly; the leading working-men, as was shown at the late Sheffield Congress, are quite alive to the mischief; the Secularists as a body will go in the same direction; so will the Comtists; so will a considerable number of rationalists; so will a considerable sprinkling of Liberal politicians; and so will even a certain proportion of the advanced Churchmen, such as Hughes, and of the clerical body. I have talked to several about the matter—Rathbone, member for Liverpool, Harrison, Morley and others—and I am about to take further steps. There is a decided sympathy felt by all I have named; and I think that it is important to move."

Probably, if I had duly borne in mind the general principle of the specialization of functions, I should have seen that my function was to think rather than to act, and should have never entertained the intention here indicated.

During the short period covered by the title of this chapter, nothing further occurred calling for mention.

In respect of punctuality, printers are not more praiseworthy than other men of business. Delay in the receipt of proofs is a standing grievance with authors, as delay in the receipt of coats and boots is a standing grievance with men at large. In this case, however, the printers proved unusually virtuous; and my anticipation above expressed, that *Ceremonial Institutions* would be ready for publication by the end of November, was more than fulfilled; for the book was nearly through the press before many days in November had passed.

But now, while the last sheets were passing under my eyes, came an event which changed the course of my life for the next three months. So marked a break may fitly be signalized by the commencement of a new division.

PART XI.

LIII. UP THE NILE.
LIV. ENDING OF THE *DESCRIPTIVE SOCIOLOGY*.
LV. *POLITICAL INSTITUTIONS*.
LVI. A GRIEVOUS MISTAKE.
LVII. COMING EVENTS.
LVIII. A VISIT TO AMERICA.
LIX. CONCLUSION.

CHAPTER LIII.

UP THE NILE.

1879—80. ÆT. 59.

ONE morning at the close of October, I received from a young lady a note saying—" Will you not come and bid me good-bye before I start for Egypt?" Of course I went forthwith.

Already I had been telling my friends that if I could get fit companionship I would again spend the winter in the South. Egypt was a country to be visited; and as I was now fifty-nine, there was not much time to be lost if I meant ever to see it. What if, instead of saying good-bye, I should become one of the party!

The party I found consisted of a clergyman, his wife, and the young lady in question; and it had been arranged that each of the ladies should choose a gentleman who, added to the rest, would make up a number sufficient to occupy a *dahabeyah* and share the cost: the intention being that the selections should be made from those in the hotel at Cairo. How the matter came about I do not remember; but it was soon perceived that I entertained the thought of joining; whereupon I was pressed to do so. As the pressure was added to by the father of the young lady, who happened to be present, I felt inclined to yield. Not then deciding, however, I took time to consider whether such a journey might be undertaken without too great a hindrance to my work, and next day assented to the proposal. An immediate departure in company with the three was obviously impracticable; for I had more than a week's revision to do on the last sheets of *Ceremonial Institutions*. But as they were going all the way by sea, and as I proposed to go by land as far as Brindisi, it was clear that I should be able to reach Cairo as soon as they did, though I started a week later. With this understanding we exchanged our temporary farewells.

During the time the negociation was pending, I said it was a pity that the party did not include one of the young lady's sisters. This remark was repeated in a letter to the mother; and, a day or two later, there came from her the question—" Will you take charge of H——?" Naturally nothing could please me better than to have such a travelling companion; and, telegraphing at once an affirmative answer, I rushed off to Leadenhall Street to engage a berth for her. A bustling interval after the young lady's arrival in town, was followed by our departure on the 11th November.

Details of the journey need not be given. Suffice it to say that, while crossing the Channel, we made the acquaintance of a gentleman and his wife who were also bound for Cairo; and I was enabled to put my charge under the lady's wing: so absolving myself from much of my responsibility; which was a great satisfaction. Our stopping places were Paris, Turin, Bologna (where we had nearly two days to spare) and Brindisi; leaving which last place by the P. & O. steamer, we reached Alexandria on the 20th and Cairo the same evening.

A good deal of merriment was caused by an occurrence which arose from the division of our party. The arrangements in pursuance of which I brought with me an additional member of it, were made after the departure of the original group. They went by a private steamer bound from Liverpool to Port Said; and they were, of course, in ignorance of what had happened. A passage written from Cairo on Nov. 23, thus narrates the consequences :—

"H—— and I, after a prosperous journey, arrived here nearly three days ago. We got here two days before her sister, whom we were to join, and who had no notion that she was coming! Last night, on her sister's arrival, we had an immense joke. H—— was dressed up as a Turkish lady, with black veil just showing her eyes. I took E—— to show her her room; and, on entering the ante-chamber, explained to her that for a night or so, it would be needful to share the double room with this Turkish lady, whom, as I assured her, she would find a nice creature, and to whom I then proceeded to introduce her. H—— drawled out some broken French; and it was great fun to watch, first E——'s horror and disgust at the prospect before her, and then her astonishment as the truth was disclosed.

The sunny weather is charming, but thus far I find my sleep much worse instead of better. I hope it may be otherwise after a while.

The population here shocks me greatly. Very picturesque, but poor ragged, dirty, diseased. I am eager to get away on to the Nile; hoping to see a less concentrated form of the misery of a long-decaying civilization."

That this experience was unique is not likely; but there cannot have been many who have had the opportunity of introducing one sister to another in disguise, two thousand miles away from home.

A fortnight in Cairo, partly spent in making arrangements for our inland voyage, and otherwise in sight-seeing, now followed. To myself it brought not much satisfaction. An imprudent meal at Alexandria established a long fit of indigestion, producing, as my diary tells me, a succession of wretched nights.

One result was that when, after a few days, we made an expedition to the Pyramids, I felt too much enfeebled to attempt the ascent, and had to content myself with rambling about their bases and inspecting the adjacent remains. The entry in my diary describes me as " much impressed." Perhaps even more than the Great Pyramid, the thing which impressed me was the tomb-temple in which we picnic'd. It is built of large polished granite blocks, so accurately fitted as not to have needed any mortar. Egyptologists say it is of greater antiquity than the pyramids themselves! More than anything else I saw, this ancient structure made me feel the mystery which enshrouds the earliest Egyptian civilization known to us.

It is needless to describe our visits to the mosques of Sultan Hassan and Mohammed Ali, the Tomb of the Kings and the Cemetery, the mosque of Talou, the Arab University, the howling dervishes and dancing dervishes, and a moonlight ride to the Tombs of the Caliphs. Suffice it to say that more or less daily sight-seeing relieved the long-drawn negotiation with a dragoman and the choice of a dahabeyah; for in the East, business-transactions, accompanied by much giving and receiving of presents, are exasperatingly slow.

During this interval the ladies of the party were taken to be presented to the Sultana (if that is the title of the Khedive's wife); and it was proposed to me to make a like visit to the Khedive. I do not remember by whom the proposal was made; but I greatly astonished the gentleman by declining, and by giving as my reason that I did not care for introductions which led to nothing. I have a great aversion to mere ceremonial interviews.

By the end of a fortnight matters had been settled, and there remained only to stock the dahabeyah with the needful supplies. My friends amused themselves by rambling through the bazaars buying oriental knick-knacks; but as I had no taste for them (I brought back nothing but photographs) this distraction was not available. Hence I was a good deal bored. One of the things I did to pass the time was to make an excursion to a suburban watering place.

This place was Helouan, some dozen miles from Cairo, on the border of the Eastern Desert, where the existence of sulphuretted springs had led the late Khedive to attempt the establishment of a resort for visitors; not, however, with much success, for the place lacked attractions.

Clearer ideas of a desert were obtained than I before had; but that which I chiefly remember is that for the first time I perceived the nature of an "after-glow." Egypt is a land in which fine sunsets are habitual—not sunsets of that gorgeous kind in which clusters of clouds are splendidly lighted up, for there are not commonly the clouds required; but sunsets fine in the sense of presenting a brightly illuminated Western sky. From the clearness and dryness of the air, it further results that habitually (as occasionally in our own climate in frosty weather), just as sunset is taking place, the Eastern portion of the heavens to some height above the horizon, becomes red. Evidently its redness is due to the fact that along with those rays which, reaching the observer, yield to his eyes the bright red of the western sky, there go the rays which pass by him and fall on the haze in the lower part of the Eastern sky. Now this illuminated haze, visible to him by reflected light, must be visible by transmitted light to people living several hundred miles below the Eastern horizon; and to them it constitutes an "after-glow." Verification is obtained by watching what takes place. As the sun goes below the Western horizon, there may be observed on the Eastern horizon (which the flatness of the desert makes visible in Egypt) a grey band, due to that portion of the Eastern haze which does not catch the red rays from the West. As the sun descends further below the Western horizon, this grey band broadens; and, at the same time, the red haze above it ascends and broadens. This process continues until eventually the red haze, becoming fainter as it broadens and rises higher, is lost in mid-heaven; where, of course, the thickness of illuminated haze, as seen from below, is insufficient to cause appreciable colour. Presently, on the other side of the heavens, this process is reversed. The diffused and faint red light extending high up, gradually descends, narrows, becomes brighter, and ends in an "after-glow".

On the morning of Dec. 12 our dragoman signaled the departure of our dahabeyah by discharging his pistol —the sole weapon of defence we had on board; and we sailed away with a fair north wind.

It seems at first surprising that the North wind should blow daily, if not with complete regularity, yet with something approaching it. I suppose the cause is that, to supply the place of the immense volume of heated air which ascends from the surfaces of the surrounding deserts when the sun begins to heat them, a current of air sets in below; and the coldest air, which is that from the North, is that which takes the place of the heated air. Be this as it may, however, the cold North wind greatly qualifies one's sensation of warmth from the sun's rays, and at the same time greatly qualifies the pre-conception one has of the climate. How cold it frequently is may may be judged from the fact that the fellahs, who, on the banks of the river, work all day with their shadoofs, raising water to irrigate their lands, habitually construct screens to shelter themselves from the blast. And, in further proof of the coldness, I may add that more than ten days' journey South of Cairo, we twice had ice formed at night on the deck of our dahabeyah.

Here let me correct another erroneous impression respecting the meteorology of Egypt, entertained, I suppose, by others in common with myself. I had always been led to believe that "it never rains in Egypt." I was completely undeceived when at Helouan; where, in the adjacent desert, besides marks of recent storms, I saw a channel which had been cut through the rock, some dozen or more feet wide, and nearly as deep, by the tremendous torrents which occasionally rushed down it.

While I am speaking of natural objects which interested me, let me name a flock of pelicans seated upon an adjacent sand-bank as we sailed by. After the melancholy-looking specimens in the Zoological Gardens, it was pleasant to see these birds in one of their natural habitats. I was puzzled to understand how, in the turbid waters of the Nile, they are able to secure a sufficiency of prey. Obscured by the suspended mud and sand, fish can be visible at but very short distances; and one would have thought that creatures requiring food in such considerable quantities, could not have obtained, by diving, a sufficiency.

Perhaps it may be that the fish are limited almost entirely to the bottom, of which there is curious evidence. As far as I remember, all the fish I saw, differing though they might in species, were alike in being provided with long pendant tentacles; showing how large a part exploration by touch played in their lives. So thick is the Nile water that at any considerable depth in it the light must be very dim; and, as the distance seen through an obstructing medium with little light can be but small, the obtainment of food in mid-water must be impracticable. Feeling about at the bottom seems the only alternative; and hence the great development of tactile organs.

But what of our life and adventures on the Nile? Well, is seems hardly worth while to say anything concerning them. As to the life, considered apart from occasional excursions to tombs and temples, it was monotonous enough. And as for the things seen, are they not described by many travellers, and delineated in the works of Egyptologists? Now-a-days, to say anything new about them would be difficult.

There is, however, a further reason why I do not give details of our journey. The dyspepsia set up at Alexandria, with its consequent bad nights, had produced a state of depression which prevented me from entering with due zest into sight-seeing; and anything I might say about what we did and saw would lack that character which only deep interest can give. Hitherto my nervous relapses had not caused any conspicuous changes in my flow of spirits, which, throughout life, had been equable—never very high, never very low. But now I had experience of a state, not uncommon with nervous subjects, in which fancies, afterwards seen to be morbid, took possession of me; leading to ill-balanced estimates and consequent unwise judgments. Already I had once decided to return, and had changed my mind; and at the first cataract I finally decided to return. As is usual, our expedition was to extend to the second cataract; but at Philæ, leaving my friends to carry out the original plan, I bade them good-bye. This decision of course added considerably to my expenses; for, beyond my share of the costs up to the second cataract and back, which of course I paid though I did not go, I had to pay the cost of the return-journey to Cairo.

This return-journey was rendered less monotonous than it would else have been by a fortunate incident. Such excursion traffic on the Nile as is not carried on in dahabeyahs, is divided between two steamers; one of which plies below the first cataract and the other above it: passengers being transferred through some five miles of desert from the one to the other. When my friends sailed away from Philæ, this upper steamer had just returned from the second cataract; and, joining those on board, I had, in common with them, to wait three days until the steamer at Assouan was ready for us. Among those thus detained was Prof. Sayce; and during these three days we had some interesting conversations. One of them concerned a general assumption of the philologists to which I demur; and I remember it in some measure because it took place as we paced backwards and forwards on the southern side of a grove of palms, to shelter ourselves from the North wind; though the place is nearly five hundred miles south of Cairo.

On our way down the river Prof. Sayce's information made more instructive than they would otherwise have been some things we saw together, and particularly the temple of Abydos.

How much was due to the aspect of things, and how much to my mood, I cannot say, but Egypt impressed me as a melancholy country. In the title of a work by Mr. Stuart Glennie, it is called "the Morning-Land": the intention obviously being to suggest that it was the land in which civilization dawned. But to me, not looking forward upon it but looking back, it seemed rather the land of decay and death—dead men, dead races, dead creeds.

Everywhere are ancient burial places to be visited—vast cemeteries like that of Sakkara, extensive sepulchral chambers such as those of the kings of Thebes, and rock-cut tombs seen in the faces of the cliffs as we sail by. Relics taken from graves are soon made familiar; and from time to time one sees fragments of mummy-cloth blown about by the winds. Here and there are shapeless mounds of *débris*, chaotically grouped, where once towns and cities stood. At some places half imbedded in these, and elsewhere otherwise imbedded, are the remains more or less ruined of the ancient temples, in which, as in the tombs, was carried on a cult that grievously subordinated the living to the dead; while, along with represented acts of sacrifice, their walls are filled with scenes of merciless slaughter of one people by another. And then, from the lifeless deserts on either hand, the winds have ever been bringing sands to bury the remains of men and their works, and to re-bury them when exhumed.

Nor does modern Egypt fail to remind one of death and decay. Vast heaps which cover up once populous towns, probably of comparatively recent date, draw one's attention close to Cairo. Tombs, as of the Caliphs and others, are here, again, among the things to be visited. Moreover there are the burial grounds now in use —unfenced places run over by children and dogs, covered by broken stones and monuments, with holes which seem to run into the graves: places so repulsive that anyone otherwise indifferent to death might shudder at the thought of being interred there.

And then there comes the thought of the miserable peoples who have lived and died in the Nile valley; from the earliest times, when the masses were slaves to the military and priestly castes, down to our own times, when unhappy fellahs are beaten by extortionate tax-gatherers to get money for supporting corrupt governments. The suffering which has been borne on the banks of the Nile by millions of men during thousands of years is appalling to think of.

Connected with these impressions, is the remembrance of a marvellous contrast between two memorials to the dead, presented at Ghizeh and at Elephantine respectively.

With the one memorial is associated the name of Cheops, or, as he is now called, Shufu or Koofoo—a king who, if we may believe Herodotus, kept a hundred thousand men at work for twenty years building his tomb; and who, whether these figures are or are not correct, must have imposed forced labour on enormous numbers of men for periods during which tens of thousands had to bear great pains, and thousands upon thousands died of their sufferings. If the amounts of misery and mortality inflicted are used as measures, this king, held in such detestation by later generations that statues of him were defaced by them, ought to be numbered among the few most accursed of men.

The other memorial I observed on the occasion of an excursion we made to the island of Elephantine at Assouan. We saw a burial place there; and noted a grave-heap recently made. Perhaps it covered the body of one who died prematurely of toil made greater by State-extortions; perhaps of a son who had laboured in support of aged parents; perhaps of a widow who had borne the burden of rearing fatherless children. But the fact which impressed me was that at the head of this grave-heap the sole mark of remembrance was a sun-dried brick stuck on end.

The contrasts between these monuments was striking when one thought of it. To a man of immeasurable guilt the biggest building which the world contains; to a man probably inoffensive and possibly meritorious a lump of parched clay!

After a day spent at Cairo in recruiting (for, as may be imagined, five nights on board a cramped Nile-steamer left me in a state of exhaustion), and after going to see the resident English physician there, Dr. Grant, I departed for Alexandria. Next morning was spent in an excursion to Ramleh, a residential suburb, to call on Mr. Hills, the international arbitrator (I don't know his official title), who had invited me to stay with him; and, in the afternoon, I went on board the "Ceylon" P. & O. steamer.

Three days took us to Brindisi; another day to Ancona; and the next morning found us at Venice. Here I suppose I ought to have remained some time; but I find by my diary, rather to my surprise, that my stay did not extend beyond three days. Doubtless my impatience to get home was the chief cause of this abridgment; joined, perhaps, with the fact that "the stones of Venice" did not produce in me so much enthusiasm as in many. Not that I failed to derive much pleasure; but the pleasure was less multitudinous in its sources than that which is felt, or is alleged to be felt, by the majority. This may be seen from the first entry in my diary:—

"Venice at 8 to 9; went to Danielli's. Saw St. Mark's, the Piazza, the Grand Canal, and some churches: fine day—very picturesque—general effect fine—individual things not."

Quarries in which men thought only of getting stone, often present picturesque effects when deserted; whereas the artificial rock-works made when trying to produce picturesqueness are always miserable failures. Venice reminded me of this. In the separate buildings in which architects aimed at beauty, they have rarely achieved it; but they have unawares achieved it in the assemblages of buildings. Houses severally placed without reference to effect, present everywhere charming combinations of forms and colours; so that, especially in the smaller canals, every turn furnishes a picture.

Astonished at these heretical opinions, the reader will doubtless ask for justifications, and I cannot well avoid giving them. Speaking generally, then, say of the palaces along the Grand Canal, my first criticism is that they are fundamentally defective in presenting to the eye nothing more than decorated flat surfaces. No fine architectural effect can be had without those advancing and retreating masses which produce broad contrasts of light and shade and yield variety in the perspective lines. This is not all. A flat *façade* has not only the defects that its perspective lines are monotonous and its contrasts of light and shade insufficient; but it has, in too conspicuous a way, the aspect of artificiality. Its decorative elements—columns placed against the surface, pilasters stuck upon it, reveals cut into it, string-courses running along it, *plaques* or medallions or carved wreaths attached in plain spaces—are all obviously designed for effect. They form no needful parts of the structure, but are merely superposed; and clearly tell the spectator that they are there simply to be admired. But any work of art is faulty if it suggests an eager desire for admiration in the artist—if it suggests that neither the thought of use nor the simple perception of beauty moved him, but that he was chiefly moved by love of applause. It is a recognized truth that that is the highest art which hides the art, and an ornamented flat surface necessarily fails in this respect; since it discloses unmistakably the fact that almost everything done to the surface is done for the sake of appearance. As illustrations of my meaning I may name the Dario, the Corner-Spinelli, and the Rezzonico palaces. The best of the flat *façades* is that of the Scuola di San Rocco; and it is so because the decorative element, less obtrusive than usual, is also subordinated to the structural element in such wise that its lines are dependent on the structural lines.

Passing from this general criticism to more special criticisms, let me single out the Ducal Palace. There are many faults which might be severally dwelt upon—the inelegant proportions of its main dimensions; the dumpy arches of the lower tier, and the dumpy windows in the wall above; the meaningless diaper pattern covering this wall, which suggests something woven rather than built; and the long rows of projections and spikes surmounting the coping, which remind one of nothing so much as the vertebral spines of a fish. But, not dwelling on these defects, let me signalize a defect of another order: the impression of weakness which the construction gives. A satisfactory architectural work, if it does not positively suggest stability, must, at any rate, avoid suggesting instability. The artist has to consider the sum total of a spectator's consciousness; and if one element of that consciousness is a feeling of insecurity, however vague, that feeling is so much deduction from whatever pleasure is yielded by the purely æsthetic characters. In the Ducal Palace we have a lower tier of arches borne on dwarf columns, and above these a tier of more numerous arches on taller and thinner columns which support foliated circles; and then, surmounting this structure, we have a large area of wall, not much lightened by openings. The general effect is that of a very heavy mass posed on an assemblage of slender supports. That the weight is not too great for them to bear, is true: the building stands. But the appearance is such as to raise the thought of a dangerous stress—an uncomfortable thought which more or less perturbs the consciousness of such beauty as there may be in the parts.

And what about St. Mark's? Well, I admit that it is a fine sample of barbaric architecture. I use the word barbaric advisedly; for it has the trait distinctive of semi-civilized art—excess of decoration. This trait is seen in an Egyptian temple, with its walls and columns covered with coloured frescoes and hieroglyphs. It is seen in oriental dresses, of which the fabric is almost hidden by gold braiding and crusts of jewellery. It is seen in such articles of Indian manufacture as cabinets and boxes, having surfaces filled with fret-works of carving. And in mediæval days throughout Europe, it was habitually displayed on articles belonging to those of rank—pieces of furniture profusely inlaid; suits of armour covered everywhere with elaborate chasing; swords, guns, and pistols, with blades, barrels and stocks chased and carved from one end to the other. The characteristic of barbaric art is that it leaves no space without ornament; and this is the characteristic of St. Mark's. The spandrils of the lower tier of arches are the only parts of the *façade* not crammed with decorative work. This is an error which more developed art avoids. Practically, if not theoretically, it recognizes the fact that, to obtain the contrasts requisite for good effect, there must be large areas which are relatively plain, to serve as foils to the enriched areas. A work of art which is full of small contrasts and without any great contrasts, sins against the fundamental principles of beauty; and a contrast above all others indispensable is that between simplicity and complexity.

Archeologically considered, St. Mark's is undoubtedly precious; but it is not precious æsthetically considered. Unfortunately many people confound the two.

My last glance at Venice was from the gondola which took me up the Grand Canal to the Railway Station, early on the 7th of February. Thence I started for the West and reached Milan in the afternoon.

Two days there were pretty fully occupied in sight-seeing: the cathedral being the chief attraction. I see by my diary that I glanced into it on the afternoon of my arrival; heard part of the Mass there next day; and, before departing the day after, "went again to admire the cathedral".

Leaving Milan on the 9th, I journeyed home *viâ* Turin and Paris, reaching London on the 12th. The entry in my diary is:—" Home at 7-10; heartily glad—more pleasure than in anything that occurred during my tour".

From a letter to Youmans written on the 13th, I may quote a passage of some interest which, though irrelevant to the subject-matter of the chapter, belongs to it by order of date:—

" I reached home last night . . . In Paris on Wednesday I saw Baillière, and he told me that the French Minister of Education was desirous of having an edition of the *Education* from which the first chapter [" What Knowledge is of most worth "] should be omitted; for that, though he himself concurred in its argument, there would be much opposition if official distribution was given to a book containing it. I agreed with Baillière to let such an edition be published in a very cheap form."

I should add that, in giving my assent to the publication of such an addition, I stipulated that the extent and nature of the part omitted should be specified in the preface. This was done, and the truncated book issued for tutorial use as desired.

CHAPTER LIV.

ENDING OF THE *DESCRIPTIVE SOCIOLOGY*.

1874—81. ÆT. 54—61.

As during a long preceding period, so during the period covered by the foregoing six chapters, there had been carried on, in addition to other occupations, the superintendence of the *Descriptive Sociology*. In chapter XLVII an account was given of this undertaking up to the stage reached at the close of 1874; and here I have to indicate the course of events connected with it up to the date now arrived at, and then to a date considerably in advance. I may most conveniently do this by stringing together a number of extracts from letters to my American friend. One of them, dated January 22, 1875, says:—

"The loss on the *Descriptive Sociology* threatens to be very great, at any rate for a long time to come. I have had the accounts of expenditures and receipts made up to the end of last year. I find that to that date, I had spent £2170 „ 12 „ 10; and that my returns amounted to £260 „ 17. To these returns I may add, as money not yet received but due, about £80 from sales of the three first numbers during the last half-year; and I suppose that the sum due from your side will, when received, swell the proceeds of sales to about £400."

A letter of 27 Feb. again touches upon the question of loss:—

"It is clear that, as things now look, I must stop. The

Savage Races now printing and in manuscript, must be published; and also the parts on which Collier, Scheppig, and Duncan, are now engaged; but after this is done I shall be disinclined to sacrifice further large sums, and give myself continued trouble, for the benefit of . . . ."

The correspondence after this contains nothing concerning the matter that is worth quoting until midsummer 1876; when, on July 10, I wrote:—

"Nos. 5 & 6 of the *Des. Soc.* are still in the press. No. 5 I hope to issue as soon as I return in the autumn; but No. 6 (the Hebrews) will not, I expect, be ready until the beginning of next year. I have abandoned the Hindoo civilization, finding that Duncan did not wish to continue the compilation, and being very glad to escape the further trouble and loss; so that I shall cease with No. 8."

I evidently looked forward to this final issue after no great delay; but I was doomed to disappointment.

For now affairs became considerably complicated, and my worries much increased, in two ways. The rate of compilation was greatly diminished by the ill-health of the compilers, brought on by over-work notwithstanding my frequent protests; and it was further diminished by the premature departure from England of one of them. Dr. Scheppig's adopted career—that of a teacher—he had, it appeared, simply intended to suspend for a time when he made his engagement with me: partly wishing to see something of English life and institutions. After three years he became impatient to resume his career; knowing that, according to German regulations, he had to pass through an ordained series of stages, and that longer delay would postpone by so much the attainment of a good position. Hence, at the beginning of 1876, he asked my permission to accept a post in Germany; representing to me that he would be able to finish the work he had in hand—the Hebrews—before leaving. The result well exemplifies the illusions caused by hope. When, towards April 1876, the time for going came, he had far from finished his task, and had to take it with him. This explanation will make comprehensible the following paragraph in a letter dated Jan. 3, 1877.

"Collier is quite broken down. He relapsed during the spring at the time when he became a candidate for that Professorship which he foolishly thought he would be able to undertake along with the completion of my work, and which, instead, sufficed, even by the excitement of the candidature, to put him wrong again. He has never got right since, and has been two months doing nothing. I had a letter from him this morning saying that he was no better. The evil is very serious, for this prostration of his state which has now lasted so long from the time since it first commenced two years ago, greatly adds to the cost of the compilation of the French Civilization. The compilation alone of this part will cost me £500 at least, if, indeed, I succeed in getting it completed, about which I begin to have my doubts. Scheppig too, I fear, is greatly out of health. His copy for the printer has been coming very slowly of late, although I was led to suppose there was not much to be done to it; and although I wrote a fortnight ago, inquiring about his health, he has not replied. I very much fear that he is worse. I repent greatly of my foolish good-nature in agreeing early last year that he should apply for the post that he now holds at Holstein. I listened to his representations that he would be able to finish the work before he went. He utterly miscalculated, was unable to anything like finish it, but took a great part of the work with him to complete there, and has not completed it by a great deal even now."

The next noteworthy report of progress is dated Feb. 16, 1878:—

ENDING OF THE *DESCRIPTIVE SOCIOLOGY*

"A few days ago I made up my annual accounts of the *Descriptive Sociology*, and I find that I have now spent £3,200 and odd, while I have got back from England and America £800 and odd. That I shall ever in any lapse of time repay even printing expenses, is obviously out of the question; for I now see that the sales of the parts that have been issued some little time do not suffice to pay interest upon the capital invested in them. As soon as No. VI, the American Races, is through the press, which it will be I hope early in the autumn, I shall go to press with the French, which will be the last. The Hebrews is still dragging its slow length along, not above two-thirds of the extracts being as yet printed. I suspect as things are going on it will be another year before that is ready."

In the slow progress of the undertaking nothing further is to be noted in correspondence until a passage dated Oct. 6, 1880, which runs:—"The printing of this part [Hebrews and Phœnicians] has cost me £320, saying nothing of the cost of compilation." And then, in a letter of Dec. 2, comes this further reference to it:—

"This number of the "Hebrews and Phœnicians" has not yet had much notice, and there has been no sign of such extra sale as I had anticipated; so you had better beware how you run to any expense in the anticipation of a demand. The stupidity of the public passes all comprehension. Here is a thing which, as Hooker says, "every parson ought to have", and yet there is no demand for it."

It seemed a reasonable anticipation that, if not to the clergy as a body, yet to a considerable sprinkling of them, a work which presented the successive phases of Hebrew life under all its aspects in a way convenient for reference, would appear worth possessing. But authors and publishers alike are often utterly wrong. Books of which they have small hopes prove great successes, and books of great promise prove failures. Neither at the above date, nor during the subsequent months or years, did this number of the *Descriptive Sociology* command greater attention than the others.

Nearly another year had to elapse before this undertaking, so disastrous to the compilers in health and to me in purse, was brought to a close. A letter to Youmans dated Oct. 27, 1881, contains the passage:—
"At length the lingering process of getting No. 8 of the *Descriptive Sociology* through the press is complete. Collier has been so prostrate that he has actually taken more than a year to get the tables corrected and printed. I enclose herewith a copy of the notice of cessation, from which you will see that the pecuniary results are sufficiently disastrous. I am heartily glad, irrespective of this, to get the business out of hand, so that it may no longer occupy my attention.

Collier has written to me respecting the proposed introduction to the *Descriptive Sociology*. He is, however, so far shattered in health that he does not think he could work at it more than an hour a day."

The " Notice of Cessation," above referred to, ran as follows:—

" With the issue of the VIIIth part, herewith, the publication of the *Descriptive Sociology* will be closed.

The collecting, classifying, and abstracting of the materials contained in the parts now completed, was commenced in 1867; and the work, carried on at first by one compiler, subsequently by two, and for some years by three, has continued down to the present time.

On going through his accounts, Mr. Spencer finds that during the fourteen years which have elapsed since the undertaking was commenced, the payments to compilers, added to the costs of printing, etc., have amounted to £4,425 15*s.* 7*d.*; while, up to the present time, the returns (including those from America) have been £1,054 12*s.* 1*d.*—returns which, when they have been increased by the amount derived from the first sales of the part now issued, will leave a deficit of about £3,250.

Even had there been shown considerable appreciation of the work, it would still have been out of the question to continue it in face of the fact that, after the small sales which immediately follow publication, the returns, so far from promising to repay expenses in course of time, do not even yield five per cent. interest on the capital sunk.

Should the day ever come when the love for the personalities of history is less and the desire for its instructive facts greater, those who occupy themselves in picking out the gold from the dross will perhaps be able to publish their results without inflicting on themselves losses too grievous to be borne—nay, may possibly receive some thanks for their pains."

Perhaps I ought to add that the above-stated loss is much less than that which would be set down by an accountant. As is implied by the figures, the amount laid out is the total which resulted from adding each year the sum spent in that year, and similarly with the proceeds: no account being taken of interest in either case. If the amount expended in successive years had been considered as otherwise invested, in securities yielding, say, 4 per cent.; and if, as I suppose they would have been by a man of business, the sums sacrificed in loss of interest on the progressively increasing total during the fourteen years, had been taken into calculation, the loss specified would have been considerably more than £4000.

Since the notice was issued the sales, small as they were, have so greatly decreased that nothing like 5 per cent. upon the capital sunk is obtained. The returns for last year (I write in 1889), after deducting trade-profits and the costs of paper, printing, and binding, yielded a little more than one per cent. on the irrecoverable outlay.

CHAPTER LV.

POLITICAL INSTITUTIONS.

1880—82. ÆT. 60—62.

ALREADY in October 1879, while the volume on *Ceremonial Institutions* was passing through the press, and there remained nothing for me to do to it beyond correcting the proofs, the next division, *Political Institutions*, had been commenced: the first half of the month having been devoted to the preparation of materials, and much of the latter part to the writing of the "Preliminary" chapter. On Oct. 8 I wrote:—

"It is a big business even to prepare the materials, and it will be a very big business to properly deal with them. In fact I feel I am about to commence the most arduous part of my undertaking—being, as it is, so immensely extensive and so immensely complex. However, the organizing ideas are making themselves fairly clear, and I have hopes that it will work out satisfactorily, and that, having worked out satisfactorily, it will be of very great importance in rationalizing people's ideas; or at least the ideas of those who are sufficiently advanced to be capable of assimilating it."

The decision, made on the 31st of the month, to go to Egypt, was joined with the intention of writing further chapters during the voyage up and down the Nile; and to this end I took with me a considerable quantity of classified extracts and memoranda: deciding that "I must revert to primitive practices and be my own amanuensis." But, as is implied by the last chapter but one, these preparations and resolves proved futile. Though one of the young ladies of our party kindly offered to write to my dictation, yet my mood was such that nothing came of the offer; and the packet of materials I had taken with me was brought back unopened: the only furtherance of my work being, perhaps, that which resulted from contact with people in a lower stage of civilization.

Concerning the course of my writing during the period covered by this chapter, not very much needs here be said. I will note only that I decided to treat the successive chapters of *Political Institutions* as I had treated those of *Ceremonial Institutions*. I decided to publish them, or at any rate a number of them, serially; and I made arrangements, like those before made, with the *Fortnightly Review* in England, with the *Popular Science Monthly* in America, and with periodicals in France, Germany, and Italy. In this case I did not extend the simultaneous publication of translations to Hungary and Russia: why I do not now remember; but I think because it did not seem worth while to take the extra trouble involved. Adding only that the first of the chapters thus published made its appearance in Nov. 1880, and the last (in England at least) in July 1881, I pass on to narrate the incidents which accompanied this portion of my work.

And here I am reminded that I have not said anything about the daily routine I went through during the years now passing. Some three chapters back, a transcribed portion of my diary presented in detail my occupations and amusements during an autumn vacation; and it seems fit that I should somewhere give a like transcript from the register of my occupations and amusements during a portion of the London season. To avoid the need for selection, I will take the interval between my return from Egypt and the end of March; omitting the first week, during which, after three months' absence, I had of course scarcely settled down into the usual order, either of work or of social life.

"*February* 22nd [Sunday]:—Reading and sorting mems; Club; dined at Busk's—Allman and wife.   23rd:—New secretary—Mr. Sutton; letters and sorting mems; Club; dined there, Hirst and Debus.   24th:—Letters and sorting mems; Athenæum committee; dined at Club—Tyndall, Hirst, and Debus.   25th:—Letters; reading French tables for extracts; business; Club; dined there—Hirst, Debus. 26th:—reading French tables for extracts; Club; dined there—Hirst.   27th:—Commenced "Political Organization"; dined at Club—Hirst, Debus.   28th:—"Political Organization"; Club; dined at Tyndall's—Huxley, Dean Stanley, Hirst, Lady Claud Hamilton, Miss Hamilton, &c.   29th [Sunday]:—Revising draft of Autobio.; dined at Club—Hirst and Debus.   *March* 1st:—"Political Organization"; Club as usual.   2nd:—"Political Organization"; Club; dined with Miss North—Holman Hunt, Fergusson, Galton, Richmond, Maskelyne, &c.   3rd: —"Political Organization"; Club; dined with Frankland— meeting Spottiswoode, Hooker, Huxley, Debus, Tyndall, &c. 4th:—"Political Organization"; Club; X dinner.   5th:— "Political Organization"; Club; dined there—Hirst.   6th: —"Political Organization"; Club; to Kew and dined with Hooker—met Siemens, Masters, and Henslow.   7th [Sunday]:—Revising Autobio.; walk with Cobb and [Arthur]

Cohen; called on Campbells; Club; dined there—Hirst and Debus.   8th:—Finished "Political Organization"; dined at Club; went to Criterion Theatre.   9th:—Arranging mems; Athenæum committee—Rule II election; called on Theresa Potter to inquire about the travellers; dined at Club—Morley.   10th:—Arranging mems; began "Political Integration"; dined at Club—Hirst; *Soirée* at Spottiswoode's.   11th:—"Political Integration"; dined at Club.   12th:—"Political Integration"; Club.   13th:—"Political Integration"; Club; dined with Lord Arthur Russell—met Lord and Lady Sligo, Lord and Lady Reay, General McCrealock, &c.   14th [Sunday]:—Miscellaneous; called on Mrs. Lewes; dined at Club—Tyndall, Hirst, and Debus.   15th:—Revising; dined at Club—Roupell, Hirst, and Debus.   16th:—Revising; Club; dined at Galton's—Romanes, Maskelyne, Strachey, Miss Lawrences, &c., &c.   17th:—Revising; dined at Club.   18th:—Correspondence with Collier all morning—no amanuensis; dined at Club.   19th:—Ditto, Ditto; Athenæum House-Committee—selecting cooks; dined at Club.   20th:—Revising; Club; dined at Smalley's—Lord Reay, A. Forbes, Lord Houghton, Elton, Cartwright, &c.   21st [Sunday]:—Unwell; dined at Club.   22nd:—Revising; dined at Club—Hirst, Debus.   23rd:—Revising; Club; dined at Harrison's—Pigott, Paul, &c.   24th:—Revising; looking after refitting of my study, and arranging books &c.; dined at Club.   25th:—Revising; dined at Club and came home to meet Lott.   26th:—With Lott to Richmond; dined there; down the Thames to Kew; home at 6½.   27th:—Revising; afternoon with Lott to Lyceum, to see Merchant of Venice; evening, called on Baileys [old friends we made in Switzerland in '53].   28th [Sunday]:—Loch came to spend the day; afternoon, called on Bishopp [an old engineering friend]; dined at St. James restaurant; evening at Busk's.   29th:—Over with Lott to Enmore Park and spent the day with Loch; walked to Crohamhurst. 30th:—Lott went home; new secretary, Mr. Edmunds; dic-

tating "Political Integration"; dined at Club. 31st:—
"Political Integration"; Club; dined there."

These entries may be taken as fair representatives, save in two respects. It seems that from the want of a secretary during part of the time, my morning's work did not proceed in the ordinary uniform way—was not indicated, as it mostly was, by the title of a chapter repeated day after day, followed after a while by the title of a subsequent chapter. And then I see no mention of music. Usually, in the space of a month, a concert, public or private, would appear in the record of my relaxations.

If I did not go to him at Easter, Lott usually came to me; and this year a special motive for coming had been to hear all about my doings in Egypt. Doubtless among the things I told him, was something equivalent to the following passage written to Youmans on April 13:—

"I am glad to report myself as well—better indeed than I have been for a long time. Notwithstanding drawbacks, the break in my ordinary life which the excursion to Egypt involved, seems to have been decidedly beneficial, and has apparently worked some kind of constitutional change; for, marvellous to relate, I am now able to drink beer with impunity and I think with benefit—a thing I have not been able to do for these 15 years or more." [Long desistance from work was probably a chief cause.]

On May 3, referring to the same subject, I wrote:—

"I was 60 on Tuesday last. My vigour is pretty well shown by the fact that I found myself running up stairs two steps at a time, as I commonly do."

It seems strange that, considering my frequent bouts of dyspepsia and perpetual bad nights, I should have retained so much vitality. The next extract, dated 21 June, concerns another matter:—

"Enclosed I send you a note which will please you, and which will furnish you with an admirable handle against the Classicists. It is from the Greek minister here; and accompanies, as you see by its contents, a Greek translation made by a late Minister of Education. The surprising and extremely telling fact is that this thing which the Greeks have first undertaken to translate, is the first chapter of the *Education*—'What knowledge is of most worth.'"

Anomalous enough! While in England the educational authorities cry "Greek Literature rather than Science," in Greece they cry "Science rather than Greek literature."

Whitsuntide found me at Clifton: duty more than pleasure being the occasion of my journey there. Since the death of my uncle Thomas, named in an early part of this volume, I have made no mention of my aunt Anna. But on looking back I count up four visits to see her, which were among those unrecorded excursions referred to in a recent chapter: two being to Hinton, where, after the death of her brother, Mr. Brooke, she lived for some years with her sister-in-law and niece; and two being to Churchill near Bristol, where she has, since the death of her sister-in-law, lived with the clergyman to whom her niece was married. Churchill is within easy reach of Clifton. On going thither I learned that she was at Weston-super-Mare. There I went next day, and found her bearing cheerfully her invalid-life in bed, borne for years before and years since—evidently consoled by those thoughts of compensation hereafter which doubtless, in the present state of the world, make the ills of life more tolerable to many than they would else be.

Before returning to town I made a *détour* to Stourbridge, with a view to finding an answer to the genealogical question named in a preceding chapter; but I failed, as before.

In the course of his career an author finds that each new book is a new hostage to fortune. Like a child of the body, to which Bacon's metaphor tacitly refers, a child of the mind becomes a source of troubles and anxieties; so that, as he advances in life, more and more of the author's time is taken up with the increasing distractions which accompany the increasing number of volumes published. I do not refer only to the fact that each additional work furnishes a further vulnerable place to antagonists; though this is of course a large part of the result. But I refer also to the fact that each additional work brings after it an extra series of transactions which augment the complications of life in subsequent years— the trouble of revision, the attention required to bring things up to date, the business of new editions.

This spring two interruptions hence arising occurred; of which the first was entailed by an apparent need for self-defence. By Mr. Malcolm Guthrie there had been published a volume, *On Mr. Spencer's Formula of Evolution*, aiming to refute the doctrine set forth in *First Principles;* and the Rev. Prof. Birks had issued a book entitled *Modern Physical Fatalism and the Doctrine of Evolution, including an examination of Mr. H. Spencer's First Principles*. Besides these major attacks, formidable if measured by bulk, there were some minor ones, less bulky, but more worthy of notice, coming from Prof. Tait, the Rev. Mr. Kirkman, Mr. Matthew Arnold, the *North American Review*, and Prof. Cliffe Leslie. A new edition of *First Principles* was called for; and, thinking it worth while to deal with these antagonists in an Appendix, I devoted to the task parts of June and July.

The other interruption had a different origin. When I agreed to publish *The Study of Sociology* in the "International Scientific Series," I stipulated that after a specified period I should be at liberty to issue an edition of the work along with my other works. The year in which I became free to do this was 1880; and for several preceding years I had, during intervals of leisure, been slowly removing such defects of expression as I found in the book, and preparing a postscript. I think I have before named the fact that so far from disliking the process of polishing, as most writers do, I had a partiality for it; and cannot let any piece of work pass so long as it seems to me possible to improve it. The library edition of *The Study of Sociology*, published in July of this year, furnished a marked illustration of this trait. I had of course revised the original MS.; I had revised the proofs before publication in the *Contemporary;* I had revised the proofs of the re-published articles forming the volume as it appeared in the "International Scientific Series"; I had revised this volume in preparation for a final edition; and, lastly, I had revised the successive sheets of this final edition as they passed through the press. Thus every sentence in the work had passed under my eye for correction five times; and each time there was rarely a page which did not bear some erasures and marginal marks. There are those who hold that changes of expression, carried even to a much smaller extent, are commonly injurious; and it may be that the first mode of expression is occasionally the best. But I am of opinion that where an alteration is also a condensation it is nearly always an improvement.

Occasionally very ludicrous effects are caused by the printing of sentences which were probably not read over after they were written. I have noted in the course of years two examples worth recording. One was in an advertisement which I cut out of *The Times*, and have now before me. It begins as follows:—

"Mr. Henry Leslie's Choir, June 11.—Programme:— Part 1. Sacred Music.—Motett, for double choir, 'The Spirit also helpeth us' (in compliance with very numerous requests), Bach."

The other was still more remarkable. Some dozen years since there arose a mania for ornamenting houses at Christmas with illuminated texts; and in response to the demand for these, there appeared an advertisement of "Marcus Ward's Christmas Wall Decorations". To guide purchasers in ordering those which would fit spaces on their walls, Messrs. Ward & Co. had specified after each text the length of the scroll occupied by it. This memorandum of length gave to more than one of them some oddity of appearance; but finally there came this:—

"'Unto you is born a Saviour.' About 6 feet long."

This advertisement, which also I have preserved, will be found in the *Athenæum* for Dec. 15, 1877, page 788.

Already I have narrated two strange coincidences that have occurred to me; and because it furnished the occasion for a third, I must say something about my visit to Scotland this autumn.

After a fortnight at Inveroran, I moved on to Loch Hourn-head. A deer-forest, spreading over some of the mountains adjacent, had been for several years tenanted by Mr. Robert Birkbeck; and by him I had been invited there. A small yacht which fetched me from Glenelg, and in which various excursions were made, added to the pleasures of the place; and partly in rambling, partly in sea-fishing, partly in yachting, a pleasant ten days was passed. During my stay, reference was made to Black's novels, the scenes of many of which lie on the west coast of Scotland. This recalled to me a curious coincidence which had occurred some years before while I was staying at Ardtornish. I was reading *A Daughter of Heth*. At intervals I had got through the first volume and commenced the second, when, one afternoon, it was announced that the Dobhran was about to start for Oban to meet friends who were arriving from Glasgow. Knowing that there would be a good deal of unoccupied time, I took with me this second volume. We arrived in Oban Bay half an hour before the steamer was due, and cast anchor. During the interval of waiting I resumed my novel. Presently I came to a part which told how the heroine was taken on a yachting excursion by her friends, and went to Oban Bay. This odd coincidence between the fictitious yachting and the actual yachting I narrated. Now comes the strange fact. If not the next day, then certainly within a few days, I took up a number of the *Cornhill Magazine* in which Mr. Black's novel, *White Wings*, was being serially published, and read a chapter containing an account of a visit paid by the heroine and her friends to Loch Hourn! The coincidence was not, on this second occasion, complete; for I was not on board Mr. Birkbeck's yacht while reading. But the yacht was lying out in the loch, within two hundred yards of the window at which I sat.

For this last of the three coincidences I have named, there is no other evidence than my own word; but of the others there exist, among my papers, documentary proofs. The one described in the first volume, showing that, at an interval of four years, I made two engagements of exactly the same kind, in which my two superiors were both of the same nationality, had the same surnames, and the same christian names, is one which might as readily have occurred to any one else as to me; and one which I suppose must from time to time be paralleled in the degree of correspondence, if not in the kind of correspondence. Now comes the lesson. There is no more reason for expecting correspondence between two such sets of facts in actual life, than between such a set in actual life and such a set in a dream. Considered as a question of probabilities, the last correspondence is just as likely as the first. See then the implication. Millions of people in Great Britain dream every night; and in the space of a year there are probably at least a hundred millions of dreams vivid enough to be recalled on awaking. Clearly, then, in view of this occasional correspondence between two sets of events in actual life, we must infer that out of this enormous number of cases there will occasionally be a correspondence between a set of events in actual life and a set of events in a dream; and when one such occurs it will appear like a fulfilment. May we not say that the alleged fulfilments are not more common than, in conformity with the law of probability, we may expect them to be?

My farewell to my friends, and to the grand scenery of Loch Hourn, was made on the 25th August, and on the next day I arrived in London.

As narrated above, there had arisen in the spring two of those eddies or backwaters by which the stream of an author's life is more and more impeded as it lengthens and broadens; and now in the autumn there arose another. Its nature is indicated in the following extract from correspondence:—

"As you have, I daresay, observed, I have been a good deal attacked by various critics as to the "incoherence", as they call it, of my psychological system, and the "confused" character of my metaphysics: the confusion which they ascribe to me, being, as I conceive, due to their own inability to co-ordinate the several aspects of the system as they are now separately stated. As I hinted in the course of my reply to criticisms, written some years ago, I had originally intended to write a division under the head "Congruities", in which the harmony existing between the several parts should be pointed out, and had refrained from doing this because I thought the harmony was sufficiently conspicuous; but that, as the criticisms passed proved that this was not the case, I might hereafter add this division. The third edition of the *Psychology*, I find, is now gone, with the exception of fifty copies; and finding this, I am inclined to prepare this additional division for the fourth edition. As this opinion concerning the *Psychology*,—that the views are not consistent with one another,—has been made widely prevalent, and is repeated by critics who know nothing about it as an established truth, it seems to me needful that I should do this; especially as I fancy the reputation of the book is somewhat damaged by this kind of opinion in the Universities."

The execution of this piece of work, commenced before I left town, occupied me for a month after my return; and then followed a short supplementary holiday. I had for several years made it a practice to take runs down to the sea-side (usually Brighton) when the state of my work enabled me to partly occupy the time in revision. So, taking with me a set of proofs of this new division of the *Psychology,* and visiting the Spottiswoodes at Coombe Bank on my way, I passed on to Minster, Margate, Westgate, Ramsgate, Sandwich, Deal, and Dover: staying a few hours at some of these places and a few days at others; and returning to town as soon as I had finished my proof-correcting.

Still another backwater now hindered me. Various criticisms, some from undistinguished persons and others from men of mark, had been made upon *The Data of Ethics:* Prof. Sidgwick being, I remember, one among these last. A new edition was called for; and, to remove certain of the misapprehensions and invalid objections, it seemed worth while to say something. The result was that I devoted nearly three weeks to writing an appendix to the book. Only in the last week of October had I freed myself from these various entanglements, and was able to resume the writing of *Political Institutions,* which thereafter made some progress.

Two months later came one of those events which, as the years roll on, happen with increasing frequency, and render life less worth living. The following extract from a letter to Lott tells what this event was:—

"You were doubtless saddened by the sudden death of George Eliot. I had seen her on the very afternoon of the day on which she was taken ill—being impelled to go in response to a note I had received the preceding day, and by the consciousness that I was leaving town and could not otherwise expect to see her for three weeks. The next I knew was the announcement of her death in Thursday's evening paper, which reached me at Hastings."

Some of the obituary notices contained an error which

had been long current without making its appearance in such form as to admit of rectification. It was now needful to rectify it, and I published the following letter in several of the daily papers.

"SIR,—Though, as one among those intimate friends most shocked by her sudden death, I would willingly keep silence, I feel that I cannot allow to pass a serious error contained in your biographical notice of George Eliot. A positive form is there given to the belief which has been long current, that I had much to do with her education. There is not the slightest foundation for this belief. Our friendship did not commence until 1851—a date several years later than the publication of her translation of Strauss, and when she was already distinguished by that breadth of culture and universality of power which have since made her known to all the world.—HERBERT SPENCER."

Information which I had, I suppose, given to my American friend during one of his visits here, led him to publish in a New York journal a letter rectifying kindred misconceptions current in the United States. This is what I subsequently wrote to him on the matter:—

"Your second letter, which concerned the notice of 'George Eliot,' reached me while away in Gloucestershire, but only this morning did I receive a copy of the *Sun*, containing your explanations.

What you have said is nearer to the truth than the current statements are, though it is still, I think, divergent, as representing my influence as greater than I think it was. In respect to the fact that I, in early days, urged her to write fiction, you are doubtless right; though it was not so much on the ground of any unfitness for philosophical writing, which I should be far from alleging, but on the ground that I thought she had in a high degree all the faculties needed for fiction. That she resisted this suggestion for some years is also true. It may be, and probably is, as you say, that she was considerably influenced all along by my books. In fact, accepting their general views as she did, it could hardly be otherwise; and it may be that the *Principles of Psychology* was a help to her in the respect of her analyses. But it never occurred to me to consider the effect so great as you suppose. Her powers in respect of introspection and sympathetic insight into others, were naturally extremely great; and I think her achievements in the way of delineation of character are almost wholly due to spontaneous intuition.

In respect of her avowed condition, she has been more a disciple of Comte than of mine; although her acceptance of Comte's views was very much qualified, and, indeed, hardly constituted her a Comtist in the full sense of the word. Still she had strong leanings to the " Religion of Humanity ", and that always remained a point of difference between us. However, during our last interview, which was on the very day she was taken ill, conversation brought out evidence that she was veering a good deal away from Comte, and recognized the fundamental divergence from the Comtist conception of society, of views of mine which she accepted. She had been re-reading, with Mr. Cross, the *Data of Ethics* and the *Study of Sociology* (the last, indeed, for the third time), and was in general sympathy with their views. So that the influence might have been more manifest in further works if she had lived to write them (she had sketched out another novel and written the first chapter).

However, you have done very well by correcting the false impressions that have been so widely diffused. Probably you have already seen that I immediately myself wrote a letter to the papers stating that there was no truth in the notion that her education had been under my direction."

To exclude a mis-apprehension likely to be strengthened by a reference made above, let me say that the mention of Comte and his doctrines had resulted during a conversation concerning *The Study of Sociology*, and was quite incidental. Positivism had always been a tacitly tabooed topic between the Leweses and myself—the only topic on which we differed, and which we refrained from discussing.

A movement was commenced to obtain for George Eliot a place in Westminster Abbey; but, before any overt steps were taken, it was concluded that undesirable comments would probably be made, and the movement was abandoned. She was buried in the Highgate Cemetery; and, though the day was continuously rainy, the funeral was attended by a very large concourse, including many distinguished men.

The mention above of *The Study of Sociology*, and the consciousness that the writing of *Political Institutions* occupied me during the period covered by this chapter, suggest the propriety of here saying something about my political opinions at the age of 60, considered in contrast with those I held in early days. Have my ideas been modified by the conservatism of advancing years, or by the wider knowledge acquired? or have both operated in causing the change from a sanguine view to a desponding view? I have sometimes startled friends by saying that I am more tory than any tory, and more radical than any radical; and the still-continued truth of this paradox shows that, while I have not relinquished my ideal of the future, I have come to see that its realization is far more remote than I had supposed. The indignation against wrong, the hopefulness of youth, and the lack of experience, had joined in me, as they do in many, to produce eagerness for political re-organization, and the belief that it needed only to establish a form of government theolly more equitable, to remedy the evils under which suffered. Hence my juvenile radicalism.

 true, as shown in *Social Statics*, that by the time I was thirty the crude notions of five-and-twenty had been considerably qualified. I had come to see that institutions are dependent on character; and, however changed in their superficial aspects, cannot be changed in their essential natures faster than character changes. It had become manifest to me that men are rational beings in but a very limited sense; that conduct results from desire, to the gratification of which reason serves but as a guide; and that hence political action will on the average be determined by the balance of desires, wherever this can show itself. It is also true, as shown in the essay on " Reform: the Dangers and the Safeguards ", that ten years later I saw that mischiefs would result from the giving of votes, unless the cost of political action, general and local, were made to fall directly and unmistakeably on all individuals who had them; and that political power can be safely extended only as fast as governmental functions are restricted.

But I myself illustrated the truth that feeling rather than intellect guides; for, apparently forgetting these conclusions, I approved that wide extension of the franchise effected by the Reform Bill of 1867. The sentiment of early years, so strongly enlisted on behalf of the seemingly-just principle of giving equal political powers to all men, proved too strong for the restraints of my calmer judgments. And then, beyond those recognized truths which feeling led me to ignore, there were other truths unrecognized which I ought not to have overlooked, and from the recognition of which further deterrents should have arisen.

I might have inferred *a priori*, that which has now become clear *a posteriori*, that the change would result in replacing the old class-legislation by a new class-legislation. It is certain that, given the average human nature now existing, those who have power will pursue, indirectly if not directly, obscurely if not clearly, their own interests, or rather their apparent interests. We have no reason for supposing that the lower classes are intrinsically better than the higher classes. Hence if, while the last were predominant, they made laws which in one way or other favoured themselves, it follows that now, when the first are predominant, they also will give legislation a bias to their own advantage. Manifest as it always was, it has now become more manifest still, that, so long as governmental action is unrestricted, the thing required is a representation of *interests;* and that a system under which one interest is overwhelmingly represented (whether it be that of a smaller or of a larger section of the community) will issue in one-sided laws. We shall presently see the injustices once inflicted by the employing classes paralleled by the injustices inflicted by the employed classes. During a long past the superior have inequitably profited at the cost of the inferior; and now one of those rhythms displayed in movements of every order, is bringing about a state in which the inferior will inequitably profit at the cost of the superior.

There was another overlooked truth which has lately become conspicuous enough. Often I have reproached politicians with contemplating only the proximate results of legislation and not seeing the remote results; and I find I have to reproach myself with a kindred blindness. I did not in early days perceive that one organic change tends ever to initiate another, and this another, occasionally bringing about a perpetual moulding and re-moulding of institutions, and a too-plastic state of society; until there eventually arrives something approaching to political disorganization.

But, as above said, while character remains unchanged, change of institutions, however great superficially, cannot be fundamentally great; and while there is going on disorganization of one kind, there goes on re-organization of another kind—while the old coercive arrangements are being relaxed, new coercive arrangements are being unobtrusively established. For the concomitant of that legislation which more and more advantages the employed classes at the expense of the employing classes, is the growth of an administrative system becoming ever more powerful and peremptory—a new governing agency which the emancipated people are unawares elaborating for themselves, while thinking only of gaining the promised benefits. Unceasing development of this, daily more rapid, has now become inevitable, for the reason that both electors and their representatives invoke with increasing urgency public help, public expenditure, and public regulation, which all imply a continually augmenting army of officials—an army which, by the restrictions and dictations its members enforce, gradually decreases the freedom of citizens, at the same time that it further decreases this freedom by demanding that more and more of their labour shall be devoted to maintaining it and paying for the work it superintends. The insidious growth of this organized and consolidated bureaucracy will go on, because the electorate cannot conceive the general but distant evils it must entail, in contrast with the special and immediate advantages to be gained by its action. For the masses can appreciate nothing but material boons—better homes, shorter hours, higher wages, more regular work. Hence they are in favour of those who vote for restricting time in mines, for forcing employers to contribute to men's insurance funds, for dictating railway-fares and freights, for abolishing the so-called sweating system. It seems to them quite right that education, wholly paid for by rates, should be State-regulated; that the State should give technical instruction; that quarries should be inspected and regulated; that there should be sanitary registration of hotels. The powers which local governments now have to supply gas, water, and electric light, they think may fitly be extended to making tramways, buying and working adjacent canals, building houses for artizans and labourers, lending money for the purchase of freeholds, and otherwise adding to conveniences and giving employment. While all this implies a wide-spread officialism, ever growing in power, it implies augmented burdens upon all who have means: constituting an indirect re-distribution of property. There is, in fact, already in force the policy which Mr. Henry George advocates, when he says we must not turn out the landlords but "tax them out".

On recognizing the universality of rhythm, it becomes clear that it was absurd to suppose that the great relaxation of restraints—political, social, commercial—which culminated in free-trade, would continue. A re-imposition of restraints, if not of the same kind then of other kinds, was inevitable; and it is now manifest that whereas during a long period there had been an advance from involuntary co-operation in social affairs to voluntary co-operation (or, to use Sir Henry Maine's language, from *status* to contract), there has now commenced a reversal of the process. Contract is in all directions being weakened and broken; and we are on the way back to that involuntary co-operation, or system of *status*, consequent on the immense development of public administrations and the corresponding subordination of citizens—a system of industries carried on under universal State-regulation—a new tyranny eventually leading to new resistances and emancipations.

There may be factors which I have overlooked. Co-operation, for example, were it successful, might do much towards checking this transformation. But so long as co-operation succeeds only in distribution and fails in production, not much is to be hoped from it. Human nature must be much better than it at present is before a much higher civilization can be established. Though I believe that, in the words of the song, "there's a good time coming," it now seems to me that the "good time" is very far distant.

Beyond the usual routine entries, varied by mention of a visit to Standish at Easter, my diary tells me nothing of note concerning the season of 1881. The following extracts from letters, however, seem worth reproducing. The first is dated Feb. 14:—

"I had from Alglave the other day a pleasant piece of intelligence which you will be glad to learn. The French Government have bought 100 copies of the translation of *the Data of Ethics* for the public libraries in France."

The next is dated May 7:—

"I inclose a letter from Morley in which, as you see, he proposes to end the series with the forthcoming chapter on 'Compound Political Heads.'"

The succeeding chapters were, however, published in America. The next passage which may fitly be quoted bears the date June 13:—

"I am glad to see that you take the same view as I do with respect to the supreme importance of the political theory, especially for you in the U.S. I do not believe that a true theory will do much good; but we may at any rate say, contrariwise, that an untrue one does a great deal of harm; and at present much mischief is going on among you as a result of untrue theories."

Utterly irrelevant though it is in subject, I am prompted to add here a passage written during this spring to my friend Lott:—

"As you say you have thoughts of coming to hear Berlioz's *Faust*, I would suggest that a much better thing in that way would be to hear his *Romeo and Juliet*, which I am glad to say is to be repeated on April 7th. This is, I am now certain, the piece a part of which so delighted me when I heard it thirty years ago, and the non-recognition of which by the critical world so exasperated me. I have been since that time aware that it was a part of *Faust* or a part of *Romeo and Juliet;* and now, having recently heard *Faust*, which did not reach my expectations, I am clear it was a part of *Romeo and Juliet*."

I must have been mistaken, however; for I did not find in *Romeo and Juliet* anything which gave me such extreme pleasure as did some music of Berlioz played during the first season of the New Philharmonic Concerts, which he then conducted. I have not been able to discover what music it was.

An occurrence too amusing to go unrecorded, requires the introduction that this autumn I decided to visit the Eastern side of the Grampians, which I had never seen. One of the results is given in the following passage from a letter to my American friend:—

"I may end with something to make you laugh. A story

is in circulation, which originally made its appearance in one of our personal journals, *The World,* that a place which I had visited during my absence has been exorcised, in consequence of my presence. It was at Braemar, where, as the paragraph states (rightly), I had been staying some days, and where a Free Church clergyman saw my name in the visitors' book. 'He was seen to shudder, and, being asked what was the matter, in tremulous accents said that Anti-Christ was living under the same roof, and straightway convened a prayer-meeting in the billiard room as a fumigatory measure.'"

Knowing the worth of newspaper statements, I gave but little heed to this story until I obtained a verification. But from a fellow-member of the Athenæum, who was in the hotel after my departure, and also from another acquaintance, I learnt that something of the kind took place.

A letter written soon after from Ardtornish, or rather from its neighbourhood, contains a quotable paragraph. It is dated " SS. Yacht Dobhran, in the Sleat Sound," 12th August:—

" As you see, I write this while out yachting on the west coast of Scotland, in a steam-yacht belonging to my friends at Ardtornish. I have brought with me, for final revision, the last of the chapters intended for serial publication, [" The Industrial Type "], and shall post it to you from some place we touch at.

It is terribly long, and I fear may entail on you some inconvenience. But it could not with justice to the subject-matter be made shorter; and the matter is of cardinal importance—indeed it is the culminating chapter of the work—and, indeed, of the Synthetic Philosophy, in so far as practical applications are concerned. It has worked out quite to my satisfaction. You will be glad to see how entire is the harmony between the concrete argument, as here set forth, and the abstract argument contained in *The Data of Ethics.*"

The fiftieth meeting of the British Association was held at York this year. Sir John Lubbock, one of our X club, was President; and this fact furnished one of the motives which prompted my departure for York after three weeks at Ardtornish. A letter to Lott, written after my return to town, gives some particulars concerning my stay there:—

"You complained in your last that I had not given you any account of my own previous doings. Well, to exclude any such complaint in your next letter, I will just indicate my movements since I wrote to you from Ardtornish. Valentine Smith took me in the Dobhran to Stranraer on my way to York [he being on his way to London], and in the course of our day's voyage we touched at Jura and called on Henry Evans to see his place. It is recently built and a very comfortable one. At York I had pleasant days: my stay at Escrick being especially enjoyable. The circle was a varied one, and everything was made more agreeable by our very charming hostess, Lady Wenlock, who is one of the most attractive women I know. At Fryson, where I afterwards spent some four days, among the guests were Lady Burdett-Coutts and her husband. She is amiable and unassuming.

From Fryson I went to Rusland, and had a quiet ten days before coming South, where I have now been for nearly a month. On the whole I had a very enjoyable holiday, and have come back all the better for it: being, in fact, in very fair condition."

And so ends the last narrative of my vacation doings with which the reader need be troubled.

The remainder of '81 and early part of '82, yielded but one incident of moment; and this proved to be of so much moment—to me, at least—that I have reserved it for separate narration in the next chapter. Too great an amount of walking, entailed by an expedition into South Wales during my stay at Standish at Christmas, considerably weakened me, and, as I see by entries in my diary after my return to town, prepared the way for the mischief which I brought on myself in February.

The only noteworthy occurrence which the beginning of 1882 brought, is described in the following passage from a letter dated Feb. 14:—

"This morning is marked by a somewhat unusual incident. I received from America, from a naturalized German named Hegeler, one of the firm of Matthieson and Hegeler, Zinc Manufacturers of La Salle, Illinois, a long letter inclosing me a bill of exchange for two hundred and odd pounds. He explained that his immediate reason for sending it was that he had read in the *Chicago Daily News,* that I am "not in easy financial circumstances"; a statement which, I presume, has taken its origin in the announcement of my loss on the *Descriptive Sociology*. I am, by this same post, returning the bill of exchange to Mr. Hegeler, with due recognition of his generosity, but with the explanation that there exists no such need as that which he supposes. He seems, by his account of himself, to have been active in the endeavour to propagate advanced ideas."

Mr. Hegeler's activity in the direction named was shown some four years later by founding and supporting *The Open Court*—a weekly paper having for its object the reconciliation of Religion and Science on the basis of Monism.

The last chapter of *Political Institutions*, commenced on Feb. 13, was not completed till the 24th of March—a delay consequent on the disturbance of health caused in a way to be presently described. Early in April the volume was delivered over to the attention or inattention—chiefly inattention—of the reviewers.

I am not sure whether I entertained some hope that the general doctrine set forth would receive consideration: probably not much if any. But if I entertained any I was disappointed. Though this doctrine, being a part of the general Theory of Evolution, might not unnaturally be regarded as having an *a priori* character, yet, since it is throughout ostensibly based on, and justified by, multitudinous facts, it has an inductive warrant which might have commended it even to those whose reasonings are limited to inferences from blue books and newspaper statistics. But conclusions to which men are averse cannot be made acceptable to them by facts any more than by arguments; and Englishmen are averse to conclusions of wide generality. Not only out of parliament, among the ignorant, but in parliament, among those supposed to be enlightened, such a question as whether there are or are not any limits to the functions of government is pooh-poohed as an abstract question not worth discussing. "Practical" wisdom is supposed to lie in the assumption that an Act of Parliament can do anything, and that it is foolish to waste time in considering whether there are any principles of social life which justify one kind of legislation and negative another. Perhaps it will some day be seen—possibly by some it is seen now—that the question of the proper sphere of government is the most "practical" of all questions; and that the fostering of false ideas concerning the things to be asked for and expected from the State, is fast leading to a social revolution which threatens to end in re-barbarization.

If I did look for some acceptance of the leading ideas

set forth in this volume, it was from the men of science that I looked for it. These general facts,—that in the course of animal evolution there arises a strong contrast between the method of co-operation among those organs which carry on the vital actions, and the method of co-operation among those organs which carry on dealings with the environment; and that there arises in the course of social evolution a kindred contrast between the mode of co-operation among the industrial structures which sustain social life, and the structures which perform actions of offence and defence against other societies (which form the social environment),—might, I thought, be recognized by the scientifically cultured, and their significance perceived. That there results the industrial type or the militant type according as one or other set of organs and mode of co-operation predominates; and that the phenomena of activity, structure, government, with the corresponding beliefs and sentiments, are determined by the relative predominance; proved to be conceptions no more appreciated by those who are in the habit of studying natural causation, than by those to whom natural causation is an unfamiliar thought.

Beliefs, like creatures, must have fit environments before they can live and grow; and the environment furnished by the ideas and sentiments now current, is an entirely unfit environment for the beliefs which the volume sets forth.

CHAPTER LVI.

A GRIEVOUS MISTAKE.

1881—82. ÆT. 61.

WHEN something like half the period covered by the last chapter had elapsed, there occurred an incident which led to the greatest disaster of my life—a disaster that resulted from doing more than I ought to have done.

During many years the materials for the *Principles of Sociology* in course of accumulation, had from time to time shown me the relation which exists between a militancy and a social organization despotic in form and barbaric in ideas and sentiments while they had simultaneously shown me the relation which exists between industrialism and a freer form of government, accompanied by feelings and beliefs of just and humane kinds, conducive in a higher degree to happiness. Near the end of Chapter LII, a passage I have quoted from a letter shows that in 1879 I had spoken to friends concerning the possibility of doing something towards checking the aggressive tendencies displayed by us all over the world—sending, as pioneers, missionaries of "the religion of love," and then picking quarrels with native races and taking possession of their lands. Sympathetic though our conversations were, they ended without result. Sometime near midsummer 1881, however, Mr. Frederic Harrison reminded me of these conversations, and asked me whether I had thought anything more about the matter. While writing *Political Institutions*, I had become still more profoundly impressed with the belief that the possibility of a higher civilization depends wholly on the cessation of militancy and the growth of industrialism. Hence I responded eagerly; and the result was a renewal of the consultations which had been dropped. Mr. John Morley joined in them, Mr. Dillwyn, M.P., Professor Leone Levi, the Rev. Llewelyn Davies, Canon Fremantle, Mr. Chesson, Col. Osborne, and others. By request I drew up an address setting forth our aims: its general idea being that while the doctrine of non-resistance, on which the Peace Society take their stand, is quite untenable, the doctrine of non-aggression is tenable. In July sundry meetings of those interested were held at the house of Sir Arthur (now Lord) Hobhouse; and matters were put in train before the close of the London season.

All this was in direct contravention of a rule I had laid down for myself. As shown by the circular quoted in a preceding chapter, I had, years before, decided to decline joining in public movements; and I had, up to this date, persevered in my refusal to give anything more than name and money in furtherance of ends of which I approved. But now my interest was such that I unhappily forgot, or disregarded, the prudential considerations which had, on all previous occasions, restrained me. Not, indeed, that I intended to take continuously an active part. It was obvious that there existed a large amount of anti-war feeling, especially among the artisan-class and the great body of dissenters; and the belief was that if this feeling were provided with some means of expressing itself, there would result a self-sustaining movement. I thought it would be practicable to join in the effort to initiate such a movement, and then leave others to carry it on. Had not my wishes so possessed me as to exclude ideas of possible consequences, I should have seen that I might not improbably be led, in spite of myself, to do more than I intended.

In the autumn our meetings were resumed; arrangements were gradually matured; further sympathizers gathered together; and on the 22 of February 1882, we held a public meeting at the Westminster Palace Hotel. Being anxious to see a successful start made, I had allowed much work to devolve upon me which should have been undertaken by others. I agreed, contrary to my original intention, to take part in the meeting, move a resolution and make a speech. With my narrow margin of nervous power it was an absurd thing to do; and still more so to persevere when, as my diary shows, I was, for several days before, breaking down. But I had put my hand to the plough and would not turn back. There was here again illustrated a trait on which I have before commented—the liability to be tyrannized over by a resolution once formed: consciousness becoming so possessed by the end in view that all thought of anything adverse is excluded.

Nothing of any moment came of our action. Some sympathy was expressed by newspapers representing the dissenters; and I remember one of them said it was a disgrace to their body that such a movement should have been initiated by rationalists. Yet neither from those who are stirred chiefly by religious motives, nor from those who are stirred chiefly by political motives, did there come any support worth naming. Though year by year filibustering colonists and ambitious officials, civil and military, were everywhere laying hands on the territories of neighbouring weaker races (" 'annexing' the wise call it ")—though consequent chronic hostilities, and multiplying salaries to new governors and their staffs, were continually swelling the national expenditure; yet the elector at home, preoccupied by disputes about local option, hours of closing public-houses, employers' liabilities, preferential railway rates, and countless small questions, would give no attention to the fact that his burdens are being perpetually made heavier, and his risks more numerous, without his assent or even his knowledge. And while the average tax-payer, bourgeois and artisan, thinking only of small proximate evils, remained indifferent to this great but remote evil, the organs of the upper classes, ever favouring a policy which calls for increase of armaments and multiplication of places for younger sons, ridiculed the supposition that it was practicable or desirable to restrain those colonial authorities who yearly commit us unawares to expensive wars and additional responsibilities.

It was, indeed, a foolish hope that any appreciable effect could be produced under conditions then existing, and with an average national character like that displayed. While continental nations were bristling with arms, and our own was obliged to increase its defensive forces and simultaneously foster militant sentiments and ideas, it was out of the question that an " Anti-Aggression League " could have any success. While promotion was accorded, and titles were given, to those who, in our dependencies, forestalled supposed hostile intentions of neighbouring tribes by commencing hostilities—while the tens of thousands of appointed teachers of forgiveness of injuries, uttered no denunciations of the implied maxim—" Injure others before they injure you "; it was absurd to expect that any considerable number would listen to the prinicple enunciated, that aggression should be suffered before counter-aggression is entered upon. With a parliament and people who quietly look on, or even applaud, while, on flimsy pretexts, the forces of our already vast Eastern Empire successfully invade neighbouring States, and then vilify as " dacoits," *i.e.* brigands, those who continue to resist them, the expectation that equitable international conduct would commend itself was irrational.

But while no good came of our movement, great evil came to me. There was produced a mischief which, in a gradually increasing degree, undermined life and arrested work.

Beyond dictating the last pages of *Political Institutions*, nothing was done during the Spring: recovery of health, not then supposed to be seriously deranged, being the chief occupation. There were visits of a few days to Brighton and one to Hastings (where the Busks were staying), with consequent improvements, and relapses on return to town and resumption of daily routine. There was a short sojourn with my friend Lott at Quorn early in April, and a longer one towards the end of May, during which he and his belongings accompanied me on a three days' excursion to Sherwood Forest. Standish, too, was visited on my way back to town; and with my stay there this time is associated the remembrance of a discussion on the question of immortality: the occasion for it being the recent death of Mrs. Potter, which had ended a friendship of nearly forty years standing. As may be supposed, my position in respect to the question discussed was agnostic—the position that on the one hand there is no evidence supporting the belief in immortality, and that on the other hand there is no evidence to warrant denial of it.

Later in the season occurred a sequence of this visit. My friend Potter was one of the directors of the Dutch Rhenish Railway Company; and there had long been entertained the suggestion that I should some day accompany him on one of his visits to Holland to attend the annual meeting. This year the suggestion took effect. Going a few days in advance, to renew my recollections of Antwerp and to give a little time to Ghent and Rotterdam, I joined my friend and two of his daughters at the Hague. Our brief stay there was followed by a visit to Amsterdam, where, as at the Hague, the picture galleries were seen, and where, of course, many adverse criticisms were passed by me. Two works only I remember—one a Burgomaster's feast by Van der Helst, which, unsatisfactory as a whole (the subject being unfitted for art), is admirable in many of its faces; the other, Rembrandt's celebrated " Lesson in Anatomy " at the Hague. This appeared to me to fail utterly in the essential point of dramatic truth. Instead of being shown as occupied in observing the professor's proceedings, or listening to what he says, or else in some intelligible bye-play, the students are shown in meaningless attitudes and with vacant expressions of face, in no way relevant to the occasion.

After a day at Utrecht (where the railway meeting was held), a short sojourn at Cologne, and a voyage up the Rhine as far as Coblenz, my friends and I parted: they continuing their journey to Switzerland, and I turning my face homewards—taking my route up the Moselle to Trèves to see the Roman remains, going thence to Metz, and from there viâ Paris to London.

No permanent benefit resulted from this any more than from previous relaxations. There had commenced a series of descents, severally caused by exceeding my diminished strength and making it still less, which brought me down in the course of subsequent years to the condition of a confirmed invalid, leading little more than a vegetative life.

This final result I refer to here, considerably in advance of its date, chiefly for the purpose of pointing a moral. The occasion is a fit one for criticizing an opinion often professed and rarely ever called in question.

We are told that the pleasurable feeling caused by the doing of right is itself a sufficient reward for the right done, and a sufficient compensation for any evil which doing right entails. Though probably many are conscious that their experiences do not verify this belief, yet the propriety of maintaining it, as well as all beliefs which apparently conduce to good conduct, seem so obvious that they keep silence. The tacit assumption made by writers on ethics, and by ordinary people who moralize on the affairs of life, is that only vice brings ill-consequences, while virtue always brings good consequences; and this creed is taught without qualification, though facts daily prove that wrong-doing often escapes punishment, alike external and internal, (conscience being callous), while right-doing often brings heavy penalties, and is followed by no such moral satisfaction as appreciably mitigate the pains to be borne. Bodies permanently enfeebled by self-sacrifices in nursing, minds injured for life by overwork in fulfilment of responsibilities, social positions damaged by the conscientious acting-out of convictions, are constantly thrust on the observation of all; and inquiries, if made, would prove that the supposed mental content obtained not only forms no adequate set off to the evils suffered, but commonly forms no appreciable element in consciousness.

Certainly this expresses my own experience; and I have no reason to suppose it exceptional. If I know my own motives, the actions I have narrated above were prompted exclusively by the desire to further human welfare. Indeed, I do not see how any other construction can be put upon them. It is obvious that I had nothing to gain in this world by the implied expenditure of time, money, and effort; and as I have no belief in anything to be gained in another world, it cannot be that other-worldliness moved me. But right though I thought it, my course brought severe penalties and no compensations whatever. I am not thinking only of the weeks, months, years, of wretched nights and vacant days; though these made existence a long-drawn weariness. I refer chiefly to the gradual arrest and final cessation of my work; and the consciousness that there was slipping by that closing part of life during which it should have been completed. For had I not been thus incapacitated, the remaining volumes of the Synthetic Philosophy might by this time have been written and published. What, then, is the quality of the consciousness produced in me by looking back on this most disastrous incident in my career? Though I still regard with approval the course I took, considered intrinsically, yet contemplating it, even when separated from its consequences, does not produce a feeling appreciably above equanimity. And when, with this lack of any pleasurable consciousness, there is joined the painful consciousness of evils entailed, and especially the consciousness of a great aim missed, the total result is a feeling the reverse of pleasurable. Habitually shunning the recollection, I shy at the rising idea as a horse shies at an alarming object, and quickly take some other course of thought. In this case, then, the accepted dogma is in every way falsified.

It is best to recognize the facts as they are, and not try to prop up rectitude by fictions. The first needful qualification of the current belief is that the good results of right conduct can be looked for only in the majority of cases, and not in each particular case. And the second needful qualification is that it is not the absolutely right conduct, but the relatively right conduct, from which, on the average, good results flow—the conduct which is duly adjusted to social conditions.

CHAPTER LVII.

COMING EVENTS.

1881—82.　ÆT. 61—62.

A LETTER quoted in the last chapter but one, under date 13 June, 1881, contained an unquoted passage which I have reserved for insertion here, as being relevant to the matters contained in this chapter. It runs as follows:—

"After my experience last year in going to and from Alexandria, on each of which occasions I had a three days voyage, my fears of sea-travelling in respect of entailed sleeplessness are somewhat diminished; and I have of late been consequently entertaining the thought that I may possibly come over to see you. If so, it will be, I think, in the latter half of next year."

In the course of the autumn the intention thus indicated gained in definiteness, and by-and-bye prompted preparations; as witness the following extract dated Jan. 10, 1882:—

"I spent Christmas week with the Potters in Gloucestershire, and during my stay was led by my friend Potter, who has been across the Atlantic some dozen times, to take time by the forelock in respect of a good berth. The result of our conversation was that he wrote to Cunard's, and that I have secured a desirable room in the "Servia", sailing on the 12th of August. Unless, therefore, the time of sailing should be altered or some disaster should happen to me, I suppose I shall see you about the 21st or 22nd of August."

Soon afterwards a further arrangement was made. On Feb. 16, I wrote thus:—

"As to my intentions when I arrive in the U.S. they are at present not very decided. . . I must not forget one piece of intelligence, namely that my intimate friend Edward Lott, of whom you have heard me speak (I am not quite sure whether you have seen him) has volunteered to accompany me, at any rate as far as New York. This will be a great addition to my pleasure, and should we arrange for him to join me in part of the tour, he may serve very advantageously as a buffer: you may depute to him in a considerable measure the function which you have volunteered to undertake."

I suppose it was his constitutional modesty which led my old friend to make his proposal tentatively, as he did; but the hesitation was quite uncalled for. He might have been sure that after a friendship commenced more than forty years before, the harmony of which had never for a moment been broken, and during which we had made together so many excursions, long and short, his companionship would gratify me more than that of anyone else.

The project having been matured thus far, various sequences presently came. Here is one, indicated in a letter written on March 8, 1882:—

"I see by a copy of the *Tribune* which he sent me two days ago, that Smalley has telegraphed particulars concerning my visit. Various mis-statements of course are becoming current. It is reported over here that I am in financial difficulties, and am going over to lecture, with a view, it is implied, of recouping myself! You may judge, if you do not otherwise know, the degree of likelihood there is of this, from the fact that a few days ago I received an application from one of your lecture-bureaux offering me terms up to $250 per lecture, which I wrote by return of post positively declining, and saying that no terms they could offer would tempt me."

A passage in a letter dated March 29, refers to another sequence:

" Your suggestion with regard to attending the meeting of the Association at Montreal, is one which I, of course, yield to; especially with the view of supporting you in your position of Chairman of the Committee of Science Teaching, and especially as you say I shall be free to leave if I find for any reason that it is too much for me.

I have been considerably knocked up by the worry of this Anti-Aggression League business, which has chiefly fallen on my shoulders, and have been in great fear of a prolonged breakdown. However, I am considerably better and hope shortly to be all right again."

This hope, alas! as already indicated in the last chapter, was doomed to disappointment. I little thought then that there had been initiated a slow and long descent to the invalid life of later years. On April 21 I again expressed myself decidely with respect to my intentions.

" I have already given in the *Athenæum* an authoritative contradiction to the rumour that I was about to lecture during my tour in America, and I do not propose to change my decision. The reply I gave to one of the lecture bureaux which made an offer to me, was that neither the offer they made, nor any other offer, would induce me. I must still make the same answer. Even the offer of £300 for me to lecture, which you communicate, fails to alter my resolution. Were lecturing my habit, as in the case of Tyndall and Huxley, there would be nothing special in my undertaking to give lectures or a lecture; and the implication would be different. But as matters stand, the giving a lecture or reading a paper, would be nothing more than making myself a show; and I absolutely decline to make myself a show.

What I do while with you I mean to make entirely subordinate to relaxation and amusement; and I shall resist positively anything which in any considerable way entails on me responsibilities or considerable excitements. I suppose you have long ago discovered that I have a faculty of saying No, and that when I say No I mean No."

Referring to the same subject, a letter of June 21 says:—

"With respect to the proposed public dinner, I must, I presume, assent. To decline would be awkward; and as I propose to limit myself a good deal in the way of social intercourse and receptions, I must, I conclude, yield to some arrangement which shall replace more detailed entertainments."

Would that my boasted ability to say "No" had been more fully justified! Now, when I look back, I recognize sundry occasions on which failure of this ability entailed mischievous results.

The ensuing six weeks brought no incident of moment not already named. Relaxations and excursions which I trusted would restore my lost balance failed to do this. A letter of July 21 says:—

"Though better, I am still not up to much work. I am looking forward to the voyage and my visit with you to raise me to a higher level of vigour."

The hope thus implied was not a very rational one. Had I called to mind past results of the wear and tear of travel, I should have anticipated mischief rather than benefit. Even had I been up to my ordinary low level of health, the expedition would have been of doubtful prudence, and in my then debilitated state it was decidedly imprudent.

But here was another case in which a plan once fixed upon becomes a tyrant over me, and dictates persistence regardless of consequences. Under the circumstances which had arisen I ought to have abandoned the projected voyage, and sacrificed my double passage money (I had taken a state-room all to myself, not daring to risk the additional hindrances to sleep entailed by the presence of a fellow-passenger): at the same time reimbursing my friend Lott for his bootless outlay. But such a course did not, I believe, even occur to me, and I unhesitatingly occupied the early part of August in completing my preparations.

On the 10th I went down to Liverpool to spend a day or two with the Holts, who had kindly proposed that I should make their house my place of departure.

CHAPTER LVIII.

A VISIT TO AMERICA.

1882. ÆT. 62.

PARAPHRASING a familiar remark, one may say,—Happy are the voyagers whose narratives are dull. Ours answered to this description. It was prosperous, and without noteworthy incident. Of entries in my diary, one made on the 16th, after only four days at sea, shows my constitutional impatience—" Getting very much bored." On the 19th there is the entry—" Magnificent sunset; the finest in colour I ever saw." And a wretched night, noted on the 18th, was accompanied by the remark—" Terrific disturbance from fog-whistle."

This last entry reminds me of an error I had made. It will scarcely be said of me that I usually accept current statements without sufficient criticism; but even I am not infrequently misled by too readily giving credence. It is commonly alleged that a berth amid-ships is the best, because the motion from pitching is there the smallest; and the berth which I took in the " Servia " was in this position. I quite forgot that, as I am a good sailor (I had not a qualm either going or returning), avoidance of much motion was of secondary moment, and that for me a state-room in the bow, where the noises are least, was the most desirable. The result of the mistake was that not only by the shrieks of the fog-whistle, which was just over my head, but by other loud sounds, my ordinarily bad sleep was made more broken than ever.

A climax was put to the mischief on the last night. We arrived too late to reach the wharf, and had to lie off Staten Island. Here the raising of the baggage and cargo, in preparation for landing in the morning, gave me, as my diary says, "a horrible night from noises;" so that, when my friend Youmans came on board at 7 on the morning of the 21st to welcome me, he found me in an unusually dilapidated state.

"I had to remind myself when entering a shop that it was not needful to speak French", said Lott a day or two after, *a propos* of the foreign aspect of the houses. It is the older part of New York which yields this impression, due, I suppose, to the prevalence of green Venetian-blind shutters, like those which prevail on the Continent.

Soon, however, when we reached its modern parts, the feeling produced by the aspect of New York was one of surprise at its magnificence. Thinking of it chiefly as a centre of business-activity, and perhaps unduly influenced by much that I had read about its ill-paved streets, I had conceived the place as having small pretensions to architectural beauty; and was consequently unprepared for the multitude of imposing edifices. My diary says—"Am astonished by the grandeur of New York". We have nothing to compare with Fifth Avenue.

Prof. and Mrs. Youmans had expected me to be their guest, and had made arrangements for my friend Lott also, in fulfilment of an invitation sent him to England.

But I was obliged to disappoint them. In my shattered state I dared not undertake the social responsibilities which would have been entailed, even in the absence of visitors. And then the interviewers had to be avoided. These quickly made their appearance, and, though put off for a time by the statement that I was too unwell to see anyone, would have soon returned. The result was that before the day was over, we migrated to the Windsor Hotel; where, my companion having a great faculty for silence when need was, I felt in his company safe against excitement.

Next day was spent in making preparations for our tour; and the morning after saw us on our way to a place of rest, which was so needful to me.

The first part of our journey was by steamer up the Hudson, which scarcely reached my expectations, save about West Point, where it is picturesque. Leaving it at Rondout Ferry, we went thence by railway and vehicle to the Kaarterskill Hotel—the place Youmans had fixed upon for us. Some 3,000 feet above the sea, this is one of those refuges to which the Americans fly in July and August from the heats of their cities. Here five days were passed beneficially.

The entry we made in the hotel-book was—"Mr. Edward Lott and friend": the intention being to avoid salutations and inquiries. Of course this mode of entry was in itself suspicious; and though the New York papers had given no clue (for they had been successfully mystified respecting my movements), the host and some of the guests, when the time for our departure came, said that from the beginning they had known who the " friend " was; but that, seeing I wished to be quiet, they had respected the *incognito*. We did not repeat the device, which was obviously useless.

Our rambles during the few days' stay on the top of this mountain (or big hill, rather, for the Catskills have not that ruggedness which the word mountains suggests) made us acquainted, among other things, with a portion of virgin forest. I was shown how erroneous was my preconception. In common, I daresay, with the preconceptions of most others, mine had been based on experiences of woods at home; and I had failed to imagine an important trait, of which we see nothing in England—the cumbering of the ground on every side with the decaying, moss-covered trunks of past generations of trees, lying prone, or leaning one upon another at various angles, and in all stages of decay.

While sitting on a ledge of rock facing the East, and looking over the wide country stretching away to the horizon beyond the Hudson, it was interesting to think that here we were in a land we had read about all our lives—interesting, and a little difficult, to think of it as some three thousand miles from the island on the other side of the Atlantic whence we had come. Not easy was it either, and indeed impossible in any true sense, to conceive the real position of this island on that vast surface which slowly curves downward beyond the horizon: the impossibility being one which I have vividly felt when gazing sea-ward at the masts of a vessel below the horizon, and trying to conceive the actual surface of the Earth, as slowly bending round till its meridians met eight thousand miles beneath my feet: the attempt producing what may be figuratively called a kind of mental choking, from the endeavour to put into the intellectual structure a conception immensely too large for it.

I may remark, in passing, that it is well occasionally thus to do, what nine hundred and ninety-nine in a thousand never think of doing—to dwell awhile on such imaginations as we can frame of those vast cosmical phenomena amid which "our little lives" are passed—to think, for example, that while the eye has been passing from the beginning of this line to the end of it, the Earth has travelled thirty miles!

On August 29, a drive, a short railway-journey, a ferry passage, and a longer railway-journey, brought us to Albany, where a few hours were spent: mainly in seeing the Capitol. In fulfilment of a pre-arrangement we then went on to Saratoga.

The pre-arrangement was that Prof. Youmans and his wife would meet us there. We found them at the United States Hotel, which my American friend wished me to see as unique—" said to be the biggest hotel in the world—1500 guests," as my diary notes. The sight was, however, partially thrown away on me. I have a vague recollection of the vast dining-room with its long ranges of tables and multitudinous persons; but the persons themselves left no impression. I am a bad observer of humanity in the concrete: being too much given to wandering off into the abstract. My habit of falling into trains of thought is at variance with the habit of watching people around. I suppose I lack a good deal of knowledge to be hence derived, and lose a good deal of amusement. In these latter years, especially, I find that I contemplate so little the faces of those whom I see at parties or elsewhere, that several meetings are commonly needful to make me remember them. Naturally, then, I did not profit much by the opportunity of criticizing a crowd of

American fashionables. Neither their manners nor their costumes, both of which would, I suppose, have called remarks from most people, called any remarks from me. Costumes, indeed, I usually notice so little that, unless they are very good or very bad, I retain not the slightest recollections of them. A simple dress which is elegant without the appearance of effort, and a dress which is tawdry, or discordant in its colours, or bad from over-elaboration, I occasionally remark. But unless as presenting one or other of these extremes, the attire of no lady at a dinner party or *soirée* ever leaves the slightest trace in my memory. Such attention as I give is given to the wearers and not to their clothes.

One person whom I saw, however, and one criticism which I passed on him, I do remember. Walking about the hotel garden was a railway magnate, said to be one of the wealthiest of Americans. He was a coarse-featured man; and, I was told, had manners to match. Before I left England, one who had business-relations with him offered me a letter of introduction; saying that, if I behaved civilly and went to dine with him, he would probably give me a free pass over the railways. But I preferred not to accept the introduction.

Two days sufficed for Saratoga; and on the morning of Sept. 1 we departed northwards by railway to Lake St. George, and by steamer to its upper end: being accompanied so far by Mr. and Mrs. Youmans, who there bade us good-bye and returned home. Lake St. George is the most picturesque thing I saw in the United States. Three of our English lakes placed end to end would be something like it in extent and scenery. A steamer up Lake Champlain delivered us at Burlington in the course of the afternoon; and the afternoon of the next day saw us on our way to Canada. Mr. Iles, the manager of the Windsor Hotel, had some months before written pressing me to stay there when I visited Montreal. He came to a station some distance down the line to meet us, and piloted us thence to our destination. During the few days of our stay, we were treated by him *en prince*.

The meeting of the British Association had ended before our arrival. On the whole this was fortunate; for, probably, had it been going on, further mischiefs would have been added to those which I had suffered. The sights of Montreal and its surroundings remained the sole attractions. There was the ascent of the hill which gives its name to the place—Mount Royal; there was a drive up the banks of the St. Lawrence to the Lachine rapids; and there were the noteworthy buildings of the city itself.

To many travellers these would, I dare say, have given more pleasure than they gave to me; for I failed to exclude the thought of certain antecedents not in harmony with a feeling of admiration. For a generation or more Canadians have been coming to England for capital to make their great lines of railway; and have put before English investors statements of costs and profits so favourable, that they have obtained the required sums. These statements have proved far more wide of the truth than such statements usually prove—so wide of it that the undertakings have been extremely disastrous to investors: impoverishing great numbers, and ruining not a few (my poor friend Lott becoming, eventually, one of these last, and dying prematurely in consequence). But while, to open up these communications which have been so immensely beneficial to their commerce and industries, the Canadians have, by exaggerated representations, got from the mother-country resources which they were supposed unable to furnish themselves, they have yet been able to build imposing cities full of magnificent mansions, and at Montreal an hotel far exceeding in grandeur anything the mother-country could, at that time, show.

Sunday and Monday having been passed at Montreal, half a day on Tuesday carried us by the Grand Trunk railway to Brockville; where, crossing the St. Lawrence, we got on board a steamer bound for Alexandra Bay—a place built for visitors to " The Thousand Islands." Here the morrow was spent with much pleasure, partly in a hired boat which took us amid the islands near at hand, and partly in an excursion-steamer which made a run of some forty miles, it was said, through the remoter islands. How the region could have been formed—how the St. Lawrence could have cut these multitudinous channels, dividing tree-covered masses of rock of all sizes,—it is difficult to understand. But it is the romance of the scene which chiefly impresses one. Obviously this trait has prompted inhabitation; for here a small hotel, and there a villa, peeps out amid the trees. It has become the fashion among wealthy Americans to have one of these small water-guarded areas as a summer abode: gratification being doubtless given to a sentiment which is active during boyhood and is not altogether dead in adult life.

Picking us up next day, a steamer for Toronto carried us through another region of " The Thousand Islands," and presently on to Lake Ontario. " In the afternoon we came unto " a town, in which it could not be said that " it seemed always afternoon "; but in which, contrariwise, the vivacity of morning seemed conspicuous. This was Kingston, where the steamer stopped for a time to take in wood. We rambled about and found, to our astonishment and shame, that though containing only ten or twelve thousand people, Kingston had the telephone in use all over the place. I say "to our shame", because at that time (1882), the telephone was scarcely used at all in London, and was unknown in our great provincial towns. I have sometimes puzzled myself over the anomaly that while, in some ways, the English are extremely enterprising, they are, in other ways, extremely unenterprising. I remember that in 1868 the hotel I stopped at in Naples had electric bells to all the rooms; though in England no such appliances had come within the range of my observation. While there exist a select few among us who are full of ideas, the great masses of our people appear to be without ideas. Or, to state the case otherwise, it seems as if the English nature (I say English, because I do not assert it of either Scotch or Irish) exhibits a wider range than any other nature between its heights of intelligence and its depths of stupidity.

A night spent on board the steamer while traversing Lake Ontario, was followed by the arrival at Toronto before mid-day; and, after a few hours spent there, another steamer took us across the lake to Niagara. Thence, after a brief railway-journey, we reached the Falls.

"Much what I had expected" is the remark in my diary. That is, the Falls neither came short of my expectations nor much exceeded them. I think, however, that the effect of closer acquaintance was to deepen the impression of grandeur. With the intermission of a day at Buffalo, a week was spent in contemplating the scene and its surroundings from all points of view. We saw everything that was to be seen, including the "Cave of the Winds"; and saw it with the deliberation needful for full appreciation and enjoyment.

I was a good deal at a loss to understand the denuding action by which the falls have cut their way back so far. Often where streams make deep gorges, they do it by the aid of stones and gravel swept down in times of flood, and serving to file the rocks. But at Niagara no hard masses are habitually carried over by the water to act as excavating tools; and though, a mile lower down, the rapids are violent enough to carry along great rocks if they came, yet the intervening space of water has a current so moderate that it could not carry along even boulders. How then is the material cut out, and in what shape transported? There seems no alternative but to conclude that the denuding force is the unaided impact of the water on the rocks at the bottom of the fall. The fall is 160 feet high; and it is calculated that it delivers 100,000,000 tons of water per hour, or more than 27,000 tons per second. As it curls over, this mass of water is probably some 20 feet thick; and though, before reaching the bottom of the water below, perhaps 30 or 40 feet down, its superficial parts must lose a good deal of their velocity, yet its central parts are probably not much retarded. At the bottom, this mass of water is subject to a lateral pressure of, say, fifteen pounds to the square inch; so that though, ordinarily, a stream falling on a hard surface disperses itself laterally, this mass of water is in great measure prevented from thus dispersing itself. Hence the rocks on which it falls have to bear the brunt of, say, 20,000 tons per second moving with a velocity of more than 100 feet per second; and we must infer that the continuous blow is so violent that simple abrasion detaches particles from the surfaces of the rocks and the current carries them away. Though the Clifton Hotel, at which we stayed, is probably a third of a mile from the Great Fall, and though my bedroom was on the opposite side of the building, its windows were in a state of constant jar; and, doubtless, this tremendous impact was the cause.

I have omitted to say that the morning after our arrival Prof. Youmans and his sister, having travelled all night from New York, came to bear us company for a few days. Their presence added much to the enjoyments of our sojourn.

Chicago, at which place Lott had some relatives, was to have been the western limit of our tour; but my state was such that I dared not undertake so long a journey. I urged my friend to proceed thither without me: proposing to stay at Niagara till his return, and representing that the company of Miss Youmans would keep me alive. But I could not persuade him: he insisted on remaining to take care of me.

Our first stopping-place after leaving the Falls on Sept. 16, was Cleveland; respecting which my diary says—" walked about; surprised by the display and bustle " in so new a place. After Cleveland came Pittsburg, boasted of as the smokiest town in the world.

Why Cleveland and why Pittsburg? may naturally be asked. The answer carries me back to our voyages across the Atlantic. On the Servia's tender at Liverpool, a letter of introduction was handed to me by Mr. Andrew Carnegie, whose iron works at Pittsburg, aided in their prosperity by protection, have made him a millionaire.

He pressed me to visit him at Cresson, a place on the Alleghanies, like the Kaarterskill Hotel on the Catskills, used as a summer refuge by over-heated Americans. I eventually yielded to the pressure; and our journey through Cleveland to Pittsburg was in fulfilment of the promise made.

The repulsiveness of Pittsburg led me to break through my resolution always to stop at an hotel; and in the evening we drove with Mr. Carnegie to the house of his brother a few miles out. After we had inspected his works next day, he took us by special carriage, which to my great comfort contained a sleeping compartment, to Cresson. It was now the 19th of September; the summer heats were over; the visitors had gone home; the hotel was closed; and Mr. Carnegie's *annexe* was unavailable. He took us to an old-fashioned inn at " Mountain Top." His departure after a day spent in showing us the neighbourhood, and our departure after a day spent in visiting the little town of Ebensburg, were followed by descent of the Eastern flank of the Alleghanies to Harrisburg. To a day spent in rambling about this not-very-interesting town, succeeded a railway-journey to Washington.

Whether the fact that the President (or rather the Vice-President, for Mr. Garfield was dead) was away at Newport, prompted the decision to go direct to Washington without stopping at Baltimore, I cannot remember; but I remember that his absence was a cause of satisfaction to me. Aversion to ceremonial interviews I have before exemplified as a trait of mine. Partly this is due to dislike of formalities, and partly to a disinclination to converse with strangers. Under ordinary circumstances, thinking is to me more pleasurable than talking; and hence, in the absence of an interlocutor in whom I feel interest, I am not tempted to talk. Some sentiment of friendship or personal regard is requisite to make conversation preferable.

The sights of Washington of course received due attention. We visited the White House, though not its occupant; we went over the Capitol, and paused for a few minutes in its then empty legislative chambers; with Major Powell as our guide we perambulated the Smithsonian Institution and its surroundings; we contemplated the Washington monument, then in course of erection; and we did some justice to the suburbs. One of our days was of course devoted to an excursion up the Potomac to Mount Vernon, famous as Washington's home and burial place; where some hours were spent in looking over rooms and relics, and wandering about the grounds. I remember we were astonished at seeing a place planted with slips of willow notified as having been brought from Napoleon's tomb in St. Helena. The incongruity struck us both as passing strange.

Was it at Washington, or was it elsewhere, or was it at all places, that I was struck with the passion of the Americans for iced water? Not only does it come up at every meal, but even in the middle of the night it must be made accessible: the habit being to place in the mouth of a jug a wedge-shaped piece of ice too large to go in, and with its narrow end downwards, so that, thawing all night and dripping into the jug, it insures an ever-ready supply of water just above freezing point. Evidently the origin of this habit is the need for a sensation, which in one form or other is universal. Everyone dislikes food that is insipid, and, when there is no natural taste in it, condiments and sweetening agents are resorted to. Drinks that have flavours, sweet or bitter, are preferred to tasteless drinks; and, if a liquid not otherwise attractive is taken, then it must be not tepid, but decidedly hot or decidedly cold. But why have the Americans especially become such lovers of iced water? Possibly the prevalent disuse of alcoholic drinks, which yield the required sensations, and which one scarcely ever sees at table in the hotels, is the cause. The sensation of taste being ungratified, the sensation of temperature is, as far as possible, substituted for it.

There can, I think, be little doubt that the habit is an injurious one. In the first place, taking an amount of liquid much exceeding that required for carrying on the bodily functions, is pretty certain to be detrimental; and in the second place, frequently taking this at a temperature so much below blood-heat, is also pretty certain to be detrimental by continually checking digestion, which is temporarily arrested by an influx of cold liquid. It is true that upon occasion cold liquid may, by reaction, stimulate the gastric circulation; but perpetually exciting the blood-vessels to reactions inevitably produces in them an abnormal state, resulting in a chronically deficient circulation.

Our arrival at Baltimore in the evening of the 28th was followed next morning by the arrival of Youmans from New York. Whether my state of health would negative the proposed public dinner, had remained an undecided question; and he came over to see what was now my state and my decision. Some improvement had taken place; and though in my diary entries of "bad nights," "wretched nights," &c., were frequent, the number of better nights had increased. Hence I thought I might venture; and, returning to New York, he thereafter busied himself in making preparations.

We went to the Mount Vernon Hotel, which was, to my thinking, the best we met with in the United States: moderate in size (small, indeed, according to the American standard) and well appointed. I detest big hotels, with vast crowds of guests: not liking to feel myself a mere unit mechanically manipulated in a great machine. I believe that at the Mount Vernon Hotel, as elsewhere, the waiters, negro and half-caste, were considerably surprised by my disregard of their dictations. Clothed with a little brief authority, they delight in exercising it; and, in the hotels everywhere, habitually fix on this or that table for a guest in a peremptory kind of way. Avoidance of draught, obtainment of light, or other reason, often led me to ignore the choice made for me, where no claims of other guests were in question. Evidently the waiters were unused to this; for Americans commonly make no demurs either to the bedrooms assigned to them by the clerk at the bureau, or to the tables they are motioned to by the head-waiter. The English have the repute among them of being grumblers, and I believe I fully maintained the character.

One of the things I saw in Baltimore was the Johns Hopkins University, which Prof. Sylvester, then engaged there, took us over; but the thing which gave me most pleasure was the Peabody Institute, remarkable for its architectural beauty, especially in the interior. The library struck me as combining use and beauty in a manner perfectly satisfactory. I can recall nothing equal to it. The name of the architect, which I inquired, has unfortunately lapsed from my memory.

Some years before, I had met in England Mr. J. W. Garrett, President of the Baltimore and Ohio Railway. He lived in Baltimore during the winter, and in summer at his residence, Montebello, a few miles out. We drove over; and by pressure I was induced to break through my rule of taking up my abode at an hotel. We spent at Montebello five pleasant and beneficial days: lounging in the garden, driving, and on one occasion being taken down the upper part of Chesapeake Bay by our host in a private steamer. As a relaxation he had taken to breeding horses, and was proud of his stud. He had many men engaged in making a private race-course, on which to test the speed of his colts.

Mr. Garrett exhibited the results, so common in America, of over-work. When I saw him in England I supposed that he was ten years or more my senior; but I found, to my astonishment, that he was my junior. To the satisfaction of his wife, I began to preach to him the gospel of relaxation—a gospel on which, a few weeks later, I enlarged in public at greater length.

Poor man! he did not live long to carry on either work or amusement. Some three years after, Mrs. Garrett, thrown from her carriage, died in a few days, and he, chronically out of health, succumbed to the shock.

The next stage in our journey brought us to Philadelphia. To it, of course, some days were to be devoted. Mr. G. W. Childs, who makes it a point to entertain all notables, would have had us stay with him, but from doing this I excused myself. In various ways, however, he conduced to our convenience. Mr. Cook, the correspondent of *The Times* at Philadelphia, being our guide, and Mr. Childs' carriage being at our disposal, we saw what was to be seen at our ease.

There were the extensive engine works of Messrs. Baldwin, where they are said to turn out a complete locomotive engine *per* day. There was the magnificent park, in a drive through which Prof. Leidy was our companion. There was an excursion up and down the Delaware River, in a steamer which Mr. Roberts, President of the Philadelphia Railway, placed at our disposal. There was the Girard College, extensive and well-appointed, but subjecting its boys to a mechanical, coercive kind of discipline which called forth from me a strong expression of disapproval. I hoped the official who showed us round would communicate it to those in authority.

Some immense municipal buildings were, I remember, among the attractions of the city. I was told by Mr. Childs that there existed a committee of citizens formed for the purpose of putting a check on the extravagance of the local authorities; and I believe that in some other American cities there are like committees. A generation ago it was commonly thought that democracy was, and would be, economical; since nothing could be more obvious than that when the people had power, they would not tolerate the wasteful expenditure of the money which they furnished. But experience is not verifying this *a priori* conclusion in America, and is not verifying it with us.

One more railway-journey, bringing us to New York, completed the tour we had made during the seven weeks of our absence. On looking at the map and seeing how small was our circuit and how enormous was the area of the States not even approached by us, I felt astonished, and almost alarmed, at the vastness of the society we were in. To be told that the dividing line between East and West, on the two sides of which the populations balance, is fast approaching the Mississippi, amazes one on remembering how short a time it is since the countries to the west of the Mississippi were inhabited only by Indians. Clearly, at the present rate of progress (unless internal dissensions should cause separation, which is quite possible), the United States will very soon be by far the most powerful nation in the world.

Our experiences of travel did not verify the impressions derived from books read in past years. Intrusiveness was a trait of Americans described and exemplified; but we found none of it. I cannot remember one occasion on which we were addressed by fellow-travellers, the only intrusiveness was that of the interviewers, who, in fulfilment of their functions, tried, at various places, to see me. As I had anticipated, my friend Lott served as an admirable buffer, and in all cases pleaded, truly enough, that I was not sufficiently well to be visible. As they could not interview me they sometimes interviewed him; and on one occasion he figured in the report as my " leonine friend ". I can understand his calm, massive face, and large beard, suggesting the epithet; and probably when occasion called for it he might be leonine enough in action; but in my long experience of him he had proved himself a very pacific lion.

Interviewers when baulked are apt to be disagreeable. Feeling bound to make some report, they pick up such details as they can from servants, and are not over particular respecting the trustworthiness of their informants. Indeed, in the accounts they thus gather of sayings and doings, food and habits, anything which admits of having a ludicrous aspect given to it is made the most of.

After my return to New York, I named to Youmans some of the annoying things that had been said: among others a reported opinion of mine about an English author then in America. It was purely fictitious; and I remarked that it would be almost worth while to have an interview for the purpose of contradicting these false statements. "By all means," said he,—" let me interview you." I acceded to the suggestion, and next morning was appointed for the purpose. The result was, however, that I practically interviewed myself. Two instances excepted, the questions as well as the answers were my own. Ever ready to make the best of the occasion, Youmans had this seeming-interview set up in type, and distributed impressions to the New York papers, and, in advance, to the Chicago papers. Hence it appeared simultaneously in whole or in part in many of them: so being unlike an ordinary interview, which is the product of the reporter for a single paper. Of course my remarks, after my manner, were mainly critical; and while not failing to recognize the greatness of American achievements, consisted largely of adverse comments on their political life. Nevertheless they were well received: I suppose because they were seen to be the criticisms of a friend anxious for American prosperity, rather than of an enemy prompted by a dislike for their institutions.

New York had now to be seen; for of course the day we spent in it after our arrival enabled us only to glance at some of its main thoroughfares. The Central Park was explored and much admired; there were two excursions to Brooklyn; some of the centres of business were visited; hours on sundry occasions were spent at the

Century Club, and some at the Lotus Club; and we went to one or two theatres and admired the acting, which we had not done at Washington or Philadelphia.

But we had still to see something of the New England States; and after nine days in New York we departed northwards.

Our first stopping-place was New Haven, where a morning was devoted to inspecting Yale College, and more especially Prof. Marsh's collection of remains of marvellous fossil mammals from the far West. Then in the afternoon we pursued our course to Newport, which we had been told before leaving England was one of the places to be visited. The chief reason assigned for visiting it, however—namely, that it was the summer resort of the fashionable world—was no longer in force; for the season was over. This we did not regret. The place has some natural attractions, and, as being composed mainly of scattered villas, is more like Bournemouth than any other of our watering-places. Six pleasant and beneficial days were spent there.

And now of course came Boston, to which we took our way on Oct. 28th, occasionally admiring as we went the fine masses of gorgeous autumn foliage.

The day of our departure for Boston was determined by an invitation to dine with the Saturday Club; which we did a few hours after our arrival. At this weekly dinner there had for many preceding years been gathered the chief notabilities of Boston and its neighbourhood—especially Concord. Until recently Emerson had presided; and now the president was Dr. O. W. Holmes. The " Autocrat of the Breakfast Table " proved himself a very genial head of the dinner table. It was pleasant to meet, in company with others less known, one whose writings had given me so much pleasure, and some copies of whose best known book I had given to friends as a book to be read and re-read.

Of course among Bostonians, one who had done so much as an expositor of the Synthetic Philosophy—Mr. John Fiske—was the first to whom attention was due; and we early went over to the suburb, Cambridge, where he lives. After luncheon with him we called on Prof. Asa Gray, and saw something of the Botanical Garden before our return to Boston and our evening at the Union Club. Exploring and admiring the city occupied us the following morning—ascending the Bunker Hill monument, visiting the Eastern suburbs &c. The day after came a visit to the Museum of Arts, and then an inspection of Harvard, with Fiske as our guide; and subsequently a drive with him through Longworthy and the Western suburbs.

Some two hours next day were spent at Lexington, which Lott was anxious to see as a typical New England village; and then we continued our journey to Concord. Our chief purpose was of course to visit Emerson's house; and here a pleasant hour was spent in company with his widow, son, and daughter. We were then taken to the cemetery. Not many months had passed since Emerson's death, and the grave-heap was undistinguished by any monument. "Sleepy Hollow" is so beautiful and poetical a spot as to make one almost wish to die at Concord for the purpose of being buried there.

And now there occurred a disaster. We were in danger of losing the train, and I thoughtlessly ran some distance at full speed. The effort, which I perceived at the moment was too much for me, did great, and I believe permanent, damage. The night which followed was so wretched as to prompt the immediate resolution to leave Boston and its excitements; and, sending to Dr Holmes, with whom I was to dine, an apology for breaking the engagement, we forthwith went back to Newport. This step was taken in the hope that a little quiet would restore me: its promptness being due to the consciousness that the time for the dinner was approaching.

Five days did a little, but only a little, towards mitigating the mischief. The dinner was appointed for the 9th; and on the afternoon of the 8th we were obliged to depart for New York.

The prospect before me was sufficiently alarming. An occasion on which, more perhaps than on any other in my life, I ought to have been in good condition, bodily and mental, came when I was in a condition worse than I had been for six-and-twenty years. "Wretched night; no sleep at all; kept in room all day", says my diary; and I entertained " great fear I should collapse." When the hour came for making my appearance at Delmonico's, where the dinner was given, I got my friends to secrete me in an ante-room until the last moment, so that I might avoid all excitements of introductions and congratulations; and as Mr. Evarts, who presided, handed me on to the daïs, I begged him to limit his conversation with me as much as possible, and to expect very meagre responses.

The event proved that, trying though the tax was, there did not result the disaster I feared; and when Mr. Evarts had duly uttered the compliments of the occasion, I was able to get through my prepared speech without difficulty, though not with much effect; for I have no natural gift of oratory, and what little power of impressive utterance I may have was in abeyance. It goes without saying that I diverged a good deal from the form of response customary on such occasions. While setting out with a due recognition of my indebtedness to American sympathy, my address was mainly devoted to a criticism of American life, as characterized by over-devotion to work. The thesis on which I enlarged was that life is not for learning nor is life for working, but learning and working are for life. And a corollary was that the future has in store a new ideal, differing as much from the present ideal of industrialism as that ideal differs from past ideal of militancy.

Of the proceedings which followed I need only say that they were somewhat trying to sit through. Compliments, even when addressed to one privately, do not give unalloyed pleasure. To be wholly pleasing, they must be indirect or more or less disguised. As may be imagined, then, unqualified eulogies uttered by one speaker after another before an audience to whose inquiring glances I was exposed on all sides, were not quite easy to bear—especially in my then state. However, they had to be borne, and by and by I became tolerably callous. When I have said that everything passed off to the entire satisfaction of my friend Youmans, I have sufficiently indicated the success of the dinner and its sequences. Ready, as usual, to make capital of everything, he prepared a little volume in which were published together the " Interview " and the report of the proceedings of the dinner, joined with letters and undelivered speeches.

Rest and preparations for departure occupied the next day; and then, on the 11th November, after lunching with Youmans—taking our last meal with him as we did our first—we went on board the "Germanic." Various friends and a sprinkling of strangers were there to see us off. Among these last was one who drew me into conversation concerning a recent election in which the "bosses" had been defeated, and asked my opinion about the result; which, taken unawares, I gave without much thought. It afterwards occurred to me that I had been out-manœuvered; and my suspicion was verified on our arrival at Queenstown, where, among many newspapers delivered to me, I found some which contained a telegraphic statement of the opinion I had expressed. Thus I was, after all, interviewed at the last moment.

Concerning our return-voyage I need say no more than is said in the following passages from a letter written on Nov. 25, after our arrival in England.

"Everything on the "Germanic" was satisfactory—attendance good, cuisine admirable, the state-room reserved for me the best possible, and every attention paid to my wishes. The only danger I ran was that resulting from the kindness of American friends. When I got down to my state-room I found that their hospitalities had not ceased, but were pursuing me out into the Atlantic! There were presents of flowers, fruit, wine, brandy, oysters, in quantities beyond the possibility of consumption. So that joined with the excellent fare of the "Germanic," there resulted some risk of excess. I was reminded by antithesis of the title of a book published some time ago, *Plain Living and High Thinking;* for high living and plain thinking would fitly have described my regimen. However, if the ocean would have continued its good behaviour to the last, I should have gained greatly notwithstanding."

This is preceded by a paragraph which gives some subsequent incidents of the voyage.

"My telegram [from Queenstown] unhappily gave a premature statement of results. At the time that I wrote it, in preparation for the delivery at Queenstown the next morning, the "Germanic" was rolling so much in a gale that I had to hold the inkstand from sliding off the table. The previous night the rolling, though less, had been such as to keep me awake a good part of the night; and the night which now followed being much worse, (Cyclones are numbered 1 to 12 in point of strength, and ours was a No. 9) I got no sleep until we were under the lee of the Irish coast, about three or four in the morning. Then the third night was worse still. We were too late to pass the bar of the Mersey, and, anchoring outside, where I thought I was going to have a quiet night, I got literally no sleep, in consequence first of the riot kept up by some men who were having farewell convivialities in their cabin, and afterwards by the noises which went on nearly all through the night in preparation for landing in the morning—chiefly raising the baggage by machinery just over my head. The mischief was not simply the negative mischief of sleeplessness, but the positive mischief of nervous irritation and wear from the perpetual rattle. And then there came the journey by the express to London. It was an immense relief to get home, and I was so delighted I scarcely realized how much I was knocked up."

And then follows an account of my prostrate state, which I omit. Suffice it to say that I did not stir out for three days, and that ten days passed before I ventured to call on friends.

Thus ended an expedition which I ought never to have undertaken. Setting out with the ill-founded hope that the journey and change of scene would improve my health, I came back in a worse state than I went: having made another step downwards towards invalid life.

CHAPTER LIX.

CONCLUSION.

1882—89. ÆT. 62—69.

MORE than six years have passed by since the incidents narrated in the last chapter; and, were I to give an account of these years after the same manner as heretofore, several more chapters would be required.

Of work, now proceeding very slowly and with long intervals during which nothing was done, certain small results would have to be described. There were four articles in the *Contemporary Review*, afterwards published under the title of *The Man* versus *The State*. There was a volume on *Ecclesiastical Institutions*, forming Part VI. of the *Principles of Sociology;* the separate publication of the last chapter of which led to a disagreeable controversy. There were two essays—or rather an essay divided into two parts—on "The Factors of Organic Evolution"; and two years after the last of these, came two short controversial articles, each of which had to be broken off in the middle from inability to proceed.

Concerning the chief breaks in my ordinary routine, there would be passages telling how, in 1883, my good friend Valentine Smith, finding that I was going North considerably before the time he had fixed for themselves, sent down to Ardtornish a staff of servants for my sole benefit, and left me for a week in exclusive possession of the place and its belongings. In 1884 would come the account of a tour through the west of Scotland, in which I took with me the daughter and niece of my friend Lott: afterwards joining the Potters at Summerfield, a new place which they had for the autumn near Ulverston. And then, in the account of 1885, would have to be told how, after a fortnight with the Potters at Stock Park on the banks of Windermere, I visited Dr. Priestley at his place on the Spey, and there, after walking about half a mile, wielding a salmon-rod for a quarter of an hour and walking back, had to pass several days in bed, and then telegraphed to my secretary to fetch me home: the journey being made with half-a-dozen breaks.

Thus was made a further great descent to confirmed ill-health and incapacity.

Passing over details, it will suffice to say that I gradually got myself into a state in which, with a greatly narrowed margin of strength, I from time to time unawares overstepped the margin, still further diminished my strength, and had thereafter to keep within a still narrower margin; and so on until an extremely low stage had been reached.

After one of these disasters, dating from the private view at the Royal Academy in the spring of 1886, and after presently having to spend some five or six weeks indoors, I took a suite of rooms at Upper Norwood, and there induced to join me as guests Mrs. Bray and Miss Hennell (George Eliot's great friends): the temporary benefits being then, as afterwards, quickly undone. Depression during a weary month indoors in London did mischief; and, fearing continuance of it, I went down to Brighton: travelling then, as ever since, in a hammock slung diagonally in an invalid-carriage. At Brighton a year and a quarter passed, with many improvements great and small, and many relapses great and small. During the last four months of my stay there, a victoria with india-rubber tyres, which I bought, enabled me to drive about more than I could otherwise have done: days and weeks, however, often passing without my being able to use it. In November 1887 I was induced by Miss Beatrice Potter to take rooms in the same house with them at Bournemouth, where they were fixed for the winter (my friend Potter having also now become an invalid). The change of scene, and still more the presence close at hand of those about whom I cared, produced a great effect; and at the end of January 1888, I returned to town, frequented the Athenæum daily for a month, and even got so far as playing a game at billiards. Then, as usual, came a catastrophe: too long and too animated a conversation brought me down with a crash, and I was unable to reach the Athenæum during the remainder of the season. Drives in the park close at hand, extended on a few occasions to the Savile Club, were all that I could achieve when able to go out. The end of June found me at Dorking, where I took up my abode with my friend Mr. Grant Allen for the summer months. There rapid advances resulted; but a little too much physical effort, followed by a little too much mental excitement, again undid all the good done. Improvements and relapses filled the time till the middle of October, when Mr. Allen was obliged to go, as he habitually did, to a warmer climate; and I, unable to move, took his house for the winter. The five months passed in it, more monotonous even than the fifteen months passed at Brighton, were made more bearable in the one place as in the other by various friends, who came to spend sometimes a few days, sometimes three weeks, with me; and especially were they relieved by two children of my friend Mrs. Cripps (*née* Potter), who in response to my inquiry—" Will you lend me some children?" let them visit me at Dorking, as they had done at Brighton. In the middle of March 1889 I got back to town; fixed myself at a quiet hotel within five minutes of the Athenæum, so as to get there with but a short drive; was improved greatly by the change; and, as usual, have, by adverse occurrences, physical and mental, again lost what good I gained. So that now, after having been in the interval much better and at other times much worse, I am below the level of three years ago, when my invalid-life commenced.

Beyond correspondence, done by proxy when possible, my sole occupation during these three years (save the two fragments of essays above named) has been the composition of this volume—an occupation which, entered upon because heavier work, even in small quantity, was impracticable, has proved in some measure a solace, by furnishing subjects of thought and preventing that absolute vacuity of life which I must otherwise have borne. How extremely slow has been the progress is shown by the fact that, when the pages of text have been duly reduced by deduction of extracts &c., the amount dictated, revised, and corrected in proof has been at the rate of a little more than fifteen lines per day —three lines less than half a page.

And now about the future? I dictate these lines on my 69th birthday; and an invalid-life like mine, due to chronic disorder unaccompanied by organic disease, is not unlikely to last some time. What then shall I do with it?

Shall I, with such small energy as it leaves me, complete, if possible, the first volume of this autobiography? Part I., giving an account of my early life and education is finished; but Parts II. and III., and IV., covering the interval between 17 and 28, and occupied chiefly with the incidents of my career as a civil engineer, remain in the form of outline draft given to them when, many years ago, I rapidly dictated my recollections to a shorthand-writer. Shall I go back upon this rude sketch, and elaborate it into a readable form?

On reflection I decide against this course. Occasional experiments have raised the hope that I may, in a rough if not in a finished way, write another portion of the *Principles of Ethics*—the most important portion, which I feel anxious not to leave undone. If I can keep in check the tendency to bestow too much attention on the expression of the ideas, and be content with a sufficiently intelligible presentation of them, it seems possible that, at a slow rate like that above described, I may execute this piece of serious work.

Here, then, at any rate for the present, I suspend this narrative of my life which has so long occupied me: intending to continue it only when I find it impracticable to do anything else.

PART XII.

LX. REFLECTIONS.

[*Written Four Years Later.*]

CHAPTER LX.

REFLECTIONS

[Written Four Years Later.]

IF we pass over that earliest conception of the supernatural which exists among various uncivilized and semi-civilized peoples, who believe in a material resurrection—who think the dead man reappears in substantial shape, has to be fought over again in battle, as the Fijians believe, or gets up from his grave at night and goes hunting, as is asserted by many savages; and if we begin with the ghost-theory under that modified form in which the double, more or less spiritualized, goes away at death, returning to the body after a shorter or longer period; we see that at the outset the idea of a relation between character and bodily structure is excluded. Along with the notion of duality there grows up the assumption that character inheres in the ghost, and that the body is merely the ghost's house, having no causal relation to it. This is the necessary implication, too, of all the various doctrines of metempsychosis. The soul which, according to some forms of the doctrine, is condemned to be encased in numerous inferior creatures, one after another, is manifestly regarded as independent of its material embodiment, and not as in any sense a product of its material embodiment.

How far back may be traced the belief that there exists

a connexion between mind and brain, it is difficult to say. It seems probable that very early the phenomena of idiocy raised the thought of some such relation, qualifying the current dualism—qualifying it, however, in an inconsistent way. For at a time when there was recognized the "narrow forehead of the fool," there was no assertion of the logical implication that a man's nature is determined by his cerebral development. Even in our own day, though this truth is recognized in the scientific world, and in a half-and-half way in the unscientific world, yet by most people it is asserted in one breath and denied in another. The same man who now speaks contemptuously of another as having no brains, now contests the doctrine that character varies with brain. Nevertheless it is clear that some sort of dependence is currently admitted.

But there remains to be made a further admission. There has still to be recognized the truth that, in both amounts and kinds, mental manifestations are in part dependent on bodily structures. Mind is not as deep as the brain only, but is, in a sense, as deep as the viscera.

Before specifying the psycho-physical connexions which more especially concern us, let me name certain subordinate ones not here in question, though they should be noted.

There are the ways in which perfections and imperfections of face and limbs have reactive influences on character. Much might be said about the mental effects of bodily deformity. One who knows that he is looked upon by those around with disfavour, can scarcely avoid being in some measure soured—cannot feel the friendship for them which he might otherwise feel. At the same time his temper is almost certain to be injuriously influenced by the consciousness of inability to compete with others in sports and games, and to obtain those satisfactions which efficiency brings: envy being a probable result. Conversely, the man of fine physique, prompted by proved strength and skill to attempt things beyond the powers of most, and to gain applause by success, has his mental attitude modified, in some respects favourably and in other respects unfavourably. Achievements produce content with himself and an increase of friendliness to those who applaud him; though, at the same time, he may be rendered haughty and unsympathetic in his other relations.

So it is with beauty and ugliness. A fine face is a letter of recommendation which usually begets more kindly treatment from all than would else be experienced; and, though a very ugly face will draw from a few special attentions, intended to dissipate the depressed consciousness accompanying it, yet in most cases this consciousness is not weakened but strengthened by others' behaviour. There is neglect, if nothing more; and this, causing a sense of social isolation, tends to repress the sympathies.

It is true that the reactive effects of these physical traits on psychical traits are variable, and sometimes opposite; according as they fall on one or another original nature. Women show us that the possession of great facial attractions may, if the nature is essentially sympathetic, conduce to increase of sympathetic manifestations; since the genial behaviour to one who has great beauty excites in such case a kindred response, and increases the natural kindliness of disposition. Conversely, a handsome woman who is decidedly egoistic is usually made worse by her handsomeness—lives chiefly for admiration, and becomes more regardless of others' claims than she would else be. So, too, great bodily powers in a man may, according to the original balance of his feelings, lead him to treat those of inferior strength either less kindly or more kindly than he would have done were he not thus distinguished. In like manner deformity or ugliness may, instead of souring those characterized by it, have, in some cases, a reverse effect. It may prompt them to make themselves attractive in other ways than by their physical traits.

All I wish here to note is that, given an inherited cerebral structure and accompanying balance of mental traits, the development of the external organs, if it departs considerably from the ordinary standard, makes the mental traits different from those which the same brain would have yielded had it been associated with ordinary face or limb.

But now I pass from indirect relations to direct relations. The psycho-physical connexions which I more especially refer to, are those existing between the mental manifestations and what we distinguish as the constitution; meaning, thereby, the sizes and qualities of the various vital organs, and those peripheral extensions of them which take the forms of arteries and veins.

Consciousness forthwith ceases if the current of blood through the brain is stopped. The amounts and kinds of the mental actions constituting consciousness vary, other things equal, according to the rapidity, the quantity, and the quality, of the blood-supply; and all these vary according to the sizes and proportions of the sundry organs which unite in preparing blood from food, the organs which circulate it and the organs which purify it from waste products.

That intellectual and emotional manifestations are changed in their kinds and amounts by changes among these factors, many know, though few recognize the implications. The quantity of mental action shown in energy of will and flow of spirits ebbs during the prostration of illness; and the quality of mental action is altered as well as the quantity. Supposing there is enough vitality to cause display of feeling (which sometimes there is not), the display frequently takes the form of irritability. We have daily proof, too, that the volume of emotion, and consequently the efflux of muscular energy, is diminished by fatigue and accompanying fall in the circulation through the brain. And everyone has seen how great are the effects on the mind of medicinal agents which change the quantity and quality of the cerebral blood-supply—the influence, now exhilarating, now stupefying, of alcohol; the primarily exciting, and secondarily sedative, results of opium; the improved spirits which tonics often produce; and the lowered mental energies following use of medicines like the bromide of potassium, which, persisted in, sometimes causes extreme depression.

But, if variations of both ability and feeling are caused by variations in those physical processes which enable the brain to act, then it follows that permanent differences in the sizes and proportions of the organs carrying on those physical processes—differences which distinguish one constitution from another—must have permanent effects on the mental manifestations, both intellectual and moral. Men's characters must be in part determined by their visceral structures.

Primarily, the question concerns the amount of life—the amount of that molecular change from which results the energy expended in both bodily activities and mental activities. The evolution of this energy depends on the cooperation of sundry vital organs, and the efficiency or non-efficiency of each one affects all the others and affects the total result: the brain being implicated alike as a recipient of more or less blood which is more or less fit in quality, and as being also a generator of nerve-force which influences the actions of the viscera. Let us look at the three sets of visceral factors separately.

First must be named the structures constituting the alimentary system, which may severally be well or ill developed. There may be inability to deal with an adequate quantity of food, or there may be slovenly digestion, having the effect that much of the food taken in is thrown away—unmasticated lumps which the over-taxed stomach gets into the habit of passing on inadequately triturated, and therefore unutilized. Or, again, there may be solvent secretions of which some are unfit in quantity or quality or both. If one or other of these causes necessitates a deficient amount of blood, the vital actions, those of the brain included, must, other things equal, go on slowly or feebly or be soon checked. It is true that the food eaten is no measure of the nutriment absorbed. But, whether smallness of the alimentary system or imperfect action of it be the reason, chronic deficiency of blood must entail chronic cerebral inactivity, intellectual and emotional. Conversely, there is evidence that an unusually active digestion may, other things equal, be a factor in unusual mental energy. Handel, so wonderfully productive, so marvellous for the number and vigour of his musical compositions, may be named in illustration.

Abundance of good blood will not be followed by vividness of thought or power of feeling, unless there is efficient propulsion of it. Great cerebral action implies great waste and rapid repair; and, if the repair does not keep pace with the waste, prostration must soon result. If the slowness of the blood-supply is temporary the activity will soon flag, and if it is constitutional there will be a low standard of mental manifestation. The emotions especially, which are relatively costly, will be feeble; and this will result in lack of energy and want of will. When, at the one extreme, we see that stoppage of the blood-supply is immediately followed by insensibility, and, at the other extreme, see that exalting the blood-supply by a medicinal agent which raises the power of the heart, produces elation of feeling and increase of vigour, it becomes manifest that permanent differences between the efficiences of the structures which carry on circulation, must cause permanent differences between the amounts of mental manifestation. Not only is power of heart a factor in power of mind, but quality of the arteries is also a factor. Those in whom the blood-vessels, inadequately contractile, soon yield under stress, have not the untiring energy of those whose blood-vessels can bear persistent action without yielding.

And then, beyond quantity of blood and circulation of blood, comes the further factor—purification of blood. Professor Michael Foster has recently been enlarging on the truth that fatigue is chiefly caused by the accumulation of waste products in the system. The depurating organs fail to get rid of these with adequate speed; and the blood becomes fuller than usual of substances which, instead of aiding the functions, tend to arrest them. A familiar example is the effect produced by great exertion in running. This increases the carbonic acid in the blood more rapidly than it can be eliminated by the lungs. The being "out of breath," as we say, and the need for temporary desistence, show us how presence of an overcharge of a poisonous substance impedes the vital actions. A corollary is that those in whom the lungs are ill-developed will have a constitutionally lower activity, bodily or mental, or both. Similarly, deficient size of the kidneys, entailing imperfect excretion of the waste products they get rid of, and consequent accumulation of them in the blood, causes hindrance to nervous action; as is implied by the fact that stoppage of the excretion produces dimness of sight, at other times deafness, and, when extreme, brings on drowsiness, torpor, and coma. So, too, it is if the liver fails in its action. Lowness of spirits, drowsiness, and torpor, are among the symptoms of liver-derangement; and these are aspects of diminished nervous energy. The implication is, then, that those who have by nature livers or kidneys below the average in development, are to that extent likely to be characterized by some failure in the genesis of nerve-force, and by consequent lack of animation.

Details apart, however, the general conclusion is undeniable. If by skin, lungs, liver, and kidneys, waste-products of the muscular, nervous, and other activities are excreted—if the existence of these depurating structures implies that, unless by their agency effete matters are got rid of, life must cease; it is a corollary that life must be impeded if one or other of them is deficient in size or quality. And it follows that the brain, depending for its action on a due supply of blood duly purified, must be affected in its efficiency by every variation in the development of this or that excreting organ.

REFLECTIONS

But now we come to the truth of chief significance. Not the quantity of mind only, but the quality of mind also, is in part determined by these psycho-physical connexions. Amount and structure of brain being the same, not only may the totality of feelings and thoughts be greater or less according as this or that viscus is well or ill developed, but the feelings and thoughts may also be favourably or unfavourably modified in their kinds. Difference of disposition is caused both directly and indirectly.

Directly, the effect of imperfect supply of blood to the brain is shown in reluctance to do many things which require energy, and in consequent failure of duty towards self and others. One of the absurdities current among both cultured and uncultured is that it is as easy for one man to be active as for another. If A is diligent and B idle, the condemnation of B always takes for granted that the cost of effort is the same to A and B. Though everyone knows that during the prostration of illness, or before good health has been recovered, it is a great trial to make even a small exertion, yet scarcely any draw the inference that the lack of energy, temporarily existing in such cases, exists permanently in other cases, and throughout life makes activity more or less difficult. Character is affected in sundry ways. Often the individual thus made inert by constitution, cannot be at the trouble of doing needful things for his own benefit, but persistently submits to a serious inconvenience rather than take measures to remove it. And if even when personal pains and pleasures are in question he will not exert himself, naturally he is reluctant to exert himself when the pains and pleasures of others are in question. A, who is constitutionally active, takes trouble in doing things for others' gratifications, and is credited as essentially altruistic; while B, though his absence of effort for others is due to constitutional inactivity, and not to want of sympathy with them, is thought essentially egoistic. Differences hence resulting may affect even the discharge of equitable obligations; for while to the man of restless energy the liquidation of a claim may present no obstacle, it may present a great obstacle to an equally conscientious man of inert nature.

But now, beyond these qualitative mental differences which arise directly from quantitative differences of mental energy, there are other qualitative differences arising indirectly—differences of disposition seemingly consequent on inherited differences of brain, but really consequent on differences between the blood-supplies to the brain. For the higher emotions are physiologically more expensive than the lower; and, when the blood-supply is deficient, fail before the lower do. In the *Principles of Psychology*, §§ 249—261, I have set down various corollaries from the truth that from cerebral actions of simple kinds, which are directly related to maintenance of life, and are, therefore, essentially egoistic, we rise by successive complications to those highest governing cerebral actions which, most involved in their compositions, arise from less fully organized structures, the actions of which are most liable to fail. Ancient and simple nervous connexions, and accompanying mental cohesions, which are primary and deep down in the nature, are more persistent than those superposed ones which are relatively modern and complex; and, consequently, when the tide of blood ebbs, these last become feeble or disappear while the first remain: the result being that the surviving egoistic feelings are no longer kept in check by altruistic feelings.

REFLECTIONS

Examples of this causation in its temporary form are familiar. When a child who is ordinarily amiable becomes pettish and fretful, the medical man suspects that the alimentary canal is not doing its duty, and finds that, the cause of failing nutrition having been removed, the mental perversions disappear. So, too, in adult life the visceral derangements produced by over-work and anxiety are often followed by ill-temper. Even the recognized differences between irritability before dinner and equanimity (sometimes joined with generosity) after dinner, suffice to show that, when flagging pulsation and impoverished blood are exchanged for vigorous pulsation and enriched blood, there results that change in the balance of the emotions which constitutes a moral change. And, if there are such temporary mental unlikenesses due to temporary physiological causes, there must be analogous permanent mental unlikenesses due to permanent physiological causes. It becomes clear that in this respect, as in other respects, the mind is as deep as the viscera.

These general conclusions are intended to introduce certain special conclusions. Often it has been a question with me why, in certain respects, I contrast unfavourably with both father and mother. Probably in chief measure the cause is of the kind just explained—a physiological cause. I have never shown the unfailing diligence which was common to them; and there has not been displayed by me as great an amount of altruistic feeling as was displayed by both. One apparent reason is that the cerebral circulation has, by certain bodily traits, been throughout life rendered less vigorous than it should be.

Besides his large brain, my father, as a part of his fine physique, had a large chest; and, as a result of well-developed thoracic viscera, had an abundant supply of energy. I have heard him say that he looked back with astonishment at the work he did when a young man; and even during later life, though his activity was not judiciously directed, he was always busy about something. In physique my mother was not of so fine a type, and the constitution, though fairly well balanced, was by no means so vigorous: the development of the thorax being rather below than above the average standard. But she had an overwhelming sense of duty, and, throughout life, was daily forced by it to expend energy in excess of the normal amount; so that, spite of all protests, she eventually brought herself to a state of chronic prostration. This overwhelming sense of duty was, doubtless, in its origin religious: the moral feelings, naturally decided, were reinforced by the religious feeling. But in me the cooperative factors were not the same as in either. The visceral constitution was maternal rather than paternal. Traits of bony structure imply that the thoracic viscera are not so well developed as they were in my father; and that, as a consequence, the circulation and aeration have not been constitutionally so good.

As far back as I can remember there have been signs that the periphery of the vascular system has not been well filled. Except in hot weather, or after walking several miles, the ends of my fingers have been inadequately distended; coldness of the hands has been an ordinary trait; and relative dryness of the skin has also shown deficient blood-supply at the surface: an obvious implication being that in the brain also, the blood-supply, when not increased by excitement, has been below par. It is true that my extraordinary feat in walking when a boy of 13, seems to prove that there was at that time no deficiency in either heart-power or lung-power; and, if we pass over the evidence from thoracic development, it might be inferred that the damage done by this enormous overtax on a half-finished body, was the primary cause of this defective function throughout after life. Certainly it seems likely to have been a part cause. Be this as it may, however, there is undeniable evidence that, either from deficient propulsive power or from some chronic constriction of the arterioles, the remoter plexuses of blood-vessels everywhere have commonly not been duly charged. Hence a somewhat deficient genesis of energy, or, at any rate, a genesis of energy not as great as that displayed in my father.

The same cause has probably operated in producing that further moral difference above indicated. In respect of negative beneficence the likeness to both father and mother is fairly well marked. In early days there was none of that tendency towards cruelty which boys so commonly display, and, throughout later life, the infliction of pain or the witnessing of pain inflicted, has ever been repugnant; save, indeed, under the excitement of argument, when I have usually shown but little regard for the feelings of opponents. But in the kind of beneficence distinguishable as positive—that which implies not passivity but activity—I perceive a decided difference between myself and my parents. My father especially, with his abundant energy, was active on behalf of others—doing things which would either give them pleasure or be indirectly beneficial. But my greater inertia, caused in the way shown, has tended to hinder such actions. The incentives to them have been commonly neutralized by dislike to taking the requisite trouble. This initial difference has doubtless originated a difference of mental tendency; for, where the yielding to sympathetic promptings has commenced, there is established the habit of so yielding, and, conversely, under opposite conditions there arises the habit of not yielding. In respect to one kind of altruistic action, however, I recognize no deficiency. The sentiment of egoistic justice is strong in me, and sympathetic excitement of it produces a strong sentiment of altruistic justice. Consequently, there is not only a readiness to join others in opposition to political injustice, but a readiness to take up the causes of individuals unjustly dealt with. Abundant energy is furnished in such cases by the anger which the sight of aggression generates in me.

A cooperative cause may be named as having accentuated the contrast between the amount of the wish to avoid giving pain and the amount of the wish to give pleasure. From time to time it has seemed to me that in families brought up from generation to generation ascetically, and acting up to the belief that the pursuit of pleasure is wrong, it happens that while there is a frequent witnessing of suffering, and familiarity with the natural language of suffering, and therefore ability to sympathize with suffering, there is a relatively infrequent witnessing of pleasure, and an unfamiliarity with the natural language of pleasure, and consequently a relative inability to sympathize with pleasure. And, if there thus results a relative inability to sympathize with pleasure, the temptation to give pleasure must be less than usual, at the same time that the desire to avoid giving pain may be as great as usual or greater. Having in my own case recognized this as a possible cause of the difference, or at least a cooperative cause, I was some years ago struck by a parallel inference drawn by the Rev. Dr. Martineau, *à propos* of his sister, in *The Daily News* for December 30, 1884:—

"That in our early home the parents were so 'cruel' as 'to starve the emotions in' their children by 'lack of tenderness in manner or feeling' (3 4), I can in no wise admit as a characteristic of that particular household, though the allegation would have a certain amount of truth if turned into a general description of the prevailing habit of the time. In old Nonconformist families especially, the Puritan tradition, and the reticence of a persecuted race, had left their austere impress upon speech and demeanour unused to be free; so that in domestic and social life there was enforced, as a condition of decorum a *retenue* of language and deportment strongly contrasting with our modern effusiveness."

An influence of this kind was certainly at work both in the Spencer family and in the Holmes family, and may have had its effect on me. But I here name it chiefly with a view to the general implication that asceticism tends to produce inability to sympathize with others' pleasures, and therefore a lack of desire to give them pleasures.

Leaving these psycho-physical interpretations of character, I pass now to those which are more especially psychical—those which depend on structure of brain rather than on the pressure at which the brain is worked. For, let me remark in passing, there are two distinguishable sources of mental power. It may result from an ordinary brain worked at unusually high pressure, or from a brain which, in some respects not ordinary, is worked at medium pressure or even low pressure: the one giving manifestations of great intensity but not special in their kinds, the other giving special manifestations. It is with the last that we are here concerned.

Whatever specialities of character and faculty in me are due to inheritance, are inherited from my father. Between my mother's mind and my own I see scarcely any resemblances, emotional or intellectual. She was very patient; I am very impatient. She was tolerant of pain, bodily or mental; I am intolerant of it. She was little given to finding fault with others; I am greatly given to it. She was submissive; I am the reverse of submissive. So, too, in respect of intellectual faculties, I can perceive no trait common to us; unless it be a certain greater calmness of judgment than was shown by my father; for my father's vivid representative faculty was apt to play him false. Not only, however, in the moral characters just named am I like my father, but such intellectual characters as are peculiar are derived from him. We will look first at three fundamental ones.

Though an intution is not inheritable, the capacity for an intuition is, and I inherited an unusual capacity for the intuition of cause. Already I have commented on the curious display of it when, as a boy of thirteen, I called in question the *dictum* of Dr. Arnott, endorsed by my uncle Thomas, respecting *inertia*. Without instruction, and without special thought, I had reached a truer insight into ultimate dynamical relations than those who were much older and far better cultured. Always my father had been prone to inquiries about causes. The habit of making them implied that the consciousness of causation was dominant in him; and often during my boyhood, as I have before said, he put to me questions about causes: not, however, questions of the fundamental kind just referred to. But the aptitude for conceiving causes, primarily inherited, had been rendered by practice unusually strong; and there had been produced a latent readiness to grasp the abstract necessity of causal relations. This has been shown in my course of thought throughout life. Though my conclusions have usually been reached inductively, yet I have never been satisfied without finding how they could be reached deductively. Alike in various detached essays and in that general doctrine which has chiefly occupied me, this fact is conspicuous; and it is equally conspicuous in my political thinking, which is pervaded by an unconquerable belief in the effects of general causes working generation after generation: exemplified, for instance, in my often repeated prophecy that a nation which fosters its good-for-nothings will end by becoming a good-for-nothing nation.

Of the two further intellectual traits inherited from my father, the first to be named is the synthetic tendency. That this was dominant in him is proved by his little work entitled *Inventional Geometry*, containing a multitude of problems to be solved by synthetic processes which pupils are to discover. Both the tendency in himself and the encouragement of the tendency in me, were seen when, during my youth, he led me through the successively more complicated problems in Perspective: requiring me to find out the modes of solving them. It scarcely needs saying that the synthetic tendency has been conspicuous in all I have done from the beginning. *Social Statics* set out with a fundamental principle, and built upon it a coherent body of conclusions. My first essay, published not long after

—" A Theory of Population, deduced from the general Law of Animal Fertility "—proved by its title that its argument was synthetic, while the same trait, manifested in many subsequently-written essays, clearly declared itself in the organization of the series of works which I commenced in 1860, and finally took an overt form in the title of that series.

But the synthetic tendency has in me been accompanied by an almost equal analytic tendency. Though in my father's mind this was less manifest, it nevertheless existed to a greater extent than it exists in most minds. Indeed, his habit of seeking for causes implied it; since the detection of a cause cannot be achieved without analysis. But in him the analytic tendency, like the synthetic tendency, was relatively limited in its range. He occupied himself much more with the concrete, and much less with the abstract, than it became my habit to do. While the analytic tendency was more pronounced in me, it also displayed itself in a wider sphere. There was an early illustration of it in the progress from the views set forth in *The Proper Sphere of Government* to those set forth in *Social Statics*. The last work grew out of the first in consequence of an inquiry for the common origin of the conclusions which the first set forth separately; and the analysis which disclosed the common principle involved in them, preceded the synthesis which constituted the body of the work. Not long after, an essay on " The Universal Postulate " furnished a more pronounced illustration of the analytic tendency; for the purpose of that essay was to identify the common character of all those beliefs, established immediately by perception or mediately by reason, which we regard as having absolute validity. So, a few years later, with the Theory of Evolution at large. It was not enough that the general transformation should be shown to arise from the instability of the homogeneous and the multiplication of effects. It was needful that these also should be analyzed and shown to be corollaries from the persistence of force—a truth defying further analysis. So that, both subjectively and objectively, the desire to build up was accompanied by an almost equal desire to delve down to the deepest accessible truth, which should serve as an unshakable foundation.

One further cardinal trait, which is in a sense a result of the preceding traits, has to be named—the ability to discern inconspicuous analogies. Of course, in the process of taking to pieces some group of phenomena, there come into view those factors which are deep-seated and necessary, as distinguished from those which are superficial and not necessary. So, too, is it in the process of building up. A coherent fabric of conclusions cannot be framed unless there is a recognition of primary and unchangeable connexions, as distinguished from secondary and changeable ones. Evidently, then, the habit of ignoring the variable outer components and relations, and looking for the invariable inner components and relations, facilitates the perception of likeness between things which externally are quite unlike—perhaps so utterly unlike that, by an unanalytical intelligence, they cannot be conceived to have any resemblance whatever. An example is furnished by the analogy between a social organism and an individual organism. A vague recognition of this analogy was seen in an article named in Chapter XV as written in 1844, in which, commenting on the propagation of the evil consequences of dishonesty among citizens, I argued that a society has a common life which implicates all its individuals. This preparedness for recognizing a definite analogy presently had its effect. When writing *Social Statics*, there was made the statement that social organizations and individual organizations are similar in their phases of development. It was pointed out that a low society, like a low animal, is made up of like parts performing like functions; whereas, as fast as societies and organisms become more highly evolved, they severally become composed of unlike parts performing unlike functions. Evidently this was a parallelism recognized only by ignoring all concrete characters of the parts and thinking only of the essential relations among the parts—an analytical process of stripping off whatever the two things had not in common. And then, when the nakedness of the essential relations in each permitted comparison of them, it became manifest that the fundamental analogy was determined by the operation of the same cause in each: this cause being the mutual dependence of parts. It became manifest that it is the mutual dependence of parts which constitutes either the one or the other a living aggregate, and that it is because of the increasing mutual dependence of parts, and consequent increasing unity and vitality of the aggregate, that there is in both cases shown an advance from a homogeneous structure to a heterogeneous structure.

To the co-operation of these intellectual tendencies, the first three of which were exhibited in my father, and apparently transmitted with increase, and the last of which, a derivative result of the others, took in me an activity not apparent in him—to these tendencies, I say, working together throughout wider ranges of thought, must be in large measure ascribed whatever I have done.

One further intellectual trait, in part derived from the foregoing and in part of more general nature, must be set down. Already there has been named the fact that in boyhood and youth I was much given to castle-building: not differing from other young people in respect of the tendency, but only in respect of its degree. The absorption which, as indicated in Chapter II, went to the extent of talking to myself as I walked through the streets, and the love of picturing adventures, nightly indulged in, which, on awaking, often made me vexed because I had gone to sleep before having had my fill, proved that ideal representation was habitual; and continuance of it under other forms in later life was shown by the fact, named in Chapter XXXI, that when out of doors I sometimes passed those living in the same house with me without knowing that I had seen them, though I looked them in the face. This activity of imagination, not greater than in many others, but in me specialized by the synthetic tendency, has had an effect which at first sight seems anomalous.

Probably many readers of the foregoing pages will have been struck by the heterogeneity in my mental occupations and objects of interest. Fully to perceive how apparently unlike one another these have been, it is requisite to bring into juxta-position sundry of the subjects of speculation occupying my later life with the appliances and improvements devised during my earlier life. The products of mental action are then seen to range from a doctrine of State-functions to a levelling-staff; from the genesis of religious ideas to a watch escapement; from the circulation in plants to an invalid bed; from the law of organic symmetry to planing machinery; from principles of ethics to a velocimeter; from a metaphysical doctrine to a binding-pin; from a classification of the sciences to an improved fishing-rod joint; from the general Law of Evolution to a better mode of dressing artificial flies.*

There is something almost ludicrous in this contrast between the large and the small, the important and the trivial; but, as facts in that natural history of myself which I have aimed to give, it is fit that they should be indicated. The almost equal proclivities towards analysis and synthesis above pointed out, seem to be paralleled by almost equal proclivities to the abstract and the concrete, the general and the special; or, otherwise regarded, equal proclivities to the theoretical and the practical. But for every interest in either the theoretical or the practical, a requisite condition has been—the opportunity offered for something new. And here may be perceived the trait which unites the extremely unlike products of mental action exemplified above. They have one and all afforded scope for constructive imagination. Evidently constructive imagination finds a sphere for activity alike in an invention and in a theory. Indeed, when we put the two together, we are at once shown the kinship; since every invention is a theory before it is reduced to a material form.

In this, as in so many other traits, I recognize inheritance from my father: in some directions with increase, and in others without. His constructive imagination was shown not only by his *Inventional Geom-*

* See Dr. E. Hamilton's *Recollections of Fly Fishing*, p. 92.

etry, but by sundry small inventions; and it was shown much more conspicuously by his *Lucid Shorthand*, in which it appears under both the analytic and the synthetic aspects. It was shown, too, by an unusual ability for solving puzzles, alike of the mental and of the mechanical kinds. In this I could not compare with him; but in both mechanical inventions and in the union of philosophical analysis and synthesis, this applied form of constructive imagination appears to have been further developed while transmitted.

And here this last remark introduces a group of facts at once striking and instructive.

When discussing the question whether the effects of use and disuse are inherited, I have sometimes been tempted to cite evidence furnished by sundry of my own traits; but have refrained because of dislike to making public statements about them. Here, however, as included in an autobiography, I may fitly set down these instances of modifications, mental and bodily, resulting from specialities of habit in ancestors.

It has been remarked that I have an unusual faculty of exposition—set forth my data and reasonings and conclusions with a clearness and coherence not common. Whence this faculty? My grandfather passed all his life in teaching, and my father, too, passed all his life in teaching. Teaching is, in large measure, a process of exposition. Hour after hour, day after day, the master of a school, or one who gives private lessons, spends time in explaining. If he is worth his salt, he does not simply listen to rote-learnt lessons, but takes care that his pupils understand what they are learning; and, to this end, either solves their difficulties for them, or, much better, puts them in the way of solving them by making them comprehend the principles on which solutions depend. The good instructor is one in whom nature or discipline has produced what we may call intellectual sympathy—such an insight into another's mental state as is needed rightly to adjust the sequence of ideas to be communicated. To what extent my grandfather possessed this intellectual sympathy I do not know; but his daily life cultivated it to some extent. My father possessed it in a high degree, and throughout life cultivated it. I possess it in a still higher degree: so, at least, I was told, when a young man, by one who had experience of my father's expositions and of mine. It appears, then, that the faculty has developed by exercise and inheritance.

No one will deny that I am much given to criticism. Along with exposition of my own views there has always gone a pointing out of defects in the views of others. And, if this is a trait in my writing, still more is it a trait in my conversation. The tendency to fault-finding is dominant—disagreeably dominant. The indicating of errors in thought and in speech made by those around, has all through life been an incurable habit—a habit for which I have often reproached myself, but to no purpose. Whence this habit? There is the same origin as before. While one-half of a teacher's time is spent in exposition, the other half is spent in criticism—in detecting mistakes made by those who are saying lessons, or in correcting exercises, or in checking calculations; and the implied powers, moral and intellectual, are used with a sense of duty performed. And here let me add that in me, too, a sense of duty prompts criticism; for when, occasionally, I succeed in restraining myself from making a comment on something wrongly said or executed, I have a feeling of discomfort, as though I had left undone something which should have been done: the inherited tendency is on its way to become an instinct acting automatically.

Similarly to be explained as resulting from inheritance, is an allied trait—disregard of authority. Few have shown this more conspicuously. As an early illustration may be remembered the incident narrated of myself as happening at the age of 13, when I called in question the doctrine of *inertia* set forth in Dr. Arnott's *Physics* and defended by my uncle, and persisted in my dissent spite of this combined authority against me. Out of illustrations furnished by later life may be named my published rejection, in 1858, of the conception of nebulæ then universally accepted in the astronomical world; and again my rejection of Owen's theory concerning the archetype and homologies of the vertebrate skeleton, at that time accepted in the biological world and taught in some medical schools. My books show submission to established authority, only in cases where my knowledge of data needed for judgment was obviously inadequate (as, say, in the higher Mathematics, or the higher Physics, or in Chemistry) and where, consequently, the opinions of experts were to be accepted. For this trait, so unusual in its degree, there is, as said above, the same explanation as before. For what is the attitude perpetually maintained by the teacher? Always in presence of his pupils he is himself *the* authority, subject to no other. All through adult life the mental attitude of subordination is made foreign to him by his function. Such contact as he occasionally has with superiors, bears but a very small ratio to the contact he has with inferiors. Hence the sentiment of submission to authority is but little exercised.

A closely-allied trait, or in part another aspect of the same trait, has to be indicated—the absence of moral fear. In the account of my life at Hinton, a passage from a letter written by my uncle to my father was quoted, commenting upon this. He said:—

" The grand deficiency in Herbert's natural character is in the principle of *Fear*. And it is only so far as his residence with me has supplied that principle in a degree unusual to him, that after a few struggles he entirely surrendered himself to obey me with a promptness and alacrity that would have given you pleasure to witness; and the more obedient I have observed him the more I have refrained from exercising authority. By *Fear*, I mean both that ' Fear of the Lord ' which ' is the beginning of wisdom,' and that fear of Parents, Tutors, &c."

Deficient fear of those superior to me in age or position, of course implied want of respect for authority; but it included a further element—disregard of the consequences which such disrespect might bring. And this trait, conspicuous in my boyhood, has been in later life shown throughout my writings; for nowhere have I betrayed any fear either of an individual or of the aggregate of individuals. It has, in fact, never occurred to me to hesitate because of foreseen mischiefs; or rather, I have not foreseen them because I have not thought about them. It has been thus even in cases where public disapprobation was unmistakable; as in my persistent opposition to State-education—an opposition expressed when 22, and expressed with equal or greater strength when 73; though for these many years past I have been conscious that almost the whole world is against me. And now observe that we have the same explanation as before. For what is the relation between a master and his pupils? It is a relation from which the sentiment of fear on his side is excluded. The school is a small society; and in it the master fears neither any one member of it nor the whole assemblage.

I pass now to a bodily trait no less significant. My hands are unusually small—smaller than the hands of a woman of less than my own height. Both in size of the bones and in development of the accompanying muscles they are considerably below what they should be. How is this? If the lives passed by my father and grandfather are considered, a cause is manifest. Both of them did nothing more, day by day, than wield the pen or the pencil, and neither of them was given to sports of any kind or to any exercises which might have served to keep up the sizes of the hands. Occasionally, when a young man, my father went fishing, and sometimes, though rarely, he did a little gardening of a light kind; but the exercise of the hands beyond that which his daily avocations entailed was scarcely appreciable. In me, then, the hands show the result of two generations of diminished action.

Thus the inheritance of acquired characters is exemplified in four mental traits and one bodily trait.

It is rightly said that a man has the defects of his qualities—that, along with certain advantages his nature yields him, there go certain disadvantages. On considering the effects of the inherited traits above enumerated, I am struck with the verification of this truth which some of them afford.

Lack of regard for authority, and fearlessness of the

consequences entailed by dissent from other men's opinions, have been part causes of what success I have had in philosophical inquiry. Such reverence for great names as most feel, and resulting acceptance of established doctrines, would have negatived that independence without which I could not have reached the conclusions I have. Never stopping to ask what has been thought about this or that matter, I have usually gone direct to the facts as presented in Nature, and drawn inferences afresh from them—occasionally, it may be, untrue inferences, but in other cases inferences which are true. Meanwhile the implied moral nature has had—especially in early life—injurious consequences. Little as the fact was recognized by my father, the insubordination shown during my childhood and boyhood was, as I have indicated, a trait indirectly caused by absence of subordination throughout his life and the life of his father. The resulting chronic disobedience, so often deplored, led not only to direct evils, but to various indirect evils: chiefly the attitude of antagonism, the alienation of feeling, the undermining of the affections, and the consequent weakening of that influence which should be exercised through them: a diminished activity of sympathy being also an accompaniment. So that this trait, advantageous to me as a thinker, was otherwise disadvantageous.

Instead of saying "was," I ought to say "has been," for I recognize certain detrimental effects extending throughout adult life. One has been a tendency to under-estimate the past as compared with the present. Doubtless this has been partly due to reaction against the over-estimating which is current. To me it has seemed obvious that boys, early impressed with the products of Greek and Roman civilization—products sundry of which appeal strongly to the instincts of the savage, dominant in them at that age—never recover from the resulting bias, but remain throughout life subject to the perverted judgments then formed. They read everything ancient with a predisposition to appreciate, and everything modern with a predisposition to depreciate.

Uninfluenced in this way, I have very likely been carried to the other extreme. Take, for example, the opinion about Plato. Time after time I have attempted to read, now this dialogue and now that, and have put it down in a state of impatience with the indefiniteness of the thinking and the mistaking of words for things: being repelled also by the rambling form of the argument. Once when I was talking on the matter to a classical scholar, he said—"Yes, but as works of art they are well worth reading." So, when I again took up the dialogues, I contemplated them as works of art, and put them aside in greater exasperation than before. To call that a "dialogue" which is an interchange of speeches between the thinker and his dummy, who says just what it is convenient to have said, is absurd. There is more dramatic propriety in the conversations of our third-rate novelists; and such a production as that of Diderot, *Rameau's Nephew*, has more strokes of dramatic truth than all the Platonic dialogues put together, if the rest are like those I have looked into. Still, quotations from time to time met with, lead me to think that there are in Plato detached thoughts from which I might benefit had I the patience to seek them out. The like is probably true of other ancient writings.

The *a priori* conclusion that reaction against current

error almost certainly leads to an opposite error, implying that, being so intensely modern, I undervalue that which is ancient, has been impressed on me a good deal of late years by recognizing the great progress made during some of the earliest civilizations—Egyptian, Babylonian, Indian. But while it has become clear that the remains left by these eastern nations prove them to have been more advanced, both in the arts and in thought, than I had supposed, and that lack of reverence for what others have said and done has tended to make me neglect the evidence of early achievements, it has also become clear that the common educational bias, against which my own bias is a reaction, has led to a like under-estimation of pre-classic progress. The great indebtedness of the Greeks to the peoples who preceded them in civilization, is yearly becoming more conspicuous.

The critical tendency dominant in me, because perpetually exercised by father and grandfather, has similarly entailed advantages and disadvantages. In presence of current opinions it has prompted examinations, often disclosing errors and causing rejections; while, as already implied, the fault-finding spirit, leading to more or less disagreeableness in social intercourse, has also partially debarred me from the pleasures of admiration, by making me too much awake to mistakes and shortcomings.

In conversation the critical tendency has constantly led to discovery of reasons for disagreement rather than reasons for agreement. To name those points in respect of which another's view coincided with my own, has not usually occurred to me; but it has always occurred to me to name the points of non-coincidence between our views.

A further effect has been to render my enjoyment of works of art less than it might else have been. The readiness to dwell upon defects has diminished the appreciation of beauties, by pre-occupying consciousness. Possibly there are perfections in various paintings of the old masters which impress me but little, because I am keenly alive to the many mistakes in *chiaroscuro* which characterize them. These force themselves on my attention in a way which they would not do were there no such constitutional aptitude for seeing the imperfections. When looking at Greek sculpture, too, I constantly observe how unnatural and inartistic is the drapery. Though in large measure I admire the more important parts of the works, my admiration is much less than it would be but for the vivid consciousness of this drawback. In some measure the like happens with music. Many years ago, when I attended the opera a good deal, I remarked to one who was frequently my companion—George Eliot—how much analysis of the effects produced deducts from enjoyment of the effects. In proportion as intellect is active emotion is rendered inactive. And a like result necessarily accompanies criticism, since the critical process involves more or less the analytical process. So is it also with my appreciation of literature—more especially poetry. In these various cases it is not that I am reluctant to admire—quite the contrary. I rejoice in admiration; and rejoice when at one with others in their admiration. But it rarely happens that the work of art of whatever kind is so satisfactory in every way as to leave no room for adverse comment.

Not in respect of works of art only, but also in respect of some works of Nature, this tendency has been shown: the works of Nature being, in this case, persons. An illustration occurred during the first year of my friendship with the Potters. Mr. Potter had a younger sister—a great beauty, alike in face and figure. During the visit of my uncle and aunt to them in Upper Hamilton Terrace, and during an evening I was spending there, my aunt said to me:—" Well, what do you think of Miss Potter?" Any other young fellow would have launched out into unmeasured praise. But my reply was:—" I do not quite like the shape of her head ": referring, of course, to my phrenological diagnosis. The incident has dwelt in my memory, because I afterwards blamed myself for the absurd way in which I had singled out a trait that did not, on theoretical grounds, quite satisfy me, and ignored all that there was calling for admiration.

It seems probable that this abnormal tendency to criticize has been a chief factor in the continuance of my celibate life. Readiness to see inferiorities rather than superiorities, must have impeded the finding of one who attracted me in adequate degree.

Lest the above anecdote should be taken to imply deficient appreciation of physical beauty, I must add that this is far from being the fact. The fact is quite the reverse. Physical beauty is a *sine quâ non* with me; as was once unhappily proved where the intellectual traits and the emotional traits were of the highest.

How difficult is the judging of character; and yet how little hesitation most people have in forming positive judgments. " What do you think of Mr. So-and-so?"

has been the question occasionally put to me concerning someone I have seen for an hour. And then, after my reply that I was unable to form an opinion so soon, there has come an expression of surprise. It is true that occasionally, where the manifestations have been clear—perhaps in a handsome woman spoiled by adulation, who makes great claims and has become distinctly selfish—my estimate has been formed forthwith, and a sufficiently strong prejudice—if it is to be so called—established. But in average cases decision is suspended until I have had considerable evidence.

Sometimes I have expressed my belief about this matter by the paradox that nobody knows himself and nobody knows any one else; meaning, by this extreme statement, that the possibilities of a nature are never disclosed until it has been placed in all circumstances, and that no nature ever is placed in all circumstances. Generally, the conditions of life have been so comparatively uniform that very few tests have been applied, and very few phases of character made visible in conduct.

An experience of early years gave me a vivid consciousness of the way in which feelings are readily determined this way or that way by accidents. It was in the days of my difficulties, when regard for economy obliged me always to travel in third-class carriages: then far less comfortable than they are now. Opposite to me, on one occasion, sat a man who, at the time I first observed him, was occupied in eating food he had brought with him—I should rather say devouring it, for his mode of eating was so brutish as to attract my attention and fill me with disgust: a disgust which verged into anger. Some time after, when he had finished his meal and become quiescent, I was struck by the woe-begone expression of his face. Years of suffering were registered on it; and, while I gazed on the sad eyes and deeply-marked lines, I began to realize the life of misery through which he had passed. As I continued to contemplate the face and to understand all which its expression of distress implied, the pity excited in me went to the extent of causing that constriction of the throat which strong feelings sometimes produces. Here, then, were two utterly antagonistic emotions aroused within a short time by the same person under different aspects. In the absence of the change described, either of these might have arisen without the other, and either of them, had it been expressed alone, would have given to other persons an untrue conception of me; an untrue conception which, indeed, I should have had of myself, had not the circumstances been varied in the way they were.

In respect of the intellectual faculties, experience shows that manifestations are often determined by accidents. Here is a skilful physician, who, in the leisure part of his later life, shows considerable ability in water-colour landscape—an ability not discovered until a vacation at the seaside in company with an artist friend, led to an attempt. One whose *forte* is mathematics, being led by accident into a musical circle, proves to have musical gifts which neither he nor others suspected. And some exceptional occasion discloses the fact that a distinguished chemist is also a born orator. But what is true of the intellectual faculties is also true of the emotional faculties. Each nature is a bundle of potentialities of which only some are allowed by the conditions to become actualities.

In this latter part of my life a personal illustration has

forced this truth upon me in a marked way. During early years, and throughout mature years, there was no sign of marked liking for children. It is true that when, as narrated, I took up my abode with a family in Marlborough Gardens, I did not make the presence of children an objection—rather the contrary. It is true, also, that during my many visits to Standish, recurring throughout a large part of my life, I was always on good terms with the bevy of little girls who were growing up. But my feeling was of a tepid kind, and, as I learned from one of them when she was adult, the belief, or at any rate her belief, was that I did not care much for children. Had it not been for a mere accident this might have remained her belief and mine also. When at Brighton in 1887, suffering the *ennui* of an invalid life, passed chiefly in bed and on the sofa, I one day, while thinking over modes of killing time, bethought me that the society of children might be a desirable distraction. The girls above referred to were most of them, at the time I speak of, married and had families; and one of them—Mrs. W. Cripps—let me have two of her little ones for a fortnight. The result of being thus placed in a nearer relation to children than before, was to awaken, in a quite unanticipated way, the philoprogenitive instinct—or rather a vicarious phase of it; and instead of simply affording me a little distraction, the two afforded me a great deal of positive gratification. When at Dorking a year afterwards, I again petitioned to have them, and again there passed a fortnight which was pleasurable to me and to them. Such was the effect that from that time to this, the presence of a pair of children, now from this family of the clan and now from that, has formed a leading gratification—

I may say the chief gratification—during each summer's sojourn in the country.

Evidently, but for the thought, and consequent experiment, at Brighton, my nature, in so far as this part of it is concerned, would have remained unknown to me and unknown to every one else.

So is it with character throughout its entire range. The remark that the manifestations of feelings are greatly changed by marriage is often made. The new circumstances initiate a new balance; and without doubt all other new circumstances have their effects in bringing out traits not before known to exist.

The motives which cause the essential actions of life are simple. No one fails to identify the appetite which normally prompts eating; though, in an invalid state, this prompting feeling may become complicated, or replaced by other feelings. So, too, with the love of children. Variations in its quality do not mask its essential nature. But when we come to those complex emotions which originate the complex actions of life, there is usually great difficulty in deciding what are the proportions among their components. The conduct which social relations daily call out, and the activities into which all are led, may be generated in various ways, and probably in no two persons are generated in exactly the same ways —in no two persons are the elements of them alike in their kinds and their ratios.

Occasionally I have asked myself what have been the motives prompting my career—how much have they been egoistic and how much altruistic. That they have been mixed there can be no doubt. And in this case, as in most cases, it is next to impossible to separate them mentally in such way as to perceive the relations of amount among them. So deep down is the gratification which results from the consciousness of efficiency, and the further consciousness of the applause which recognized efficiency brings, that it is impossible for any one to exclude it. Certainly, in my own case, the desire for such recognition has not been absent. Yet, so far as I can remember, ambition was not the primary motive of my first efforts, nor has it been the primary motive of my larger and later efforts. The letters on *The Proper Sphere of Government* were prompted solely, I believe, by the desire to diffuse what seemed to me true views. That this was a chief motive to the rationalization and elaboration of them constituting *Social Statics*, seems implied by the fact that, had it not been for the publisher, Mr. Chapman, I should have issued the work anonymously. And of later evidences there is that furnished by the *Descriptive Sociology*, on which I continued to spend money and labour after the absence of public appreciation became manifest.

Still, as I have said, the desire for achievement and the honour which achievement brings, have doubtless been large factors. Where I have been forestalled in the promulgation of an idea, I have unquestionably felt some annoyance; though the altruistic sentiment acting alone would have made me equally content to have it promulgated by another as by myself. In controversy, again, the wish for personal success has gone along with the wish to establish the truth—perhaps has predominated over it, as I fancy it does in most. For fighting excites the personal feeling so as to make it primary rather than secondary. Nor can it be denied that, in the prosecution of my chief undertaking, I have been throughout stimulated by the desire to associate my name with an achievement. Though from the outset I have had in view the effects to be wrought on men's beliefs and courses of action—especially in respect of social affairs and governmental functions; yet the sentiment of ambition has all along been operative.

Two other prompters have had shares. There has been the immediate gratification which results from seizing and working out ideas. As I once heard a scientific friend say, the greatest satisfaction he knew was that yielded by a successful day's hunting—figuratively thus expressing the discovery of facts or truths. And it has been with me a source of continual pleasure, distinct from other pleasures, to evolve new thoughts, and to be in some sort a spectator of the way in which, under persistent contemplation, they gradually unfolded into completeness. There is a keen delight in intellectual conquest—in appropriating a portion of the unknown and bringing it within the realm of the known.

Of these two remaining prompters the other, allied to the last though distinguishable from it, is the architectonic instinct—the love of system-building, as it would be called in less complimentary language. During these thirty years it has been a source of frequent elation to see each division, and each part of a division, working out into congruity with the rest—to see each component fitting into its place, and helping to make a harmonious whole. That the gratification of this instinct has been a not unimportant factor, I find at the present moment clear proof. As soon as I have ended this series of reflections, I am about to commence Part VII of the *Principles of Sociology*—" Professional Institutions "—in the hope that after finishing it I may be able to finish also the next part—"Industrial Institutions," and so complete the third volume. What spurs me on to this undertaking? Though the genesis of the professions constitutes a not uninteresting subject, it does not seem that a coherent account of it, showing how the general process of evolution is afresh illustrated, is of any public importance. Nor can I suppose that by executing this piece of work I shall add in any appreciable degree to my own reputation: this will be practically the same whether I do the work or not. Clearly, then, my desire to do it is the desire to fill up a gap in my work. My feeling is analogous to that of the architect when contemplating the unfinished wing of a building he has designed, or one of the roofs only half-built. Like the restless desire he would feel to supply these missing structures, is the restless desire I feel to complete these divisions now wanting.

Though it is partly included in the last factor, there should be definitely named a further factor—the æsthetic sentiment. There appears to be in me a dash of the artist, which has all along made the achievement of beauty a stimulus: not, of course, beauty as commonly conceived, but such beauty as may exist in a philosophical structure. I have always felt a wish to make both the greater arguments, and the smaller arguments composing them, finished and symmetrical. In so far as giving coherence and completeness is concerned, I have generally satisfied my ambition; but I have fallen short of it in respect of literary form. The æsthetic sense has in this always kept before me an ideal which I could never reach. Though my style is lucid, it has, as compared with some styles, a monotony that displeases me. There is a lack of variety in its verbal forms and in its larger components, and there is a lack of vigour in its phrases. But the desire for perfection has in this, as in the building up of arguments, prompted unceasing efforts to remove defects.

Here I am struck with a proof that this architectonic instinct and this æsthetic sentiment, now chiefly operative as stimuli, must be very dominant; since they are making me persevere spite of strong deterrents. With a brain lamed when I was five and thirty, and since that time so frequently put wrong by over-work, or other excitement, as to have been made almost incapable of bearing activity, I am, at seventy-three, urged on to do a little more of the task I set myself thirty-three years ago.

My state of brain is now such that I am obliged to break the small amount of work I do into short lengths. I dictate for ten minutes and then rest awhile; and, as I have observed this morning (July 24, 1893), I do not usually repeat this process more than five times, making a total of fifty minutes. Very frequently (as at the time I am revising this in proof) I dare not do more than three times ten minutes or twice ten minutes; and often I dare do nothing. When above my average, there is the addition of a little revising in the afternoon, done in a similar manner—a few sentences at once. Throughout the rest of the day the process of killing time has to be carried on as best it may.

Walking has to be restricted to two or three hundred yards when at my best, and occasionally has to be given up altogether. A drive of an hour and a quarter or an hour and a half, in a carriage with india-rubber tyres, is all the further exercise practicable; and continually a little excess in this produces injurious effects, now and then demanding entire desistence. Reading, even of the lightest kind, is almost as injurious as working. Everyday the temptation to read has to be resisted: a few pages at once being alone practicable. Very often forgetfulness leads to a transgression of the limits; bringing, as a penalty, a night worse than usual. So is it with conversation. When I am below my average, this has to be given up altogether, and when at my best has to be kept within narrow bounds. Even much listening is negatived. I make use of ear-stoppers, which when I cannot conveniently leave the room, enable me to shut out the voices of those around sufficiently to prevent me from understanding what is said; for damage results from the continuous attention which listening involves.

The mischief caused by continuous attention prevents use of the microscope, in which I had this year hoped to occupy a little time while here (Pewsey). A small amount of it produced general disturbance, which lasted several days; and now I find that three or four minutes at a time is as much as I can bear. Games, too, of all kinds are rendered impracticable. Even the simple child's game of spillicans, requiring intent observation and careful action of the muscles, proves too much for me. Cards are quite out of the question; and I have not tried backgammon since 1887, when, being at the time in a low condition, two games caused a serious relapse.

Of course this constitutional state, varying within wide limits, usually forbids social intercourse. I have not been at a *soirée* for these ten years; and only on a few occasions since 1882 have dared to dine out: the last occasion being nearly two years since, when the imprudence was severely punished. Public amusements are rigorously excluded. When in the United States in 1882, I went to a theatre, but never since. Concerts, too, are negatived. Half-an-hour proved more than enough the last time I attended one. Nor can any considerable amount of drawing-room music be borne. When, two years ago, Mr. Carnegie presented me with a piano, I made arrangements with a professional lady to give me an hour's performance upon it weekly; but two experiments sufficed to cause desistence. I got no sleep afterwards on either occasion.

Thus the waking hours have to be passed in an unexciting and, by implication, in an uninteresting way—lying on the sofa or lounging about, and, when the weather and the place permit, as now, sitting very much in the open air, hearing and observing the birds, watching the drifting clouds, listening to the sighings of the wind through the trees, and letting my thoughts ramble in harmless ways, avoiding as much as possible exciting subjects. But of course, debarred, as I thus am, from bodily and mental exercise and most kinds of pleasures, no ingenuity can prevent weariness.

When I speak of the waking hours, meaning of course the day, as passed in this manner, I apparently imply that the hours of the night are not waking hours. But in large measure they are. If the day has been gone through with prudence, and I have taken my dose of opium ($1\frac{1}{2}$ grains) at the right hour, then between half-past ten and perhaps one, perhaps two, perhaps half-past two, broken sleep is obtained—never continuous sleep. After that come hours of sleeplessness and tossing from side to side; mostly followed, but sometimes not followed, by more broken sleep before the servant comes with my breakfast in the morning, at 8. And then the dreams accompanying such sleep as I obtain, though not bad in the sense of being dreadful or horrible, are usually annoying.

Yet this state which I have brought myself to by forty years of brain-work—a brain-work which would have been by no means too much had I not at the outset overstrained myself—I am impelled to maintain by this desire to continue the task I have undertaken. This architectonic instinct tyrannizes over me. Such more comfortable life as I might lead if I would cease altogether to tax myself, I decline to lead. And this I suppose for the reason that, though more comfortable in one sense, it would be on the whole less comfortable. Besides being debarred from that slight pleasurable excitement given me by the trifling amount of work I am able to do daily, there would be the perpetual consciousness of something left undone which I wanted to do. The weariness would become still worse had I to spend the whole day in killing time, with such small means of doing it.

Contemplation of these physical consequences of my career leads me to think of the other consequences— the question,—What advice would I give to an aspirant, pecuniary, social, &c.; and the thought of them raises who, in early or middle life, thought of devoting himself to philosophy, or to some other division of grave literature: prompted to do so by the belief that he had something important to say? Supposing the something to be really of importance (against which, however, the probabilities are great, notwithstanding his own confident opinion), deterrent advice might fitly be given.

In the first place, unless his means are such as enable

him not only to live for a long time without returns, but to bear the losses which his books entail on him, he will soon be brought to a stand and subjected to heavy penalties. My own history well exemplifies this probability, or rather certainty. Had it not been for the £80 which, in 1850, I proved to the printer was coming to me under the Railway Winding-up Act, I should have been unable to publish *Social Statics*. Only because the bequest from my uncle Thomas made it possible to live for a time without remunerative labour, was I enabled to write and publish the *Principles of Psychology*. For two years after *The Synthetic Philosophy* had been projected, no way of bringing it before the world was discoverable. When, at length, mainly by the aid of scientific friends, without whose endorsement I could have done nothing, it became possible to get together a sufficient number of subscribers, it was presently proved that, partly because of my inability to keep up the intended rate of publication, and partly because of losses entailed by numerous defaulters, I should have been obliged to desist before the completion of *First Principles*, had it not been that the death of my uncle William, and bequest of the greater part of his property to me, afforded the means of continuing. Not even then were my difficulties ended. Six years' persistence in work which failed to yield such returns as, added to other sources of income, sufficed to meet my modest expenses of living, brought me, in 1866, to an impending cessation. After finding that in the course of the years devoted to philosophical writing, I had sunk more than £1100, and was continuing to lose, I announced that when the volume then in hand was completed I should discontinue. Only because the necessity for discontinuance was removed, partly by the American testimonial and partly by my father's death, which diminished the responsibilities coming upon me, was the notice of cessation cancelled. Even after that, several years elapsed before the returns from my books became such as put me quite at my ease. And only in subsequent years did my income become ample. Evidently it was almost a miracle that I did not sink before success was reached.

As the difficulties of self-maintenance while pursuing a career analogous to mine, are almost insuperable, the maintenance of a wife and family must of course be impossible. One who devotes himself to grave literature must be content to remain celibate; unless, indeed, he obtains a wife having adequate means for both, and is content to put himself in the implied position. Even then, family cares and troubles are likely to prove fatal to his undertakings. As was said to me by a scientific friend, who himself knew by experience the effect of domestic worries—" Had you married there would have been no system of philosophy."

If the prompting motive is the high one of doing something to benefit mankind, and if there is readiness to bear losses and privations and perhaps ridicule in pursuit of this end, no discouragement is to be uttered; further than that there may be required greater patience and self-sacrifice than will prove practicable. If, on the other hand, the main element in the ambition is the desire to achieve a name, the probability of disappointment may still be placed in bar of it. Adequate appreciation of writings not adapted to satisfy popular desires, is long in coming, if it ever comes; and it comes the more slowly to one who is either not in literary circles, or, being in them, will not descend to literary "log-rolling," and other arts by which favourable recognition is often gained. Comparative neglect is almost certain to follow one who declines to use influence with reviewers, as I can abundantly testify.

Even should it happen that, means and patience having sufficed, the goal is at length reached and applause gained, there will come nothing like the delights hoped for. Of literary distinction, as of so many other things which men pursue, it may be truly said that the game is not worth the candle. When compared with the amount of labour gone through, the disturbances of health borne, the denial of many gratifications otherwise attainable, and the long years of waiting, the satisfaction which final recognition gives proves to be relatively trivial. As contrasted with the aggregate of preceding pains, the achieved pleasure is insignificant. A transitory emotion of joy may be produced by the first marks of success; but after a time the continuance of success excites no emotion which rises above the ordinary level. It is, indeed, astonishing to what an extent men are deluded into pursuit of "the bubble reputation," when they have within their reach satisfactions which are much greater: supposing, at least, that the endeavours to gain these greater satisfactions are not disappointed, which unhappily they very often are.

And, then, beyond the fact that literary success when it comes, if it ever does come, brings pleasures far less than were anticipated, there is the fact that it brings vexations and worries often greatly exceeding them. While the approbation looked for often does not come, there often comes instead undeserved disapprobation.

REFLECTIONS

Adverse criticisms of utterly unjust kinds frequently pursue the conscientious writer, not only during his period of struggle but after he has reached his desired position. Careless mis-statements and gross misrepresentations continually exasperate him; and if he measures the pains produced by these against the pleasures produced by due appreciation, he is likely to find them in excess.

Beyond the evils which the aspirant will have to bear in the shape of blame for ascribed oversights which do not exist, and ascribed errors which are not committed, and ascribed absurdities which are in truth rational conclusions, he may have to bear graver evils. If his writings are of kinds which arouse antagonisms, political, religious, or social, there will be visited upon him the anger of offended prejudices, or of threatened interests, or both.

Already, in giving an account of my uncle Thomas, I have pointed out the extent to which the *odium theologicum,* joined with the animosity caused by attack on class-interests, may prompt grave calumnies. One who raised his parish from a low and neglected state to a state of relative culture and prosperity; one who spent all his spare time in efforts to benefit the working-classes by lectures and writings; one who, returning from the scenes of his philanthropic exertions, always reached home on Saturday night so as to give his two services on the Sunday; one who for discharge of his clerical duties, and for activities which went far beyond them, received the pittance of £80 a year; was actually described as a sinecurist! One whose efforts were devoted to the moralization of men so strenuously that he eventually killed himself by them, was described as not even expending the efforts which an ordinary parish priest devotes to the mechanical performance of his routine functions in return for a good income! While doing an excess of work, he was stigmatized as doing none!

From theological antagonism I have myself suffered but little; and, indeed, have met with an amount of forbearance and sympathy which has surprised me. On me, however, there have of late come the effects of political animosity. In my first work, *Social Statics,* it was contended that alienation of the land from the people at large is inequitable; and that there should be a restoration of it to the State, or incorporated community, after making due compensation to existing landowners. In later years I concluded that a resumption on such terms would be a losing transaction, and that individual ownership under State-suzerainty ought to continue. In his *Progress and Poverty,* Mr. Henry George, quoting the conclusion drawn in *Social Statics,* made it a part-basis for his arguments; and, when my changed belief was made public, his indignation was great. There resulted after some years a work by him entitled *A Perplexed Philosopher,* in which he devoted three hundred odd pages to denunciation, not only of my views but of my motives, and assailed me as a traitor to the cause of the people. He alleged that my change of opinion must have resulted from a wish to ingratiate myself with the landed and ruling classes: applying to me Browning's lines in *The Lost Leader*—" Just for a handful of silver he left us, just for a ribbon to stick in his coat." This he did in face of the fact that in works quoted by him, I have spoken disrespectfully of the two most conspicuous members of these classes, Mr. Gladstone and Lord Salisbury

(*Study of Sociology,* chap. xvi, and *Principles of Ethics,* §130); and have thus spoken of each at the time when he was Prime Minister, and had in his hands the dispensing of honours and patronage! Then, turning his fiction into a fact, and working himself into a fury over it, Mr. George does not scruple to manufacture evidence in its support. He says:—

The name of Herbert Spencer now appears with those of about all the Dukes in the kingdom as the director of an association formed for the purpose of defending private property in land (p. 201).

I am a member of but one political body. This body, which I was in part instrumental in establishing, was subsequently joined by sundry men of title, and among them two dukes. This body is the London Ratepayers Defence League!

Mr. George's book, circulated in the United States and in England, has been reviewed in various journals which have accepted its statements; and many have quoted its denunciations, apparently supposing that there was ground for them. Even *The Times* cites, without any condemnation of it, Mr. George's charge that I have "abandoned the necessary inferences, from motives less abstract and considerably less creditable, than those founded on sound logic and the truth of things." (January 12, 1893.)

Here, then, are lessons for one who, dealing with theological, political, or social subjects, says candidly what he believes. If his career leads him to set forth views exciting class-animosities, or individual-animosities, he may count upon greater evils than are entailed by the stupidities and misinterpretations of critical journals; and must take into account the possibility, if not the probability, that he will be injured by utterly false interpretations of his motives and by consequent vilifications.

Is it then that these various dissuasives, had they been put before me when I began my career, would have stopped me; or do I regret that I was not stopped by such dissuasives? I cannot say yes. If at the outset the many chances against success had been specified, it is doubtful whether desistence would have resulted. Nor even had I seen clearly the evil to be entailed in the shape of ill-health, would this further deterrent have sufficed. Once having become possessed by the conception of Evolution in its comprehensive form, the desire to elaborate and set it forth was so strong that to have passed life in doing something else would, I think, have been almost intolerable. The perpetual consciousness of a large aim unachieved would have been a cause of chronic irritation hardly to be borne.

Little, then, as I should encourage another to follow my example and throw prudence to the winds, it will readily be understood that, as things have turned out, I find no reason to regret the course I took and the life I have passed: very much the contrary, indeed. Nearly all men have to spend their energies, year after year, in occupations which are more or less wearisome, if not repugnant, simply that they may gain the means of living for themselves and their dependents; and have not the daily satisfaction of working towards a greatly-desired end. The artist of genius may, indeed, be named as one whose labour subserves the double purpose of bringing him material support and realizing his conceptions: the pleasurableness of the last being doubtless very great. The born musician, or painter, or poet, experiences an intensity of pleasure in his work which no other man does. But omitting these, men at large have to pass their days in duties from which they would gladly be excused. Quite different has been my lot: my chief complaint having been that state of brain every day forbade me to continue when I wished to do so. Even taking into account chronic disturbance of health, I have every reason to be satisfied with that which fate has awarded me.

Moreover, these disturbances of health have not been of a kind so difficult to bear as those borne by many who have no compensations for them. They have not entailed on me any positive suffering; unless, indeed, the weariness and irritation of perpetual bad nights come under that name. I have not been subject to much positive pain: less, I think, than most are. And then, during the greater part of the time since my break-down in 1855, the constitutional state, which seems to have become adapted to a small amount of broken sleep, has not been such as to negative many of the pleasures within reach. It is true that, reading to any considerable extent being injurious, light literature has been almost wholly cut off, and restriction of evening excitements has been imperative; but otherwise, up to the age of 62, the deprivations were not great. Only during the last ten years, and especially during the last six years, have I been more and more cut off from most relaxations.

And here let me exclude some misapprehensions likely to be caused by what has been said above. Naturally it will be inferred that the chronic perturbations of health described, and especially those which of late years have brought me to what may be called an invalid life, must be indicated by an invalid appearance. This is far from being the case. Neither in the lines of the face nor in its colour, is there any such sign of constitutional derangement as would be expected. Contrarywise, I am usually supposed to be about ten years younger than I am. And this anomalous peculiarity conforms to a medical observation which I have seen made, that nervous subjects are generally older than they look.

Thus, if I leave out altruistic considerations and include egoistic considerations only, I may still look back from these declining days of life with content. One drawback indeed there has been, and that a great one. All through those years in which work should have had the accompaniment of wife and children, my means were such as to render marriage impossible: I could barely support myself, much less others. And when, at length, there came adequate means the fit time had passed by. Even in this matter, however, it may be that fortune has favoured me. Frequently when prospects are promising, dissatisfaction follows marriage rather than satisfaction; and in my own case the prospects would not have been promising. I am not by nature adapted to a relation in which perpetual compromise and great forbearance are needful. That extreme critical tendency which I have above described, joined with a lack of reticence no less pronounced, would, I fear, have caused perpetual domestic differences. After all my celibate life has probably been the best for me, as well as the best for some unknown other.

And now, having made these reflections concerning my own nature and its relation to the work I have done, what have I got to say concerning things at large? Besides those products of experience which, in my books, have been organized into a coherent whole, what further products have been collaterally formed. In these my declining days, what noteworthy differences have arisen in the aspects which the world around presents to me?

Not very much has to be said beyond emphasizing what has been already said. In various of my later books there have been indicated those modifications of views which mature years had brought concerning political, religious, and social affairs. The years which have since elapsed have served but to make these modifications more marked. All that remains is to set them forth in their accentuated shapes, after asking what probability there is that the opinions formed in this closing part of life are nearer to the truth than those formed in its earlier part.

The comparative conservatism of old age has various factors. In part it results negatively from diminished energy. Strength prompts action; and action, resulting in change, familiarizes the mind with changes and makes the effecting of them relatively attractive: enterprise is a trait of youth. Not diminished strength only, but hardening habit also, tends to make changes less and less attractive. To break through the usages of thought and conduct gradually established, becomes at once difficult and repugnant. Then, to these obstacles resulting from constitutional alteration are added others arising from what is in one sense mental growth. Things which in early life look simple and easy to deal with, are found, as life goes on, to be complex and deeply rooted. In what appeared wholly evil there are discovered elements of good below the surface; and what once seemed useless or superfluous is discovered to be in some way beneficial, if not essential. In each man as he grows old such factors act in various proportions and combinations: those due to senility being usually the chief.

In myself those due to wider observation and longer

thought are, I believe predominant. I believe this because the aversion felt in early days for the older types of social organization survives. Now, as at first, not only is autocracy detestable, but there persists a dislike to that form of personal rule seen in qualified monarchical governments. I still sometimes think to myself, as I thought fifty years ago, how ludicrous would be the account given by some second *Micromegas* who, looking down on the doings of these little beings covering the Earth's surface, told how, to some member of a particular family, they assigned vast revenues and indulgences beyond possibility of enjoyment, ascribed beauty where there was ugliness, intelligence where there was stupidity, traits of character above the average where they were below; and then daily surrounded these idealized persons with flattering ceremonies, accorded to them extensive powers, and treated with contumely any who did not join in the general worship. Holding that true loyalty consists in honouring that which is intrinsically honourable, and showing reverence for a worth demonstrated by conduct and achievement, I feel at present, as in the past, irritated by such observances as those which lately showered multitudinous wedding presents, and contributions of money from countless men and women, on two young people who, enjoying luxurious lives, have neither benefited their kind nor shown the least capacity for benefiting them. Hence it is clearly not because of any change of sentiment that I look with greater tolerance on monarchy; but simply because wider knowledge has led me to perceive its adaptation to the existing type of man. Institutions of every kind must be regarded as relative to the characters of citizens and the conditions under which they exist; and the feelings enlisted on behalf of such institutions must be judged, not by their absolute fitness but by their relative fitness. While the average feelings of people continue to be those which are daily shown, it would be no more proper to deprive them of their king than it would be proper to deprive a child of its doll.

Chiefly, however, the greater contentment I feel now than of old with established governmental forms, is due to the strengthened belief that there is a necessary connexion between the natures of the social units and the nature of the social aggregate. A cardinal doctrine of M. Comte and his disciples, is that individual men are products of the great body in which they exist—that they are, in all their higher attributes, created by that incorporated humanity called by Comte the supreme being. But it is no less true, or rather it is much more true, that the society is created by its units, and that the nature of its organization is determined by the natures of its units. The two act and re-act; but the original factor is the character of the individuals, and the derived factor is the character of the society. The conception of the social organism necessarily implies this. The units out of which an individual organism builds itself up, will not build up into an organism of another kind: the structure of the animal evolved from them is inherent in them. So, too, is it in large measure with a society. I say " in large measure " because the relations between the two are less rigid. In an animal the units and the organism have worked together, acting and reacting, for millions of years; but in a society for only a few thousands of years, and in the higher types of societies for only a few hundreds of years. Hence the character of the society inheres in the characters of its units far less deeply. Still, it inheres in so considerable a degree that complete change from one social type to another is impracticable; and a suddenly-made change is inevitably followed by a reversion, if not to the previous type in its old form, yet to the previous type in a superficially different form.

Illustrations of this truth are arising before our eyes. While old kinds of coercive government are dissolving, new kinds of coercive government are evolving. The rule of the monarch and the landed class, unqualified in feudal days, and in part replaced by the rule of the middle class after the Reform Bill, has since then been in larger part replaced by that of the working class, which is fast becoming predominant. But the temporary freedom obtained by abolishing one class of restraints, which reached its climax about the middle of the century, has since been decreased by the rise of another class of restraints, and will presently be no greater than it was before. We have been living in the midst of a social exuviation, and the old coercive shell having been cast off, a new coercive shell is in course of development; for in our day, as in past days, there co-exist the readiness to coerce and the readiness to submit to coercion.

Here, then, I see a change in my political views which has become increasingly marked with increasing years. Whereas, in the days of early enthusiasm, I thought that all would go well if governmental arrangements were transformed, I now think that transformations in governmental arrangements can be of use only in so far as they express the transformed natures of citizens.

Less marked, perhaps, though still sufficiently marked, is a modification in my ideas about religious institutions, which, indicated in my later books, has continued to grow more decided. While the current creed was slowly losing its hold on me, the sole question seemed to be the truth or untruth of the particular doctrines I had been taught. But gradually, and especially of late years, I have become aware that this is not the sole question.

Partly, the wider knowledge obtained of human societies has caused this. Many have, I believe, recognized the fact that a cult of some sort, with its social embodiment, is a constituent in every society which has made any progress; and this has led to the conclusion that the control exercised over men's conduct by theological beliefs and priestly agency, has been indispensable. The masses of evidence classified and arranged in the *Descriptive Sociology,* have forced this belief upon me independently: if not against my will, still without any desire to entertain it. So conspicuous are the proofs that among unallied races in different parts of the globe, progress in civilization has gone along with development of a religious system, absolute in its dogmas and terrible in its threatened penalties, administered by a powerful priesthood, that there seems no escape from the inference that the maintenance of social subordination has peremptorily required the aid of some such agency.

Much astonishment may, indeed, reasonably be felt at the ineffectiveness of threats and promises of supposed supernatural origin. European history, dyed through and through with crime, seems to imply that fear of hell and hope of heaven have had small effects on men. Even at the present moment, the absolute opposition between the doctrine of forgiveness preached by a hundred thousand European priests, and the actions of European soldiers and colonists who out-do the law of blood-revenge among savages, and massacre a village in retaliation for a single death, shows that two thousand years of Christian culture has changed the primitive barbarian very little. And yet one cannot but conclude that it has had some effect, and may infer that in its absence things would have been worse.

At any rate, it is clear that, with men as they have been and are, the ultimate reasons for good conduct are too remote and shadowy to be operative. If prospect of definite eternal torture fails to restrain, still more must prospect of indefinite temporal evil fail. When we study the thoughts of the average British elector, who can conceive no reason for voting thus or thus save some material advantage to be gained, we may see that threats and promises of intense pains and vivid pleasures are alone likely to influence his conduct in marked ways.

Then, again, there is the truth, which is becoming more and more manifest, that real creeds continually diverge from nominal creeds, and adapt themselves to new social and individual requirements. The contrast between mediæval Christianity and the present Christianity of protestant countries, or again the contrast between the belief in a devil appointed to torment the wicked, strenuously held early in this century, and the spreading denial both of a devil and of eternal punishment, or again the recent expression of opinion by a Roman Catholic that there may be happiness in hell, suffice to show the remoulding of what is nominally the same creed into what is practically a quite different creed. And when we observe, too, how in modern preaching theological dogmas are dropping into the background and ethical doctrines coming into the foreground, it seems that in course of time we shall reach a stage in which, recognizing the mystery of things as insoluble, religious organizations will be devoted to ethical culture.

REFLECTIONS

Thus I have come more and more to look calmly on forms of religious belief to which I had, in earlier days, a pronounced aversion. Holding that they are in the main naturally adapted to their respective peoples and times, it now seems to me well that they should severally live and work as long as the conditions permit, and, further, that sudden changes of religious institutions, as of political institutions, are certain to be followed by reactions.

If it be asked why, thinking thus, I have persevered in setting forth views at variance with current creeds, my reply is the one elsewhere made:—It is for each to utter that which he sincerely believes to be true, and, adding his unit of influence to all other units, leave the results to work themselves out.

Largely, however, if not chiefly, this change of feeling towards religious creeds and their sustaining institutions, has resulted from a deepening conviction that the sphere occupied by them can never become an unfilled sphere, but that there must continue to arise afresh the great questions concerning ourselves and surrounding things; and that, if not positive answers, then modes of consciousness standing in place of positive answers, must ever remain.

We find, indeed, an unreflective mood general among both cultured and uncultured, characterized by indifference to everything beyond material interests and the superficial aspects of things. There are the many millions of people who daily see sunrise and sunset without ever asking what the Sun is. There are the university men, interested in linguistic criticism, to whom inquiries concerning the origin and nature of living things seem trivial. And even among men of science there are those who, curiously examining the spectra of nebulæ or calculating the masses and motions of double-stars, never pause to contemplate under other than physical aspects the immeasurably vast facts they record. But in both cultured and uncultured there occur lucid intervals. Some, at least, either fill the vacuum by stereotyped answers, or become conscious of unanswered questions of transcendent moment. By those who know much, more than by those who know little, is there felt the need for explanation. Whence this process, inconceivable however symbolized, by which alike the monad and the man build themselves up into their respective structures? What must we say of the life, minute, multitudinous, degraded, which, covering the ocean-floor, occupies by far the larger part of the Earth's area; and which yet, growing and decaying in utter darkness, presents hundreds of species of a single type? Or, when we think of the myriads of years of the Earth's past, during which have arisen and passed away low forms of creatures, small and great, which, murdering and being murdered, have gradually evolved, how shall we answer the question—To what end? Ascending to wider problems, in which way are we to interpret the lifelessness of the greater celestial masses—the giant planets and the Sun; in proportion to which the habitable planets are mere nothings? If we pass from these relatively near bodies to the thirty millions of remote suns and solar systems, where shall we find a reason for all this apparently unconscious existence, infinite in amount compared with the existence which is conscious —a waste Universe as it seems? Then behind these mysteries lies the all-embracing mystery—whence this universal transformation which has gone on unceasingly throughout a past eternity and will go on unceasingly throughout a future eternity? And along with this rises the paralyzing thought—what if, of all that is thus incomprehensible to us, there exists no comprehension anywhere? No wonder that men take refuge in authoritative dogma!

So is it, too, with our own natures. No less inscrutable is this complex consciousness which has slowly evolved out of infantine vacuity—consciousness which, in other shapes, is manifested by animate beings at large—consciousness which, during the development of every creature, makes its appearance out of what seems unconscious matter; suggesting the thought that consciousness in some rudimentary form is omnipresent. Lastly come the insoluble questions concerning our own fate: the evidence seeming so strong that the relations of mind and nervous structure are such that cessation of the one accompanies dissolution of the other, while, simultaneously, comes the thought, so strange and so difficult to realize, that with death there lapses both the consciousness of existence and the consciousness of having existed.

Thus religious creeds, which in one way or other occupy the sphere that rational interpretation seeks to occupy and fails, and fails the more the more it seeks, I have come to regard with a sympathy based on community of need: feeling that dissent from them results from inability to accept the solutions offered, joined with the wish that solutions could be found.

THE END.

APPENDICES.

A NOTE.

[*Where to place the following two letters has been a question not easily answered, for no place seems quite appropriate. After much consideration I have decided that they should be inserted here rather than elsewhere.*]

5 *Percival Terrace,*
Brighton,
Nov. 21, 1900.

DEAR MR. HUXLEY,

On further reading your very interesting Life of your father, I find some statements of personal concern which will cause much misapprehension.

Through inadvertence, passages on pages 333 of vol. I. and 266 and 68 of vol. II. convey the impression that the criticism of my proofs by your father extended to my writings at large; and a phrase of yours on page 133 of vol. II. implies that you have yourself derived this impression. It is an erroneous one. Beyond *First Principles* your father read in proof *The Principles of Biology,* a biological essay, and some chapters concerning the nervous system. There was peremptory need for expert criticisms on these, and he very kindly gave me his; but I did not ask his critical aid when writing the seven volumes dealing with Sociology, Psychology, and Ethics, or the six volumes of my miscellaneous works, save the 15 pages of " diabolical dialectics " (ii. 185), and a chapter entitled " Religious Retrospect and Prospect." This is in a measure implied by my letter accompanying the proofs of the essay on " The Factors of Organic Evolution "—a letter in which I spoke of habitually submitting " my biological writing to your [his] castigation " (ii. 127) ; for had the practice been general I evidently should not have limited the statement to biological writing.

A word concerning the unpublished Autobiography. Reading of proofs by friends (your father being one) was to be a check on errors of taste. The parts your father saw amounted to about a third.

When saying, *à propos* of his rôle of " devil's advocate," that " there is no telling how many brilliant speculations I have been the means of choking in an embryonic state," your father was venting one of his facetious exaggerations. A comparison between the original MSS. and the printed books, made by my secretary to whom I dictate this letter, shows that in the three volumes above named there are four passages of a speculative kind in the MS. which have disappeared from the printed text. [Let me add that of the two omitted from *The Principles of Biology* one concerned the derivation of the vertebrate type from the ascidian type—a speculation which not long after received support from the discoveries of Kowalewsky. I afterwards gave it a place in Appendix D of vol. II.]

As shown by a letter you have partly quoted, I have expressed my grateful sense of your father's " invaluable critical aid," but naturally I do not wish this to be understood as having been far greater than it was.

Whatever changes you may make in future editions for the purpose of preventing misapprehensions, cannot of course be known to readers of the current edition. Yet

NOTE

I am not content that they should remain in error. What should be done?

Yours truly,
HERBERT SPENCER.

In response to this appeal Mr. Huxley published the following letter in *The Athenæum* for December 8, 1900.

HUXLEY'S LIFE.

November 28, 1900.

It has been suggested to me by Mr. Herbert Spencer that a phrase of mine in the *Life and Letters of T. H. Huxley* (vol. II. p. 133) might give rise to a false impression touching the extent to which my father used to criticize the proofs of Mr. Spencer's published writings. The words " from whom [viz., Mr. Spencer] he had, according to custom, received some proofs to read," refer, of course, to the " biological writings " mentioned in Mr. Spencer's letter quoted on p. 127. Besides such biological writings, my father read in proof only *First Principles* and two small fragments amounting to thirty-two pages. I do not suppose that those who have any knowledge of the subject will imagine that he criticized the proofs of Mr. Spencer's writings at large; but I should be sorry to think that I had possibly suggested a false notion to others.

Your readers will hardly need telling that epistolary humour is not always to be taken literally, and that the phrase about his being " devil's advocate " to Mr. Spencer (i. 333)—" There is no telling how many brilliant speculations I have been the means of choking in an embryonic state "—is meant rather as a consolation for a

APPENDICES

young worker in biological science, to whom my father proposed to act in the same useful, if ungrateful capacity, than as a definite statement as to Mr. Spencer's biological writings, in which, I understand, a comparison of the MSS. with the printed volumes shows the removal of but four* such speculative passages during the proof stage.

But the period assigned to this " devil's advocacy," going back " thirty odd years " from 1884 to the beginning of my father's acquaintance with Mr. Spencer, indicates that the playful allusion must be as much to the informal dialectics of conversation as to serious written work, for the reading of proofs referred to above only began with the Synthetic Philosophy in 1860.

L. HUXLEY.

It is manifestly needful that I should give a permanent place to these letters. Were they to disappear, the one privately and the other in an ephemeral publication, the first edition of Professor Huxley's *Life and Letters* would establish everywhere the belief that my writings at large had had the benefit of his criticisms, and that had it not been for his restraints I should have set forth numerous ill-based speculations in the thirteen volumes treating of Psychology, Sociology, Ethics, and miscellaneous subjects.

[* Not quite correct. There were two in *First Principles* and two in the Biology.]

APPENDIX A.

[*The following programme of the Synthetic Philosophy, issued in the spring of 1860, though quoted in the preface to "First Principles," is given here as being a biographical document. A further reason for re-quoting it is that opportunity is afforded for appending the names of the first subscribers, which are not without interest.*]

A SYSTEM OF PHILOSOPHY.

MR. HERBERT SPENCER proposes to issue in periodical parts, a connected series of works which he has for several years been preparing. Some conception of the general aim and scope of this series may be gathered from the following Programme.

FIRST PRINCIPLES.

PART I. THE UNKNOWABLE.—Carrying a step further the doctrine put into shape by Hamilton and Mansel; pointing out the various directions in which Science leads to the same conclusions; and showing that in this united belief in an Absolute that transcends not only human knowledge but human conception, lies the only possible reconciliation of Science and Religion.

II. LAWS OF THE KNOWABLE.—A statement of the ultimate principles discernible throughout all manifestations of the Absolute—those highest generalizations now being disclosed by Science, which are severally true not of one class of phenomena but of *all* classes of phenomena; and which are thus the keys to all classes of phenomena.*

---

* One of these generalizations is that currently known as "the conservation of force;" a second may be gathered from a published essay on "Progress: its Law and Cause;" a third is indicated in a paper on "Transcendental Physiology;" and there are several others.

APPENDICES

[*In logical order should here come the application of these First Principles to Inorganic Nature. But this great division it is proposed to pass over: partly because, even without it, the scheme is too extensive; and partly because the interpretation of Organic Nature after the proposed method is of more immediate importance. The second work of the series will therefore be—*]

THE PRINCIPLES OF BIOLOGY.
Vol. I.

PART I. THE DATA OF BIOLOGY.—Including those general truths of Physics and Chemistry with which rational Biology must set out.

II. THE INDUCTIONS OF BIOLOGY.—A statement of the leading generalizations which Naturalists, Physiologists, and Comparative Anatomists, have established.

III. THE EVOLUTION OF LIFE.—Concerning the speculation commonly known as " The Development Hypothesis "—its *a priori* and *a posteriori* evidences.

Vol. II.

IV. MORPHOLOGICAL DEVELOPMENT.—Pointing out the relations that are everywhere traceable between organic forms and the average of the various forces to which they are subject; and seeking in the cumulative effects of such forces a theory of the forms.

V. PHYSIOLOGICAL DEVELOPMENT.—The progressive differentiation of functions similarly traced; and similarly interpreted as consequent upon the exposure of different parts of organisms to different sets of conditions.

VI. THE LAWS OF MULTIPLICATION.—Generalizations respecting the rates of reproduction of the various classes of plants and animals; followed by an attempt to show the dependence of these variations upon certain necessary causes.*

---

* The ideas to be developed in the second volume of the *Principles of Biology* the writer has already briefly expressed in sundry Review Articles. Part IV. will work out a doctrine suggested in a paper on "The Laws of Organic Form," published in the *Medico-Chirurgical Review* for January 1859. The germ of Part V. is contained in an essay on "Transcendental Physiology: " See *Essays*, pp. 280-90. And in Part VI. will be unfolded certain views crudely expressed in a ''Theory of Population," published in the *Westminster Review* for April 1852.

THE PRINCIPLES OF PSYCHOLOGY.
Vol. I.

Part I. THE DATA OF PSYCHOLOGY.—Treating of the general connexions of Mind and Life, and their relations to other modes of the Unknowable.

II. THE INDUCTIONS OF PSYCHOLOGY.—A digest of such generalizations respecting mental phenomena as have already been empirically established. [This proved to be a very inadequate description.]

III. GENERAL SYNTHESIS.—A republication, with additional chapters, of the same part in the already-published *Principles of Psychology*.

IV. SPECIAL SYNTHESIS.—A republication, with extensive revisions and additions, of the same part, &c. &c.

V. PHYSICAL SYNTHESIS.—An attempt to show the manner in which the succession of states of consciousness conforms to a certain fundamental law of nervous action that follows from the First Principles laid down at the outset.

Vol. II.

VI. SPECIAL ANALYSIS.—As at present published, but further elaborated by some additional chapters.

VII. GENERAL ANALYSIS.—As at present published, with several explanations and additions.

VIII. COROLLARIES.—Consisting in part of a number of derivative principles which form a necessary introduction to Sociology.*

THE PRINCIPLES OF SOCIOLOGY.
Vol. I.

Part I. THE DATA OF SOCIOLOGY.—A statement of the several sets of factors entering into social phenomena—human ideas and feelings considered in their necessary order of evolution; surrounding natural conditions; and those

---

* Respecting the several additions to be made to the *Principles of Psychology*, it seems needful only to say that Part V. is the unwritten division named in the preface to that work—a division of which the germ is contained in a note on page 544, and of which the scope has since been more definitely stated in a paper in the *Medico-Chirurgical Review* for Jan. 1859.

APPENDICES

ever-complicating conditions to which Society itself gives origin.

II. THE INDUCTIONS OF SOCIOLOGY.—General facts, structural and functional, as gathered from a survey of Societies and their changes: in other words, the empirical generalizations that are arrived at by comparing different societies, and successive phases of the same society.

III. POLITICAL ORGANIZATION.—The evolution of governments, general and local, as determined by natural causes; their several types and metamorphoses; their increasing complexity and specialization; and the progressive limitation of their functions.

Vol. II.

IV. ECCLESIASTICAL ORGANIZATION.—Tracing the differentiation of religious government from secular; its successive complications and the multiplication of sects; the growth and continued modification of religious ideas, as caused by advancing knowledge and changing moral character; and the gradual reconciliation of these ideas with the truths of abstract science.

V. CEREMONIAL ORGANIZATION.—The natural history of that third kind of government which, having a common root with the others, and slowly becoming separate from and supplementary to them, serves to regulate the minor actions of life.

VI. INDUSTRIAL ORGANIZATION.—The development of productive and distributive agencies, considered, like the foregoing, in its necessary causes: comprehending not only the progressive division of labour, and the increasing complexity of each industrial agency, but also the successive forms of industrial government as passing through like phases with political government.

Vol. III.

VII. LINGUAL PROGRESS.—The evolution of Languages regarded as a psychological process determined by social conditions.

VIII. INTELLECTUAL PROGRESS.—Treated from the same point of view: including the growth of classifications; the evolution of science out of common knowledge; the advance from qualitative to quantitative prevision, from the indefinite to the definite, and from the concrete to the abstract.

IX. ÆSTHETIC PROGRESS.—The Fine Arts similarly dealt

with: tracing their gradual differentiation from primitive institutions and from each other; their increasing varieties of development; and their advance in reality of expression and superiority of aim.

X. MORAL PROGRESS.—Exhibiting the genesis of the slow emotional modifications which human nature undergoes in its adaptation to the social state.

XI. THE CONSENSUS.—Treating of the necessary interdependence of structures and of functions in each type of society, and in the successive phases of social development.*

THE PRINCIPLES OF MORALITY.

VOL. I.

PART I. THE DATA OF MORALITY.—Generalizations furnished by Biology, Psychology and Sociology, which underlie a true theory of right living: in other words, the elements of that equilibrium between constitution and conditions of existence, which is at once the moral ideal and the limit towards which we are progressing.

II. THE INDUCTIONS OF MORALITY.—Those empirically-established rules of human action which are registered as essential laws by all civilized nations: that is to say—the generalizations of expediency.

III. PERSONAL MORALS.—The principles of private conduct—physical, intellectual, moral and religious—that follow from the conditions of complete individual life: or, what is the same thing—those modes of private action which must result from the eventual equilibration of internal desires and external needs.

---

* Of this treatise of Sociology a few small fragments may be found in already-published essays. Some of the ideas to be developed in Part II. are indicated in an article on "The Social Organism," contained in the last number of the *Westminster Review;* those which Part V. will work out, may be gathered from the first half of a paper written some years since on "Manners and Fashion;" of Part VIII. the germs are contained in an article on the "Genesis of Science;" two papers on "The Origin and Function of Music" and "The Philosophy of Style," contain some ideas to be embodied in Part IX.; and from a criticism of Mr. Bain's work on "The Emotions and the Will," in the last number of the *Medico-Chirurgical Review,* the central idea to be developed in Part X. may be inferred.

APPENDICES

Vol. II.

IV. JUSTICE.—The mutual limitations of men's actions necessitated by their co-existence as units of a society—limitations, the perfect observance of which constitutes that state of equilibrium forming the goal of political progress.

V. NEGATIVE BENEFICENCE.—Those secondary limitations, similarly necessitated, which, though less important and not cognizable by law, are yet requisite to prevent mutual destruction of happiness in various indirect ways; in other words—those minor self-restraints dictated by what may be called passive sympathy.

VI. POSITIVE BENEFICENCE.—Comprehending all modes of conduct, dictated by active sympathy, which imply pleasure in giving pleasure—modes of conduct that social adaptation has induced and must render ever more general; and which, in becoming universal, must fill to the full the possible measure of human happiness.*

In anticipation of the obvious criticism that the scheme here sketched out is too extensive, it may be remarked that an exhaustive treatment of each topic is not intended; but simply the establishment of *principles,* with such illustrations as are needed to make their bearings fully understood. It may also be pointed out that, besides minor fragments, one large division (*The Principles of Psychology*) is already, in great part, executed. And a further reply is, that impossible though it may prove to execute the whole, yet nothing can be said against an attempt to set forth the First Principles and to carry their applications as far as circumstances permit.

It is proposed to publish in parts of from five to six sheets octavo (80 to 96 pages). These parts to be issued quarterly; or as nearly so as is found possible. The price per part to be half-a-crown; that is to say, the four parts yearly issued to be severally delivered, post free, to all annual subscribers of Ten Shillings.

* Part IV. of the *Principles of Morality* will be co-extensive (though not identical) with the first half of the writer's *Social Statics.*

THE PRINCIPLES OF MORALITY

Should an adequate sale be insured (on which contingency however the execution of the projected works wholly depends) the first part will appear in July next.

LONDON, March 27, 1860.

Those who wish to take in the proposed serial are requested to fill up, cut off, and forward (without delay) the following form to Mr. MANWARING, 8, *King William Street, Strand, London, W. C. This form commits the subscriber to the* first *volume only, of the series. Lest the guaranteed circulation should prove insufficient, no subscription should be paid until the issue of the first part shows that the design will be carried out. Copies of this Circular, for distribution, may be had of* Mr. MANWARING.

———————————1860.

Sir,
    Please put down my name for one copy of the first of Mr. *Herbert Spencer's projected series of works; and let the successive parts be directed to me as below.*

                        Name———————————
                        Address———————————

Mr. Manwaring, &c., &c.

APPENDICES

List of names sent in up to the date at which this circular is issued:—

JOHN STUART MILL, ESQ.
GEORGE GROTE, ESQ., F.R.S.
RIGHT HON. LORD STANLEY, M.P.
CHARLES DARWIN, ESQ., F.R.S., F.L.S., F.G.S.
PROF. HUXLEY, F.R.S., F.L.S., Sec. G.S.
NEIL ARNOTT, ESQ., M.D., F.R.S.
ERASMUS DARWIN, ESQ.
W. B. CARPENTER, ESQ., M.D., F.R.S., F.L.S., F.G.S.
GEORGE ELIOT, ESQ.
R. MONCKTON MILNES, ESQ., M.P.
OCTAVIUS H. SMITH, ESQ.
PROF. SHARPEY, M.D., Sec. R.S., F.R.S.E.
PROF. DE MORGAN
E. JOHNSON, ESQ., M.D.
E. S. DALLAS, ESQ.
J. LOCKHART CLARKE, ESQ., F.R.S.
CHARLES BABBAGE, ESQ., F.R.S., F.R.A.S., &c.
W. H. RANSOM, ESQ., M.D.
PROF. GOLDWIN SMITH.
O. DE BEAUVOIR PRIAULX, ESQ.
W. H. WALSHE, ESQ., M.D.
HEPWORTH DIXON, ESQ.
DR. FRANKLAND, F.R.S.
T. SPENCER BAYNES, ESQ., LL.B.
J. CHAPMAN, ESQ., M.D.
PROF. GRAHAM, F.R.S., F.G.S., D.C.L., &c.
T. L. HUNT, ESQ.
H. FALCONER, ESQ., M.D., F.R.S., F.L.S., F.G.S.
REV. CHARLES KINGSLEY, F.L.S., F.S.A., &c.
SIR CHARLES LYELL, F.R.S., F.L.S., F.G.S., &c.
R. G. LATHAM, ESQ., M.D., F.R.S.
J. D. HOOKER, ESQ., M.D., F.R.S., F.L.S., F.G.S.
PROF. TYNDALL, F.R.S.
SIR JOHN TRELAWNEY, BART., M.P.
PROF. BUSK, F.R.S., F.G.S., F.L.S.
HENRY T. BUCKLE, ESQ.
PROF. F. W. NEWMAN, M.A.
G. H. LEWES, ESQ.
H. BENCE JONES, ESQ., M.D., F.R.S.
H. DUNNING MACLEOD, ESQ.
PROF. MASSON, M.A.
H. G. ATKINSON, ESQ., F.G.S.
J. D. MORELL, ESQ.
E. H. SIEVEKING, ESQ., M.D.
COL. SIR PROBY T. CAUTLEY, K.C.B., F.R.S.
R. W. MACKAY, ESQ.
PROF. H. D. ROGERS, F.R.S., F.G.S., F.R.S.E., &c.
DR. TRAVIS.
REV. W. G. CLARK.
GEORGE LOWE, ESQ., C.E., F.R.S., F.G.S., &c.
ALEXANDER BAIN, ESQ.
G. DRYSDALE, ESQ., M.D.
PROF. LAYCOCK, F.R.S.E.
E. S. PIGOTT, ESQ.
SIR JAMES CLARK, BART., M.D., F.R.S.
J. A. FROUDE, ESQ.
SIR HENRY HOLLAND, BART., M.D., F.R.S., F.G.S., &c.
SIR JOHN HERSCHEL, BART., F.R.S., F.R.A.S., F.G.S., &c.

M. CHARLES DE RÉMUSAT, de l'Académie Française, Ancien Ministre, &c., &c.
M. JULES SIMON, Ancien Professeur de Philosophie au Collége de France, Ancien Conseiller d'Etat, &c.
M. EMILE D. FORGUES.
M. AMEDÉE PICHOT, D.M., Directeur de la Revue Britannique.

APPENDIX B.

[*The following is the letter to Mr. G. H. Lewes, referred to at the close of chapter xxxvi, as having resulted from the publication of the "Reasons for dissenting from the Philosophy of M. Comte".*]

29 Bloomsbury Sq. W.C.
March 21st, 1864.

My dear Lewes,

Thanks for your criticisms, some of which are important as saving me from an over-statement that would have been mischievous. With respect to the others I will briefly reply to the most important; and after troubling you to read these replies and my comments on the propositions contained in your two notes, I will say no more on the matter.

I was wrong in the assertion that Comte repudiated the science of mind: I should have said the subjective analysis of mind. That he does this I take on your own evidence; since you quote John Mill against him on this point.

The proposition which I oppose to Comte's proposition of the three successive states, theological, metaphysical, and positive, you say is "by no means a counter-proposition". When Comte says that the three methods are "different and even *radically opposed,*" while I say that the method is one that continues essentially the same; and when he says that there are three possible terminal conceptions while I say there is but one possible terminal conception; it seems to me that the term counter-proposition is well warranted.

APPENDICES

I have not read Littré. Harrison named the fact that he had replied to me, and I have as yet only skimmed the chapter in which he does this and sought elsewhere for my name to see whether he anywhere regards me as a partial adherent. As he does not do so I conceive that the note is justified. But I have put a note recognizing your criticism respecting ideas and emotions; and meeting it.

You say I have not recognized Comte's "conception of sociology as a *science*" among his distinctive doctrines. I do not see that it is distinctive of him. The *conception* that there is a social science was surely, as Masson shows, entertained by Vico and Kant—vaguely if you like. That which is distinctive of Comte is his *elaboration of the conception*. Surely, too, you will not deny that there have been other conceptions of social science among the German thinkers, however wild and untenable. Unless you can show that before Comte no one believed that social phenomena conform to law, you cannot say that the *conception* of social science is *distinctive* of Comte.

You ask, too, why I do not put down, as among his distinctive doctrines, the idea of a philosophy constructed out of the sciences. I do not admit this to be distinctive any more than the other. I refer you to your own *History of Philosophy* (p. 348), in proof that Bacon had an idea of such a philosophy; and, as far as it goes, a very true one. I hold that his assertion that "unless natural philosophy be drawn out to particular sciences; and again, unless these particular sciences be brought back again to natural philosophy," involves a more correct conception of the relations of the sciences to each other than Comte's elaborated hierarchy of the sciences. Bacon's conception is *vague and true*: Comte's conception is *definite and untrue*. I really cannot see that the notion of an organization of the sciences into one whole can be claimed for Comte.

You protest against my representing Comte as excluding the recognition of *cause* from the positive philosophy. If

APPENDIX B

he does not do so what becomes of his alleged distinction between the perfection of the metaphysical system and the perfection of the positive system.

In your first note you say "when Comte insists on the *relativity* of knowledge he thereby *postulates* an Absolute, as you do." I do not see how you can say this if you mean that he *consciously* or *avowedly* does so. Have I not myself joined issue with Hamilton and Mansel on this very point; and endeavored to show that the existence of an Absolute is necessarily postulated *though they have not recognized this necessity?* And if Hamilton and Mansel assert the relativity of knowledge and do not recognize the implied consciousness of existence transcending knowledge, is it not legitimate to say that Comte does the same when there are his own words to show it?

One of the implications of your first note, and of our conversations, is that I ought to recognize myself "indebted to Comte as one independent thinker may be indebted to a predecessor." I do not admit that I am reluctant to recognize indebtedness to predecessors: it is a question of *the* predecessor. If anyone says that had von Baer never written I should not be doing that which I now am, I have nothing to say to the contrary—I should reply it is highly probable. But because I am deeply indebted to one predecessor, I do not see that I am called upon to admit indebtedness to another when I am unconscious of it.

You say that you may have thought that my antagonistic attitude towards Comte has tended to suppress the growth of any consciousness of indebtedness to Comte. Possibly. But allow me to point out, on the other hand, that the attitude of Comte's disciples, and your own attitude in particular as expositor, is one which inevitably tends to generate an exaggerated estimate of Comte's influence, and inevitably tends to make you assume indebtedness on insufficient grounds.

You say that Comte's ideas have reached hundreds who

never saw his works. This is perfectly true. If you mean to imply that any such diffused influence affected me before I wrote *Social Statics,* I say it is out of the question; for my reading up to that time had been wholly confined to the special sciences, and to party-politics, joined with miscellaneous light reading and an occasional glance into the elder writers on philosophy. The only book, which, so far as I know, was a means of diffusing any of Comte's ideas was Mill's *Logic;* and this I did not read until at least two years after *Social Statics* was written—a fact of which you will I believe find evidence without going far. [Referring to George Eliot, who had presented me with a copy of Mill's *Logic*.]

I fancy that you and other partial adherents of Comte mistake as an atmosphere of Comtean thought, what is nothing else than the atmosphere of scientific thought. Those whose education has been mainly literary, are unable to realize the mental attitude of those whose education has been mainly scientific—especially where the scientific education has been joined to scientific tendencies, and a life of practical science continually illustrating theoretic science, as in my own case. How little influence Comte's teachings have had on scientific thinking in England, will be shown by the accompanying paragraph; which I suppressed from my appendix from the desire to avoid seeming needlessly hostile.

And now let me deal with your two most specific points, taking first the question of the Sociology. You say—" Was not Comte the one who attempted to construct a Sociology on the positive method—and is not that your aim also?" If you say that here is a resemblance, you say truly. If you say that here is priority on the part of Comte, you say truly. If you say that here is indebtedness on my part, I do not admit it. If you believe that I was acquainted with Comte's ideas before *Social Statics* was written, you may suppose that I derived the notion of a social organism (which is the only point of community between us) from him; but if you do not

APPENDIX B

suppose this, I do not see what grounds you have for the assumption that I am here in any way indebted to Comte. The conception of Social Science which I have now, differs in nothing except further development from the conception set forth in *Social Statics*. With the exception of quite minor ethical propositions, I hold to all that is in *Social Statics;* and in the various political essays which I have since written, have shown its further development by the addition of conceptions which I have proved, by the analysis I sent you, to be neither allied to those of Comte nor suggested by them. I contend that, starting with *Social Statics,* passing through these several steps to the wider generalization of social phenomena given in the essay on Progress, and from thence by other steps to the views which I now hold, there is a development on lines of organization that cannot be traced to him; but are manifestly traceable to the extension of von Baer's principle, and to the rationalization of it which I have since attempted. [This statement, along with some preceding and succeeding ones, and along with a passage in the " Reasons for dissenting from the Philosophy of M. Comte," make it clear that I had, in 1864, forgotten some of the ideas reached in 1850; for on pp. 451-53 of *Social Statics,* where individual organisms and social organisms are shown to be similar in the respect that progress from low types to high types is progress from uniformity of structure to multiformity of structure, there is, in so far, and in other words, a recognition of the law which von Baer formulated in respect of the development of each organism, as a progress from homogeneity to heterogeneity.]

The other important point is that raised in your question— " Was not Comte the man who first constructed *a* Philosophy out of the separate sciences—and is not that your aim also"? Here, it seems to me, is the chief source of difference between us. I venture to think that you are assimilating two wholly different things—endeavouring to establish a lineal descent between systems which are not only generically distinct or ordinally distinct, but which belong to distinct classes. What is Comte's professed aim? To give a coherent account of the progress of *human conceptions.* What is my aim? To give a coherent account of the progress of the *external world.* Comte proposes to describe the necessary, and the actual, filiation of *ideas.* I propose to describe the necessary, and the actual, filiation of *things.* Comte professes to interpret the genesis of *our knowledge of nature.* My aim is to interpret, as far as it is possible, the genesis of the *phenomena which constitute nature.* The one end is *subjective.* The other is *objective.* How then can the one be the originator of the other? If I had taken the views briefly set down in *The Genesis of Science,* and developed them into an elaborate system showing the development and coordination of human knowledge in pursuance of a theory at variance with that of Comte; then you might rightly have said that the one was suggested by the other. Then you might rightly have asked—" Was not Comte the man who first constructed a Philosophy out of the separate sciences—and is not that your aim also?" A philosophy of the sciences has a purely abstract subject-matter. A philosophy of nature has a purely concrete subject-matter, and how the one can beget the other I do not see. A concrete may beget an abstract; but how an abstract begets a concrete is not manifest. Comte's system is avowedly an Organon of the Sciences. The scheme at which I am working has been called by Martineau a Cosmogony. Surely in the generation of thought, an Organon should give origin to an Organon and a Cosmogony to a Cosmogony. If you look for my predecessors, and if you point to the Cosmogonies of Hegel and Oken as being conceptions which may have influenced me, I do not say nay: I knew the general natures of Hegel's and Oken's Cosmogonies, and widely different as their conceptions are from my own, they are conceptions of the *same class,* and may very possibly have had some sug-

APPENDIX B

gestive influence.* But why, in seeking the parentage of the Cosmogony at which I am working, you should pass over antecedent Cosmogonies, and fix on an Organon of the Sciences for its parent, is more than I understand.

And now, having pointed out what I conceive to be the fundamental difference between the natures and aims of Comte's scheme and my own (which your question assumes to be the same in nature and aim) let me take a further step. Looking at it from this new point of view, glance through the essay on Progress. Having done this, ask yourself, in the first place, whether you see any Comtean inspiration in that—whether you see in it anything more than the extension of von Baer's principle and the endeavour to interpret that principle deductively? You must I think answer—No. In the second place, ask yourself whether there are not in that essay the rudiments of the scheme which is developed in *First Principles*. You cannot but answer—Yes. And then, in the third place, ask, is it so foreign to my nature to go on further developing ideas, that you cannot believe that the last of these has grown out of the first? In the essay on Progress there is a rudimentary Cosmogony. In *First Principles* there is a more elaborated Cosmogony. Is it unnatural that the one should in the course of some years have evolved the other?

Even while I write I am reminded of evidence on this point, which, however inconclusive it may be to others, is perfectly conclusive to myself; and makes me more than ever certain of the truth of my denial. You may remember that at the end of 1858 or beginning of 1859, I made an effort to obtain some appointment, which should give me sufficient means and leisure to do that which I am now

* Sixteen years after this letter was written, the analogy between the Synthetic Philosophy and the system of Hegel, in so far as the subject matter is concerned, was alleged by Mons. Carrau. In an article published in the *Revue des Deux Mondes* on 1st April, 1880, he said:—
" C'est l'Encyclopédie de Hegel refaite au point de vue de la méthode expérimentale."

doing. I have a distinct recollection of then explaining to Mr. Grote, who took some interest in the matter, that my purpose was to elaborate the ideas contained in the essay on Progress, which had then taken a larger development. And if Mr. J. S. Mill keeps his letters, I am greatly mistaken if it cannot be shown by the correspondence I then had with him, that I gave him the same explanation of my aims.*

Whether you do or do not continue to think as you did on this matter, you will at any rate see that the amount and kind of evidence which (to myself) warrants my continual denial, is abundant and definite. And unless there is virtue in saying that you are indebted when you are not conscious of being indebted, I think I am not only warranted in making the denial but bound to make it.

In brief, then, my position is this:—Until it is shown that the views of social science I now hold, differ from those contained in *Social Statics,* by something more than difference of development—until it is shown that a Cosmogony is not to be rightly affiliated on preceding Cosmogonies but is to be rightly affiliated on an Organon of the Sciences—until it is shown that the essay on Progress does not contain the rudiments out of which *First Principles* has naturally developed—until it is shown that I have adopted some general view of Comte's, or been led by his teaching to abandon some view I previously held; I shall continue to assert that I am uninfluenced by Comte, save in those minor views of his which I avowedly accept, and by the influence of antagonism. And until some such specific evidence is assigned, I shall continue to think the opposite assertion unwarranted.

Sincerely yours,
HERBERT SPENCER.

[* Fortunately he had kept my letter. He returned it to me and I have quoted it in Chapter XXX.]

APPENDIX C.

[*Documents concerning the intended cessation of the issue of the Synthetic Philosophy, and concerning the measures taken to prevent it.*]

Private.
London, April 8th, 1866.

Sir,

The subscribers to Mr. Herbert Spencer's System of Philosophy have been informed through a circular from the Publisher, that owing to the present insufficiency of Subscriptions its publication must be discontinued.

Mr. Spencer having declined several offers of direct contributions towards the expenses of publishing his great work, the only alternative remaining would appear to be, that those to whom its discontinuance would be a matter of deep regret, should subscribe for a sufficient number of copies to secure the author from loss.

It is estimated that 250 additional Subscriptions would suffice for this purpose.

Should you be disposed to join the undersigned in taking additional copies, you are requested to fill up the enclosed form and send it to Messrs. Williams & Norgate.

GEORGE BUSK, JOHN LUBBOCK,
JOHN TYNDALL, J. S. MILL,
T. H. HUXLEY.

APPENDICES

To Messrs. WILLIAMS & NORGATE,
   14 *Henrietta Street, Covent Garden, London, W.C.*
Enter my name as a Subscriber to the 4th and following volumes of Mr. Herbert Spencer's System of Philosophy;
* *Number of Subscriptions* _____
   Name _____
   Address _____

Messrs. Williams & Norgate are ready to take charge of, and keep for the subscribers the copies they may subscribe for for the present purpose, if directed to do so.

The second of the two circulars named in Chapter XXXVIII here follows:—

The Royal School of Mines, Jermyn Street,
May 18th, 1866.

My dear Sir,

I think it is desirable that a copy of the accompanying letter addressed to me by Mr. Spencer, should be sent to all those who have expressed a wish to co-operate with Mr. Busk, Sir John Lubbock, Mr. Mill, Prof. Tyndall, and myself, in carrying out the plan suggested in our circular of April 8th last.

Mr. Spencer's letter appears to me to preclude us from any corporate action in promoting the pecuniary success of his works; but so stout a champion of personal liberty, can, I am sure, make no objection to efforts on the part of individuals, who reflect that his time and his labours are still bestowed without remuneration, to extend the list of subscribers.

I am, yours very faithfully,
T. H. HUXLEY.

Sydney Williams, Esq.

* The subscription for each copy being 10 shillings per annum (or rather for each issue of four parts) £5— ,, — ,, — would represent Ten Subscriptions £10— ,, — ,, — Twenty Subscriptions, &c.

APPENDIX C

17 Wilmot Street, Derby,
13th May, 1866.

My dear Huxley,

You are aware of the sad event which brought me down here some three weeks ago. This event has consequences respecting which it seems proper that I should write to you without further delay.

When, along with the last number of the *Biology*, I issued a notice of cessation, to take place on the completion of the volume now in progress, I did so because I felt that I was not justified in continuing to sink what little property I possess, as I have been doing year by year since I began publishing. My position is now so far changed, that it will be possible for me to persevere, without making any other sacrifice than that of my time.

As you know, I reluctantly assented to the measures that had, unknown to me, been taken by friends interested in the continuance of my work, only because otherwise the alternatives were, discontinuance of it or prospective ruin. Now that these are no longer the alternatives, my reason for assenting disappears. I shall feel much more at my ease in going on with my serial as heretofore, than I should feel with the help of that additional circulation of it proposed to be secured—in however delicate a way.

Will you, therefore, be kind enough to see that the arrangements lately entered into are cancelled—not, however, without expressing my acknowledgments to those who have entered into them. While I regret that you, and others who have co-operated, should have spent so much time and trouble in devising a plan now to be abandoned, the conclusive proofs of sympathy with my aims that have been thus given, will ever be a gratifying remembrance to me.

Very sincerely yours,
HERBERT SPENCER.

APPENDIX D.

[*An account of the invalid-bed, as given by the "British Medical Journal" for July 27, 1867.*]

A NEW INVALID-BED.

There is now on view at the establishment of Mr. Ward, the invalid chair-maker, Leicester Square, a new invalid-bed, admitting of a much greater variety of movements than any of those at present in use. The upper framework has adjustments similar to those of an ordinary fracture-bed; permitting the body to be raised to various inclinations, and the knees to be bent to various angles. But the peculiarity is, that this frame-work is supported, under its centre, on a large ball-and-socket joint, which allows the whole framework, with its variously adjustable parts, to be moved about bodily in all directions; so as to be inclined longitudinally, laterally, or both, and to be moved round so as to face all points of the compass. By means of a simple locking apparatus, the framework is firmly fixed in any attitude that may be desired: a few turns of the handle sufficing again to release it, and any other attitude to be assumed. Among the advantages obtained are these:—

The patient may be taken out of bed, and put into bed again, without the effort ordinarily required. The ball being unlocked, and the bed being gently tipped forwards, so that its lower end reaches the floor, the patient comes upon his feet; and after the sheets have been changed, or some needful act performed, he is placed with his back against the inclined surface of the bed, which, being then made to revolve backwards, he lies as at first.

By a lateral, instead of a longitudinal inclination of the bed, the patient may be turned over from the back on to the side, or contrariwise; saving the labour and pain often entailed by this change.

The longitudinal inclination of the bed being changeable at pleasure, the patient may lie, or may sleep, at any angle that he may prefer, or that is prescribed; either with the head higher than the feet, or, as it is sometimes desirable, with the feet somewhat higher than the head: the inclination being of course adjustable to a nicety, and changeable at will.

The moveable framework which supports the trunk, being raised, so that the trunk and legs form an angle (which may be varied to any extent up to a right angle) the whole bed may then be moved longitudinally round its centre of support, so that the body in this bent position may have the head and feet placed at all varieties of relative elevation. For example, while the trunk is horizontal the legs may be greatly inclined upwards, an attitude that is desirable where injury of the foot or knee renders it proper to diminish the pressure of blood.

The framework that bends the knees being raised, as well as that which inclines the trunk, the same longitudinal rotation of the framework gives a great variety of partly-reclining, partly-sitting postures. The patient may be placed, without any effort to him, in all attitudes between that of lying horizontally, and that of sitting upright in an easy chair.

These movements may, of course, be all of them joined with any such degree of lateral inclination of the bed as is desired; so that, supposing the framework has been adjusted somewhat into the form of an easy chair, and tilted forwards or backwards so as to bring a wounded arm or foot to the right height, the bed may be at the same time tilted sideways, so as to bring this wounded arm or foot on the uppermost side, into the most convenient position for dressing the wound.

At the same time the movement of horizontal rotation being brought into play, the whole bed may be moved round until the injured part is turned towards the light: this same horizontal rotation being, at other times, available for giving the patient change of view, enabling him to look out of the window when raised in the sitting posture, or to have his face turned away from the light if it is distressing.

To the side of the framework is fixed a moveable arm, carrying a small table, to support a plate or basin, and this table, by a slight change of position, also becomes a reading-easel.

One of the advantages of the bed not originally foreseen, but which has come out in practice, is that of being able to make certain changes in a patient's position quite suddenly. When the ball-and-socket joint is but partially locked, so that a moderate force applied to the head or foot of the bed will change its position, the patient, previously lying back, may be instantly raised into the sitting posture if a coughing fit come on.

One further use that may be named is, that when the ball-and-socket joint is completely unlocked, so as to permit perfect freedom of movement, two attendants, seizing the handles on the opposite sides of the bed, may give the patient a little exercise, by rocking the bed from side to side in the manner of a cradle.

Beyond the special advantages above described, there are some general advantages. The ability to change the posture of the patient in such a variety of ways and degrees, without any effort to him, must tend to diminish that pain, weariness, and irritability, caused by long continuance of the same attitude, or by small choice of attitudes, and must so conduce to convalescence. A further result to be antici-

A NEW INVALID-BED

pated, is, that bed sores may be avoided, the points of chief pressure being changeable at will, and as often as is desired.

This bed, devised by Mr. Herbert Spencer, the distinguished biologist and philosophical writer, for a member of his own family, has been in use between four and five months, and has so far answered his expectations that he has had a second made, with sundry improvements, hoping that it may be of service to others. Mr. Spencer has refrained from patenting it: not wishing to place any obstacle in the way of its general use.

APPENDIX E.

[*A letter concerning the feeling in England at the time when there began the American War between North and South— a letter written for publication in the "New York Tribune," and which, though withheld at the time, was published in that Journal some years later.*]

MY DEAR YOUMANS: When you were here I told you that the Americans wholly misconceive the feeling with which England at first regarded the quarrel between North and South. To others of your countrymen I have, from time to time, made the same statement; and I have urged more than one of them to examine for himself the evidence furnished by our press, and to publish the results of his examination. Nothing has come of my suggestions, however. Whether those I spoke to thought it impossible that the truth could be so entirely at variance with their belief as I represented, or whether they preferred cherishing a belief which seemed to justify their indignation, I cannot say: probably both causes conspired with their dislike to the required trouble.

The importance of disabusing the American mind on this matter is increasingly manifest. That hostile feeling toward us which has for years been displayed by your journals and your orators, has been largely if not mainly caused by the impression that gratuitous ill-will was felt by us from the outset; and I cannot but think that were this erroneous impression removed, there would be less difficulty in coming

APPENDIX E

to an understanding on disputed questions. Failing to find any one else to do what it seems to me should be done, I have myself had collected the requisite materials, with the view of affording to Americans the means of judging how far they are warranted in cherishing that animosity which has lately been exhibited more violently than ever.

In the first place let me show you the public opinion that existed in England at the time that secession was impending, as that opinion was expressed in the columns of the press.

"In South Carolina, and Alabama, and Georgia, an appeal is to be made to the last powers vested in the State Constitution, with a view to disunion, on no ground whatever, that can be discovered, except that they do not like Mr. Lincoln. * * * To all our political notions there is no more reason for the violences reported from the Southern States than there would be for the electors of Southwark refusing to pay assessed taxes because Lord Palmerston had declared against the ballot. * * * The Southern States certainly would not mend matters by a separation. * * * Anything is better than dividing State against State, house against house, and servant against master in the most rising nation in the world."
[*Times,* Dec. 5, 1860.

"Without sharing the opinions, much less using the language, of the Abolitionists with respect to Slavery, which bad though it be, must remain for many years an institution of the United States, we look upon the conduct of South Carolina in this matter as disgraceful in the last degree. To gratify their pique against those of opposite politics, and to advance their local interests, the Slave-owners would destroy a Constitution under which their country has enjoyed singular prosperity." [*Times,* Dec. 11, 1860.

"The Americans may confidently assure themselves that there is no party in this kingdom which desires anything but the maintenance and prosperity of the Union. * * * We cannot disguise from ourselves that, apart from all political complications, there is a right and a wrong in this question, and that the right belongs, with all its advantages, to the States of the North." [*Times,* Jan. 4, 1861.

"The proposal of secession is so wild, so absurd, that it

could not be put forth by men sensible enough to conduct public affairs unless they were so dishonest as to be unworthy of the trust. The threat is either an outbreak of mad passion, or a device to obtain concessions from the fears and affections of the North." [*Daily News,* Jan. 2, 1861.

" Granted that the United States of America are beset with peculiar difficulties in treating this question [Slavery]— when are these difficulties to vanish, when are they to be lessened under the domination of the South? Have not the Southern states gone on from iniquity to iniquity? * * * *

" We must not forget that slave-owners are necessarily aggressive in every sense, and that in the United States they have been as a minority not only dominant and aggressive, but turbulent, insolent, and overbearing even towards the majority of their own race and nation."

[*Morning Herald,* Dec. 27, 1860.

" If the Southern States were the advocates of a cause less pernicious and detestable than the extension of slavery, we should still think their proceedings foolish and suicidal; but, under existing circumstances, they can have neither the sympathy nor good wishes of any man, either in America or in England, who has the slightest regard for the progress of civilization and the interests of humanity."

[*Morning Post,* Dec. 5, 1860.

" We must persist in the opinion that this Southern agitation is false in its pretences, and will be proved a blunder by its results; but, if now, or at any future time, the slave states should break away from the Union, we might await with confidence the day when the Northern confederacy, stronger in its liberty, in its moral power, and in its physical manhood, would rise and overwhelm its sullen rival, and crush the system of slavery for ever."

[*Daily Telegraph,* Dec. 3, 1860.

" We see also how intolerant slavery makes its votaries. They have enjoyed a long lease of power; they have had the advantage of a large number of pro-slavery Presidents, as well as of supple majorities in Congress; and from the admission of Texas into the Union, as a Slave State, down to the repeal of the Missouri compromise, their demands, monstrous and unjust as they have been, met with a too ready compliance. But now, because they have received a check, and their opponents, whose rights they have so often violated, have succeeded in climbing into power, they have the

APPENDIX E

effrontery to put on an air of injured innocence, and to pretend that the legitimate triumph of the North is an act of aggression against them."
[*Morning Star,* Nov. 27, 1860.

"They [Slave States] dare not go out of the Union with their slaves, for they have nowhere to go to. They are a great deal safer in the friendship and alliance of the North."
[*Express,* Nov. 20, 1860.

"The election of Abraham Lincoln will be hailed everywhere as a declaration that the great Republic is not a slave Republic. * * * England will now approve of the general course of the United States policy; and with the dominancy of the Slave power half the causes of irritation between the two countries will cease. England must ever be an anti-slavery country, and its Government of any party an anti-slavery Government." [*Sun,* Nov. 19, 1860.

"But will the South really carry out their threat, and secede from the Union? We believe that all their loud talk is but bluster, and that they will do nothing so utterly mad as this. * * * We are persuaded that the North have little to lose by the change, the South everything. * * * With the feeling of the whole world against them; standing alone in their assertion of a principle which Christianity and civilization have condemned, the Southern states of America—abundant in land, bankrupt in everything else—would sink rapidly to a lower and lower level, till they had become as degraded as Mexico."
[*Standard,* Nov. 24, 1860.

"If we augur rightly, the Southern rebellion will splutter a great deal and then subside. It rests upon grounds not tenable in an Anglo-Saxon community; for it does not rest upon any violation of the Constitution, the common law or the statute book. It rests upon arrogance and ill-temper, too weak a foundation for a Southern confederacy."
[*Spectator,* Dec. 1, 1860.

The English "nation may be trusted to consent to almost any sacrifice rather than that the Slave-trade should exceed its present inevitable limits."
[*Saturday Review,* Dec. 29, 1860.

This universal condemnation of the South and sympathy with the North, uttered through the English journals before

APPENDICES

the news of Secession reached us, was uttered afterwards in even stronger language. Here are the proofs:

"For our own part, whatever opinions Americans may have of English policy, we beg to assure them that in this country there is only one wish—that the Union may survive this terrible trial. Should Providence decree it otherwise, we earnestly pray that the separation may be an amicable one. Civil war in a flourishing country and among a kindred people can never be contemplated without horror by a nation like ours, and we trust that neither the violence of the people nor the weakness of their leaders will bring this calamity on the American Union." [*Times*, Jan. 18, 1861.

"Without law, without justice, without delay, she [South Carolina] is treading in the path that leads to the downfall of nations and the misery of families. The hollowness of her cause is seen beneath all the pomp of her labored denunciation, and surely to her, if to any community of modern days, may be applied the words of the Hebrew Prophet—'A wonderful and horrible thing is committed in the land. The Prophets prophesy falsely, and my people love to have it so.'"
[*Times*, Jan. 19, 1861.

"We should be thankful to see reason to hope that the South could throw off her madness, and agree now to terms which she must accept at last." "If the seceders do not make the most of that time [*i.e.* the remaining six weeks of President Buchanan's term of office] to negotiate a return, there seems to be no other prospect than that of coercion—unwilling as the North sincerely is to resort to it."
[*Daily News*, Jan. 21, 1861.

If the Southern States succeed in establishing a separate Union, they will form a State "insignificantly small and hated among mankind, for lack of those moral attributes without which in this age no Power can claim or receive the respect of civilized and free communities."
[*Morning Post*, Jan. 9, 1861.

"No one desires to witness the dismemberment of a great, friendly, and cognate nation; but if this object should be accomplished the blame will rest with the people of the South, whose treason and rebellion have been aided and abetted by the temporizing and cowardly policy of Mr. President Buchanan." [*Morning Post*, Jan. 12, 1861.

If war should arise "we must once more rely on the

APPENDIX E

natural laws of justice, and predict that the slave Secessionists will be humbled, if not trampled under foot."
[*Daily Telegraph,* Jan. 19, 1861.

" Every man who deserves the name throughout the civilized world gives his hearty sympathy to the North."
[*Daily Telegraph,* Jan. 15, 1861.

" The free States are purging themselves from the contempt of the civilized world for past submission to the slave oligarchs; and whatever may be the intentions of Mr. Lincoln in reference to the issues agitating the thirty-three states of the Union, there is ample evidence in the tone of the Northern press that the doom of Slavery is sealed."
[*Morning Herald,* Jan. 28, 1861.

" We deplore the infatuation which impels the Cotton States to a course so unjustifiable and dangerous. * * * We sympathize with our brethren of the North in the trial of principle and temper to which they are subjected."
[*Morning Star,* Jan. 15, 1861.

" We may well suppose that the Southern men *make themselves believe* their cause a good one—but the men of the North *know* theirs to be so. It requires no tampering with conscience to enjoy the faith that extension of slavery ought to be repressed; and *that* is the present creed of the North. It demands the subversion of all Christian instincts to believe in the right of property in man, and to think slavery an institution of Heaven; and *that* is the creed of the South. No artifice can make this professed creed a *faith.* Think of dying for slavery!"   [*Sun,* Jan. 19, 1861.

" The spectacle presented in the United States * * * of successful rebellion in the South, with timidity and almost daily change of men and measures in the Government of Washington, is one which all Englishmen must regard with pain."   [*Globe,* Jan. 14, 1861.

" In our estimation the South has all to lose and nothing to gain by disunion; and unhappily the rest of the world may lose, too, by conduct which seems to spring from no source but political pride and passion."
[*Globe,* Jan. 18, 1861.

" There remains no course open to the friends of the Union but an appeal to the sword. * * * We hold it to be perfectly clear that the act of secession is rebellion, and that the Government which neglects by every means in its power to prevent so dire a calamity is guilty of treason to

APPENDICES

the Federal constitution. But, in the present instance the enormity of the crime of the state of South Carolina is magnified by the absence of any reasonable ground for their withdrawal from the Union." [*Standard,* Jan. 19, 1861.

"On the South rests the whole guilt of this fratricidal strife; and on the South will fall the worst consequences of the conflict it has provoked." [*Standard,* May 2, 1861.

"We can only say that the South *is* mad—mad in the way that is caused by passion acting on ignorance and a morbid self-will." [*Express,* Jan. 24, 1861.

"The Southerners * * * are fighting, not to be let alone, but for the preservation and maintenance of the Slave System, to which everything must be subordinated."
[*Spectator,* Jan. 5, 1861.

"It is the dread of being inclosed in a ring fence, a vital article in the Republican programme, which fills the Southerns with dismay, and urges them on in their mad progress towards anarchy." [*Spectator,* Jan. 26, 1861.

"There is little danger that Englishmen will look on the dissolution of the United States with languid curiosity or malicious satisfaction. We have plenty of selfish reasons, if we had no others, for regarding it with something like dismay. In fact, the event which South Carolina has recklessly precipitated may be said to have involved this country in the very same embarrassments with which the Northern United States have so long struggled."
[*Saturday Review,* Jan. 12, 1861.

"The Northern States are fully justified in arming for the support of the Constitution."
[*Saturday Review,* Feb. 2, 1861.

Such was the display of English feeling in the daily and weekly papers of all political parties. The journals of extreme Toryism joined those of extreme Liberalism in this unqualified reprobation of the South. *Not a single expression of sympathy with the South has been discovered in the course of the examination.* One expression of the kind was, I am told, published in a monthly magazine, and protested against as being in absolute opposition to the current of public opinion. Just that cordial approval which the anti-Slavery party of the North expected to have from England,

and which they afterwards so loudly complained that they did not get, was at first shown to them in the clearest manner, even by those least friendly to American institutions.

How came all this to be changed? When once a sentiment has been established throughout the whole nation, it is a difficult thing to alter it; and the transformation of it into an opposite sentiment in the course of a few months, implies some very unusual and very strong influence. After the English people had unanimously condemned the South and wished success to the North, it is impossible that a large part of them should have turned round without a cause. What was that cause? I know of none but your behaviour to us. At the very outset, even before Secession had taken place, there was a predisposition to put an unfavourable construction on all we said and did. The loud utterances of a fellow-feeling with you, of which I have given examples that might be indefinitely multiplied, seem either to have passed unnoticed by your papers, or to have produced no effect on you; while, on the other hand, ready credence seems to have been given to "stories of the joy expressed by Englishmen travelling in the United States at the prospect of the Constitution collapsing," which appeared in your papers as early as December, 1860, and which I find protested against in our papers as incredible. Men who are biassed, very generally can see only the facts which they expect to see; and I suppose that the traditional bitterness against England, encouraged, if I am rightly informed, even by the lessons in your school-books, made you ready to believe and remember all allegations of unfriendly feeling on our part, while you were unready to believe, and very soon forgot, the clear proofs of our friendly feeling. Thus only is it possible to account for the fact that, out of the enormous mass of evidence to the contrary, you extracted materials for the conviction that we bore you ill-will. Thus only is it possible to account for the fact that, in response to our manifestations of sympathy, there came insinuations respecting our intentions and our motives; false statements of what we were doing or were about to do; assertions that our interests were on the side of the South, and that therefore we were sure to go with the South; charges of mean selfishness based on the assumed truth of these assertions; ending in invectives that became daily more violent. Friends who are treated as enemies are not likely to remain friends; and your persistent misrepresentations, by alienating some and producing resentment in others, eventually aroused among us the hostile sentiment with which we were wrongly charged. I leave you to judge of the truth of this inference after telling you how I was myself affected. It has been said of me by some of your writers that I am in feeling more an American than an Englishman; and the statement is in a considerable degree true. Moreover, at the time in question (though in a still greater degree afterward), my relations with individual Americans and with the American public were such as to heighten my preëxisting sympathies. Nevertheless, I confess that your behaviour toward us wrought in me a change similar in kind to that which I saw wrought in those around me, though not so great in degree. Irritated day after day by seeing ascribed to Englishmen ignoble motives which certainly were not prevalent, if they existed at all, the strength of my fellow-feeling with the North gradually diminished. Nothing could have made me sympathize with the South; but I can well understand how those whose detestation of Southern institutions and Southern conduct was less intense than mine, were at length so much incensed by your undeserved reproaches that they changed sides. I do not defend this. I do not think any were justified in wishing well to your antagonists because they felt themselves calumniated by you; and perhaps I ought myself to have kept uncooled my originally warm interest in your success. But it is not in ordinary human nature to respond to hard words by unflagging good wishes.

APPENDIX E

Was there not a reason for our hard words, you will say? Did not the premature proclamation of neutrality justify our interpretations? I cannot enter at length into this vexed question. I will only say that, had such a proclamation been made by a people who were displaying unfriendly sentiments to you, you might have had some reason to regard it as an act of hostility; but coming as it did along with the reprobation—I might almost say execration—of your antagonists, it could not reasonably be interpreted otherwise than as a step taken in pursuance of our established foreign policy. That the step was taken sooner than was necessary for the avoidance of entanglements, may or may not be true; but even if true, it is surely strange that an error of judgment on the part of a Minister should have made you forget the manifestations of good feeling from an entire nation.

No doubt there existed here some who willingly found provocation in your treatment of us. Their social position, their class-interests, their traditional opinions, have always predisposed our "upper ten thousand" to look coldly on a society like yours. And irritated as they frequently were by having the success of American institutions held up to them as a reproach, it is not surprising that they were ready to say and do unfriendly things whenever the opportunity offered. Hence it became the policy of their journals to reproduce here everything you said against us; and when the Trent affair and your adverse tariff gave occasion, the comments of their journals were, of course, such as to increase, as much as possible, the growing alienation. Affording, as the language of your Press continued to do, abundant materials for generating it, this hostile sentiment, which was at first limited to a small minority, spread until it became the prevailing sentiment among the influential classes, though not among the mass of the people. And this it was which led to the angry speeches made by certain members of our Legislature; this it was which at length produced openly-avowed partisanship with the South; this it was which made possible the unfortunate Alabama business.

I have laid before you little else than indisputable facts; and from these facts such inferences as I have drawn are, I think, irresistible. It is a fact which any one may verify by referring to the files of our papers in New York, that for months after the commencement of your troubles, the unanimous sympathies of the English with the North were expressed in the most unqualified manner. It is a fact that my own originally warm interest in the success of the North was gradually cooled by the groundless suspicions and undeserved reproaches with which you responded to our good wishes; and if it be an inference that what changed me from an ardent sympathizer into a lukewarm sympathizer, changed others from friends into enemies, the inference is one which scarcely admits of question. The conclusion is, I think, inevitable, that but for the revolution of feeling brought about by your behaviour to us, there would never have been prompted any of those private acts of aid to the Confederates of which you complain, nor would there have happened that gross official negligence which allowed that aid to be given. I am, very sincerely yours,

HERBERT SPENCER

No. 37 Queen's Gardens, Bayswater, May 22, 1869.

APPENDIX F.

A NEW FISHING-ROD JOINT.

[*From " The Field" newspaper for January* 14, 1871.]

Sir,—During the late salmon-fishing season, I had the opportunity of trying a rod with a new kind of joint, which I had made for me in the spring. The results having been satisfactory, a description of it may be of interest to fishermen who care about improved appliances.

This new form of joint may be generally described as a combination of the splice and the socket; possessing, as I think, the advantages of both without their inconveniences.

In the figure, A B represents a splice made with a shoulder at C—the effect of the shoulder being that, so long as the halves of the splice are held together laterally, they cannot be drawn apart longitudinally. The halves of the splice are held together laterally by a sliding socket or collar, D E, of such length and diameter that when it is drawn down till the bottom of it, E, comes to the point B, or rather to the dotted line just below B, the splice is tightly inclosed by the collar throughout its whole length: the tightness, of course, resulting from the slight taper of the rod and the corresponding taper of the collar. The advantages of this arrangement are these:—

1. Decrease of weight. Instead of the usual metal socket and the metal bracket fitting into it, which have to bear all the strain, and therefore must be of considerable thickness,

APPENDICES

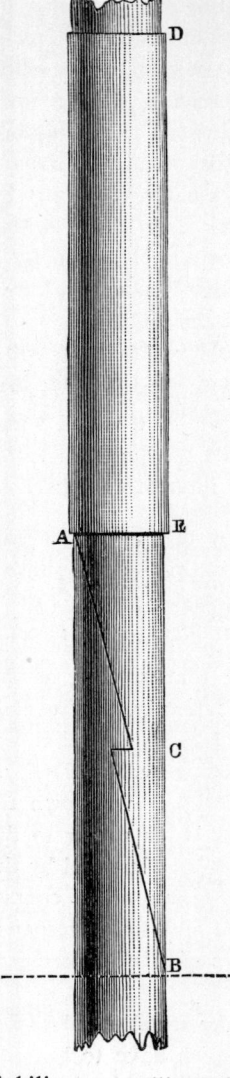

there is only a single collar, which may be made comparatively thin; since the strain it has to bear is no greater than that which is borne by the wrapping of silk ordinarily covering a splice.

2. Quickness of adjustment. When the rod is being put together, no time is required to adjust the line of the runners. The fixing of the splice itself fixes the line of the runners, which cannot afterwards go awry. A further and greater economy of time and trouble, results from dispensing with the usual link of wire or string, needful to prevent the loosening of the joints by continual casting.

3. Avoidance of entanglements. The existing form of socket joint, needing its tying of wire or string to prevent loosening, causes inconvenience and irritation by often catching the line or the flies. This collar-splice joint, as it may fitly be called, offers nothing against which the line or the flies can catch.

4. It is quickly taken to pieces: requiring no untying, and not being liable to bind.

This last assertion may perhaps be received with scepticism, since it seems obvious that as, in rainy weather, water will get into this joint as into the ordinary one, the liability to swelling of the wood and consequent binding will be as great, if not greater. But, anticipating this difficulty, I had especial care taken that the wood should be made waterproof. Soaking it in hot boiled oil and subsequent varnishing, rendered it impermeable; so that though, during my fishing of last season, exposure to rain for many hours repeatedly occurred, I never had any inconvenience from binding. I may add that, as an additional precaution, I rubbed the surface of the splice, outer and inner, with tallow. [This was a mistake. I forgot that "verdigris" would result from contact of tallow with brass. I afterwards used oil. Perhaps vaseline would answer.]

It may be well to meet a further doubt which some will feel—whether the sliding collar will not be loosened by continual casting, as the ordinary socket is. Recognizing this possibility before the rod was made, I concluded that there would be little danger of such an evil. The common rod is apt to get loose at the joints, because at each cast the momentum given to the upper parts of the rod tends to pull them out of their sockets; but in the joint I have described, the shoulder of the splice effectually prevents this momentum of the upper parts from producing any effect, so long as the collar keeps its place; and there is no tendency to loosening of the collar, save that resulting from its own momentum, which is not sufficient to overcome the friction. Experience verified this anticipation: when the collar was thrust into its place with moderate tightness, it never stirred.

Being much simpler than the ordinary joint, it ought, I should think, to be considerably cheaper; though I cannot say that the advantage of cheapness was realized in my experience. But of course anything made for the first time is much more costly than when it is habitually made. Mr. Alfred Carter, of St. John's Street Road, Islington, was the maker; and, on the whole, he carried out my plans satisfactorily.

37, Queen's Gardens,   HERBERT SPENCER.
    Bayswater, Jan. 3.

APPENDIX G.

OBITUARY NOTICE OF J. S. MILL.

[*From the " Examiner" newspaper for May* 17, 1873.]

To dilate upon Mr. Mill's achievements, and to insist upon the wideness of his influence over the thought of his time, and consequently over the actions of his time, seems to me scarcely needful. The facts are sufficiently obvious, and are recognized by all who know anything about the progress of opinion during the last half-century. My own estimate of him, intellectually considered, has been emphatically, though briefly, given on an occasion of controversy between us, by expressing my regret at "having to contend against the doctrine of one whose agreement I should value more than that of any other thinker."

While, however, it is almost superfluous to assert of him that intellectual height so generally admitted, there is more occasion for drawing attention to a moral elevation which is less recognized; partly because his activities in many directions afforded no occasion for exhibiting it, and partly because some of its most remarkable manifestations in conduct, are known only to those whose personal relations with him have called them forth. I feel especially prompted to say something on this point, because, where better things might have been expected, there has been, not only a grudging recognition of intellectual rank, but a marked blindness to those fine traits of character which, in the valuation of men, must go for more than superiority of intelligence.

It might, indeed, have been supposed that even those who

never enjoyed the pleasure of personal acquaintance with Mr. Mill, would have been impressed with the nobility of his nature as indicated in his opinions and deeds. How entirely his public career has been determined by a pure and strong sympathy for his fellow-men—how entirely this sympathy has subordinated all desires for personal advantage—how little even the fear of being injured in reputation or position has deterred him from taking the course which he thought equitable or generous; ought to be manifest to every antagonist, however bitter. A generosity that might almost be called romantic was obviously the feeling prompting sundry of those courses of action which have been commented upon as errors. And nothing like a true conception of him can be formed unless, along with dissent from them, there goes recognition of the fact that they resulted from the eagerness of a noble nature, impatient to rectify injustice and to further human welfare.

It may, perhaps, be that my own perception of this pervading warmth of feeling has been sharpened by seeing it exemplified, not in the form of expressed opinions only, but in the form of private actions. For Mr. Mill was not one of those who, to sympathy with their fellow-men in the abstract, join indifference to them in the concrete. There came from him generous acts that corresponded with his generous sentiments. I say this not from second-hand knowledge, but having in mind a remarkable example known only to myself and a few friends. I have hesitated whether to give this example; seeing that it has personal implications. But it affords so clear an insight into Mr. Mill's character, and shows so much more vividly than any description could do how fine were the motives swaying his conduct, that I think the occasion justifies disclosure of it.

Some seven years ago, after bearing as long as was possible the continued losses entailed on me by the publication of the *System of Philosophy,* I notified to the subscribers that I should be obliged to cease at the close of the volume

then in progress. Shortly after the issue of this announcement I received from Mr. Mill a letter, in which, after expressions of regret, and after naming a plan which he wished to prosecute for reimbursing me, he went on to say:—
"In the next place . . . what I propose is, that you should write the next of your treatises, and that I should guarantee the publisher against loss, *i.e.* should engage, after such length of time as may be agreed on, to make good any deficiency that may occur, not exceeding a given sum, that sum being such as the publisher may think sufficient to secure him." Now though these arrangements were of kinds that I could not bring myself to yield to, they none the less profoundly impressed me with Mr. Mill's nobility of feeling, and his anxiety to further what he regarded as a beneficial end. Such proposals would have been remarkable even had there been entire agreement of opinion. But they were the more remarkable as being made by him under the consciousness that there existed between us certain fundamental differences, openly avowed. I had, both directly and by implication, combated that form of the experiential theory of human knowledge which characterizes Mr. Mill's philosophy; in upholding Realism, I had opposed in decided ways, those metaphysical systems to which his own Idealism was closely allied; and we had long carried on a controversy respecting the test of truth, in which I had similarly attacked Mr. Mill's positions in an outspoken manner. That under such circumstances he should have volunteered his aid, and urged it upon me, as he did, on the ground that it would not imply any personal obligation, proved in him a very exceptional generosity.

Quite recently I have seen afresh illustrated this fine trait—this ability to bear with unruffled temper, and without any diminution of kindly feeling, the publicly-expressed antagonism of a friend. The last evening I spent at his house was in the company of another invited guest, who, originally agreeing with him entirely on certain disputed questions, had some fortnight previously displayed his change of view —nay, had publicly criticized some of Mr. Mill's positions in a very undisguised manner. Evidently, along with his own unswerving allegiance to truth, there was in Mr. Mill an unusual power of appreciating in others a like conscientiousness; and so of suppressing any feeling of irritation produced by difference—suppressing it not in appearance only, but in reality; and that, too, under the most trying circumstances.

I should say, indeed, that Mr. Mill's general characteristic, emotionally considered, was an unusual predominance of the higher sentiments—a predominance which tended, perhaps, both in theory and practice, to subordinate the lower nature unduly. That rapid advance of age which has been conspicuous for some years past, and which doubtless prepared the way for his somewhat premature death, may, I think, be regarded as the outcome of a theory of life which made learning and working the occupations too exclusively considered. But when we ask to what ends he acted out this theory, and in so doing too little regarded his bodily welfare, we see that even here the excess, if such we call it, was a noble one. Extreme desire to further human welfare was that to which he sacrificed himself.

HERBERT SPENCER.

APPENDIX H.

HERBERT SPENCER AND HIS AMERICAN FRIENDS.

[*Letter published by Prof. Youmans to correct erroneous impressions current in America.*]

To the Editor of The Tribune.

SIR: I ask a portion of your space to correct certain misstatements which have appeared in the newspapers in reference to the assistance given to Mr. Herbert Spencer from this country in publishing his works. Repeated contradictions of these erroneous statements have already appeared in your columns, but they seem to have failed of their purpose, as the following extract from a recent evening paper will show. The writer said: "The considerable sums that have been transmitted to Mr. Spencer from his American publishers have been the means, as he himself has borne witness, of enabling him to apply himself in singleness of purpose to the one great life-work. If Mr. Spencer should be spared to us only long enough to complete this work (the philosophical system) it is significant to consider it will be to his American revenue that the saving from frittering bread-and-butter work, which would otherwise have been a necessity, of fruitful years sufficient to its completion will be due."

It is no doubt a creditable thing that a few persons in this country, seeing the great public importance of Mr. Spencer's labors, and learning that they were in peril of interruption for lack of support, contributed liberally to prevent a result which they believed would be a public calamity; but if the matter is to be talked about and boasted of as a national honor, it becomes important to know exactly how the case stands. A glance at the facts will show that the writer above quoted claims altogether too much. The circumstances were these.

During the early part of his career as a philosophical writer, Mr. Spencer was habitually a loser by his labors; not simply in devoting time without return, but in having to spend in publication sums which were only in part repaid by sales, and he was consequently forced to make repeated inroads upon his property. His projected philosophical system was a formidable undertaking which he expected to occupy twenty years of time, and which would involve heavy expenditure, which no publisher would undertake. To meet this he chose the form of subscription as the only plan holding out any inducement of enabling him to prosecute the work. Accepting the assurances he received that it would be sustained, he commenced publication in 1860, with about 450 English subscribers and about 250 from this country. But owing to causes which need not be named the enterprise was not sustained. In two or three years the English subscription fell off to about 300 and the American ceased entirely. His American publishers paid him a copyright on his books, but that, with the proceeds from the English subscriptions, was insufficient to protect him from loss. Early in 1866 he found, upon examining into his affairs, that spite of every effort to economize he had, in the course of his literary career, frittered away nearly $6,000, and that if he went on much longer in the same way nothing would be left; and so, with much reluctance, he announced the discontinuance of the serial.

But English thinkers were by no means indifferent to the fate of the undertaking. Mr. Mill made a noble proposal, offering to assume the entire pecuniary responsibility of going on with the work, but Mr. Spencer declined it. A movement was afterward made by certain leading scientific men to secure an artificial increase in the circulation of his serial. This Mr. Spencer at first resisted, but was afterwards induced to consent to the arrangement in a qualified form. While the matter was pending, however, the sudden death of Mr. Spencer's father occurred, and altered the aspect of the case; so that he at once canceled the arrangement, and resolved to continue the work at his own expense.

Meantime, moved by the announcement that Mr. Spencer's series was to stop for lack of support, and knowing that he had been a heavy loser by the publication of works of great value to the public, some of his American friends contributed a sum to repay his losses, and help the project on; and in July, 1866, when going to England, I was commissioned to hand over to Mr. Spencer the documents showing that $7,000 had been invested in his name in American securities. The funds were not sent to him as a largess, or because he was personally in want of them, but they were sent to aid in carrying on an extensive and very important work which was threatened with arrest because of non-support. Mr. Spencer was not consulted, and the thing was so done that he had no choice but to acquiesce in the arrangement. The spirit in which he did it is shown in the following letter:

MY DEAR SIR: Though my friend Dr. Youmans, by expressions in his letters, had led me to suppose that something was likely to be done in the United States with the view of preventing the suspension of my work, yet I was wholly unprepared for anything so generous as that which I learned from your letter of June 25. In ignorance of the steps that were being taken, I had thought that possibly a revival and extension of the American list of subscribers would be attempted; and my thought having taken this direction, the unexpected munificence of my American friends quite astonished me, as it has astonished all to whom I have named it. Not simply the act itself, but also the manner in which the act has been done, is extremely gratifying to me. Possibly you are aware that while on the one hand I had decided that I ought not to continue sacrificing what little property I possess, I had, on the other hand, resolved not to place myself in any questionable position; and, in pursuance of this resolve, I had negatived sundry proposals made here in furtherance of my undertaking. But the course adopted by my American friends is one which appears to give me no alternative save that of yielding. Already in the case of the profits accruing from republished works, which I declined to receive unless the cost of the stereotype plates had been repaid to those who furnished the funds, they defeated me by saying that if I did not draw the proceeds they would remain in Messrs. Appleton's hands; and I foresee that were I now to be restive under their kindness, they would probably take an analogous step. I therefore submit, and I feel less hesitation in doing this because the strong sympathy with my aims which has from the beginning been manifested in the United States, makes me feel that impersonal rather than personal considerations move those who have acted in the matter, and should also guide me. Will you, therefore, be so good as to say to all who have joined in raising this magnificent gift, which more than replaces what I have lost during the last 16 years, that I accept it as a trust to be used to public ends, and that, at the same time, feelings of another kind compel me to express my gratitude as well as my admiration. Let me add that while the material results of their act will be that of greatly facilitating my labors, the approval conveyed by it in so unparalleled a way from readers of another nation, cannot fail to be a moral stimulus and support of great value to me. Believe me, my dear Sir, very sincerely yours,

HERBERT SPENCER.

ROBERT B. MINTURN, *Esq., New-York.*

Mr. Spencer's statement that the action of his American friends would have the effect of greatly facilitating his labors, soon proved true, and in a way that he himself hardly anticipated. Instead of continuing to employ a youth as an amanuensis, he was able to engage a gentleman of university education to give him assistance of a higher kind. Not, indeed, that he wanted this assistance to carry on his regular philosophical series; but he foresaw that in dealing with the "Principles of Sociology" (the great work of his system in three volumes), he would require the collection and classification of a very large amount of materials. This was begun in 1867, simply with a view of facilitating his own work, but it quickly proved to be so important that Mr. Spencer decided to have it carried out for general use. Though subsidiary to his main enterprise this was an immense undertaking, and one which is destined to prove of great public moment. Mr. Spencer wanted the most comprehensive and accurate knowledge concerning all the diversified phases of human society, as a basis of inquiry into the laws of its development. Devising a method by which the different orders of sociological facts could be tabulated, and readily compared, he divided the races of mankind into three great groups—the existing savage races, the existing civilized races, and the extinct civilized races—with the view of working out the whole subject in the most exhaustive manner. He has engaged three gentlemen of the requisite qualifications to take each a division of the work and devote to it five years of research. The work is already considerably advanced, and portions of the "Descriptive Sociology," as it will be called, have been slowly passing through the press for the last two years, and Mr. Spencer hopes to be able to issue the first numbers in the course of the Autumn.

These statements will make manifest the nature of the misapprehension that has arisen. When, a few months ago, in a letter to Mr. Appleton, part of which appeared in *The Evening Post,* Mr. Spencer said that his chief reason for gratification at the increase of returns from this country, was that he would be able to push forward more rapidly the sociological tables, the allusion was to this supplementary undertaking. Of course the outlay implied by it, including the cost of printing only, to be returned after a considerable time, is great; and the rate of progress is determined by his ability to meet this cost. The reference of the above-quoted writer to Mr. Spencer, as having himself borne witness to the importance of his American receipts, must therefore be interpreted by these facts. Although he has received probably more sympathetic encouragement from this country than from his own, and although more of his books have been sold here than there, yet it is neither true that he has received more money from his American than from his English sales, nor that his American income could have alone sustained him, nor that the continuance of his "System of Philosophy" was dependent upon assistance from the United States. Mr. Spencer is very far from underrating the great benefits he has derived from American appreciation and American generosity; but if claims are to be made as to who shall have credit in the matter, he has a right to ask that no injustice be done to his English friends, who were equally appreciative of his work, and equally generous in their proposals to sustain it.

New York, June 5, 1872. E. L. YOUMANS.

INDEX

Adam Bede, authorship of, ii. 44.
Adventure on a railway, i. 151.
Advertisements, ludicrous, ii. 424.
Advice to aspirants, ii. 531 *et seq.*
Air-pump, Spencer improves, i. 127.
Alcohol, effects of, i. 366.
Allen, Grant, ii. 484.
Amanuensis, use of one begun, ii. 40.
Amberley, Lord and Lady, ii. 141.
Americans, testimonial from, ii. 166.
Amusements, ii. 48.
Analysis and synthesis, proclivities toward, ii. 260.
Animal worship, origin of, essay on, ii. 253.
Appleton, D., & Co., publish Spencer's works, ii. 111 *et seq.*
Appleton, William H., ii. 265; Spencer's portrait painted for, 275.
Architectural effects, criticism of, ii. 405.
Architecture, study of, i. 227.
Ardtornish estate, ii. 77.
Arnott, Dr., quoted, i. 116; ii. 47.
Athenæum Club, Spencer elected to, ii. 207; life at, 262.
Attacks on Spencer's "First Principles," ii. 422.
Autobiography begun, ii. 334.

Bagehot, Walter, i. 589.

Bain's "Emotions and Will," review of, ii. 54.
Baltimore, ii. 471.
Banking crisis, article on the, ii. 5.
Baptism of infants, i. 71.
Bath Magazine, Spencer writes for, i. 127.
Baynes, T. S., ii. 117.
Bed for invalids invented by Spencer, ii. 173.
Berlioz, M., ii. 437.
Bernard, C. E., i. 159.
Billiards, ii. 263.
Binding of books, ii. 363.
Binding-pins, difficulty of manufacture and sale, i. 353, 369.
Biology, the volumes of, ii. 131.
Birks, Professor, book by, ii. 422.
Bishop, G. D., i. 159.
Blanc, Louis, i. 535.
Boarding, in a private family, i. 582.
Bodichon, Madam, i. 399, 434.
Book, Spencer's first, i. 406; difficulties of publication, 410.
Books, sale and distribution of, i. 454.
Boston, Mass., visit to, ii. 476.
Botanizing, i. 404.
Bournemouth, sojourn at, ii. 484.
"Boy, be a, as long as you can," ii. 358.
Boyhood pleasures, i. 79 *et seq.*
Boyhood traits of Spencer, i. 89 *et seq.*
Bradley family, i. 533.
Bradshaw's Guide, i. 146.
Braxton, Carter, i. 17.

INDEX

Bray, Mrs., ii. 483.
Brettell family, i. 4; Jane, i. 17.
Bridge designed, i. 203.
Bridges, spiral courses in, i. 168.
Bright, John, i. 251.
British Association, meeting of, 1870, ii. 256.
Bromley, John, i. 18.
Bromsgrove, work at, i. 196.
Brooke, Harold, i. 114.
Brunel, Isambard, his work, i. 376.
Brunetière, Comptesse de, i. 378.
Bryant, Edwin W., offer of assistance, ii. 314.
Buckle, Henry T., i. 600; ii. 4.
Burdett-Coutts, Lady, ii. 439.
Burgess, J. B., his character as an artist, ii. 275.
Burr, Mrs. Higford, ii. 327.
Busk, Mr. and Mrs., ii. 81.
Buxton, Charles, ii. 108.

Caird, Principal, ii. 301.
Cairnes, J. E., ii. 139.
Canadian railways, as investments, ii. 463.
Carlyle, Thomas, note from, i. 265; characteristics, 440 *et seq.*
Carnegie, Andrew, i. 424; ii. 467, 530.
Castle-building, Spencer's, i. 85.
Causation, ii. 6.
Cephalograph, a proposed, i. 634.
"Ceremonial Institutions," ii. 356.
Chartism, i. 249.
Chamberlain, Joseph, ii. 304.
Chapman, Dr., i. 398.
Chemistry, Spencer's first study of, i. 97.
Children, training of, essay, ii. 21, 23; borrowed, ii. 485, 523.
Childs, George W., ii. 472.
Chloride of nitrogen, experiment with, i. 98 note.
Circle, a property of the, i. 135.
Circles, described by natural means, ii. 187.

Clifford, Professor, ii. 136.
Clough, Arthur Hugh, ii. 70.
Club, dining, of scientists, ii. 133.
Club, railway, i. 173.
Coincidences, i. 527; ii. 425; deduction from, 426.
Coleridge's "Idea of Life," i. 402.
Collier, James, ii. 308.
Colors, names of, i. 355.
"Complete Suffrage Movement," the, i. 249.
Comte, his philosophy, i. 517; visit to, 578.
Concord, Mass., visit to, ii. 477.
Conder, Frank, i. 147.
Conway, Moncure D., ii. 245.
Conyngham, Mr., i. 599.
Cooper, Lady White, quoted, i. 56.
Copyright commission, the, ii. 347.
Correspondence, plan for diminishing, ii. 291.
Cotswold Hills, scenery of, i. 495.
Creeds, ii. 546.
Creuze, Mr., killed, i. 209.
Criticisms and replies thereto, ii. 301.
Crole, Sarah, verses, i. 17.
Cross, John, ii. 53.
Cross, Miss, ii. 53.
Crystal Palace, the, i. 433, 523.
Cumming, Dr., his preaching, i. 502.
Curiosity lacking in the uncultivated, i. 557.
Cyclograph, a, i. 169.

Darwin, Charles, letter to, ii. 279.
Darwin, Erasmus, ii. 104.
"Data of Ethics" begun, ii. 369; finished, 380.
"Data of Psychology," work on, ii. 232.
Deacon, A. O., i. 541.
De Beauvoir, Sir John, i. 327.
Decimal system, the, i. 248.
Deepdene, i. 186.
Delmonico's, dinner at, ii. 478.

INDEX

Derby, home at, i. 71, 79.
Descriptive Sociology, work on, ii. 305 *et seq.*; ending of, 410 *et seq.*
Development hypothesis, essay on, i. 448.
Devonshire, sojourn in, i. 556.
Diagnosis of Spencer's physical peculiarities, ii. 500.
Diary, Spencer begins a, ii. 185; extracts, 385, 418.
Disestablishment discussed, ii. 303.
Dorking, sojourn at, ii. 484.
Drawing, Spencer learns, i. 85.
Dreams, effect of morphia on, ii. 203.
Drowning, Spencer in danger of, i. 83.
Duncan, David, becomes Spencer's secretary, ii. 201; goes to India, 252.
Dymond, Jonathan, his essays, i. 351.

E. A. B., i. 202; quoted, 33, 224, 253; letter on faith, 316.
Earl Soham, visit to, i. 503.
Earth, form no proof of original fluidity, i. 641.
"Economist," the, i. 378; Spencer's connection with, 383.
Editing a Suffrage Union paper, i. 284 *et seq.*
Education, Spencer's early, i. 100; established systems of, 387; methods, 507; defects, ii. 307.
Electric lighting, ii. 328.
Electrolysis, i. 222.
Electro-magnetic action, i. 207, 216.
Eliot, Charles W., ii. 327.
Eliotson, Dr., editor, i. 261.
Elliot, Sir Frederick, ii. 330.
Emerson, Ralph Waldo, his essays, i. 278, 399.
Engineering, Spencer begins, i. 141 *et seq.*; resumes, 294.
Entomology, Spencer's study of, i. 84.
Equivalents, scale of, i. 613.
Euclid, Spencer's study of, i. 104.

Evans, John, verses by, ii. 387.
Evans, Marian, i. 455 *et seq.*, 577; first stories, ii. 44; witticisms, 236, 237; death, 428; character and beliefs, 429.
Evarts, William M., ii. 478.
Evolution, first consideration of, i. 201.
Evolution, organic, ii. 115.
Exhibitions, international, i. 433; ii. 88, 366.
Exorcism, story of, ii. 438.
Eyre controversy, the, ii. 167.

"Factors of Organic Evolution," ii. 482.
Faith, discussion on, i. 27.
Family traits, ii. 500 *et seq.*
Fiction, Spencer's reading of, i. 87.
"First Principles," writing of, ii. 69 *et seq.*; translated into Russian, 147; development of, 194; translated into French, 264.
Fishing by moonlight, i. 135; fly, 569; views of, ii. 249 and *passim*.
Fiske, John, ii. 477.
Flood, report on a, ii. 232.
Florence, visit to, ii. 229.
Flying machine, a, i. 346.
Force of Expression, essay on, i. 468.
Form of the Earth, essay on the, i. 360.
Foster, Michael, ii. 495.
Fox, Charles, i. 74, 119, 146, 319.
France, Spencer's works adopted by Ministry of Public Instruction, ii. 383; buys them, 436.
Fraser, Professor, i. 566.
Freedom, erroneous ideas of, i 509.
French, study of, i. 340.
Froude, James A., i. 399.

Galton, Francis, ii. 139.
Garrett, J. W., ii. 472.
Garrison, William Lloyd, breakfast to, ii. 185.

INDEX

Genealogies, vanity of, i. 3; Spencer family, ii. 189.
Genesis of Spencer's greatest work, ii. 16 *et seq.*
Geology, study of, i. 200.
Geometrical theorem, i. 606.
George Eliot. *See* Evans, Marian.
George Henry, his tax policy, ii. 435; criticisms by and of, 536.
Germanic, passage on the, ii. 480.
Gift of money from Mr. Hegeler, ii. 440.
Girders, strength of, i. 221.
Gladstone, W. E., ii. 244.
Glyphography, i. 222.
Golf, Spencer's only game of, ii. 269.
Government, proper sphere of, Spencer's pamphlet on, i. 263.
Grammar, Spencer's ignorance of, i. 123.
Gray, Asa, ii. 136, 477.
Grazebrook, Sidney, quoted, i. 4.
Greeley, Horace, i. 399.
Greg, W. R., i. 425.
Grote, historian, ii. 22; characterized, 182.
Grove, Sir William, ii. 168.
Growth, physical, effect of, i. 129.
Gull, William, ii. 255.
Guthrie, Malcolm, book by, ii. 422.
Gutta-percha, i. 359.

Hallam, John, i. 20.
Harris, George, i. 148.
Harrison, Frederic, i. 292.
Haunted room, a, i. 562.
Haydn's "Creation," i. 315.
Haythorne Papers, i. 471.
Health, Spencer in search of, i. 541 *et seq.*
Heane, Agnes, i. 10.
Hegeler, Mr., sends money to Spencer, ii. 440.
Helmholz, Professor, ii. 136.
Hemus, family name, i. 7.
Hennell, Miss, ii. 483.

Hensman, H., i. 159.
Henzey family, i. 4.
Herbarium, making a, i. 217.
Herbert, name chosen, i. 72.
Heyworth, Lawrence, i. 252, 280, 297; elected to Parliament, 362.
Higgins, Mr., ii. 104.
Highlands of Scotland visited, ii. 52, 108.
Hinton Charterhouse, journey to, i. 102; described, 113; revisited, 233.
Hiring fair, a, i. 593.
Hirst, Dr., ii. 269.
Hodgson, Shadworth, ii. 301.
Holland, visit to, ii. 448.
Holland, Sir Henry, ii. 23.
Hollander, Bernard, quoted, i. 283.
Holme, George, i. 83; ii. 343.
Holmes family, i. 3, 4.
Holmes, Harriet, described, i. 63.
Holmes, John, business, i. 15.
Holmes, Oliver Wendell, ii. 476.
Honorary degrees, remarks on, ii. 273.
Hooker, Sir Joseph, ii. 168.
Hope, H. T., i. 186.
Household utensils, senseless changes in, ii. 238.
Howitt, William, i. 338.
Hudson, Professor, i. 55.
Hughes, Thomas, ii. 138.
Hugo, Victor, i. 567.
Humphreys family, i. 113.
Huth, Alfred, ii. 104.
Huth, Henry, ii. 104.
Hutton, R. H., i. 589; ii. 244.
Huxley, L., correspondence with, ii. 553.
Huxley, Thomas H., i. 465 and *passim.*

Ice-water, American passion for, ii. 469.
Iliad, the, criticism of, i. 300.
Illogical Geology, essay, ii. 50.
Inertia discussed, i. 116.
Injunctions, ethical and legal, i. 14.

INDEX

International Scientific Series, the, ii. 266; trip to Paris for, 270.
Intuitions, ii. 98.
Inventional geometry, i. 54.
Inventions, i. 346.
Isle of Wight, excursion to, ii. 251.
Italy, tour in, ii. 208 *et seq.*

Jackson, G. W. B., i. 160, 203; misfortunes, 212; quoted, 229, 254; goes to New Zealand, 430.
Jersey, island, visit to, i. 533.
Johnson, Dr. Edward, i. 479.
Jones, Dr. Bence, ii. 106.
Jones, Thomas Rymer, i. 74.
Judgment perversions of, i. 409.

Kant's "Critique of Pure Reason," i. 289.
Kentish Town, i. 402.
Kingsley, Charles, i. 472.
Knowledge, value of different kinds of, ii. 40.
Knowles, Herbert, his poem, i. 72.
Knowles, Mr., ii. 244.

Lace manufacture, i. 77.
Lake George, ii. 462.
Lanes, peculiarities of, ii. 377.
Language, universal, i. 247, 617.
Lankester, E. Ray, prize essay by, ii. 252.
Laugel, Auguste, his review of "First Principles," ii. 127.
Laughter, Physiology of, ii. 56.
Laws of Organic Form, essay, i. 436.
"Leader," the, writing for, i. 447.
Lecturing, invitations declined, ii. 454 *et seq.*
Legacy, an opportune, ii. 72.
Legible shorthand, i. 245.
Leslie, Cliffe, ii. 141.
Letter, a strange, ii. 292.
Levelling, agreeableness of, i. 328; appliances, 631.
Lewes, George Henry, i. 399, 435; characteristics of, 437;

ramble with, ii. 79; his home, 84; edits the "Fortnightly," 140; death, 374; devotion to George Eliot, 374; letter to, 565.
Lewis, Sir George Cornewall, i. 523.
Library privileges, i. 99.
Life, conduct of, i. 476.
Literary distinction, value of, ii. 534.
Littré, M., i. 533.
Loch Etive, its beauties, ii. 250.
Loch, W. F., discussions with, i. 302.
Lockyer, J. N., ii. 138.
Locomotives, American, i. 204.
London, Spencer's first visit to, i. 119.
Lord, anecdote of a, ii. 337.
Lott, Edward, i. 219; letter to, 305; letter from, 323 and *passim.*
Lovat, Lord, his fishing, ii. 341.
Lowe, Robert, ii. 136.
Lubbock, Sir John, ii. 82, 439.
Lucid shorthand, i. 61.
Lushington, Godfrey, ii. 108.
Lynn-Linton, Eliza, i. 399.
Lyttleton, Canon, ii. 35.

McLennan, J. F., ii. 75.
Magazines, writing for, i. 258 *et seq.*
Mail-bags, device for picking up, i. 169.
Malvern House, life at, ii. 3.
"Man versus State," ii. 482.
"Manners and Fashion," essay, i. 513.
Mansel, H. L., ii. 301.
Marriage, opinions on, i. 306 *et seq.*; discussed, 428; difficulties, 559; impossible, ii. 540.
Marsh, O. C., his collections, ii. 476.
Martineau, Harriet, her "Tales of Political Economy," i. 125.
Martineau, James, i. 589; ii. 244; on evolution, 287.
Masson, David, i. 481; ii. 136; visited, 186.

INDEX

Mather's school, i. 95.
"Meddling system," article on the, i. 597.
Metaphysical Society, formation of, ii. 244.
Method of work, ii. 325.
Methodists and Quakers, Spencer brought up between, i. 94.
Metropolitan Anti-State Church Association, i. 272.
Miall, Charles, i. 272.
Miall, Edward, i. 237, 249; note from, ii. 303.
Microscope, gift of a, i. 472; work with, ii. 147, 148.
Militancy, discussion of, ii. 387, 444.
Mill, John Stuart, his "Logic," i. 277, 431; Spencer's reply to, ii. 141; his characteristics, 142; offer of assistance, 156; death, 289 and *passim*.
Milnes, Richard Monckton, ii. 23; characterized, 109.
Minturn, Robert B., ii. 165.
Misrepresentations in the United States of Spencer's work, ii. 311.
Mistake, a grievous, ii. 443.
Mitchell, Mrs., ii. 343.
Modeling, i. 235.
Models, Spencer makes, i. 85.
Molesworth, Sir W., i. 431.
Monarchy, views of, ii. 542.
Montreal, ii. 463.
Moorsom, Captain, i. 159.
Morals, basis of, i. 351.
Morley, Samuel, i. 427.
Mother of Herbert Spencer, i. 64 *et seq.*
Mountain climbing, ii. 88.
Mountain scenery, first view of, i. 364.
Mozley family, i. 74.
Mozley, T., quoted, i. 28, 49 *et seq.;* his misstatements, 645.
Music, essay on, i. 594; criticism of, ii. 49; expression, 279.
Mussy, Dr. de, ii. 105.
"Mynheer van Dunck," glee, ii. 346.
Mystery, the universal, ii. 547.

Names of subscribers, ii. 564.
Nasmyth, James, i. 205.
Nebular hypothesis, ii. 25.
Newman, Francis W., i. 399.
Newport, R. I., ii. 476.
New Radford, home at, i. 75.
New York, impressions of, ii. 458.
New Zealand, comparative advantages, i. 429.
Niagara Falls, ii. 465.
Nightingale, Florence, i. 434.
Nile, voyage up the, ii. 393 *et seq.*
"Nonconformist," the, letters written for, i. 237 *et seq.*
Nonconformists, i. 12.
Novel-reading, i. 402.

"Œnone," Tennyson's, read aloud by Huxley, ii. 136.
Office-seeking, ii. 27, 45, 52.
Old masters, opinions concerning, ii. 219.
"Open Court," the, ii. 440.
Opera, first attendance at, i. 314; criticised, 394.
Opium, ii. 106.
Orchardson, Mr., artist, i. 269.
Ordish, Edward, his inventions, i. 82.
Organic form, laws of, ii. 33.
"Origin of Species" read, ii. 57.
Osteology, i. 426; ii. 29.
Over-legislation, essay, i. 490.
Owen, Professor, lecture, i. 539.
Oxenford, John, i. 399.

Pageants, royal, aversion to, i. 432.
Paget, James, ii. 255.
Paris, first visit to, i. 531.
Parkes, Bessie, i. 399.
Peabody Institute, ii. 471.
Pedestrian tour in Scotland, a, ii. 89.
Perspective, Spencer studies, i. 121.
Pheasant-shooting, ii. 267.
Philadelphia, ii. 472.
"Philanthropist," the, i. 274.
"Philosopher," the, projected, i. 274.

610

INDEX

Philosophy of Style, i. 258.
Phonography, i. 244 *et seq.*
Phrenology, i. 228, 282.
Piano, gift of a, ii. 530.
Pickpocket, capture of a, ii. 210.
Picnic party given by Spencer, ii. 357.
Pigott, E. S., i. 436.
" Pilot," the, i. 291.
Pittsburg, ii. 467.
Planing engine, i. 361.
Poem, plan to write a, i. 259.
Poetry, tastes in, i. 299; and science, 485.
" Political Institutions " begun, ii. 416.
Political theories, ii. 433 *et seq.*
Politics, Spencer's view of, ii. 146.
Pollock, Frederick, ii. 139.
Pompeii, visit to, ii. 215.
Poor law, the, i. 118.
" Popular Science Monthly " founded, ii. 286.
Population, theory of, i. 449.
Portraits, making, i. 225; Spencer sits for his, ii. 275.
Potter, Mr. and Mrs., described, i. 298; at Gayton Hall, 357 and *passim.*
Powell, John W., ii. 469.
Powick, Spencer's life at, i. 178 *et seq.*
Preaulx, Osmond, ii. 104.
Priestley, Dr., ii. 483.
" Principles of Morality " begun, ii. 369.
" Principles of Psychology," its reception and analysis, i. 546.
" Prison Ethics," essay, ii. 56.
Pritchard, W. B., i. 271; his schemes, 326.
" Progress," essay on, i. 584.
Promotion in engineering work, i. 155.
" Psychology," first volume completed, ii. 257.
Psycho-physical connexions, ii. 491.
Publishing, difficulties of, i. 539; unfortunate, ii. 80; cost of, 312.
Pyne, J. B., artist, i. 267.

Queen's Gardens, Spencer's home in, ii. 170.
Questions for study, ii. 377.

Railway, first ride on, i. 145; the mania, 325; work on plans, 333 *et seq.*
" Railway Morals," essay on, i. 522.
Rambles in the country, i. 436.
Ransom, Dr. W. A., i. 555.
" Reader, The," ii. 138.
Reciprocal dependence in animal and vegetable creations, i. 624.
Rector of St. Andrews, Spencer nominated for, but declines, ii. 271.
Religion, Spencer's view of, i. 171.
Renan, Ernest, letter from, ii. 147.
Rendu, M., i. 487.
Renunciation, the doctrine of, i. 321.
Retriever, anecdote of a, ii. 277.
Reviews, general erroneousness of, ii. 153.
Revisions of manuscript, i. 48; of work, ii. 423.
Rhythm, universality of, ii. 23.
Riviera, the, visited, ii. 378.
Roe, Mary, i. 525.
Rolleston, George, i. 531.
Roman civilization in England, ii. 328.
Rome, impressions of, ii. 218.
Running away from school, i. 106 *et seq.*
Ruskin, John, criticised, i. 403.

St. John's Wood, i. 402.
Sales, diminished, ii. 154.
Sanitarium, Spencer goes to a, i. 521.
Saratoga, ii. 461.
" Sartor Resartus," i. 277.
Saturday Club, the, ii. 476.
Sayce, A. H., ii. 401.
Scale of equivalents, i. 189.
Scarborough, visit to, ii. 107.
Scheppig, Richard, ii. 310.
Schliemann, Dr., ii. 349.

INDEX

Sciences, classification of, ii. 123 et seq.
Scotland, excursions to, i. 364, 568.
Sea, first sight of, i. 220.
Secretaryship, Spencer accepts a, i. 176.
Self-sacrifice discussed, ii. 107.
Sellar, Professor, ii. 53.
Shelley's poetry, opinion of, i. 308.
Sidgwick, H., ii. 301.
Silchester, ii. 327.
Silsbee, E. A., ii. 61, 96.
Simmons, Captain, i. 114.
Singing lessons, i. 223.
Skew arches, i. 603.
Smith, Benjamin L., i. 434.
Smith, Goldwin, ii. 359.
Smith, Miss Leigh, i. 399.
Smith, Octavius, i. 434, 574; death, ii. 268.
Smith, Valentine, ii. 360, 482.
Smith, William, i. 434.
Snowdon, ascent of, ii. 117.
Soar, Elizabeth, i. 10.
Social Organism, the, ii. 55.
"Social Statics," origin of, i. 242; published, 414; described, 415.
"Sociology," use of the word, i. 292; considered, ii. 296.
South Wales, journey in, i. 310.
"Specialized Administration," article on, ii. 271.
Speech, Spencer's first, i. 174.
Spencer, Henry, i. 23; quoted, 45.
Spencer, John, 2d, i. 26.
Spencer, Mary Ann, i. 23.
Spencer, Mathew, i. 10; described, 18.
Spencer, Mrs. (Herbert's mother), death, ii. 175.
Spencer, Thomas, i. 27 et seq.; sketch of, 35; resigns his charge, 368; removes to London, 395; last days, 479.
Spencer, William, i. 43; his school, 95; death, ii. 72.
Spencer, W. A., i. 26.
Spencer, William George (Herbert's father), described, i. 48, 74 et seq.; death, ii. 162 and passim.
Spencer genealogy, i. 9.
Spottiswoode, W., ii. 133.
Stages of Spencer's work explained, ii. 6 et seq.
Standish, visit at, ii. 49.
Stanley, Dean, ii. 244.
Stephen, Leslie, ii. 266.
Stephens, Sir J. F., ii. 244.
Stereotyping, advantage of, ii. 191.
Strath Spey, its climate, ii. 294.
Strauss's "Life of Jesus," character of, i. 304.
Studies, Spencer's, i. 115 et seq.
"Study of Sociology," writing and publication of, ii. 285; profits of, 298.
Sturge, Joseph, i. 249; quoted, 280; described, 287.
Style, theory of, i. 182.
Subscription, publishing by, ii. 58.
Survey made by Spencer, i. 134.
Swanwick, Anna, i. 399.
Switzerland, tours in, i. 496; ii. 277.
Sylvester, Professor, ii. 471.
"Synthetic Philosophy," programme of, ii. 557.
"System of Philosophy," apology for, ii. 118.

Tact, Spencer's want of, ii. 329.
Taylor family, i. 3.
Teacher's profession, the, i. 136.
Teaching, Spencer, i. 138.
Telephone, the, ii. 465.
Tenby visited, i. 553.
Tennyson, Alfred, quoted, i. 576; ii. 244.
Text-books, Spencer's works used as, at Oxford, ii. 242.
Thackeray, William M., i. 535; ii. 104; his daughters, ii. 266.
Theatres discussed, i. 120.
Theological liberalization, ii. 289.
Thought, method of, i. 463.
Thousand Islands, the, ii. 464.

INDEX

"Times," London, its dishonesty, i. 377 note.
Tintern Abbey visited, ii. 254.
Tombs, contrasted, ii. 403.
Trade, morals of, ii. 34.
Tragedy, Spencer's idea of, i. 467.
Translations of Spencer's books into Italian, ii. 327; into Russian, 338, 362.
Trelawney, Sir John, ii. 22.
Tréport, i. 529, 533.
Trevanion, Mrs., i. 502.
Trussed beams, i. 186.
Turner, Francis C., i. 54.
Turner, J. M. W., criticism of, i. 267.
Type, new method of making, i. 279.
Typographical errors, curious, ii. 72, 535.
Tyndall, John, i. 485; his address, ii. 531.

"Ultimate Laws of Physiology," essay on, i. 590.
Umberslade Hall, i. 521.
Undulations, luminiferous, ii. 336.
United States, Spencer's visit to the, ii. 452 *et seq.*
Universal Postulate, the, i. 481 *et seq.*
Utilitarianism, ii. 100.

Valentines, i. 64.
Vaughan, Dr., his "Age of Great Cities," i. 58.
Vegetal physiology, ii. 148.
Vegetarian, Spencer becomes a, i. 401.
Velocimeter, i. 188, 609.
Venables, G. S., ii. 104.
"Vestiges of Creation," i. 308.
Vesuvius, ascent of, ii. 212.
Vincent, Henry, to lecture, i. 250.

Wagner, Richard, criticism of his work, ii. 349.
Wales, visit to, i. 542.
War, civil, in the United States, English feeling concerning, ii. 245 *et seq.*
Ward, F. O., i. 472, 545.
Washington, D. C., ii. 469.
Watch, American, presented to Spencer, ii. 167.
Watches, construction of, i. 279.
Watford, visit at, i. 119.
Waves, peculiarities of, ii. 331.
Wesley, John, i. 8.
Westbourne Grove, i. 400.
Westminster Review, writing for, i. 445.
Wetherall, F. H. P., i. 176.
Whittington Club, the, i. 392.
Whitty, Captain, i. 176.
Wife chosen for Spencer, i. 422.
Wigham, Mr., i. 487.
Wilson, James, letter from, i. 283; edits "The Economist," 378.
Wordsworth, criticism of, i. 301.
Wye, places on the, visited, ii. 254.

X Club, the, ii. 134.

Yachting, i. 565; ii. 360.
Youmans, Edward L., character of, ii. 61; visits England, 95, 335, 377; dinner to, 143; carries a testimonial to Spencer, 165; tour in Wales, 169; plan for remuneration to authors, 265; assistance on "Descriptive Sociology," 310; in Spencer's American tour, 461 *et seq.;* letters from Spencer to, ii. *passim.*
Young lady, acquaintance with a, i. 191.

DARWIN'S LIFE AND LETTERS.

More Letters of Charles Darwin.

Edited by FRANCIS DARWIN. Two vols., 500 pages each. Eight photogravures and eight half-tones. Uniform with "The Life and Letters of Huxley." Cloth, gilt top, deckle edges, boxed, $5.00 net.

The two volumes will in no way disappoint readers, for it will soon be discovered that Francis Darwin's biography of his father, while made up largely of letters, left unprinted an extremely valuable epistolary collection. The new letters are not alone scientific in the subjects they treat of; they are often personal, and delightfully so. They reveal in Darwin that persuasive and irresistible charm which men of real eminence always possess when to great talent they join simplicity and unaffected sincerity. One could quote indefinitely from this correspondence fine examples of a rare spirit which every one who came in contact with has reported to have been most charming. There ought to be wide interest in these new letters. Everything that Darwin wrote bore the impress of his sincere and gentle spirit. Even his learned treatises disclosed the man as very charming. In his letters readers meet with that attractive personality which no one that ever came under its spell can forget.

"In these letters Darwin has given a personal charm and biographical interest, which, although hitherto unused material, will serve as almost a complete record of Darwin's work."—*Washington Post.*

Life and Letters of Charles Darwin.

Including an autobiographic chapter. Edited by his son, FRANCIS DARWIN. With Portraits and Views of "Down House," Darwin's residence, etc. Two vols., 12mo. Cloth, $4.50; cloth, gilt, $5.00; half calf, $9.00.

"Of such a man, of so rare a genius and so lofty a nature, the record cannot fail to be of deep and abiding interest for us all. With a truly remarkable literary skill the man and his work are so presented as never to be dissociated."
—*London Spectator.*

D. APPLETON AND COMPANY, NEW YORK.

THE PERENNIAL CONFLICT.

The Warfare of Science with Theology.

A History of the Warfare of Science with Theology in Christendom. By ANDREW DICKSON WHITE, LL. D. (Yale), L. H. D. (Col.), Ph. D. (Jena), late President and Professor of History at Cornell University. 2 vols. 8vo. Cloth, $5.00.

"Able, scholarly, critical, impartial in tone and exhaustive in treatment."—*Boston Advertiser.*

"The most valuable contribution that has yet been made to the history of the conflicts between the theologists and the scientists."—*Buffalo Commercial.*

"A work which constitutes in many ways the most instructive review that has ever been written of the evolution of human knowledge in its conflict with dogmatic belief."—*Boston Beacon.*

"The same liberal spirit that marked his public life is seen in the pages of his book, giving it a zest and interest that can not fail to secure for it hearty commendation and honest praise."—*Philadelphia Public Ledger.*

"Such an honest and thorough treatment of the subject in all its bearings that it will carry weight and be accepted as an authority in tracing the process by which the scientific method has come to be supreme in modern thought and life."—*Boston Herald.*

"The story of the struggle of searchers after truth with the organized forces of ignorance, bigotry, and superstition is the most inspiring chapter in the whole history of mankind. That story has never been better told than by the ex-President of Cornell University in these two volumes."—*London Daily Chronicle.*

"It is graphic, lucid, even-tempered—never bitter nor vindictive. No student of human progress should fail to read these volumes. While they have about them the fascination of a well-told tale, they are also crowded with the facts of history that have had a tremendous bearing upon the development of the race."—*Brooklyn Eagle.*

D. APPLETON AND COMPANY, NEW YORK.